Families That Work

Families That Work

Policies for Reconciling Parenthood and Employment

Janet C. Gornick and Marcia K. Meyers

Russell Sage Foundation • New York

The Russell Sage Foundation

The Russell Sage Foundation, one of the oldest of America's general purpose foundations, was established in 1907 by Mrs. Margaret Olivia Sage for "the improvement of social and living conditions in the United States." The Foundation seeks to fulfill this mandate by fostering the development and dissemination of knowledge about the country's political, social, and economic problems. While the Foundation endeavors to assure the accuracy and objectivity of each book it publishes, the conclusions and interpretations in Russell Sage Foundation publications are those of the authors and not of the Foundation, its Trustees, or its staff. Publication by Russell Sage, therefore, does not imply Foundation endorsement.

Library of Congress Cataloging-in-Publication Data

Gornick, Janet C.
    Families that work : policies for reconciling parenthood and employment /
Janet C. Gornick and Marcia K. Meyers.
        p.   cm.
    Includes bibliographical references and index.
    ISBN 0-87154-356-7
    1. Work and family—United States.   2. Children—Services for—United States.
3. United States—Social policy.   4. Social policy—Cross cultural studies.
I. Meyers, Marcia.   II. Title.

HD4904.25.G67 2003
306.3'6—dc21   2003045836

Text design by Suzanne Nichols

RUSSELL SAGE FOUNDATION
112 East 64th Street, New York, New York 10021
10 9 8 7 6 5 4 3 2 1

"We are sowing winter wheat,
which the coming spring will see sprout
and which other hands than ours will reap and enjoy."

Elizabeth Cady Stanton
1893

Contents

About the Authors

Janet C. Gornick is associate professor of political science at the Graduate Center and Baruch College at the City University of New York.

Marcia K. Meyers is associate professor of social work and public affairs at the University of Washington.

—— Acknowledgments ——

WE ARE THANKFUL to several colleagues who have critiqued our work over the years and published portions of it in various venues, especially Tim Smeeding, Lee Rainwater, Diane Sainsbury, Bob Kuttner, Sheila Kamerman, and Al Kahn. We also thank participants at a number of seminars for their valuable comments on elements of the book—including Fran Blau, Jody Heymann, Ellen Bravo, Heidi Hartmann, Theda Skocpol, Shelly Lundberg, Elaina Rose, Julie Brines, Bob Plotnick, Becky Pettit, Heather Boushey, Randy Albelda, and Joan Williams. Other friends and colleagues contributed generously along the way, including Nancy Folbre, Paula England, Suzanne Bianchi, Nancy Segal, Jay Bainbridge, Katherin Ross Phillips, Jodie Levin-Epstein, and Willem Adema.

We especially thank our colleagues with whom we collaborated on empirical work presented in this book, including Harriet Presser, Anne Gauthier, Jerry Jacobs, and Elena Bardasi.

We are grateful to our excellent research assistants, especially Karrie Snyder, Keri-Nicole Dillman, Shahid Chaudhary, Lisa Kahraman, Amy Bailey, Elisha Breshears, and Se-Ook Jeong. We thank Dan Cahill for contributing his editing skills and for reminding us to write in English.

We are grateful to the staff of the Luxembourg Income Study for their generous assistance on many occasions, including Caroline de Tombeur, Paul Alkemade, and Kati Foley.

Several scholars helped us check our social policy facts, including Shirley Gatenio, Michelle Neuman, and—from the individual countries—Koen Vleminckx and Georges Hedebouw (Belgium), Shelley Phipps (Canada), Jytte Juul Jensen (Denmark), Katja Forssen (Finland), Christophe Starzec (France), Irene Dingeldey and Heike Trappe (Germany), Monique Borsenberger (Luxembourg), Laura Den Dulk (the Netherlands), Charlotte Koren (Norway), Johan Fritzell (Sweden), and Lucinda Platt (the United Kingdom). We give our thanks to them all. All remaining errors are entirely our responsibility.

We are grateful to the Alfred P. Sloan Foundation, and especially Kathleen Christensen, for supporting our research on family leave policy.

We are especially thankful to Eric Wanner and the Russell Sage Foundation for financial and intellectual support. We are grateful to Suzanne Nichols for her input along the way and for securing three anonymous reviewers whose attention to our manuscript surpassed our wildest dreams.

We also thank our extended families, our friends, and our partners for inspiring us to become researchers and teachers, for showing us that women and men are more alike than different, and for teaching us to treasure children, especially those born without the privileges that we have had. We are also deeply grateful to them for listening to us, for arguing with us, and for holding our hands as we worked for too long on this book.

Chapter 1

Introduction: The Conflicts Between Earning and Caring

I MAGINE A WORLD in which mothers could take a few months away from their jobs following the birth or adoption of a child, without sacrificing either job security or their paychecks. Imagine a world in which both mothers and fathers could spend substantial time at home during their child's first year, while receiving nearly all of their wages. Imagine a world in which mothers and fathers could choose to work part-time until their children are in primary school without changing employers or losing their health benefits. Imagine a world in which the normal workweek was thirty-seven or even thirty-five hours, and parents had the right to take occasional days off, with pay, to attend to unexpected family needs. Imagine a world in which all parents had the right to place their children in high-quality child care provided by well-educated professionals. Imagine a world in which this child care was provided at no cost or very low cost to parents.

A world such as this, indeed, can only be imagined by American parents. It is a reality, however, for parents in several countries in Europe. Parents throughout the United States and Europe share the common challenge of balancing responsibilities on the job and at home; mothers and fathers everywhere struggle with establishing divisions of labor at home that are fair and economically viable. Many parents in Europe benefit from public policies that distribute the costs of caring for children across society and require employers to accommodate parents' caregiving responsibilities. American parents are grappling with these challenges in

1

a world that is much less supportive. For the most part, they are left to craft their own solutions.

We have spent the past several years studying what parents need to balance paid work with caregiving and analyzing social and labor market policies in other countries that are relatively similar to the United States. In this book we describe what we have learned and draw policy lessons that are meaningful in the American context.

During the writing of this book, we have become keenly aware of several overlapping but surprisingly distinct conversations about work and family life in the United States. These parallel but nonintersecting conversations converge in recognizing that there is a problem. They diverge substantially, however, in their definition of the problem and their proposed solutions.

One conversation has evolved out of growing concerns for the well-being of children. Researchers in public health and education tell us that American children are doing poorly on a number of dimensions, from early school readiness to later school achievement and adolescent childbearing. Research on child development, including important new findings about early brain development, has focused much of this discussion on the role of the family in determining child outcomes. Although the causes of these problems are multiple, many observers point to the absence or diminished attention of parents—who are more deeply engaged than ever in responsibilities outside the home—as an important contributing factor.

A second conversation has been animated by rapid changes in women's engagement in the labor market. Following the sharp rise in the employment of women with children during the 1960s and 1970s, a somewhat different group of social scientists, policy analysts, and advocates began a conversation about the conflict between work and family. This conversation has focused on the problems of working parents, whose competing responsibilities leave them penalized in the workplace and overburdened and exhausted at home. Although the research is not exclusively focused on the problems of women—men too complain about a lack of time with their families—it is mothers who are viewed as most burdened and conflicted by multiple roles.

A third conversation has grown out of the second wave of the women's movement. Since the 1960s, when activists began to argue that "the personal is the political," many feminists have taken a hard look at the role of the nuclear family in the subjugation of women. Feminists concerned with the family have concluded that persistent gender inequality in the labor market is both cause and consequence of women's disproportionate assumption of unpaid work in the home. This conversation revolves around the ways in which men's stronger ties to the labor market carry social, political, and economic advantages that are denied to many women, especially those who spend substantial amounts of time caring for children.

There has been surprisingly little meeting of the minds among participants in these separate but related conversations. Their conversations seem most at odds in the solutions they propose to the problem. Research on child well-being stresses the importance of parents' availability, and many interpret this research to suggest the need for policies—such as child tax credits and maternity leaves—that would allow mothers of young children to opt out of the labor market.[1] Much of the literature on work-family conflict also stresses women's connection to children and locates the conflict in women's lives; solutions focus on policies that allow women both to work for pay and to spend time at home caring for their children—such as part-time work, job sharing, telecommuting, and flextime. In contrast, feminists have typically identified the problem as women's intermittent connection to employment and men's lagging contributions at home. Feminists argue that women will not and cannot achieve parity with men as long as they shoulder unequal responsibilities for unpaid care work. Along with policies that reduce employment barriers and discrimination, feminists typically advocate for alternatives to maternal child care—such as more and higher-quality out-of-home child care and an expansion of options for paternity leave.

We came to this collaboration as interdisciplinary social scientists with a shared interest in social welfare policy. Our backgrounds also differ in ways that mirror these larger divides: one of us was steeped in feminism, the other had a long-standing concern with the care and well-being of children. Not surprisingly, we clashed over several issues, especially those related to maternal employment when children are very young. One of us worried about symmetry between women's and men's engagement in the world outside the home, arguing that women's emancipation depends on their reaching parity with men in the public spheres of employment and politics. The other worried about poor-quality care for children, pointing out that children need their parents' time and that, in many families, that need might be incompatible with full-time maternal employment when children are young.

The challenge of reconciling these apparent tradeoffs is at the heart of this book. For the most part, we now write from a shared perspective. This perspective has been profoundly influenced by lessons we have learned from other countries. Those lessons have come partly from feminist theorizing about societal outcomes that reconcile earning, caring, and gender inequality and partly from comparative social policy studies. The more we looked abroad, the more convinced we became that our disagreements reflected false dichotomies that are socially constructed by existing family, labor market, and social policy arrangements. Our comparative research has convinced us that other countries have developed policies that help reconcile what we in the United States too often understand to be irreconcilable. Our goal in this book is to relate the lessons we have learned on our own intellectual journey.

One of the most important steps in this journey was the articulation of an end vision that honors the importance of both earning and caring, both child well-being and gender equality. The most pressing conflicts of interest arise not between men and women, nor between parents and children, but between the needs of contemporary families and current divisions of labor, workplace practices, and social policies. To resolve these conflicts in the United States, we do not need to choose sides; rather, we need to focus our attention on an end vision of what an earning, caring, egalitarian society that promotes the well-being of children might look like.

This end vision is reflected in the title of chapter 4 in this volume: the dual-earner–dual-carer society. It is a vision of a fully gender-egalitarian, economically secure, caring society. We do not suggest that this end vision is a prediction for the near future. We recognize that it embodies a long-term, perhaps even impossible, social transformation. We are convinced, however, that articulating an end vision is critical not only for resolving arcane academic debates but, more important, for establishing the principles against which we evaluate new social and labor market policies. American parents need and want more support from government. If we respond to these needs as if they embody fundamentally irreconcilable demands, we will create policies that perpetuate tradeoffs between the interests of mothers, fathers, children, and employers. If we reject the assumption that these conflicts are irreconcilable, we can hope to develop policies that advance the interests of each.

Recent decades have seen a profound transformation in the organization of employment and caregiving arrangements in the American family. The "traditional" model of a male breadwinner and female homemaker has been replaced by a model of highly gendered partial specialization in which men invest their time primarily in the workplace and women combine employment with unpaid work in the home. In the United States, in particular, government plays a minimal role in supporting parents' dual responsibilities in the home and workplace. This model assumes, and perpetuates, a long-standing belief that caregiving is a private, and largely female, concern.

This resolution of employment and caregiving demands is failing American parents and their children. Many of the problems besetting American families are less acute in other industrialized countries that have more extensive public policies that help families manage competing demands from the home and the workplace without sacrificing gender equality. Although none of the countries we have studied can be characterized as having achieved a fully egalitarian, dual-earner–dual-carer society, some provide useful examples of the ways in which government can support families in their efforts to share earning and caring work.

Our goal in this comparative exercise is to move current policy debates in the United States beyond fragmented conversations that treat child well-being, the conflict between work and family life, and gender equality as separate issues and beyond the belief that caregiving is a wholly private concern. Cross-national comparisons can help move the debate by suggesting new conceptual and practical models for policy design. They can expand our options by demonstrating that policies that appear politically or economically infeasible in the context of the United States are in fact well established and successful elsewhere. Cross-national comparisons can also provide specific lessons about policy design. Because the difference between policy success and failure often turns on details—including rules about coverage, eligibility, benefit levels, duration, and financing—the experience abroad offers valuable lessons about the nuts and bolts of policy design. In the remainder of this chapter, we preview our analytical framework and our key findings.

WHAT IS THE PROBLEM?

In chapter 2, we argue that American parents are navigating uncertain new terrain, caught between traditional conceptions of caregiving and new demographic, economic, and social realities. In the wake of rapid changes in family composition and women's employment, parents are struggling to organize their working lives and their partnerships in new ways. They are doing so, however, in a society in which many members reap the benefits of family caregiving while doing little to share the burden. The gender revolution remains unfinished, leaving women with a disproportionate share of paid and unpaid care work. Out-of-date workplace practices constrain parents' ability to devote time to the care of their children. Government provides only the most meager assistance and targets much of that assistance on those at the margins of self-sufficiency. The resulting mismatch between parents' needs and society's response strains family life, disadvantages mothers, and leaves many children with inadequate care.

Contemporary problems facing parents, especially mothers, are rooted in long-standing gendered divisions of labor. In the late nineteenth century, industrialization and the rise of waged labor sparked a massive economic and social reorganization. As most men—but few women—moved their labor from the agricultural to the industrial and commercial sectors, a family that included a male breadwinner and a female homemaker came to be defined as the ideal. Men and women assumed increasingly separate roles, with men engaging in paid work and women taking responsibility for unpaid work—most especially, the work of caring for children. This arrangement remained fairly stable through the first half of the twentieth century but began to unravel later in the century with the sharp increase in women's labor force participation and the growth of single-parent families. The waning of the breadwinner-homemaker family increased women's opportunities. New arrangements for work and family, however, including the dominant contemporary model of partial specialization between mothers and fathers, have created new tensions for many families. One tension arises because the large increase in maternal employment, and more modest increases in working hours, leave many families squeezed for time. With the majority of both fathers and mothers in the labor force, many families simply lack sufficient hours in the day to care for their children. A second tension arises from the fact that, even with high and rising employment rates, women remain the primary caregivers for children. Women have increased their ties to the labor market, but men's contributions to work in the home have not increased at a corresponding rate. Women, far more than men, now juggle dual responsibilities in the home and the workplace.

Although these tensions are not unique to the United States, they create more acute dilemmas here because we have done comparatively little to distribute the costs of caregiving throughout society. Industrialized countries have traditionally characterized childbearing and child rearing as private concerns. In reality, caregiving work—performed overwhelmingly by women—creates broadly shared benefits. As Nancy Folbre and Paula England have argued, women's caring labor creates what economists call "public goods" in the form of children who are well nurtured (Folbre 1994; England and Folbre 1999b). Children's capabilities, which result in large measure from sustained caring and nurturing, provide public benefits (what economists term "positive externalities") by enriching today's society and providing economic benefits for the next generation. Women who provide care in the home pay the costs of that work, in the form of time, energy, and forgone market wages. Others in society reap the benefits—in the form of children who are prepared to learn in school, adults who are prepared to engage in productive employment, and neighbors who are prepared to create civil society—but they do not necessarily share the costs. In other words, others in society free ride on women's care work.

Ours is not the only society that free rides on the unpaid work of families, and of women in particular. The United States is exceptional, however, in the extent to which it has failed to develop welfare state structures that distribute these costs more broadly. The American welfare state is often characterized as a laggard in cross-national terms. The United States does far less than many similarly rich countries to redistribute and equalize income or to actively manage labor markets. We also do much less to socialize the costs of caregiving—through government policies that redistribute income to families with children, public services that reduce employment penalties associated with devoting time to caregiving, or labor market regulations that protect parents' time with children. We benefit as much as any society from families' and women's caregiving work, but we do much less to spread the costs.

This exceptionally private conception of family life leaves American families to craft individual solutions to what is essentially a social dilemma: If everyone is at the workplace, who will care for the children?

Families are inventing a variety of creative arrangements to reconcile high rates of parental employment with their children's need for care. Many families reduce the labor market attachment of one parent—usually the mother. Many mothers engage in various forms of underemployment, opting for jobs that demand less of them than their skills would otherwise warrant or working part-time or intermittently (or both). Some families arrange to work opposite hours: one parent leaves for the workplace as the other returns home. Others make extensive use of nonparental care, placing children in substitute care starting in early infancy.

Although these private solutions are often adaptive for individual families, they also exacerbate long-standing problems of gender inequality at home and in the labor market. Because of their caregiving commitments, women with children earn far less, as a group, than their male counterparts, rendering them economically dependent, lacking in bargaining power at home, and at risk in the event of family dissolution. Comparatively weak labor market ties have also left women vastly underrepresented in positions of commercial and political leadership. Private solutions are also creating new social problems. For some families, nonstandard employment schedules disrupt home life, increase the risk of marital dissolution, and compromise children's well-being. For others, child care costs strain financial resources. The search for inexpensive child care solutions both reduces the quality of children's care and impoverishes child care providers. For a disturbingly large number of families, the combination of partial labor market attachment and limited government assistance leads to economic insecurity. In the end, these "private" problems create social costs, as economic insecurity, inadequate caregiving time, and poor-quality child care combine to jeopardize the well-being of many children.

ARE PARENTS AND CHILDREN DOING BETTER ELSEWHERE?

It is clear that American parents are struggling. What is less clear is the extent to which the problems they confront are inevitable. The collision between new realities and traditional conceptions of family life are evident in all industrial and postindustrial societies. Families in other countries are also struggling to balance the demands of paid work with the needs of their children and to reconcile the interests of women with those of men. In many relatively similar countries, however, the resulting problems are less acute.

In chapter 3 we compare the United States with other countries on a number of well-being indicators. In several other industrialized countries—including those with male and female employment rates that are higher than those of the United States—employed parents spend less time in paid work and incur less-costly penalties for part-time work. In some other countries, gender inequality in the labor market is less pronounced, and men do a larger share of nonmarket work. In all of our eleven comparison countries, fewer parents work nonstandard hours, and families headed by employed parents are less likely to be poor. Children in many of these countries are also doing better on dimensions ranging from infant birth weight to adolescent childbearing. This suggests that while the challenges of reconciling the demands of the home and employment are common across similar countries, the extent to which they exacerbate gender inequality, work-family conflict, and compromises to child well-being is not inevitable.

ENVISIONING A NEW SOLUTION

A comparison of the United States with other industrialized countries suggests that families' private solutions to the competing demands of the workplace and the home are exacting a particularly heavy toll from American families. As we describe in chapter 4, the discourse about these problems has also been narrower and more fragmented in the United States than in many countries in which families face similar dilemmas. Public debates about the problems of child well-being, work-family conflict, and gender equality in the United States characteristically focus on the family itself as the source of the problem. These debates fail to recognize the common origin of many of the dilemmas facing contemporary families in our willingness as a society to share the benefits of women's unpaid caregiving work without distributing the costs. These debates suggest various responses for meeting the needs of children, mothers, and families. In the absence of a new conceptualization of the collective dimensions of family caregiving, however, most solutions fail to resolve tradeoffs between earning and caring or between child well-being and gender equality.

Many observers in the United States suggest that we should shore up the male-breadwinner–female-homemaker model by increasing supports for women in their caregiving roles. With sufficient financial remuneration and social approbation, it is argued, women may be persuaded to forgo employment opportunities that are equal to men's and to retain the primary responsibility for the care and nurturing of children. This is the solution favored by many social conservatives who advocate the implementation of unrestricted child tax credits and other forms of support for the "traditional" family. It is an approach that has also been favored by some feminists, who propose rewarding women in their caregiving roles by adopting generous paid family leaves, public payments for the care of dependents ("wages for caring"), and the extension of social insurance credits to full-time caregivers.

This approach would free women to devote themselves to the

care and rearing of children. It may have much to recommend it from the perspective of children, who would be guaranteed more time with their mothers. From the perspective of gender equality, however, this approach is deeply flawed. However well compensated, the relegation of women to unpaid care work can only reinforce gendered divisions of labor and the low value placed on caring work. Women would continue to incur the economic, social, and civic penalties associated with their withdrawal from the labor market. Men would continue to miss out on caregiving opportunities. Children would continue to miss the active presence of their fathers.

An alternative possibility would be to move more caregiving work out of the home. In a universal-breadwinner society, all parents would be in the workforce full-time, and children would be cared for largely by other adults, paid for by the family or the government. This is the solution advocated by many liberal feminists, who argue that women will not obtain social and economic parity with men until they achieve equality in the labor market. It is also the solution suggested by some conservative social reformers, who place a premium on engaging low-income parents in the labor market.

This approach could go a long way toward achieving gender equality in employment, but it, too, is fundamentally flawed. It would limit mothers' and fathers' opportunities to be fully present during the critical early years of their children's lives, and it would deprive children of sustained contact with their parents throughout their lives. It would continue to devalue caring work by valuing market work above unpaid care work. Moreover, to the extent that child care remains market based, this approach would perpetuate the social and economic disadvantages of having a heavily feminized and poorly paid caregiving workforce.

Debates in the United States have vacillated for many years between these two alternatives. In the one, we are asked to sacrifice gender equality in the name of children's well-being; in the other, to sacrifice the interests of children for the sake of gender equality. What is constant is that many individuals and families are asked to sacrifice their interests to perpetuate a system in which the care of children is overwhelmingly defined as a private, and largely female, responsibility.

In chapter 4 of this book, we draw on comparative social welfare and feminist scholarship to suggest an alternative end vision. The work of several European writers has convinced us that the interests of men, women, and children cannot be reconciled by asking families to make more accommodations to the tensions inherent in the gendered model of partial specialization between fathers and mothers. These tensions cannot be resolved without fundamental transformations in divisions of labor, workplace arrangements, and the role of government. If Americans hope to create a society that values both paid work and unpaid caregiving, we will need to transform gender relations so that women and men face symmetrical opportunities and responsibilities for employment and caregiving. If we want men and women to have the opportunity to engage in caregiving work without undue economic and career sacrifice, we will need new employment arrangements that allow time for caregiving. If we hope to enhance the well-being of children and to promote gender equality, we will need to distribute the cost of caregiving more equally within society and to call on government to help make this a reality.

One version of such a transformed society has been labeled a "dual-earner–dual-carer" society by the British sociologist Rosemary Crompton (1999). This is a society that recognizes the rights and obligations of women and men to engage in both market and care work and one that values children's need for intensive care and nurturance during their earliest years. In a dual-earner–dual-carer society, parents would spend substantial amounts of time at home when their children are infants, relying more heavily on substitute care as their children grow. Parenting would be degendered; fathers and mothers would share responsibility for earning and caregiving symmetrically, with support from both employers and society more broadly.

What would it take to realize a dual-earner–dual-carer society? It would require three transformations that would reduce our historic free riding on women's unpaid labor and increase our collective support for caregiving work. First, and most fundamental, its realization rests on the dissolution of today's gendered divisions of labor. For mothers and fathers to share the caring, men (on average) would need to shift an appreciable number of hours from the labor market to the home when their children are young. For men and women to share the earning, women (on average) would need to shift a more modest number of hours from the home to the market. Mothers and fathers would essentially meet in the middle. Second, it would require the creation of a more family-friendly labor market. Both women and men would need employment that allows them to take temporary breaks, especially when their children are young. Both women and men would need access to new employment arrangements that allow them to carry out parenting responsibilities without excessive penalties in wages, benefits, and job advancement—including high-quality, reduced-hour jobs.

Third, it would depend on the expansion of government policies that support caregiving work and socialize the costs of rearing children. Families and employers alone cannot bring about these transformations in the home and workplace. For a dual-earner–dual-carer society to become a reality, government will have to take a more active role in helping both women and men to blend employment with caregiving by providing benefits such as paid family leave and child care. Policies are also needed that secure workplace changes through labor market regulations—for example, legislation that reduces standard working hours and grants workers the right to temporary periods of leave.

AN EXPANDED ROLE FOR GOVERNMENT

The development of a caring, gender-egalitarian society rests on three related changes: the dissolution of gendered divisions of labor, the emergence of new workplace practices, and the redistribution of the costs of caregiving through government policies. The subject of this book is the third of these three: the development of a new and expanded role for government. We lay out the contours of an "earner-carer" policy package that would both support families today and facilitate the development of a dual-earner–dual-carer society in the future. This package has three elements: publicly regulated and financed paid family leave, regulation of working time, and public early childhood education and care programs.

Before turning to the details of these policies (in chapters 5 through 7) or the evidence of their effectiveness (chapter 8), we consider two challenging questions. The first is whether American men and women want to share caregiving work more equally. Academics have advanced at least two theoretical rationales for gendered specialization. Essentialist arguments suggest that women's disproportionate commitments to caregiving reflect the higher value that they place on this work; neoclassical economic arguments assert that men and women elect to specialize because it is efficient and raises total family utility. These arguments are difficult to counter precisely because of the absence of a counterfactual: Women's and men's choices can be observed only in the context of contemporary views about appropriate gender roles and the limited institutional support available for caregivers. It is impossible to know what American women would prefer, or how American families would behave, in a society that valued both earning and caregiving and that allowed both women and men to blend labor market attachment and caregiving without costly penalties.

The second challenging question, particularly for Americans, is whether government *should* assume a more prominent role in supporting families. The policy package described in this volume includes family leave and child care programs that involve several forms of redistribution—from nonparents to parents, from smaller to larger families, and from well-off to less affluent households, to name a few. The package also includes labor market regulations that could be seen as restrictive to employers—for example, requiring them to shorten their standard work hours or to pay part-time and full-time workers the same hourly wage. This raises important normative questions about whether it is legitimate and appropriate to use the power of government to redistribute the costs of caring for children.

We argue that government has a central responsibility in this area because, as England and Folbre (1999b) argue, many individuals and institutions enjoy the fruits of parental caregiving without contributing to the costs. Society, through government, has at least two reasons for sharing the costs of caregiving. The first is related to efficiency. Because children's capabilities generate positive externalities, private investments in children will fall below levels needed to produce economically and socially optimal outcomes. Public programs that help to defray the costs of child rearing, such as paid family leave and high-quality substitute care, constitute important investments in today's children and in the next generation of adults.

The second reason concerns equity. To the extent that all members of society reap the benefits of child rearing, all members of society—not just mothers—should share the costs (England and Folbre 1999b; Budig and England 2001). Labor and consumer markets cannot bring about this sharing of costs; for this, we must rely on the redistributive and regulatory power of government. The failure to share caregiving costs has still other implications for equity among children. To the extent that we rely on parents' private resources, children in poor families receive far less than their more affluent counterparts; government supports could help equalize children's opportunities.

POLICY MODELS FROM OTHER COUNTRIES

We do not have to begin from scratch in the design of a policy package that would support families and facilitate the development of a dual-earner–dual-carer society. Family policies in several European countries, especially the Nordic countries of Denmark, Finland, Norway, and Sweden as well as France and Belgium—and even in neighboring Canada—provide models of what government can do to help families resolve the tensions between workplace and caring responsibilities while promoting greater gender equality. Although none of these countries has made the transition to a fully egalitarian dual-earner–dual-carer society, several have taken important steps in this direction, and their policy designs suggest useful lessons for the United States.

Chapter 5 describes family leave policies that grant employed parents time for caregiving, with compensation, especially during their children's first three years. Policies in countries that do the most to support a dual-earner–dual-carer society grant nearly all employed mothers job security and wage replacement around the time of childbirth. Following maternity leaves, parental leave rights and benefits provide both parents periods of paid leave during their children's preschool years. Gender disparities in the take-up of these policies remains problematic, however, leading some countries to strengthen incentives for fathers to make use of leaves. Mothers and fathers also have the right to some time off, with pay, to attend to short-term and unpredictable needs that arise throughout their children's lives. The financing of these leaves distributes the costs across society and minimizes the burden for individual employers.

Chapter 6 provides examples of labor market policies that protect parents' time for caregiving. In the countries that do the most to support families in their earning and caring roles, public measures limit weekly employment hours, often setting the standard full-time workweek at thirty-five to thirty-nine hours, below the American forty-hour standard. Labor market measures are in place to improve both the availability and quality of part-time work and to limit parents' employment during nonstandard hours or to compensate workers who work those schedules (or both). Public vacation policies ensure parents four to five weeks' time with their families each year—twice the amount of time available to most American workers.

In chapter 7, we describe public policies that provide alternatives for the care of children while their parents are at the workplace, through public early childhood education and care (ECEC) programs and school scheduling that is compatible with parents' employment schedules. The most supportive countries provide or finance inclusive ECEC services for a large share of one- and two-year-olds and nearly all older preschool children. The costs of these services are shared between government and families, with government assuming most of the cost and scaling parental fees to family income. Quality is ensured through public-sector staffing and regulations that require high levels of preparation—with appropriate compensation—for private and public child care workers. For older children, school scheduling policies in the most supportive countries ensure that children's school schedules are well matched to parents' hours of employment.

DOES POLICY MATTER?
LINKING POLICIES TO OUTCOMES

We have argued that an expanded role for the U.S. government can be justified both as an investment in the healthy development of children and as a means for more equitable sharing of the costs of caregiving. This assumes that these policies are effective in achieving these outcomes. In chapter 8 we review in some detail what is already known and what remains to be learned about the extent to which these policies promote gender equality and enhance child and family well-being.

The employment effects of family leave policy have received substantial research attention. The empirical evidence suggests that access to leave has the potential to reduce labor market inequalities between men and women by facilitating continuous employment and reducing wage penalties associated with motherhood. Other research suggests that access to family leave may have health benefits for children as well, especially in the form of reduced infant mortality. Evidence is less consistent as to how children benefit on other dimensions from the presence of a parent at home, although the most recent research suggests that high levels of maternal employment during the first year of life are associated with worse outcomes for at least some groups of children and that these effects persist well into grade school.

Many researchers have examined the effects of early childhood education and care on women's employment and on children's well-being. This research has produced substantial evidence that high child care costs depress mothers' employment; policies that reduce these costs have been shown to increase maternal employment, potentially closing employment and wage gaps between mothers and fathers with young children. A substantial empirical literature has also established the contribution of child care quality to children's health, cognitive, and socioemotional outcomes. The most disadvantaged children appear to benefit the most from high-quality care and to suffer the most from poor-quality care.

A small body of research has also assessed the effects of multiprogram policy packages such as we describe. These studies provide encouraging evidence that public policies aimed at either increasing gender equality or easing work-family tensions can increase women's employment rates, reduce employment discontinuity in connection with child caregiving, and lessen the extent to which employment interruptions for caregiving penalize mothers' wages later in life.

CAN FAMILY POLICY MODELS FROM ABROAD WORK IN THE UNITED STATES?

We close, in chapter 9, by addressing several common objections to the adoption of "European-style" policies in the United States. Those who are skeptical of drawing lessons from abroad often point to the extreme diversity within the American population and to particular social and economic challenges, such as the prevalence of both single parents and low-wage workers. Others are concerned that these programs are actually harmful. In particular, some fear that generous social programs may have problematic consequences for family formation; others warn that public provisions have undermined the European economies and that they would do the same in the United States. Still others argue that Americans' preferences are fundamentally incompatible with public, especially national, social programs. Other skeptics raise concerns that are not about differences between the United States and other countries. They argue that many men simply do not want to become committed caregivers, employers are likely to resist or undermine public policies that require them to accommodate parents' needs for caregiving time, or that comprehensive work-family policies would simply be too expensive.

In our concluding chapter, we address each of these concerns. We argue that these concerns do not have to constitute insurmountable barriers to providing more public supports for American families. The reality is that many of the European countries with high levels of social provision are also quite diverse, some with immigration rates as high as or higher than the U.S. rate. In fact, part of the rationale for generous social policies in some of the high-providing countries is to contribute to the integration of diverse populations into a united citizenry. Moreover, though high rates of single parenthood and low-wage employment are indeed vexing problems in the United States, they are not unique to this country. The policies described here play a crucial role in supporting families in other countries, and they operate outside the realm of traditional "welfare" programs, which have received the most sustained criticism in the United States.

Frequently voiced concerns about the unintended consequences of work-family policies are often exaggerated. Although recent fertility declines in Europe are troublesome, there is no evidence to suggest that the programs described here have contributed to this decline by encouraging women to choose employment over childbearing. In fact, the countries with the highest fertility rates are among those with the most generous work-family reconciliation policies that allow parents to combine parenting with employment. Nor is there reason to worry, as many Americans do, that these programs would increase childbearing among single women without labor force ties. The incentives created by work-family policies are in precisely those directions most widely supported by Americans: employment, parental caregiving, and paternal involvement.

Other Americans argue that generous social programs have damaged the European economies; their contribution to high unemployment rates has been widely reported in the American media. More-scholarly assessments conclude that there is little evidence for such a causal link. More important, nearly all of the European economies rebounded during the 1990s, and these recoveries unfolded as governments across Europe expanded public family leave and child care provisions and passed new laws aimed at reducing working time and increasing protections for part-time workers.

We would also argue that social policy analysts and advocates have been too quick to conclude that public work-family programs will not play in the political heartland of the United States, or are too costly, thereby reinforcing the inevitability of their defeat. In fact, public-opinion research suggests that a large share of Americans support paid parental leave, regulations aimed at shortening the workweek, public investments in child care, and longer school hours. There is no question that these benefits would be costly. A comparative analysis suggests, however, that comprehensive leave and child care benefits would cost only about half of what the United States now spends on primary and secondary education.

Finally, broadening the end vision of family policy to include support for a gender-egalitarian society has the potential to close political cleavages that have hampered the adoption of family policies in the past. Formulating leave, child care, and labor market policies to explicitly include fathers as well as mothers has the potential to engage men's support. Designing these policies to support both employment and caring, shared equally by women and men, holds promise for closing the schism between feminists oriented to reducing gender differentials, especially in the labor market, and those focused on rewarding caregiving in the home. A policy package that enables parents to care for young children at home also holds promise for bridging the gap that often separates feminists working toward gender equality from advocates concerned with children's well-being. Embracing the vision of the earner-carer society may help to mobilize widespread support for family policy expansion in the United States.

ABOUT THE SELECTION OF FAMILIES

We focus in this book on the problems of reconciling employment with the care of children. We choose to focus on families with children because the problems they face are so pressing and the consequences of failure are so great. Many of the problems we consider, however, and some of the solutions we describe are equally relevant to other caregiving demands and other family forms. The care of elderly parents, for example, creates many similar dilemmas, and a growing number of families are finding themselves "sandwiched" by the need to care for both young children and elderly parents. Although we do not address these additional caregiving challenges, many of our policy lessons are equally relevant to them.

We also focus our discussion and examples primarily on two-parent families, implying married or cohabiting heterosexual adults who are jointly caring for children. We focus on heterosexual couples because one of our key concerns is the gendered division of labor within contemporary families, but nearly all of the policies that we identify would bring nearly the same advantages for same-sex couples. In fact, same-sex couples raising children are, in some sense, the model dual-earner–dual-carer families insofar as paid and unpaid work hours are not allocated by gender. The policies that we describe as supporting dual-earner–dual-carer families are also relevant for single-parent families, who are likely to have even greater needs for caregiving and income support.

ABOUT THE SELECTION AND COMPARISON OF COUNTRIES

Most of the empirical analyses and policy discussions in this book are explicitly cross-national and comparative. Cross-national comparisons help to challenge the belief that the family-level outcomes and policy designs observed in the United States are the only ones possible, and they provide models for alternative policy designs. By linking policy designs to outcomes, we are also able to benefit from a "natural experiment" that sheds light on the consequences of policy for the outcomes that most concern us.

When selecting countries for cross-national studies, comparativists face two fundamental decisions: how many countries to study and their degree of homogeneity. A smaller number of countries allows more intimate knowledge of each case, whereas a larger number of countries ensures more variation—a factor that is crucial for any research that aims to tease out policy impacts. Selecting more similar countries (say, the United States and Canada) allows comparativists to assume some degree of similarity between them that controls for omitted variables, such as political culture. In contrast, choosing countries that are more different (say, the United States and France) provides more variation but also exacerbates the problem of dealing with multiple differences that co-vary. Choosing countries that are extremely different (say, the United States and China) pushes the limits of comparative-policy research, as overarching contextual factors are so different that policy translation becomes nearly impossible.

We have chosen a compromise strategy. Our group of countries comprises twelve relatively similar countries: the United States, Canada, and ten European countries. Twelve countries is few enough to allow us to learn about them in a reasonable amount of detail and just enough to enable us to draw some inferences about policy effects. The European countries—especially the Nordic countries—give us a window on generous, egalitarian social welfare policies that exist only in these countries, whereas Canada and even the United Kingdom allow a comparison of the United States with its most similar counterparts. Taken together, these countries offer a range of comparators, from our nearest neighbor, Canada, to countries considerably more remote.

We have excluded many countries in which families are grappling with the same concerns. The most noteworthy exclusion is that of industrialized countries in two rapidly changing regions: the former Eastern Europe and the Pacific Rim. Our omission of these countries is explained partly by severe data limitations and partly by their very differences in the area of family policy. State supports for families in the Eastern European countries, once common, have been wholly or partially dismantled following economic liberalization; similar supports are exceedingly limited, or radically different in structure, in the Pacific Rim. Policy developments in these countries are worthy of study but are largely outside the scope of our comparative framework.

We organize our presentation of these comparisons by grouping our eleven comparison countries into three fairly homogeneous groups. These groups include the four Nordic European countries of Denmark, Finland, Norway, and Sweden; the five Continental European countries of Belgium, France, Germany, Luxembourg, and the Netherlands; and two English-speaking countries, the United Kingdom and Canada.[2]

This grouping reflects the theoretical and empirical work of the Danish sociologist Gosta Esping-Andersen, as presented in his book, *The Three Worlds of Welfare Capitalism* (Esping-Andersen 1990). Esping-Andersen classifies the major welfare states of the industrialized West into three clusters, each characterized by shared principles of social welfare entitlement and relatively homogeneous outcomes. He and subsequent authors using this framework characterize social policy in the Nordic countries as generally organized along social democratic lines, with entitlements linked to social rights. Social policy in the Continental countries is typically tied to earnings and occupation, and public provisions tend to replicate market-generated distributional outcomes. In the Continental countries, social policy is also shaped by the principle of "subsidiarity," which stresses the primacy of the family and community for providing dependent care and other social supports. Social benefits in the English-speaking countries are usually organized to reflect and preserve consumer and employer markets, and most entitlements derive from need, based on limited resources.

In the 1990s, many critics (including us) charged Esping-Andersen with ignoring gender issues, such as variation in the provision of family leave and child care, and the roles of paid and unpaid work in establishing welfare-state entitlements. Yet subsequent empirical efforts to establish welfare-state typologies that incorporate gender have largely confirmed Esping-Andersen's classification. That suggests that the welfare-state principles underlying these clusters are highly correlated with those that shape family policy. In the Nordic countries, the social-democratic principles that guide policy design are generally paired with a commitment to gender equality; the market-replicating principles in the Continental countries are often embedded in socially conservative ideas about family and gender roles; in the English-speaking countries the principles of the market nearly always take precedence.

The Esping-Andersen regime types provide a useful and robust organizing framework. We make use of them in this volume because they push us to think theoretically about social policy and help us to identify empirical patterns across our comparison countries. Working with these well-known groupings will also allow comparativists to situate our findings within the larger welfare-state literature.

Chapter 2

The Changing American Family and the Problem of Private Solutions

AMERICAN FAMILIES ARE struggling. In the United States, fragmented contemporary discourses about the family cast these struggles alternately as the failure of parents to provide adequately for their children, as the difficulties women encounter in finding a balance between the demands of the workplace and the home, or as the failure of society to achieve the ideal of gender equality envisioned by many feminists. Each of these fragments captures an important dimension of the struggle. Yet they fail to suggest satisfactory solutions because they fail to situate families' dilemmas in a broader context.

The ongoing struggle of many families to find a manageable and equitable balance between work life and family life is rooted in a long history of gendered divisions of labor and in the United States' resolutely private conception of caregiving work. The contemporary social and economic organization of the American family has been shaped by two hundred years of dramatic change in the nature and location of economic activity and in gender roles. As first men and later women moved into waged work, families have had to create new arrangements for the unpaid domestic and caregiving work that has traditionally been performed by women. Although society as a whole has continued to reap the benefits of women's care work, we have done little, collectively, to help defray its costs. Families, and particularly women, have been left to craft private solutions that have exacerbated gender inequality and created new social problems.

The contemporary family model—highly gendered partial specialization between men and women—has created new demands in the form of a time crunch for families and a disproportionate caregiving burden for women. The limited provisions of the American welfare state, combined with the widespread view that caregiving is a private concern, have left families to devise their own resolutions to these tensions. These private solutions have had serious consequences for gender equality and for family and child well-being.

THE TRANSFORMATION OF THE AMERICAN FAMILY

Although the family made up of a male breadwinner and a female homemaker is often called "traditional," this family arrangement is actually relatively recent. The social and economic organization of the family has changed repeatedly during the past two hundred years and particularly dramatically in recent decades. The transformation of the American family—from the agrarian arrangements of earlier centuries to the model of partial specialization between mothers and fathers that dominates today—provides an important context in which to understand the needs of contemporary families and the highly gendered distribution of labor between women and men.

The First Transformation: From the Family Farm to Separate Spheres

From the colonial period until the middle of the nineteenth century, the great majority of American families lived agrarian lives. The family was the primary economic unit; nearly all goods and services that the family consumed were produced at home, with home production supplemented by limited market exchange, much of it through barter. All family members—men and women, children and adults—participated in the household economy by contributing directly to production or by selling some household and agricultural goods in the market.

In what Frances Goldscheider (2002) calls the "old gender balance" of agrarian society, men and women engaged in joint—

albeit different—economic activities tied to agricultural and home production. In the nonslave population, men did most of the agricultural work and women handled what would later be called "light manufacturing," along with other domestic and caregiving tasks (Blau, Ferber, and Winkler 2002). Although gender roles were different and unequal in many respects, men and women were engaged in a joint economic enterprise, and the interdependence of household members was obvious. In the slave economy, the roles of men and women were even more similar, as both worked in the fields.

Between about 1840 and 1890, the processes of industrialization and urbanization changed the economic organization of the family. During those years, many family farms and family shops were replaced by factories and commercial enterprises. Increasingly, goods and services were produced away from home, and the family changed from a production to a consumption unit. This economic transformation had enormous consequences for gender roles. As men moved rapidly away from home-based work and away from the daily lives of their children, the vast majority of women remained behind. Although some wives continued to perform farmwork, many became full-time homemakers whose work was increasingly limited to housework and the care of their husbands and children. These changes gave rise to a new family form—what we now call the "traditional" family—with highly differentiated gender roles and extreme economic specialization.[1] This social and economic restructuring also turned the household into a locus of redistribution in which husbands transferred market income to their dependent wives and children (Blau, Ferber, and Winkler 2002; Goldscheider 2002).

By the turn of the century, this traditional family had become the most common and most revered model for family life, especially among middle- and upper-income families. In 1900 nearly 85 percent of men were in the paid labor force, compared with 18 percent of women—and only 5 percent of married women (Blau, Ferber, and Winkler 2002). Employment among women, especially mothers, was associated with economic need and was generally viewed as a sign of hardship. Not surprisingly, work roles shaped up differently for married women whose husbands' earnings were low—including women of color and those in immigrant families. In 1900 almost a quarter of African American wives were employed, primarily as domestics or farmworkers; many immigrant wives also worked for pay, typically in factories (Blau, Ferber, and Winkler 2002). Single mothers, mostly widows during these years, were also likely to be at work for pay. When husbands earned sufficient income, however, the breadwinner-homemaker arrangement prevailed.

The Second Transformation: From Separate Spheres to Partial Specialization

The idealized breadwinner-homemaker arrangement dominated the American family landscape until the middle of the twentieth century. In 1940, on the eve of the Second World War, married women's labor force participation was still only 14 percent, a relatively small increase from the 5 percent at the turn of the century (Blau, Ferber, and Winkler 2002). This division of labor worked well for employers and for many men. Women's unpaid work in the home, estimated at about fifty hours a week throughout the first half of the century (Blau, Ferber, and Winkler 2002), freed men to commit themselves fully to market work. Women's absence from the labor market helped to push up male wages by reducing competition and strengthening men's ability to negotiate for a "family wage." Throughout the heyday of the breadwinner-homemaker family, trade unions worked hard to support traditional divisions of labor and offered little aid to employed women.[2]

The "traditional" family, however, would turn out to be remarkably short lived. In the second half of the twentieth century, dramatic changes in female employment and family formation brought about a second transformation in the economic and social organization of the family and the near demise of the breadwinner-homemaker family.

The first challenge to the traditional family arose as women followed men into paid work. After 1940, the percentage of women who were in the labor force rose sharply, increasing from 28 percent in 1940 to 38 percent in 1960 and reaching 60 percent in 2000; during those sixty years, the difference between women's and men's labor force participation narrowed by nearly forty points. The growth in women's employment was especially consequential for the traditional family because the most dramatic increase was among married mothers. In 1960, just over a quarter of married mothers were employed; by 2000, that figure had nearly tripled.[3] The employment rate for married mothers with children under the age of six grew most rapidly, more than tripling during that forty-year period (Blau, Ferber, and Winkler 2002; U.S. Bureau of the Census 1995, 2001).

What caused this revolutionary rise in women's employment? One important catalyst was the Second World War itself. Many women entered the paid workforce to replace the household income of their departed wage earners and to support the war effort; women's participation rate rose from 28 to 36 percent between 1940 and 1945 alone (Blau, Ferber, and Winkler 2002). Moreover, although many of the new entrants left the labor force once the war had ended, about half did not. The indirect effects of the war on later employment trends may have been even more powerful than its direct effects, in that the temporary employment shock set in motion irreversible changes in attitudes toward the employment of married women.

A number of social, demographic, and economic factors contributed to subsequent growth in women's labor force participation. Liberalized ideas about gender roles raised women's educational expectations and attainment. Between 1940 and the middle 1990s, high-school completion rates among women increased from 26 to 81 percent, and college completion rates rose from 4 to 20 percent (Blau, Ferber, and Winkler 2002). Increasing education raised women's potential market wages and the opportunity cost of staying home, propelling many women into the labor market and encouraging further investments in education.

Women were also pulled into the labor market by the rising demand for clerical work and the shift from manufacturing to services. These new occupations exerted a pull on women, especially married women, partly because their fairly low skill requirements were relatively compatible with the combination of employment and child rearing. They were also less physically demanding and less dangerous than blue-collar work, and for this reason they may have attracted some married women who would otherwise have remained out of the labor force (Blau, Ferber, and Winkler 2002). As clerical and service jobs became sex-typed as female work, both the supply of and the demand for women workers rose further. The influx of women into service employment, in turn, fueled the further expansion of the sector, as employed women began to pay others for service-related work that they had once done themselves. During the 1960s and 1970s, the women's movement in the United States accelerated the transformation of norms and expectations about women's work. Feminist activists emphasized the drudgery of housewifery, the value of economic independence, and the importance of employment as a gateway to political and civic life. Changing expectations for women were institutionalized in antidiscrimination and affirmative action policies that opened jobs, occupations, and industries long dominated by men.[4] Changing social norms about men's caregiving potential complemented new images of women in the public world. In addition, the introduction of the birth-control pill in 1960 was consequential. As women gained near-total control over their fertility, many chose to postpone childbearing or to space their children to pursue education or employment—options that until that time had been limited.

While these social and labor market forces were pulling women out of the home, other forces were creating new forms of economic insecurity that pushed women into employment. During and after the recession of the early 1970s, declining and stagnant male wages made it difficult for families to maintain or raise their standard of living with only one adult—usually an adult male—in the workforce (Mishel, Bernstein, and Schmidt 2001). Between 1979 and 1995, male wages fell by an estimated 16 percent in real terms, and many families responded by moving more adults into the workforce (Katz and Autor 1999). Between 1979 and 1989, for example, the average income in married-couple families with children rose by about 5 percent, but without the increase in wives' earnings, average family income would have actually fallen by 3 percent; even in the boom years of 1989 to 1999, when average family incomes rose by 15 percent, most of increase was contributed by the earnings of wives (Mishel, Bernstein, and Schmidt 2001).[5]

In addition to declining wages, substantial numbers of wives were pushed into paid work by the growing threat of marital dissolution. Between 1970 and 1996, the divorce rate in the United

States rose sharply, and the number of divorced people more than quadrupled (Saluter and Lugaila 1998). Newly divorced women were often compelled to work by economic necessity; given the declining certainty of marriage, those who remained married had new incentives to invest in their own careers and future earning potential. Greater economic independence and the growing social acceptance of divorce probably had mutually reinforcing effects, with greater financial means and new social permission enabling women to leave unsatisfactory marriages.[6]

The traditional breadwinner-homemaker family model was challenged on a second front during these years as the share of women who were unmarried—owing to divorce or nonmarriage—rose sharply. Between 1963 and 1997, the percentage of women who were never married nearly tripled (from 6 to 17 percent), and the percentage previously married (mostly divorced) doubled from 10 to 19 percent. The steep rise in divorce and an increase in nonmarital childbearing greatly increased the number of families headed by single mothers. During these same years, the percentage of children living with an unmarried parent rose from 9 to nearly 28 percent (Waite and Nielsen 2001). Employment is a particularly pressing economic necessity for single parents. In 2000 a larger share of single mothers with children under the age of six were in the labor force (71 percent) than married mothers with children of the same age (63 percent) (Bureau of the Census 2001).

The growth in married mothers' employment and the rise of single parenthood have fundamentally altered the profile of American families. Women's employment has reduced their presence in the home, in much the same way that the presence of men had been reduced a hundred years earlier (Goldscheider 2002). In 1930 only a minority of children lived in families in which both parents worked for pay; 55 percent lived in a two-parent family with a breadwinner father and homemaker mother. By the end of the century, a two-parent, single-earner family was the exception rather than the rule: 70 percent of children lived in a family in which both parents or the single parent were in the workforce (Hernandez 1994).

The social and economic organization of the American family changed dramatically during the latter half of the twentieth century. In terms of gender equality, however, the transformation was incomplete. The male-breadwinner–female-homemaker model rested on a nearly complete specialization of economic roles within those families that could afford to have a full-time homemaker. It has been replaced by a new arrangement in which most men invest their time primarily in earning while many women split their time between earning and caregiving. In economic terms, total specialization has been replaced by partial specialization. Partial specialization has created new opportunities for women to join men in the "public sphere" of commercial and civic activity, but it has not been accompanied by a corresponding shift of men's time from the labor market to the "private sphere" of caregiving in the home.

NEW DEMANDS ON FAMILIES AND WOMEN

The incomplete transformation of the family to an equal partnership between fathers and mothers has created new demands on American families. As families have moved more adults into the workforce, they have had to forfeit much of the time that mothers had previously spent with children. American parents, both men and women, have reason to complain about the time crunch created by long hours at the workplace. However, it is women, far more than men, who must combine their employment hours with major commitments to caregiving in the home. The gendered nature of contemporary partial specialization between fathers and mothers creates particularly acute demands on mothers.

Increased Parental Time in the Labor Market

There is considerable debate about whether the amount of time Americans spend working for pay has risen in recent decades (see Figart and Golden 1998, for a review). What is absolutely certain is that the rise in mothers' employment rates, in both married and single-parent families, means that more families now have all adults in the workforce. Among married couples, the share in which both partners were employed grew from 36 to 60 percent between 1970 and 1997 (Jacobs and Gerson 2001). During the same years, the employment rate of single mothers increased as well, and it increased again after the 1996 welfare reform, rising to 74 percent by 2000 (Bureau of the Census 2001).

In most families all adults are now in the workforce, and in recent decades two labor market trends have compounded the time squeeze within these families. First, among the employed the number of hours worked each week has increased slightly. The increase has been primarily among employed women, whose average weekly hours rose by 3 percent between 1968 and 1998 (Burtless 1999). This modest increase affected the joint weekly hours of parents in dual-earner couples, whose combined hours rose from an average of seventy-seven hours in 1970 to eighty hours in 1997; three-quarters of that increase was attributable to the rise in married mothers' average weekly hours worked.[7] During that same period, the percentage of dual-earner couples with children who worked very long hours (one hundred or more hours a week) rose from 8 to 13 percent (Jacobs and Gerson 2001).[8]

A second factor increasing demands on parents' time is a more substantial increase in weeks worked each year, primarily among women. Between 1967 and 1998, the average work year of American workers rose from forty-three to forty-seven weeks. There is some controversy among work-time scholars as to what has driven the increase in weeks worked a year. Jerry Jacobs and Kathleen Gerson (2001) argue that much of the increase in weeks worked is an artifact of women's increasing participation in the labor force. However, Laura Leete-Guy and Juliet Schor (1992) suggest that after thirty years of progress toward increasing paid time off, the hours of vacation, holidays, sick leave, and personal days for American workers fell roughly 15 percent in the 1980s.[9]

Who works for pay such long hours? The most common image is that of overworked but highly paid professionals driven by workplace culture and personal ambition. In fact, two recent studies on working time suggest that long hours of paid work are the norm across income, occupational, and educational groups. Jacobs and Gerson (forthcoming), using the 2000 Current Population Survey (CPS) data, report that though male "professional, managerial, and technical workers" work an average of forty-six hours a week, male workers in "all other occupations" report average workweeks of nearly forty-two hours. Moreover, whereas more than a third of this professional group logs fifty or more hours a week, so does more than a fifth of the workers in other occupations. Jacobs and Gerson document similar patterns by education: male workers with college degrees average forty-six weekly hours, but their counterparts with only high-school degrees average only a slightly lower forty-three hours weekly. In related research, Lawrence Mishel, Jared Bernstein, and John Schmitt (2001) find that on average married male heads of household, in every income quintile except the lowest, worked more than two thousand hours a year (the equivalent of forty hours a week for fifty weeks). Assessing the employment hours of couples in this same group by race, they find that black married couples jointly worked longer hours than their white counterparts within every income quintile (using the same income cutoffs).[10]

Women, who frequently loosen their labor market attachments to care for children, work an average of four to six fewer hours a week than men within all occupational and educational groups.[11] The gender gap in hours is largely attributable to the fact that a much higher percentage of employed women hold part-time jobs; 21 percent of working-age women, in contrast to 3 percent of men, work fewer than thirty-five hours a week. Among full-time workers, women workers report weekly hours that are nearly as long as men's (forty-two versus forty-five) (authors' calculations, based on CPS 2000).

Although highly educated, high-earning professionals may work the longest hours, they and their families have no monopoly on the time squeeze. Moreover, though adults with children are not the only overworked Americans, they are particularly likely to experience a squeeze on their time due to the movement of more women into the labor force and the modest increase in Americans' working hours. Time is finite: if adults spend more hours in employment, their time for caregiving work in the home will necessarily be reduced. As Jacobs and Gerson explain it,

> Because dual-earner couples are becoming more common and male breadwinners less common, husbands and wives may experience a sharp increase in the shared workweek even if the average individual working time shows little change. . . . Single parents, who are predominately mothers, are likely to experience an even greater time burden than are

dual-earner couples. It is not the amount of working time but rather the loss of someone to take care of domestic needs that links single mothers with dual-earner couples. (Jacobs and Gerson 2001, 46)

Women's Disproportionate Responsibility for Caregiving

Both men and women have been affected by changes in the social and economic organization of the family; and both fathers and mothers face the time crunch created by the absence of a full-time caregiver in the home. However, women, far more than men, experience this as competing demands on their time because the contemporary pattern of partial specialization between mothers and fathers remains highly gendered and creates particularly acute demands on women who are combining work in the market with their traditional responsibility for unpaid work in the home. When men left the farm for paid work at the turn of the century, they largely exited the unpaid domestic economy. When women made a similar transition, nearly a century later, they largely maintained their obligations in the home, particularly for the care of children and other dependents. Although men have increased their hours of domestic work somewhat in recent decades, the increase has been far too modest to close the substantial gender gap in unpaid work.

On average, mothers who are in the labor market work longer total hours than do their male counterparts. A large body of research suggests that women and men (parents and nonparents combined), overall, work about the same number of total hours each week, when time devoted to both paid market work and unpaid work in the home are included. In an extensive review of the literature, Francine Deutsch concludes that slightly more than half of published studies find either that American men and women spend the same amount of total time working or that men work longer hours, whereas about 40 percent conclude that women's total work time is greater than that of men. When the workdays of employed parents are compared, however, most studies suggest that women work more hours than men. As Deutsch concludes, "Perhaps the gender gap does not exist for all groups of men and women. In fact, women who are housewives may work fewer total hours than their husbands. But it is clear that among parents with young children who work at full-time jobs, women are working a lot harder than their husbands" (Deutsch 1999, 258).

Women, particularly employed mothers, experience heavy demands on their time and attention because they continue to do a disproportionate share of the unpaid work at home. The gender gap in hours devoted to unpaid work has diminished in recent decades, as men's contribution to household labor has increased modestly and women's has declined substantially (Gershuny and Robinson 1998; Bianchi et al. 2000; Bianchi 2000; Robinson and Godbey 1997). Although there has been some convergence, women continue to devote far more of their time to unpaid work. Various studies suggest that as much as 62 to 70 percent of American women's total work hours are devoted to home production, in contrast with as little as 26 to 39 percent of men's work hours (Gershuny 2000; Goldschmidt-Clermont and Pagnossin-Aligisakis 2001).

The result is a substantial gender gap in the performance of unpaid domestic and caregiving work. As of the middle 1990s, women devoted about twice as much time to housework as men— creating a gender gap of more than fifteen hours a week (Bianchi et al. 2000). Women clearly do the greater share of housework, and their workload grows along with their family commitments. Suzanne Bianchi and her colleagues (Bianchi et al. 2000) estimate that being married is associated with an estimated five additional hours a week in unpaid work at home for women but no increase among men. The presence of children in the home increases the hours spent doing housework (not including caring for children) for both men and women; but the increase in housework associated with the presence of young children (under the age of twelve) is more than three times greater for wives than for husbands.[12]

The gender gap remains particularly wide with respect to unpaid time spent caring for dependent children (Bianchi 2000; Robinson and Godbey 1997). Bianchi (2000) documents that the time married fathers in the United States spend with their children has risen in recent years. However, she estimates that they still spend just 56 percent of the time married mothers spend in primary child care activities, 45 percent of the time mothers spend in either primary or secondary activities, and about two-thirds the time in activities with children present.[13] Thus married fathers' time with children still lags behind that of mothers by a wide margin.[14]

Gender gaps in domestic and caregiving work are a source of tension in and of themselves. They also contribute to persistent gender gaps in paid work. As a result of spending so much time in domestic work, married women spend substantially less time in paid work than their partners. Many mothers, especially those with very young children, exit the labor force altogether for periods of time; 40 percent of mothers with children under the age of three are out of the labor force (Bureau of the Census 2001). Others work in part-time jobs, which usually bring lower hourly wages and other losses in job quality. Still others select occupations that permit flexibility, trading parenting time for flat wage schedules, fewer benefits, and the absence of career ladders. Employed parents also report frequent cutbacks in their working hours or days to attend to children's daily needs, and, like other employment reductions, women experience more of these work interruptions than do men (Heymann 2000).

What is important is that these reductions in employment are linked to motherhood but, for the most part, not to fatherhood. In fact, the presence of children is associated with weaker labor market ties for women and *increases* in men's labor market attachment. Compared to men without children, fathers are more likely to be employed and to be employed full-time (Gornick 1999a), and their hourly wages are higher (Lundberg and Rose 2001).

THE RELUCTANT AMERICAN WELFARE STATE: OPTING OUT OF PUBLIC RESPONSIBILITY

Economic, social, and demographic changes in the latter half of the twentieth century combined to destabilize the traditional model of family organization. However, the economic and social arrangements of families have been only partially transformed. The new model of partial specialization allows women to join men in the economic sphere; but it is also creating a time crunch for many families, increasing demands on employed mothers, and perpetuating gender inequalities. To understand the implications for American families, it is necessary to review another chapter of American history. The demise of the traditional family, the competing demands on parents, and continued gender inequality are problems not unique to the United States. The economic and social transformations of the past two centuries have created unprecedented opportunities and expectations for women and new challenges for families in all of the industrialized countries. In many countries that industrialized at about the same time as the United States, however, particularly the countries of western and northern Europe, these transformations have been accompanied by the development of welfare state programs and collective-bargaining arrangements that shift a portion of the cost of caregiving from the family to the larger society. The United States has lagged behind its European counterparts in welfare state development and industrial relations for more than a century, creating a legacy that defines caregiving in exceptionally private terms.

Between 1880 and 1930, the first large-scale welfare state programs were enacted in Europe, largely in response to new and heightened forms of economic insecurity resulting from industrialization and urbanization. By the early 1930s, when an economic downturn swept through Europe, nearly all countries had enacted most of the four broad programs that would become the core of the European welfare state: old-age, disability, and survivors' pensions; workers' compensation; unemployment compensation; and health, sickness, and maternity benefits. In the 1930s and 1940s, the later-developing European welfare states established the rest of these programs, and nearly all countries added a fifth—family allowances. By 1960, the last of the major European welfare states had enacted a family allowance program (Hicks 1999).

In comparison with most of the European countries, the United States has been characterized as having a reluctant, residual, or only partial welfare state (Katz 1986, 1989; Patterson 1986; Trattner 1994). While most European countries were developing universal social protections for their citizens, the United States continued its colonial tradition of localized, charity-based assistance for the "deserving poor" and forced work—or destitution—for those considered able-bodied and undeserving of charity. During the first two decades of the twentieth century, several of the American states established public income supports, including workers' compensation and mothers' pensions, but the national government took no substantial responsibility for protecting Americans from economic hardship. In 1935, largely as a response to the Great Depression, the United States became one of the last Western countries to establish a national program of old-age, disability, and survivors' pensions, along with unemployment insurance. When the architects of the New Deal initiated the American welfare state, however, they opted out of crucial elements of the European policy package—including national health insurance, sickness pay, and maternity benefits. In subsequent years, when family allowances were established across Europe, policy makers in the United States once again chose not to follow suit.

The divergent histories of welfare state development in Europe and the United States reflect fundamentally different conceptions of the role of the state. The institutional histories of the United States and most of Europe also differ on the important dimension of unionization. Most of the European countries combine legislated programs with benefits and job protections that are collectively bargained. In many countries, organized labor is inseparable from government; employer-employee negotiations over working conditions and social benefits are regulated, and the state often participates directly in negotiations. When the needs of European workers and their families are not met through public programs, large numbers have access to employer-based options, negotiated through representative bodies that have substantial bargaining power.

The United States has predicated its social protection system on a far more limited role for the state, a greater reliance on employer-based provisions, and much weaker institutions for worker representation. Entire programs that are wholly or primarily public in many other countries, including health insurance, sickness pay, and maternity benefits, are largely privately provided—by employers—in the United States. The majority of working-age Americans who have access to these benefits obtain coverage through employment, sometimes as part of a standard employee-benefit package, sometimes through individualized negotiation.

Where the United States does provide public social benefits, it often restricts eligibility or benefits (or both) to an exceptional degree in comparative terms. The United States' national Old-Age, Survivors, and Disability Insurance program is the most universal of our programs, providing pensions to most aged and disabled workers and their surviving spouses and children. Most other U.S. social-welfare programs are highly restricted categorically, or pay low benefits, or both. In place of universal health-insurance coverage, for example, the United States grants public insurance only to elderly, disabled, and low-income citizens. The American unemployment-compensation system is also unusually meager; it was ranked seventeenth out of nineteen industrialized countries in a recent study of benefit generosity (see Gornick 1999b).

Americans also obtain far fewer social benefits through collective bargaining than their European counterparts. As the United States developed a residual rather than a comprehensive welfare state, it also crafted public institutions that limit the role of unions and collective bargaining. The role of collective bargaining is limited partly because only a small fraction of the workforce is either unionized or represented by unions—about 15 percent overall, 10 percent in the private sector—and partly because bargaining is highly decentralized, generally affecting only one employer at a time. In most European countries, collective bargaining is both more widespread and much more centralized; agreements often affect whole industries—and sometimes nearly all workers in the country.

Unions are less developed in the United States than in many other industrialized countries for a number of historical, geographic, institutional, and cultural reasons.[15] Although cultural preferences may play a role, the legal rules that govern collective bargaining in the United States effectively reduce both union coverage and union power.[16] Furthermore, some nonunion forms of worker representation that are widespread in Europe are essentially disallowed by U.S. labor law. For example, Richard Freeman (1994) notes that the so-called works councils—bodies of workers that consult with employers at the enterprise level—would violate the terms of the primary U.S. labor law, the National Labor Relations Act. Although the causes underlying the limited development of unionization in the United States are subject to debate, the consequences are clear: when American parents turn to their employers for work-family benefits, they have a weak collective voice and little bargaining power.

Welfare state and collective-bargaining institutions have had particularly important consequences for families with children, in both Europe and the United States. Throughout western and northern Europe, the reorganization of the family in the twentieth century has been accompanied by the growth of social policies for parents and children. In most countries, the major welfare state programs—pensions, workers' compensation, unemployment, health, maternity, and family allowances—have been supplemented by housing assistance, lone-parent allowances, "sick-child days," paid parental leaves for mothers and fathers, and substantial public provisions for early childhood education and care starting at the age of three or even younger. This comprehensive package of programs protects working families from income shocks associated with bearing and caring for children. In addition, family leave and child care programs facilitate maternal employment, potentially reducing gender inequalities in the labor market and the home. All of the major family policies also have important redistributive effects. Because family policy benefits are financed largely by general revenues or contributory social insurance funds, they redistribute a portion of the costs of child rearing—across the life span, across generations, between more- and less-affluent households, and between families with and those without children.

The American state has taken a much more confined role in supporting families, especially families with children below school age. Outside of public education, the public sector in the United States has largely resisted redistributing the costs of child rearing. While the European countries were adding universal family allowances, the United States pieced together means-tested (and now time-limited) cash assistance for poor families, supplemented by modest child credits for families with tax liabilities and (later) a refundable Earned Income Tax Credit (EITC) for low-income employed parents. While many of the countries of Europe were establishing child- or parent-based entitlements to public child care, the United States developed a child care market for parents who could afford to purchase substitute care and limited public programs for poor families. While our European counterparts were enacting paid family leave schemes, the United States left the vast majority of workers to negotiate with their employers for wage replacement following childbirth.

The extent to which the United States lags behind the social-welfare states of Europe in using the power of government to socialize some of the costs of caregiving is neatly summarized in a comparison of expenditures on family-related benefits, including family allowances, family-support benefits, lone-parent allowances, paid family leave, and refundable tax credits for families (see table 2.1). Most of the European welfare states spend in the range of 1.5 to 2.2 percent of gross domestic product (GDP) on these family cash programs; that translates to about $1,400 to $2,300 for each child under the age of 18. The United States, in

TABLE 2.1 **Cash Benefits for Families, 1998**

Country	Expenditures as Share of GDP (Percentage)	Expenditures per Child Under the Age of Eighteen
Nordic Countries		
Denmark	1.5	$1,822
Finland	1.9	$1,883
Norway	2.2	$2,249
Sweden	1.6	$1,417
Continental Countries		
Belgium	2.1	$2,265
France	1.5	$1,390
Germany	2.0	$2,247
Luxembourg	2.4	$4,270
Netherlands	0.8	$884
English-Speaking Countries		
Canada	0.8	$793
United Kingdom	1.7	$1,557
United States	0.5	$650

Sources: Expenditures data from OECD (2001b); population data from Bureau of the Census (2002a).
Note: Expenditures include cash benefits for families, that is, programs targeted on families (family allowances for children, family support benefits, and lone-parent cash benefits) as well as paid family leave and refundable tax credits for families. Approximately 60 percent of the expenditures in the United States is accounted for by the EITC. Expenditures are in $U.S. 2000, ppp-adjusted.

contrast, spends only 0.5 percent of GDP (including the EITC), and average spending for each child is just $650.

THE RESPONSE OF FAMILIES: PRIVATE SOLUTIONS

The reluctant American welfare state, combined with the weak collective-bargaining strength of American workers, does little to redistribute the costs of caring for children or to support families who are combining employment and caregiving. In the United States, far more than in most European countries, families have been left to their own devices to craft solutions to the demands of balancing work in the home and in the labor market. More parents work for pay than a generation ago, and many are at work for more hours, yet their responsibilities in the home remain largely unchanged. Parents (mostly mothers) are expected to provide care for children and other family members without compensation and generally without adjustments in employment schedules. They are expected to find alternative care and supervision for children while they themselves are at work, largely without assistance from government. Families are left to craft private solutions when paid work and child rearing create competing demands on their resources.

Contemporary families have demonstrated considerable resourcefulness in crafting these private solutions. One solution chosen by many families is to reduce the employment of one parent. As reported earlier, it is still overwhelmingly women who make this accommodation by reducing hours of work or withdrawing from employment altogether. Although the labor force participation of mothers has risen steeply in recent years, women with young children are still less likely to be employed, and they are likely to work fewer hours (for pay), than either women without children or men.[17] When children are young, most mothers continue to resolve the competing demands of employment and home by limiting their time in the labor market.

Other families balance competing demands by arranging "split-shift" parenting. A substantial share of two-parent families organizes their schedules so that one parent is employed while the other cares for their children; the second parent goes to work after the first returns home. Many single mothers arrange their employment hours similarly, sharing caregiving shifts with another adult, usually their own mothers; Harriet Presser (forthcoming) reports that one-third of grandmothers who provide child care for their grandchildren have other jobs themselves.

Presser (forthcoming) estimates that one in five employed Americans now works nonstandard hours (evenings, nights, or on rotating shifts), and one in three works Saturdays or Sundays, or both. Why is there so much employment during nonstandard hours? The growth in nonstandard-hour work is usually explained by changes in employer demand (Presser forthcoming; Kimmel and Powell 2001). The majority of workers with nonstandard hours are employed in the rapidly expanding and relatively low-skilled, low-paying service sector. Moreover, in the modern twenty-four-hour economy, the services provided by these workers—cashiers, waiters and waitresses, janitors and cleaners, nurses, orderlies, and nursing attendants—are demanded at all hours.

Although demand-side factors seem to drive the overall prevalence of round-the-clock employment, many workers seek nonstandard hours to accommodate their caregiving needs. Parents with young children are the most likely to work nonstandard hours: in 35 percent of couples with a child under the age of five, and in 31 percent of dual-earning couples with a child under the age of fourteen, at least one adult works nonstandard hours or weekends (or both) (Presser forthcoming). This accommodation is extensive: Presser (1995b) estimates that the presence of a pre-school-age child increases mothers' likelihood of working non-day hours by 46 percent. When asked directly, more than one-third (35 percent) of mothers reported that child care is the primary reason for working nonstandard hours; another 9 percent indicated care for another family member as their primary reason (Presser forthcoming). This proportion may be even higher if the majority of women who indicate "job-related reasons" as the primary reason for nonstandard hours have elected to work in occupations that allow or require them to work during hours when other family members are available for child care.

Finally, many families also accommodate competing market and caregiving demands by shifting a portion of child care out of the home. More than three-quarters of preschool-age children with employed mothers are now cared for in nonparental child care settings; one-half of these children are in care for thirty-five or more hours a week (Capizzano, Adams, and Sonenstein 2000). Some of this care is provided by relatives, but nearly half of pre-school-age children are cared for in child care centers or family child care homes. The use of child care has increased steadily with maternal employment, and recent increases have been particularly steep for very young children. Two-thirds of children with employed mothers are in nonparental care before their first birthday, as are three-quarters of two- and three-year-old children (Ehrle, Adams, and Tout 2001).

School-age children also spend a considerable number of their out-of-school hours in nonparental care. Among children between the ages of six and twelve with employed mothers, nearly half spend an average of 12.5 hours a week in nonparental care arrangements other than school (Capizzano, Tout, and Adams 2000). Parents of school-age children are also much more likely than parents of younger children to leave children without supervision (in "self-care") for at least some portion of their employment hours. According to parents' reports, about 5 percent of six- to nine-year-old children are in self-care for some hours of the week; by the age of ten, about 23 percent are in some hours of self-care; and by the age of twelve, nearly half spend some time on their own (Capizzano, Tout, and Adams 2000). Because parents may be reluctant to report that they leave children, particularly young children, on their own, these survey-based estimates are likely to be conservative.

THE PROBLEM OF PRIVATE SOLUTIONS

Reductions in maternal employment, split-shift parenting, and the extensive use of nonparental care and self-care for children are some of the most significant private responses to the competing demands of the home and the workplace. In the absence of assistance provided by the state or negotiated through collective bargaining, however, these and other accommodations can do little to resolve the fundamental contradiction that arises from society's willingness to benefit from families' caregiving work and its unwillingness to share the costs. Families' solutions are often adaptive in the short term; but they are also creating new financial, time, and social problems for families while exacerbating long-standing problems of gender inequality.

Gender Inequalities in the Labor Market

One of the most significant problems associated with private solutions to work-family dilemmas is that women's withdrawal from employment to care for children (and to perform other domestic work) reinforces deep and costly gender inequalities in employment. Table 2.2 compares the average employment hours of American mothers and fathers as of 2000. (These averages include parents employed for zero hours—that is, they conflate gender differences in both employment rates and hours.) What is perhaps most striking is the constancy of fathers' hours with respect to the ages of their children. Fathers in two-parent families work for pay an average of forty-four hours a week, regardless of the ages of their children. In sharp contrast, partnered mothers' hours fall steadily with their children's ages and, presumably, the children's needs for care and supervision. As a result, fathers' weekly hours in the labor market exceed those of mothers across all children's age groups—and by as much as twenty hours a week for those with the youngest children.

Anecdotal evidence often attributes gender gaps in employment only to the most advantaged families (because women can afford to opt out of employment) or to those who are less advantaged (because women have fewer incentives to enter employment). A disaggregation of the data suggests otherwise. Gender gaps are similar when we compare women and men in families at different income levels (table 2.2). In every income group, fathers' hours are largely invariant across the stages of childhood, whereas mothers adjust their labor force attachments to the demands of parenthood. Similar patterns emerge when the data are disaggregated by education (table 2.3); fathers at every educational level spend substantially more time in the labor market than do their female partners.[18]

These care-related reductions in employment have far-reaching consequences for women. When women weaken their labor

TABLE 2.2 **Average Weekly Hours Spent in Market Work by Mothers and Fathers in Two-Parent Families, by Income Quartile, 2000**

Age of Youngest Child (Years)	Mothers (A)	Fathers (B)	Total (A + B)	Difference (B − A)
All two-parent families				
Birth to two	24	44	68	20
Three to five	24	44	68	20
Six to twelve	28	44	72	16
Thirteen to seventeen	31	44	75	13
Low-income families (bottom quartile)				
Birth to two	16	40	56	24
Three to five	19	39	58	20
Six to twelve	21	38	59	17
Thirteen to seventeen	22	35	57	13
Middle-income families (middle two quartiles)				
Birth to two	26	45	71	19
Three to five	26	44	70	18
Six to twelve	30	44	74	14
Thirteen to seventeen	32	43	75	11
High-income families (top quartile)				
Birth to two	27	47	74	20
Three to five	27	47	74	20
Six to twelve	30	47	77	17
Thirteen to seventeen	34	48	82	14

Source: Authors' calculations, based on data from CPS.
Note: Data refer to parents aged twenty-five to fifty. Hours refer to "usual hours worked per week," exclusive of commuting time and lunch breaks. Average hours include persons spending zero hours in market work.

force ties to provide care work at home, they incur penalties in wages and opportunities for advancement that last well beyond the early child-rearing years. These employment reductions are the primary factor underlying gender inequality in both employment and earnings. Ann Crittenden (2001) has labeled the reduction in earnings owing to women's disproportionate caregiving responsibilities the "mommy tax" (Crittenden 2001). A number of researchers have estimated the magnitude of this tax. One approach examines the hourly wage penalty associated with mother-

TABLE 2.3 **Average Weekly Hours Spent in Market Work, Mothers and Fathers in Two-Parent Families, by Educational Level, 2000**

	Mothers (A)	Fathers (B)	Total (A + B)	Difference (B − A)
Less than high school	21	39	60	18
High school graduate	27	42	69	15
Some college	28	43	71	15
College graduate	27	45	72	18
Postgraduate degree	30	47	77	17

Source: Authors' calculations, based on data from CPS.
Note: Data refer to parents aged twenty-five to fifty. Hours refer to "usual hours worked per week," exclusive of commuting time and lunch breaks. Average hours include persons spending zero hours in market work.

hood. Jane Waldfogel (1998), for example, finds that after controlling for various individual characteristics, young childless women earned 90 percent as much as men, but mothers earned only 70 percent as much as men. Using longitudinal data and a research design that rules out capturing spurious effects, Michelle Budig and Paula England (2001) estimate that mothers pay a wage penalty of about 5 percent an hour for each child.

Other researchers have estimated the mommy tax as the total reduction in earnings over a woman's entire working life. Crittenden (2001) estimates that the total lost earnings over the working life of a college-educated woman can easily top $1,000,000. In a middle-income family—for example, one in which a father earns $30,000 a year in full-time work and a mother $15,000 in part-time work—the mommy tax will still exceed $600,000. Although the mommy tax is highest for highly educated women, who can command high market wages, it exacerbates gender inequality in the labor market at all levels of income. For families at the bottom of the skills and earnings distributions, particularly single-mother families, it greatly heightens the risk of economic instability and poverty. As Crittenden suggests, "There is increasing evidence in the United States and worldwide that mothers' differential responsibility for children, rather than classic sex discrimination, is the most important factor disposing women to poverty" (Crittenden 2001, 88).

In sharp contrast, men's lesser engagement in care work advantages them in the labor market. A recent study by Hyunbae Chun and Injae Lee (2001), for example, finds that having a wife raises a married man's hourly wage by about 12 percent on average and by more than 30 percent if the wife is a stay-at-home partner. They conclude that wage gains for men are explained by the degree of specialization within marriage. In other words, it is not the selection of high-ability (and potentially high-earning) men into marriage that explains the marriage wage premium; rather, it is the likelihood that wives shoulder a significant share of household tasks.

The resulting differences in mothers' and fathers' earnings are immense. Among working-age adults with no children, American women take home 41 percent of all labor market earnings each year; among married parents with children, however, women command only 28 percent of total labor market earnings (authors' calculations, based on CPS 2000). This means that among families with children, fathers earn almost three dollars for every one earned by mothers. In families headed by couples, this inequality translates into wives' economic dependency and unequal power in the home.[19] In single-parent families, which are overwhelmingly headed by women, it translates into lower incomes and higher poverty rates. For older women, who have contributed less to public and private retirement pensions during their working years, it heightens the risk of economic insecurity.[20]

The concentration of women's work in the home has other, noneconomic consequences as well. Men's lesser engagement in the home not only advantages them in the labor market; it also invests them with disproportionate power in the family and positions them to engage more fully in civic and political activities. As the British sociologist Ruth Lister observes, "Women's caring and domestic responsibilities in the private sphere make it very difficult for many of them to participate as citizens in the public sphere" (Lister 1990, 457). Women without strong ties to paid work are less likely to participate in civic activities such as arts and cultural groups, neighborhood or civic groups, and volunteer work (Caiazza and Hartmann 2001). Robert Putnam (2000) finds, similarly, that working inside the home reduces women's participation in public forms of civic engagement.

Gender Inequalities in the Home

Private solutions to work-family demands that rest on women's disproportionate assumption of household and caregiving work have other problematic consequences. Although women's hours of unpaid work have declined with rising employment, their hours in domestic work and caregiving at home continue to exceed men's by a large margin. This leaves many mothers with more total work time and less leisure time than either childless women or men. Moreover, though the cost of gender specialization in the home appears to be steepest for women, men also pay a price, in the form of absences from their children's lives.

Women's disproportionate assumption of caregiving work leaves them little time for other activities when they have dependent children. As described earlier in this chapter, many mothers adjust to the presence of children by reducing their hours in market work. Mothers who are employed also appear to manage the time demands of the workplace and their children by reducing hours devoted to everything else (Robinson and Godbey 1997; Bianchi 2000). Employed mothers spend more than seven fewer hours each week on housework than their nonemployed counterparts. Employed mothers also spend less time sleeping (fifty-five compared to sixty-one hours a week), less time on personal care (sixty-nine compared to seventy-four hours), and much less time in leisure activities (twenty-nine compared to forty-one hours) (Bianchi 2000).

Women spend more time on housework and family caregiving than their male counterparts; and the quality of this time also differs. As of the mid-1990s, women spent about twice as many hours on housework as men. Among married women, 81 to 89 percent of these hours (depending on the data source) were spent on core housework tasks such as cooking, cleaning, and laundry. Among married men, in contrast, 50 to 64 percent of the hours were spent on discretionary tasks such as repairs, paying bills, and car maintenance (Bianchi et al. 2000). Men and women also differ in how they spend their time with children—and when. Mothers, for example, devote an average of nearly thirty-five hours a week to direct child care, in contrast to less than twenty hours a week for men. Of the hours spent in direct care, married mothers are one-and-a-half times as likely as fathers to spend those hours during weekdays, when conflicts with employment are most intense. During those weekdays, one-third of the time women spend in direct care are devoted to children's personal-care activities (for example, bathing, dressing, changing diapers, or feeding) or having meals with children—twice the share of men's hours devoted to these tasks (Fuligni and Brooks-Gunn 2001).

Gender gaps are also evident with respect to "free time"—the time that remains after paid work, housework, child care, and self-care are all completed. Time-diary data suggest that American men and women do not differ greatly in their total hours of free time each day. In their study of the gender gap in free time, Marybeth Mattingly and Suzanne Bianchi (forthcoming) report that men have an average of about five and a half hours' free time each day, while women have about a half hour less—a small but significant difference. On the other hand, though this difference is minimal on a daily basis, Mattingly and Bianchi point out that, if extended throughout the year, men's additional free time adds up to 164 hours a year—the equivalent of more than four weeks of vacation (at forty hours a week). In addition to having somewhat less total free time, women have significantly fewer hours of both "pure" free time (time that is not contaminated by nonleisure secondary activities) and "adult" free time (time with no children present).

Women appear to pay the steepest economic and personal costs when families solve work-family dilemmas by allocating a disproportionate share of the care work to women. However, gender inequalities, particularly in the care of children, may have costs for men as well. Most important, the gendered divisions of labor in unpaid work have marginalized men's engagement in the home, including the care and nurturing of their children. The "absent father" problem is most extreme in the growing number of families headed by a divorced, separated, or never married mother. Yet in a substantial number of two-parent homes, resident fathers are nearly as absent from their children's lives as fathers who live elsewhere.

Working Nonstandard Hours: Split-Shift Parenting and Disrupted Family Life

Many of the one-quarter to one-third of couples in which one parent works nonstandard hours rely on what Presser (forthcoming) calls "split-shift" or "tag team" parenting to provide child care for their young children. Split-shift and tag-team parenting, like other aspects of the work-family balancing act, have a gendered cast. Adapting work schedules to respond to caregiving needs remains the domain of women. Mothers are four times as likely as fathers to cite caregiving responsibilities as the primary reason for working nonstandard hours (Presser forthcoming). In addition, though men's likelihood of working evenings, nights, and weekends is unaffected by the presence or ages of children in the home, women are much more likely to work nonstandard hours when they have a preschool child (Presser 1995b). As Presser observes, "Women generally are the adapters who arrange their work hours around those of their husbands rather than vice versa. . . . Men are accepters: they are willing to care for children when mothers are employed" (Presser 1989a, 531).

Is split-shift parenting a viable solution to the problem of balancing work and family obligations? Is it just one more symptom of the problem? In terms of gender equality, split-shift parenting has the potential advantage of engaging men more fully in the care of their children. Whether by choice or necessity, fathers are more likely to care for preschool children if their work hours are different from those of mothers (Presser 1989a; Brayfield 1995).[21] For example, among dual-earner couples with preschool-age children, two-thirds of families in which the mother is at her job for ten hours or more when the father is not at his job rely primarily on the father to provide child care during those hours (Presser forthcoming).

Although split-shift parenting may help reduce gender inequalities in the provision of care for children, it does so at a high cost to workers and their families. A large body of research from Europe and the United States finds that working nonstandard hours—especially night work and rotating shifts—is associated with workers' likelihood of suffering coronary disease, sleep disturbances, gastrointestinal disorders, and chronic malaise (ILO 1995; Presser 1999); round-the-clock employment also raises the likelihood of workplace accidents (Kauppinen 2001).

What Presser (forthcoming) calls the "social consequences" of nonstandard work schedules are also troublesome for families. She finds that non-day employment is associated with lower marital quality, especially when there are children, and more-limited interactions between parent and child. Nonstandard schedules are associated with increased likelihood of marital separation or divorce, even controlling for couples' total employment time and time spent together. Married fathers who work fixed night shifts are six times more likely than their counterparts who work days to face marital dissolution; for married mothers, fixed nights increase the odds by a factor of three (Presser 1999).[22]

There is also disturbing evidence that children whose parents work night and weekend shifts fare much worse than other children. Mothers who work nonstandard hours with infants have higher levels of depression, which may diminish the quality of the attention and care they provide to children; preschool-age children whose parents work nonstandard hours are also less likely to be cared for in formal child care settings that may provide important school-readiness experiences (Han 2002). Parents who work nonstandard hours, particularly those working evenings and weekends, have less time to spend with their school-age children (Heymann 2000; Presser 1986), and this may translate into less supervision, help with homework, and other positive inputs. In a study of the effects of nonstandard employment on the cognitive development of infants, Wen-Jui Han (2002) concludes that children whose mothers have ever worked nonstandard hours—and particularly those who work more than thirty hours a week in evening, night, or variable shifts—perform significantly worse on cognitive outcomes at one, two, and three years of age. Examining the effects of nonstandard work on older children, Jody Heymann (2000) finds that, after controlling for other family and parental characteristics, each hour that a parent works between six and nine in the evening corresponds with a 16 percent increase in the likelihood that their children score low in mathematics at school. Children of parents who work nights are also nearly three times as likely to get suspended from school.

Child Care Costs for Parents, Children, and Providers

Many families solve the competing demands of the workplace and the family by shifting a portion of children's care from the family to the market. The movement of women from the home to the labor market when their children are young has greatly increased both the demand for and the supply of nonparental child care. Like other private solutions, however, extensive use of child care has created as many problems as it has solved.

Most nonparental care arrangements in the United States are market based in both provision and financing, and the use of private child care imposes steep financial costs on families. Among working families with children under the age of thirteen, about half pay for child care during their working hours. Across all families, these costs average $286, or 9 percent of family earnings, each month; the share of family income devoted to child care is much higher among families with lower earnings (Giannarelli and Barsimantov 2000). Child care costs are as high as or higher than tuition at public colleges in many states. Unlike the parents of college-age children, however, parents of young children are unlikely to have accumulated savings to pay these expenses.

Reliance on consumer markets for child care has other consequence for the quality of care that children receive. A number of observational studies conclude that the quality of most child care in the United States is low; most estimate that more than half of settings provide care that is "adequate" to "poor" and only about one in ten provide developmentally enriching care (Helburn et al. 1995; Galinsky et al. 1994; NICHD 1997b). The generally poor quality of care received by American children reflects the inability or unwillingness of parents to pay the full cost of high-quality care by well-trained professionals. This creates another, often overlooked problem in the American child care market: the impoverishment of a large, low-wage child care workforce dominated by women. Ironically, though market care is costly relative to family budgets, child care professionals are among the most poorly paid of all workers in the United States. Most also work without either employment benefits or realistic opportunities for career advancement. By way of comparison, the average earnings of workers in child care centers are about the same as—and those of family child care providers are barely half of—the wages earned by parking-lot attendants (Whitebook 1999).

Economic Insecurity and Poverty

The movement of many more women into the labor market during recent decades has created new time demands and other social pressures. We would surely expect that this increase in household labor supply was good for families' economic well-being. Indeed, throughout most of the 1990s, the United States experienced one of the longest sustained periods of economic growth in recent history. For a period of several years, the standard economic indicators seemed to convey only better and better news: the economy was growing, stock prices were climbing, unemployment rates were low, and inflation was minimal.

Although many families fared well during the 1990s, many others experienced a different economic reality. The percentage of children living in poverty decreased slightly starting in the late 1990s, but this drop only succeeded in returning the United States to the poverty rates of the 1970s. At the end of the decade, more than 18 percent of children between the ages of six and seventeen, and 22 percent of those under the age of six, were living in families officially defined as poor (Shirk, Bennett, and Aber 1999).

That nearly one in five children lives in poverty is sobering enough. It is even more troubling when we consider just how poor these children are. The formula for setting the poverty threshold in the United States has been under fire for many years. Critics point out that the underlying formula, adopted in the 1950s, was never designed to set the threshold for a reasonable standard of living and has not been updated to reflect nearly a half century of changing household-consumption patterns. The current poverty-line formula also fails to take into account several forms of government assistance—such as food stamps and the EITC—and to account for necessary expenses such as out-of-pocket payment for child care and health insurance. Updating the poverty line to respond to these criticisms suggests that poverty is an even more pervasive problem. For example, applying a "family budget" methodology to estimate the income needed to avoid economic hardship, researchers Heather Boushey and her colleagues of the Economic Policy Institute estimate that whereas 10 percent of families with children were "officially" poor in the late 1990s, nearly 30 percent had incomes below the level required for a safe and decent standard of living (Boushey et al. 2001).

The causes of persistent poverty and economic insecurity in the United States are complex. Like gender inequality, they have roots in both the economic transformations of the industrial and postindustrial eras and the resolutely private American conception of responsibility for children, especially children below school age. Of particular importance for the issues in this book, economic insecurity is heightened for many families with children by the loss of earnings associated with childbirth and early caregiving. Although some workers have the right to unpaid leave at the time of childbirth under the Family and Medical Leave Act (FMLA), the limited availability of paid leave means that many parents cannot take advantage of their right to withdraw from employment to care for infants. Nearly 80 percent of employees who do not take FMLA leave when needed report that the reason is that they could not afford to lose their pay for the period of leave (DOL 2000). The relatively small share of women estimated to have some paid maternity benefits under state temporary-disability insurance programs receive, on average, only $140 to $270 a week in benefits (Wisensale 2001), well less than enough to keep a family out of poverty. Others, lacking even these protections, rely on public-assistance benefits while on leave (DOL 2000). Once mothers are able to return to paid work, many face losing a substantial portion of their earnings to child care. Despite recent expansions in public child care programs, as few as 10 to 15 percent of income-eligible families are estimated to be receiving child care subsidies (DHHS 2000). In the absence of assistance, child care costs keep some mothers out of employment and push many near-poor families deeper into poverty.

Private Solutions and Child Well-Being

American parents are struggling to resolve competing demands from employment and caregiving, and the evidence is strong that their private solutions impose a variety of economic and social costs. For many, these solutions also fail to provide reasonable economic security. The costs for families are not solely economic, however; another body of scholarship suggests that these private solutions may be compromising children's well-being as well.

Chronic poverty, material hardship, and related problems pose some of the most direct threats to children's well-being. Persistent income poverty places children at risk for problems ranging from poor health to compromised cognitive development, poor school achievement, and early childbearing (Danziger and Waldfogel 2000; Brooks-Gunn, Duncan, and Aber 1997; Kamerman et al. forthcoming.)

Reduced parental availability during children's earliest years may pose another, more subtle risk. Inflexibility in working hours, lack of paid parental leaves, and economic necessity combine to create a limited set of choices for many parents: full-time paid work or no paid work. During the first three years after childbirth, for example, Christopher Ruhm notes that most women either do not hold jobs or work for many hours (Ruhm forthcoming). For many children, this means many hours of each day are spent without the direct care and attention of either, or the sole, parent during their earliest and most developmentally sensitive years. Although parental employment is generally good for children, providing both income and role models, some research suggests that long hours of parental employment during a child's first year of life may be associated with worse developmental outcomes (see Ruhm forthcoming for a review). Lack of parental (or other) supervision owing to employment schedules may be a risk factor for older children as well. Rates of juvenile crime triple during afternoon hours, when many young adolescents are unsupervised, and research suggests that juveniles are especially likely to experiment with drugs, sex, and other risky behaviors during these unsupervised hours (David and Lucile Packard Foundation 1999).

Although still inconclusive, research is suggesting what many parents understand intuitively: children do better when they have sufficient time with their parents, and that is especially true during the first year of life. This is precisely the input into child development that is compromised by many families' private solutions to work-family demands.

CONCLUSION

American families are struggling to resolve tensions arising from new economic and social arrangements in the family and the labor market. Women expect, and are expected, to participate with men in the labor market; they are also expected to provide most care work in the home. Most parents are employed, but workplaces and social policies are still designed for workers with minimal family responsibilities. Families have increased their labor supply, but many have experienced little real economic progress or have even fallen further behind. Many parents are working nonstandard hours as a child care strategy. Others are purchasing child care in the market and, despite spending an appreciable share of their earnings, are leaving their children in care of mediocre or poor quality. Families are being forced to make compromises, and these compromises have a distinctly gendered cast: women continue to pay steep wage penalties for motherhood, to experience high rates of poverty, and to care for children for either no or for miserably low wages. These compromises may be imposing still other penalties on children, who get too little of their parents' time when they are very young and care of uncertain quality when their parents are at work.

Although families are facing the challenges of work-family balance in all industrialized countries, families in the United States are doing so in a context of limited public responsibility for the private costs of rearing children. Problems of income and time poverty, gender inequality, questionable child care arrangements, and poor outcomes for children may not be inevitable, however. In the next chapter, we use cross-national data from multiple sources to compare the U.S. to other industrialized countries on several of these outcomes. We then turn to the question of how satisfied U.S. parents are with the time that they have available for their families in comparison to their counterparts in other countries.

— Chapter 3 —

The United States in Cross-National Perspective: Are Parents and Children Doing Better Elsewhere?

A MERICAN FAMILIES ARE not alone in the demands they encounter on their time and energy. In all industrialized and industrializing countries, working families are at the epicenter of tensions arising from changing gender norms, social supports, and labor market opportunities. However, cross-national comparisons suggest that American families face heavier demands and receive less external support than do families in other equally rich industrialized countries. The characteristically American approach of expecting private forces to solve social problems has created especially pressing burdens in this country.

On many indicators of family and child well-being, the problems confronting American families are more acute than elsewhere. American working parents are squeezed for time and pay a comparatively higher penalty for working reduced hours than do parents in our comparison countries.[1] Relative to these other rich, high-employment countries, the United States has achieved only moderate levels of gender equality, especially among parents. And our families and children fare much worse than their counterparts in other countries on several other dimensions of well-being.

THE TIME SQUEEZE

American parents have good reason to feel that they are squeezed for time. Nearly all fathers and a substantial share of mothers in the United States are employed. Those who are employed are averaging long weekly hours in the workplace; and compared with their counterparts in other countries, many of them are spending extremely long hours at work.[2]

Among married and cohabiting American parents aged twenty-five to fifty years old, 93 percent of fathers and 69 percent of mothers are employed either full-time or part-time (figure 3.1); workers on paid leave are generally counted as employed.[3] The employment rates for fathers actually vary little across our twelve countries, ranging from 88 to 97 percent, with most of that variation explained by variability in the unemployment rate for this age group (during the mid-1990s). Mothers' employment rates vary enormously, from as low as 40 percent in Luxembourg to as high as 85 percent in Sweden. Relative to this group of countries, the employment rates of American parents—both fathers and mothers—are just about equal to the cross-country average. The employment rate for American mothers lags behind those reported in all of the Nordic countries, but it exceeds mothers' rates in all of the Continental countries.[4]

The United States is exceptional, in comparative terms, with respect to the number of hours worked among those who are employed. According to the International Labour Organization (ILO 1999), the American workforce reports the longest annual hours of any in the industrialized world. American workers spend an average of 1,966 hours a year at work. Average annual work hours in the United States exceed those reported all across Europe; Americans "outwork" workers in Sweden (1,552), France (1,656), Germany (1,560), and the United Kingdom (1,731 hours). American workers log nearly six more weeks of work a year than their Canadian counterparts (at 1,732 hours), and their hours exceed even those of the notoriously work-intensive Japanese (1,889 hours) (ILO 1999). Moreover, annual work hours continue to rise in the United States, while they have been declining in nearly every other country in the industrialized world (ILO 2001).

FIGURE 3.1 **Employment Rates Among Married or Cohabiting Mothers and Fathers, Mid-1990s**

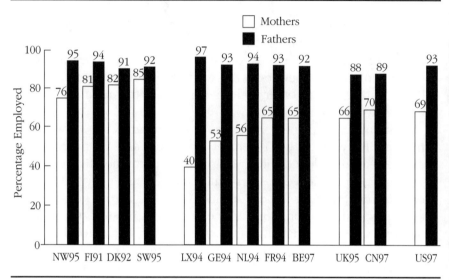

Source: Data from LIS.
Note: Employment comprises both part-time and full-time work.

As described earlier, the time crunch for many families results from the combination of moderately high levels of parental employment and long hours at the workplace. To compare the severity of the time squeeze among working parents, it is useful to examine the joint work hours of dual-earner couples with children and to consider weekly hours—rather than annual hours, which conflate work hours with vacation time.[5]

The results, displayed in figures 3.2 and 3.3, are clear: American working parents spend exceptionally long hours each week in market work.[6] American parents in dual-earner families spend an average of eighty hours a week at the workplace (figure 3.2). Similar couples in the United Kingdom log almost nine fewer hours a week, and a typical Swedish working couple works for pay about eleven fewer hours each week.

What is even more remarkable about the working time of American couples with children are the high percentages logging very long hours (figure 3.3). Nearly two-thirds of American dual-

FIGURE 3.2 **Mean Joint Weekly Work Hours Among Dual-Earner Couples with Children, Mid-1990s**

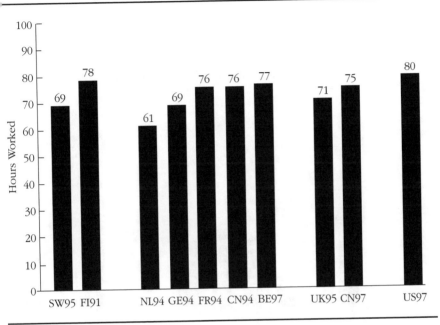

Source: Data from LIS.

earner couples with children report joint workweeks of eighty hours or more. This is an exceptionally large share in comparative terms. Other than in Canada, no more than one-third of couples in our comparison countries spend this much time at the workplace. Ten percent of dual-earning parents in the United States jointly work one hundred or more hours a week, in contrast to 6 percent in neighboring Canada and less than 1 percent in Sweden.[7]

Finland provides an especially interesting comparative case. Finnish couples work nearly the same average hours as Americans, despite higher rates of maternal employment in Finland. The difference between the countries lies in the distribution of working hours. In Finland, couples' usual working hours are more tightly clustered. Fewer than a third of employed Finnish couples log eighty hours or more a week, and only 6 percent spend one hundred or more hours a week at the workplace.

FIGURE 3.3 **Prevalence of Long Joint Weekly Work Hours Among Dual-Earner Couples with Children, Mid-1990s**

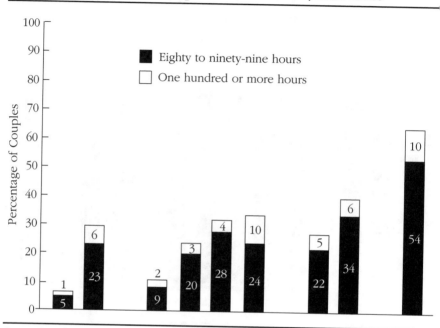

Source: Data from LIS.

WAGE LOSSES ASSOCIATED WITH WORKING PART-TIME

American workers work long hours, in part, because they pay a higher penalty for reducing their hours than do workers in other countries. About 26 percent of American mothers in the labor market are employed part-time, defined as fewer than thirty-five hours a week (authors' calculations, based on CPS 2000). For most of these mothers, the decision to work part-time means a reduction in their hourly wages. After controlling for basic differences in human capital between part- and full-time workers, women in the

FIGURE 3.4 **Wage Gaps Between Part-Time and Full-Time Employed Women, Mid-1990s**

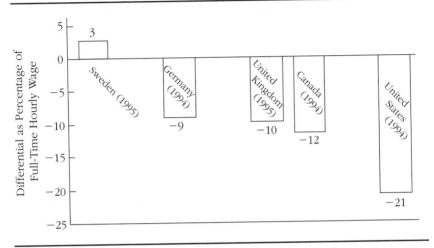

Source: Data from LIS.
Note: Gap adjusted for human-capital differences between part-time and full-time workers.

United States who work part-time earn about 21 percent less an hour, on average, than their full-time counterparts (figure 3.4).

In contrast, women's part-time wage penalty is about half that magnitude in at least three other countries: Canada (12 percent), the United Kingdom (10 percent), and Germany (9 percent).[8] Women who work part-time in Sweden earn about 3 percent more an hour, controlling for human-capital differences, than their full-time counterparts.

Clearly, part-time work is particularly costly for women in the United States. Little research has been conducted on the reasons for cross-national variation in part-time wage penalties, but two factors appear to be influential. One is the degree of occupational segregation between part-time and full-time workers—that is, the extent to which the two groups of workers work in separate occupations. The second is the overall degree of wage dispersion in the labor market; a large wage spread always widens pay gaps between more- and less-advantaged groups of workers. Both factors are comparatively high in the United States (Bardasi and Gornick 2002). Segregation between part-time and full-time workers is particularly high in the United States partly because full-time workers have relatively little access to part-time work without changing jobs, employers, occupations, or all three.

GENDER INEQUALITY IN THE LABOR MARKET

As reported in chapter 2, in the United States women lag behind men on several indicators of labor market attachment. That is especially true among parents, because American mothers are much more likely than their male counterparts to withdraw from employment to care for children, especially children below preschool age.

American mothers are more likely than American fathers to leave the labor force because they have young children than are mothers in most of our comparison countries. To assess this, we consider the effect of having a preschool-age child (aged three to five years) on the probability of employment for mothers and fathers in each of our countries. This "preschooler effect" is measured as the percentage difference in the probability of being employed associated with having a youngest child aged three to five, relative to parents of the same sex in the same country whose youngest child is aged thirteen to seventeen. Comparing employment rates between parents who live in the same country but with children of different ages helps to control for country-specific factors that influence employment rates overall, and it allows us to isolate the effect of having responsibility for young children specifically.[9]

The preschooler effect on mothers is relatively large in the United States (figure 3.5). Whereas the presence of a preschool-age child is associated with a slightly higher likelihood of employment among American fathers (relative to fathers with older children), American mothers with young children are 19 percent less likely to be employed than are their counterparts with older children. The preschooler effect for mothers is larger in the United States than in seven of the ten comparison countries, including all of the Nordic countries as well as France, Belgium, and our near neighbor Canada.

FIGURE 3.5 **Preschooler Effect on Mothers' and Fathers' Employment, Mid-1990s**

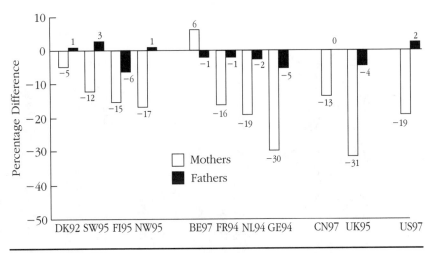

Source: Data from LIS.
Note: The preschooler effect is measured as the percentage difference in employment rates between parents with youngest child aged three to five and parents with youngest child aged thirteen to seventeen.

The same is not true of American fathers. The preschooler effect on the employment of American fathers is small, and the pattern is reversed—fathers are more likely to be in the workforce when they have younger children. The United States also has moderately gender-egalitarian outcomes, in comparative terms, on several other measures of parents' labor market attachments.

The ratio of mothers' to fathers' employment rates provides one measure of equality (see figure 3.6)[10] The use of a ratio helps to isolate cross-national variation that cannot be explained by factors that affect both men and women, such as national "tastes" for paid work and employer demand.[11] A ratio of 1 indicates complete gender equality.[12] By this measure, the United States ranks in the middle of our comparison countries. American mothers are 75 percent as likely as their male counterparts to be employed. This ratio is equal to that reported in the United Kingdom, four to five points higher than the results in Belgium and France, and 15

FIGURE 3.6 **Ratio of Married or Cohabiting Mothers' to Fathers' Employment Rates, Mid-1990s**

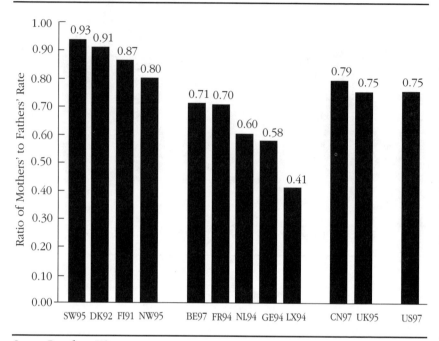

Source: Data from LIS.

to nearly 35 points higher than in the three lowest (or most un-equal) countries. However, the female-to-male employment-rate ratio for the United States is five to nearly twenty points below the ratios in the more egalitarian Nordic countries of Sweden, Denmark, Finland, and Norway, where mothers' employment rates approach parity with men's.

The employment ratio is a useful indicator of parents' labor market attachment, but it does not reveal other dimensions on which mothers' and fathers' employment patterns differ. It is possible, for example, that in the countries in which mothers' employment rates approach those of fathers, there are large gaps in hours worked among those employed. Alternatively, countries may have achieved greater parity in employment rates and hours while maintaining larger wage differentials between mothers and fathers.

In all of the countries for which we have data on weekly hours, married and cohabiting mothers' average hours spent in paid work are less than those of fathers (figure 3.7). In the United States, employed mothers work 78 percent as many hours, on average, as their male partners, the same ratio that is reported in Canada. Although the degree of gender equality in hours worked in the U.S. ratio is higher than that reported in about half the comparison countries, it lags behind the ratio reported in three other countries—France, Sweden, and especially Finland. That the United States is relatively egalitarian on this indicator is not surprising, given the comparatively low rates of part-time work in the United States. What is remarkable here is the Swedish result. Despite higher rates of part-time work in Sweden, mothers' and fathers' average hours are more equal—because many mothers who work part-time work "long part-time" (about thirty hours a week) and because Swedish fathers spend fewer hours in the workplace than do fathers elsewhere. In the Netherlands, in contrast, many mothers also work part-time, but weekly part-time hours are often very low; the gender differential in hours worked is extreme.

American working mothers also lag behind mothers in some of our comparison countries when we consider gender equality in hourly wages. As reported in figure 3.7, married and cohabiting American mothers earn approximately 67 cents for each dollar earned by the average American father.[13] That ratio is somewhat higher (more favorable for mothers) than the outcomes in the United Kingdom and Germany, but it lags behind the ratio reported in all of the other countries. The gender ratio in hourly earnings exceeds .70 in Canada and Finland and .80 in France and the Netherlands; it reaches .93 in Belgium.[14]

Finally, we consider a composite indicator—married mothers' share of total labor market earnings commanded by all married parents—which conflates gender differentials in employment rates, hours, and wages. By this measure, if mothers and fathers command equal shares of total earnings, mothers would take home 50 percent of earnings; female-to-male employment, hours, or wage ratios of less than 1 will each contribute to lowering the total share of earnings earned by mothers.

Mothers' share of family earnings lags behind that of fathers by

FIGURE 3.7 **Ratio of Married or Cohabiting Mothers' to Fathers' Average Weekly Work Hours and Average Hourly Wages, Mid-1990s**

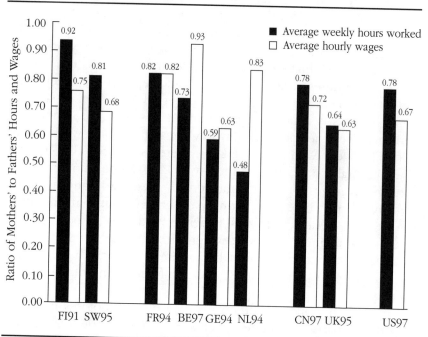

Source: Data from LIS.
Note: Results pertain to part-time and full-time workers, combined.

a wide margin in all of our comparison countries. As reported in figure 3.8, American mothers earn 28 percent of parents' total labor market earnings, which places the United States about in the middle of our group of countries. According to this composite measure, American mothers lag behind their counterparts in Canada and in six other countries, where mothers take home about 31 to 38 percent of parental labor market income.[15] The United States' fairly low cross-national ranking on this indicator (eighth place out of twelve) is shaped by all three dimensions of mothers' labor market attachment relative to that of their male partners—a moderate employment ratio (tied for six out of twelve), a relatively

FIGURE 3.8 **Mothers' Share of Labor-Market Earnings Among Married or Cohabiting Parents, Mid-1990s**

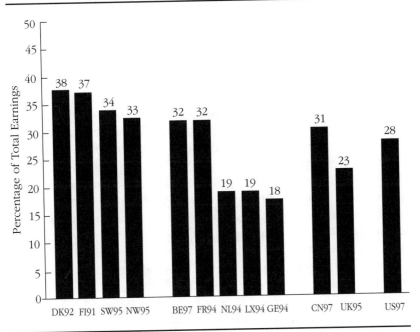

Source: Data from LIS.

egalitarian hours ratio (tied for fourth of nine), and a comparatively unfavorable gender wage ratio (seven out of nine).

Relatively high levels of equality on this indicator in the Nordic countries may seem surprising, because these countries have high levels of female employment but substantial gender differentials in other aspects of labor market attachment. In Sweden, Denmark, and Norway, in particular, many women work part-time, large numbers take up family leave options, and labor markets are relatively gender segregated by occupation (see, for example, Rubery, Smith, and Fagan 1999). On balance, however, these potentially inegalitarian patterns appear to be offset by other, equalizing factors—including the high employment rates, the long hours worked by part-time workers, and the favorable levels of pay.[16] Women in these countries, and in Finland, come closer to parity with men, in the share of labor market earnings they control, than women in the United States and in all of our other comparison countries.

GENDER INEQUALITY AT HOME

Gender inequalities in the labor market are intimately tied to gender inequalities in the home because the time women spend in unpaid domestic—and particularly caregiving—work in the home reduces their availability for employment. Given evidence that the United States ranks in the middle of our comparison countries on labor market equality, it is not surprising to discover that the United States also lags behind a number of other countries on measures of gender equality in unpaid work in the home.

Researchers use time-use diaries to measure individuals' allocation of time to various forms of paid and unpaid work. Using such data, we calculate the ratio of men's to women's hours in unpaid work, providing a measure of gender equality that parallels the ratio measure of gender equality in labor market attachments. (On this measure, complete gender equality would produce a ratio of 1). By comparing time-use data of men and women within the same country, this ratio isolates differences between men and women who are likely to share country-specific characteristics that also influence their time allocations, such as cultural expectations about time spent with children or preferences for a clean house.

According to Multinational Time Use Study (MTUS) data from the 1980s and 1990s, American employed parents with children under school age appear to be relatively inegalitarian in the allocation of time to unpaid work in the home (figure 3.9).[17] Employed mothers and fathers in the United States both spend less time in unpaid work than their counterparts in most of the countries for which we have comparable data, which may reflect the exceptionally long hours that American parents spend at the workplace. Relative to mothers, however, fathers spend less time in unpaid work in the United States than in any other of the countries studied except the Netherlands. In the most egalitarian countries—Sweden and Norway, and our neighbor Canada—fathers spend about 55 to about 60 percent as much time as mothers in

FIGURE 3.9 **Mean Daily Hours Spent in Unpaid Work by Employed Mothers and Fathers, 1985 to 1992**

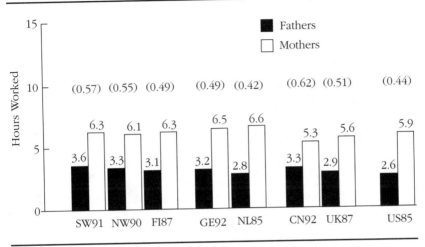

Source: Data from MTUS.
Note: Results pertain to employed adults who are married or cohabiting. Numbers in parentheses are the ratios of fathers' hours to mothers' hours.

unpaid work; in the United States, they spend only 44 percent of the time mothers spend in such work.

When we disaggregate the measures to consider three types of unpaid work in the home separately, gender inequalities are striking in the type of unpaid work performed by men and women in all of these countries (figure 3.10). Fathers in all of our comparison countries are closest to mothers in the hours spent on nonroutine housework, such as home repairs. The United States is one of only three countries in which mothers' time exceeds fathers' in this category. In contrast, American fathers spend only about one-quarter of the time reported by mothers in routine housework, such as laundry and cleaning, placing the United States in about the middle of the multicountry range. Considering time spent caring for children as the primary activity (using the MTUS definition), American fathers spend only 39 percent of the time that mothers do. Fathers in five of the seven comparison countries—Norway and Sweden, Germany, Canada, and the United Kingdom—take responsibility for larger shares of child care time.

FIGURE 3.10 **Gender Equality in Mean Daily Hours Spent in Unpaid Work by Employed Mothers and Fathers, by Category of Work, 1985 to 1992**

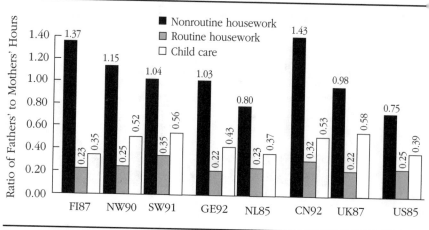

Source: Data from MTUS.
Note: Results pertain to employed adults who are married or cohabiting.

NONSTANDARD WORKING TIME

Many American parents currently meet their child care needs through split-shift caregiving arrangements in which one parent works nonstandard hours during evenings or nights or on weekends. Although this solution is not uniquely American, parents in the United States are more likely to work these nonstandard hours than are parents in all of our comparison countries.

About 12 percent of American working parents usually work in the evening or at night (figure 3.11). Late shifts are almost as common among parents in the United Kingdom (11 percent). Substantially fewer parents work late hours in the five other European countries for which we have comparable data; rates of evening and night work in these countries range from about 8 percent (in Germany and the Netherlands) to about 5 percent (in Belgium and Luxembourg).[18] American working parents are also more likely than others to work weekend shifts. In the United States, 28 percent of working parents usually work on the weekend, in contrast to only about 10 to 20 percent of parents in France, Germany, Luxembourg, and Belgium.

FIGURE 3.11 **Prevalence of Evening, Night, and Weekend Work Among Employed Parents, 1997**

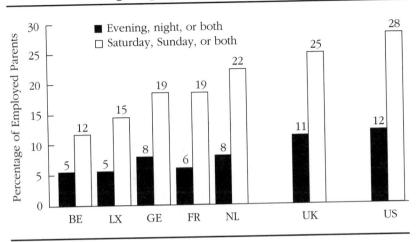

Source: Data from European LFS and U.S. CPS.

FAMILY POVERTY

Despite high levels of employment and long average working hours, a high proportion of American families live in poverty. The U.S. poverty rate among families with children is exceptional in cross-national terms (figure 3.12). We define poverty using a relative poverty rate: families are poor if total family income (labor market earnings plus cash and near-cash transfers, net of income and payroll taxes) falls below 50 percent of the median family income in one's own country.[19] By this measure, 17 percent of all American families with children were poor in 1997. Outside of the other English-speaking countries, which also had relatively high poverty rates, fewer than half as many families were poor in the rest of the countries. In the Nordic countries, poverty rates were only 2 to 4 percent.

American family poverty rates are particularly high, in cross-national terms, among working families. To net out cross-national variation in family composition—especially the high rate of single parenting in the United States—we compare poverty rates for employed two-parent and single-parent families separately. Among

FIGURE 3.12 **Poverty Rates Among Families with Children, Mid-1990s**

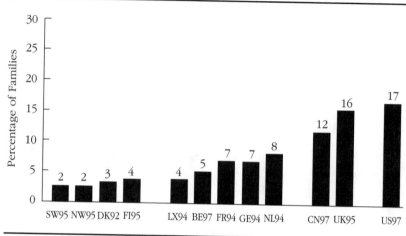

Source: Data from LIS.
Note: Poverty is defined as having household income below 50 percent of the country median.

two-parent families in which both parents are employed, 8 percent of American families have incomes at or below one-half of median income (figure 3.13). The poverty rate for families in the United States is the highest across our twelve countries; in ten of these countries, poverty rates among two-parent working families are 2 percent or lower.

Cross-national variation is even more striking for single-parent families in which that parent is employed (figure 3.13). In all countries, these families are mostly headed by women. In the United States, nearly one-half of these families are poor, despite their labor market attachment. Families headed by employed single parents are also at heightened risk for poverty in many of the Continental European countries and in Canada, but poverty rates are considerably lower (from 15 to 30 percent). In the Nordic countries and Belgium, no more than 10 percent of single-parent families with employed heads of household live in poverty.

The high family poverty rate in the United States is difficult to reconcile with its relatively high parental employment rates and long working hours. It can be explained in part by high rates of single parenthood and by comparatively high rates of withdrawal

FIGURE 3.13 **Poverty Rates Among Employed Single-Parent and Two-Parent Families, Mid-1990s**

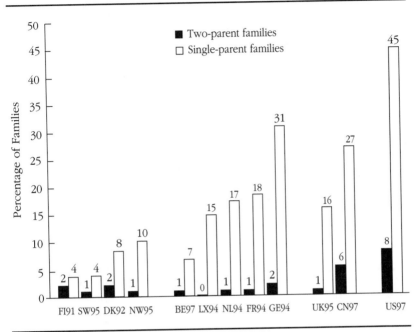

Source: Data from LIS.
Note: Poverty is defined as having household income below 50 percent of the country median. Results pertain to families in which all parents are employed.

from the labor market among both single and married mothers when their children are young. The United States also has a large low-wage employment sector in comparative terms and unusually meager government benefits for low earners. These factors combine to produce both high rates of poverty and exceptionally high levels of income inequality.

CHILD WELL-BEING

These comparisons suggest that families in the United States are faring less well than families in other countries on several measures. Whether the tensions created by long hours of work, persistent gender inequalities, poverty, and income inequality are the private concerns of families or a shared public concern depends in part on the consequences for children. In fact, cross-national data suggest that American children are not faring well relative to children in other high-income countries, with the youngest American children at particularly high risk.

Data gathered by the United Nations International Children's Emergency Fund (UNICEF 2001) reveal that poor outcomes begin in the prenatal period; the United States has the highest percentage of low-birth-weight babies (less than twenty-five hundred grams) reported across these countries, matched only by the United Kingdom (figure 3.14). At 7 percent, the rate in the United States is one to two points higher than in most of our comparison countries and nearly double the rate in Finland and Norway. American children also have the highest rates of infant mortality (deaths before the age of one year) and young-child mortality (deaths before

FIGURE 3.14 **Prevalence of Low Birth Weight, 1995 to 1999**

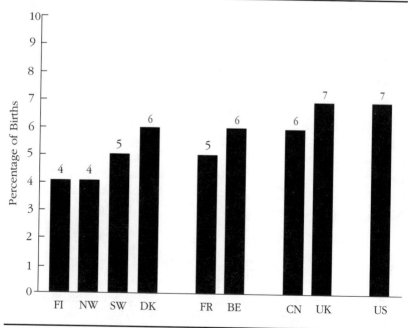

Source: Data from UNICEF (2001).

FIGURE 3.15 **Mortality Rates Among Infants and Young Children, 1999**

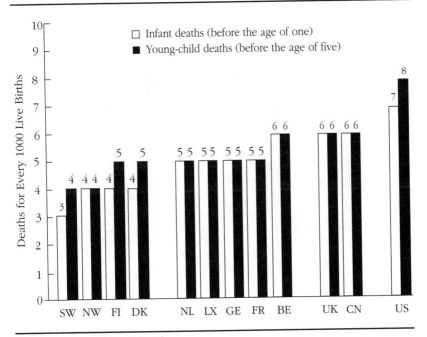

Source: Data from UNICEF (2001).
Note: Mortality rates are rounded to nearest whole number.

the age of five)—at seven and eight deaths, respectively, for every thousand live births (figure 3.15).

American children also fare relatively poorly during their school years. American children are doing worse than most children in educational achievement. Data from the Third International Mathematics and Science Study reveal that eighth graders in the United States are ranked near the bottom on standardized tests in mathematics (only the United Kingdom is lower) and lowest in science achievement (figure 3.16) (NCES 2001). American children may be falling behind in school because they spend more hours each day watching television. In a recent World Health Organization study of television watching (Currie et al. 2000), the percentage of eleven-year-olds who watch four or more hours of television a day was highest in the United States among the ten of our com-

FIGURE 3.16 **Eighth-Grade Achievement Scores in Science and Mathematics, 1999**

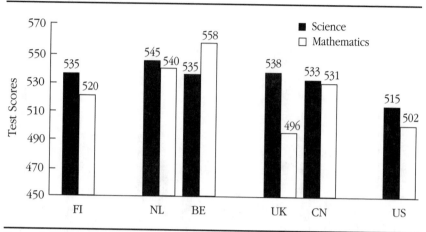

Source: Data from NCES (2001).

parison countries for which data were reported. More than a third of American children spend four or more hours a day in front of a television, fully two-and-a-half to three times the rate reported in France, the country in which hours of television watching are lowest (figure 3.17).

American children fare relatively poorly during their later teenage years as well. One of the most striking and troubling indicators is the exceptionally high rate of adolescent pregnancy in the United States. Data reported by Susheela Singh and Jacqueline Darroch (2000) for the middle 1990s indicate that eighty-three of every one thousand young American women between the ages of fifteen and nineteen became pregnant; of these, fifty-four gave birth and twenty-nine terminated their pregnancies (figure 3.18). These rates are truly extraordinary in cross-national terms. American teen pregnancy rates are more than triple the average rate reported across the Nordic countries and four to seven times as high as those in the countries of Continental Europe. Exceptionally high levels of adolescent pregnancy are worrisome in their own right as a health risk for young women and their babies. Moreover, they are an important factor in the high levels of poverty and disadvantage in the United States.

FIGURE 3.17 **Percentage of Eleven-Year-Olds Who Report Watching Television Four or More Hours per Day, 1997 to 1998**

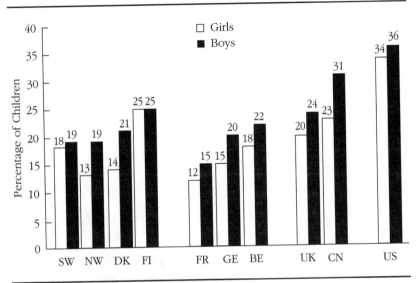

Source: Currie et al. (2000).

THE PARENTAL TIME SQUEEZE

The United States has one of the most productive economies in the industrialized world. Yet it fails to excel on many of the dimensions Americans claim to prize most highly. Not surprisingly, American parents also turn out to be more dissatisfied, relative to their counterparts in other countries, with the time they have available for their families.

Many Americans report dissatisfaction with their ability to balance work and family life. According to a recent national survey conducted by the Families and Work Institute (Galinsky, Bond, and Kim 2001), more than half (53 percent) of American workers report that they experience conflict "in balancing work, personal life, and family life."[20] Compare this with responses from a 2000 survey of working conditions across the European Union: when parents were asked, "In general, do your working hours fit in with your family or social commitments outside work very well, fairly

FIGURE 3.18 **Teenage Pregnancies and Pregnancy Outcomes, Mid-1990s**

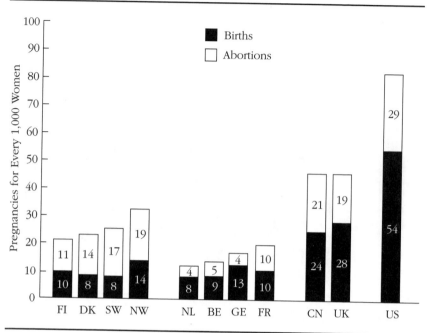

Source: Data from Singh and Darroch (2000).

well, not very well, or not at all well?," a remarkable 80 percent of parents across the fifteen European Union countries responded that their work hours and private commitments fit "very well" or "fairly well" (European Foundation 2001).

Some observers take issue with the claim that Americans are working more than they want.[21] They argue that Americans work longer hours because they like to work long hours, relative to Europeans. The evidence for this conclusion is mixed. Recent studies suggest that to the extent that it is true, it seems to be driven by concerns about compensation. John Evans, Douglas Lippoldt, and Pascal Marianna (2001) report that when asked if they would choose shorter hours (with less pay) or longer hours (with more pay), fewer Americans than Europeans choose shorter hours. When the pay tradeoff is dropped from the question, how-

FIGURE 3.19 **Preference for Having More Time with Family, Among Parents with Children at Home, 1997**

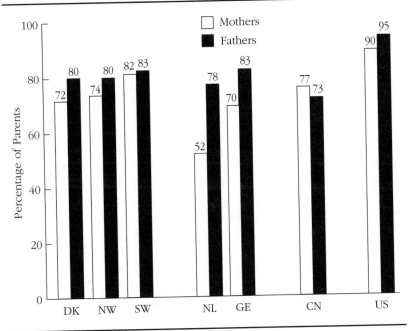

Source: Data from ISSP.

ever, a higher percentage of Americans, relative to Europeans, report that they would choose to reduce their hours.[22]

The desire for more time away from the workplace is particularly salient for parents. To place the parental time squeeze in comparative perspective, figure 3.19 compares responses to identical questions in seven industrialized countries; these data come from a supplement to the 1997 International Social Survey Programme (ISSP) data.[23] When asked if they would like to have more time to spend with their families, large proportions of both mothers and fathers in all of these countries report that they would like "a little or a lot" more time with their families. American parents appear to feel more "time poor" with regard to family life than do their counterparts in other countries. Fully 95 percent of fathers and 90 percent of mothers in the United States reported that they wished they had more time with their families. This rate among fathers is the highest of all of these countries by a considerable margin. The rate among American mothers is also nearly 10 percentage points higher than in the next-highest country (Sweden) and nearly 15 percentage points higher than among parents in nearby Canada.

CONCLUSION

Although the challenges of balancing work and family life are not uniquely American, many of the resulting problems are particularly acute in this country. These comparisons suggest that the heavily gendered compromises that families in the United States are forced to make are not inevitable. In other industrialized countries, employed parents are less squeezed for time, there is less gender inequality with respect to paid work, fewer families are in nonstandard-hour employment, rates of family poverty are much lower, and better outcomes for children can be expected. Moreover, parents in other countries appear to be more content with their balance of work and family life.

The traditionally private conception of caregiving is not working well for American families. Many working parents are dissatisfied with their ability to balance the demands of paid work and family. The United States has lagged behind many of its European counterparts in the development of policies that help families by distributing some of the costs of caregiving more broadly. Welfare-state scholars and academic feminists, working mostly in Europe, have been grappling for many years with the question of what constitutes a "woman-friendly" welfare state. Starting from the basic principles of citizenship rights, they have suggested new ways of thinking about the reciprocal responsibilities of the family and the state.

One of the most promising of these new approaches imagines a new model of society—a dual-earner–dual-carer society—in which men and women engage deeply and symmetrically in paid work in the market and caring work in the home. Achievement of a dual-earner–dual-carer society would require fundamental transformations in gendered divisions of labor and workplace practices. It would also require that government play a new, more active role in helping families resolve conflicts in their earning and caring roles. In the next chapter, we consider this theoretical framework and its implications for the organization of paid and unpaid work and for the role of government in supporting earning and caring families.

—— Chapter 4 ——

Reconciling the Conflicts: Toward a Dual-Earner–Dual-Carer Society

I N RECENT DECADES, feminist social theorists—mostly in Europe—
have engaged in a critical reexamination of the concept of social citizenship. Feminist scholars argue that a crucial shortcoming
in twentieth-century citizenship theory, beginning with the influential work of the British sociologist T. H. Marshall, has been the
failure to recognize the consequences of women's disproportionate assumption of unpaid care work. One of their central insights
is that women's socially constructed responsibilities in the private
sphere bar their full participation as citizens in the public sphere.

A crucial schism has emerged out of this scholarship. Some
feminists argue that women's attainment of equality or "sameness"
vis-à-vis men, especially in the labor market, is a prerequisite to
their attainment of full citizenship status. Others call instead for
new conceptions of citizenship that recognize and value women's
"difference," rooted in their unique responsibilities for care work.
These two perspectives differ sharply in their vision of what society might look like if women were to acquire full citizenship rights.
They also suggest alternative contours for what Helga Hernes has
labeled the "woman-friendly" welfare state (Hernes 1987, 10).
Whereas the "sameness" or "employment" perspective focuses on
state policies aimed at strengthening women's attachment to the
labor market, the "difference" or "care" perspective calls for social
policies that recognize and reward women's caregiving work, especially in the home.[1]

The tension between these two feminist vantage points—employment and care—evokes similar divides among those concerned with work and family in the United States. As we observe in chapter 1, three overlapping but surprisingly distinct conversations about work and family are underway in the United States—among feminists, among work-and-family scholars and advocates, and among child-development experts. For the most part, American feminists have taken the "employment perspective," setting their sights on gender parity in paid work. In contrast, many in the work-family and child-development fields have focused on granting women time and support for caregiving. Although these latter scholars and advocates are not necessarily working from within a feminist framework, many of them share with "care" feminists the goal of enabling women to engage more fully in caregiving.

In this chapter, we trace the employment-care split to its roots in citizenship theory and argue that its resolution can be found in the model of a dual-earner–dual-carer society that we introduced in chapter 1. Because the earner-carer model values both gender equality and caregiving, it has the potential to resolve the fundamental tensions between the employment and care perspectives.[2] It achieves this by imagining two important changes in gender relations and family arrangements. The first is symmetrical engagement by men and women in both paid work in the labor market and unpaid work in the home. In an earner-carer society, men and women would "halve it all" (as American psychologist Francine Deutsch [1999] evocatively phrases it) by sharing equally in the costs and benefits of parenting. The second is the allocation of substantial parental time to the care of very young children. In an earner-carer society, parents would shift the balance between caring for their children and the use of substitute child care with their children's changing needs. For very young children, most caring would be located in the home; for older children, larger amounts of care would be provided outside the home in public child care settings and in school. Throughout their children's dependent years, parents would have more time for caregiving, and children would "have" more of their parents, particularly during their developmentally sensitive early years.

The earner-carer model moves beyond the contemporary model of gendered, partial specialization between mothers and fathers. It also moves beyond the long-standing American conception of

caregiving as an exclusively private family concern. The reallocation of time suggested by the earner-carer model—between mothers
and fathers and between the labor market and the home—assumes that parents have the option to reduce their employment
hours when caregiving demands are high. It also assumes that
parents have access to affordable, high-quality child care alternatives while they are at the workplace. This suggests an important
role for public policy, both as a support for individual families and
as a mechanism for changing social norms.

CITIZENSHIP AND SOCIAL RIGHTS: RECONSIDERING GENDER, WORK, AND CARE

Since the 1980s, many European feminist social theorists and welfare state scholars have located their analyses of gender equality,
and the "woman-friendly" welfare state, in the literature on citizenship and social rights (Bussemaker and van Kersbergen 1994;
Crompton 1999; Ellingsaeter 1999; Fraser 1994; Lister 1990, 1997;
O'Connor 1996; Orloff 1993; Pateman 1988; Pfau-Effinger 1999;
Sainsbury 1994, 1999). In recent years the Western world has seen
a resurgence of interest in citizenship. This reemergence is rooted
in a number of contemporary processes—including democratiza-
tion in several regions around the world, the rise of ethnic and
nationalist conflicts, economic strain and a reconsideration of the
capacity of social policy, and global migration to the wealthy
countries. Feminists have been active participants in the new debates about the meaning and practice of citizenship.

    Probably the most influential feminist citizenship theorist has
been the British social policy scholar and activist Ruth Lister. Lister
argues that feminist welfare state scholars have much to gain from
citizenship theory because a citizenship approach helps clarify the
nature of achieved rights, the goals and consequences of social
provisions, and fundamental problems of exclusion. Lister holds
that feminists should reclaim citizenship as a concept because of
its strategic value in bringing "political and intellectual excitement"
to feminist social theory. As she notes, a feminist embrace of citizenship theory necessarily involves a critical rethinking of many
of its central concepts: "The combination of its salience and con-

tested nature underlines the importance of a sustained feminist analysis of the meaning, limitations and potential of the notion of citizenship. . . . A feminist project to (re)appropriate citizenship does not, however, imply an uncritical acceptance of its value as a concept" (Lister 1997, 3).

Feminist citizenship theorists take as their starting point T. H. Marshall's (1950) influential work, *Citizenship and Social Class.*[3] Marshall proposed three core elements of citizenship in the modern welfare state: civil rights, political rights, and social rights. Marshall understood the civil element of citizenship, achieved mainly in the eighteenth century, to encompass the rights necessary for individual freedom, including the rights to freedom of speech, thought, and faith. His political element, largely secured in the nineteenth century, encompassed the right to vote and the right to seek political office in free elections.

By the social element of citizenship, or social rights, Marshall referred to "the right to share to the full in the social heritage and to live the life of a civilized being according to the standards prevailing in the society" (Marshall 1950, 10–11). Marshall's social citizenship, which took hold in the twentieth century with the development of the welfare state, refers primarily to individual rights to economic welfare and social security—in common parlance, the right to live a decent life. Social rights are understood to be the fundamental concept underlying the development of the welfare state and, in turn, are granted and secured by law through the welfare state.[4] As the American political theorist Carole Pateman describes it, "The moral basis of the welfare state lies in the provision of resources for what T. H. Marshall called the 'social rights' of democratic citizenship" (Pateman 1988, 235).

When feminists revisited Marshall's concept of citizenship, they found his exposition of social rights wanting with respect to women's complex relationships to both family and market. Gillian Pascall notes that "while Marshall asserts the rights of citizenship, nowhere does he analyze the problematic relationship between citizenship and dependency in the family" (Pascall 1986, 9). As Lister notes, women were nearly invisible in Marshall's framework because he failed to appreciate the implications of women's lack of access to and integration in the labor market and their disproportionate assumption of caregiving work in the home.

The principal weakness of Marshall's conception of social rights is its failure to appreciate that women's unequal burden of caregiving constrains not only their participation in market work but also their access to employment-based welfare state provisions. Women's social rights are constrained in that entitlements for income-securing benefits—from unemployment compensation to old-age pensions—are linked to past or current employment. Pateman (1988) notes that in the democratic welfare state, employment is "the key to citizenship." She argues that "theoretically and historically, the central criterion for citizenship has been 'independence,' and the elements encompassed under the heading of independence have been based on masculine attributes and abilities" (Pateman 1988, 238). As long as women's standing as "workers" is limited and precarious, so will be their standing as democratic citizens in modern welfare states. Julia O'Connor also reconsiders Marshall and concludes that women on the whole experience exclusion from political rights—women are "grossly under-represented in the formal political system and at the decision-making level in public policy bodies" (O'Connor 1996, 50)—and from social rights as well.

The link between women's exclusion from citizenship theory and welfare state provisions is brought into relief with Gosta Esping-Andersen's (1990) cross-national analysis of social welfare provisions, *The Three Worlds of Welfare Capitalism*. Esping-Andersen compares welfare states on the extent to which individuals are protected from the vicissitudes of the labor market. This concept, which he terms "decommodification," draws heavily on Marshall's idea of social citizenship. The publication of *Three Worlds* evoked considerable feminist criticism, much of it a familiar echo to the criticism of Marshall's work (see, for example, Lewis and Ostner 1991; Orloff 1993; Sainsbury 1994). The central criticism has been that as long as women, as a group, are not fully commodified (that is, engaged in market work), decommodification is hardly emancipatory. Hence, according to this argument, the core dimension along which cross-national welfare state achievements are compared in this influential work entirely misses key programs, such as public child care, that strengthen women's social rights.

EMPLOYMENT VERSUS CARE

A deep and consequential split has emerged among feminists grappling with "engendering" mainstream citizenship and welfare state theory. One group argues that because women's access to a full range of citizenship rights rests on labor market attachment, women's emancipation requires that female employment be strengthened until gender equality in the labor market is achieved. From this "women's employment" or "universal breadwinner" perspective, the role of the "woman-friendly" state is to support women's employment opportunities and achievements.

An opposing "care" or "caregiver-parity" perspective rejects the mainstream equation of citizen with wage earner and calls instead for new concepts of citizenship that stress women's unique caregiving responsibilities. "Care" feminists call for reconstructing citizenship so that it recognizes, values, and rewards women's care work. From this perspective, the ideal role of the state is to grant women "the right to time for care" and to remunerate women for care work performed in the home—in essence, to render "women's difference costless" (Fraser 1994, 611).

Although the care perspective focuses primarily on women's rights, many care-oriented feminists also emphasize the value of care for those who receive it—first and foremost, children. As Trudie Knijn and Monique Kremer, two leading care theorists, note, "To receive informal care from a relative [who] has the right to time for care is often a good solution for both the person in need of care and the caregiver" (Knijn and Kremer 1997, 333).[5] The call from some European feminists to secure women's "right to care" resonates with many Americans in the work-family field and with many child-development experts and advocates as well. All three perspectives share a skepticism about policies aimed exclusively at tightening women's ties to the labor market.

"Employment-perspective" feminists argue that the care perspective may value and reward women's unpaid work in the short term but works at cross purposes with reducing gender inequalities in the long term by reinforcing gendered divisions of labor. They contend that a surer route to valuing caregiving work is to distribute it more equally between men and women. They predict that as gender divisions in paid work disappear over time, gender divisions in care and other household work will also erode. Care-perspective feminists reply that failing to support women as care-givers neglects women's heterogeneity by disregarding many women's desires to engage deeply in care work. They argue that the exclusive focus on equality in the workplace forecloses op-tions for protecting and remunerating women's caregiving time. Moreover, they argue, the employment perspective neglects the well-being of dependent family members, particularly children.

RESOLVING THE TENSION:
THE DUAL-EARNER–DUAL-CARER SOCIETY

The dual-earner–dual-carer model suggests a resolution of these tensions. Rosemary Crompton (1999) illustrates a continuum of models from the traditional male-breadwinner–female-carer ar-rangement to current partial modifications to an idealized earner-carer society (see figure 4.1). Crompton emphasizes that "the point of this exercise is not to provide a matrix, or static taxon-omy, within with nation states may be precisely located. Rather, the aim is to develop a flexible framework through which change

FIGURE 4.1 **Gendered Divisions of Labor, from Traditional to Idealized**

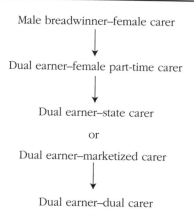

Male breadwinner–female carer

↓

Dual earner–female part-time carer

↓

Dual earner–state carer

or

Dual earner–marketized carer

↓

Dual earner–dual carer

Source: Based on Crompton (1999).

may be conceptualized" (Crompton 1999, 202–3). Although largely theoretical in its conception, this continuum also serves as a useful tool for comparing, across countries, current resolutions to the schism between employment and care. The top of the continuum illustrates the traditional division of labor, with a male breadwinner and a full-time female homemaker—the arrangement that was dominant in the United States, and in many other Western countries, in the first half of the twentieth century. The second arrangement represents a partial modification of the male breadwinner model. This gender-differentiated arrangement has emerged strongly in some countries, most especially the United Kingdom and the Netherlands, where most men are employed full-time and many women combine part-time employment, often at very low hours, with substantial hours spent in care work in the home.

At the third point on the continuum are two alternative dual-earner–substitute-carer arrangements. Both models leave a substantial share of caregiving to substitute (that is, nonfamily) caregivers. In some societies in which most employed women are employed full-time, high levels of substitute care are provided in a state sector. This model was almost universally in place in the former state-socialist countries of eastern Europe, which provided extensive public child care. To a lesser extent, this is also the model in some of the Nordic countries, especially Finland. Alternatively, widespread full-time maternal employment can be combined with child care provided in the market. This arrangement approximates that in the United States, with its relatively high rate of maternal employment, especially full-time employment, and the heavy reliance on marketized care. As Crompton notes, because many women succeed economically in the marketized-carer model, this arrangement can be consonant with greater gender equality. On the other hand, high levels of market care can have a bifurcating effect as large numbers of women purchase care, often at a low price, from a highly feminized workforce.

THE DUAL-EARNER–DUAL-CARER SOCIETY

The other extreme of the continuum in figure 4.1 suggests a distinct egalitarian social arrangement: the dual-earner–dual-carer society. This model differs from the others in two key respects. First, unlike the first two arrangements, it envisions a social and economic arrangement in which men and women engage symmetrically in both paid work and unpaid caregiving; as such, it is fundamentally gender egalitarian. Second, unlike the third arrangement, it places primary responsibility for the care of very young children in the home rather than in the hands of out-of-home carers.

Various portraits of the earner-carer society have been painted by other feminist scholars, including Ruth Lister, also in the United Kingdom; Birgit Pfau-Effinger in Germany; Anne-Lisa Ellingsaeter in Norway; and Diane Sainsbury in Sweden. In an influential article, the American political theorist Nancy Fraser argues that the "sameness" and "difference" perspectives on transforming gender relations are both unsatisfying. She suggests that "a third possibility is to induce men to become more like most women are now—that is, people who do primary care work. . . . The key to achieving gender equity in the postindustrial welfare state, then, is to make women's current life patterns the norm" (Fraser 1994, 611). Despite Fraser's contribution, images of the earner-carer society have not compelled anywhere near as much attention in the United States as they have in Europe.[6]

The earner-carer model laid out by Crompton offers a social and economic end vision that resolves many of the conflicts identified in the early chapters of this book. As we worked our way through the European literature on the earner-carer society, however, we identified an additional element that is particularly critical in the American context: affordable, high-quality early childhood education and care during the years between intensive, in-home parental care and the start of public school. For many European feminists and welfare state scholars, the state's commitment to providing or financing quality child care is taken as a given. Public care for younger children (those under the age of three) is widespread in some countries and growing in others; a commitment to universal preschool enrollment for three- to five-year-olds is in place across much of Europe. Thus the call for more parental time for young children embodied in the European earner-carer model must be understood as a shift from substitute care back to more parental care.[7]

The contemporary reality is very different for American parents, who have inherited the legacy of our semi-welfare state. Crompton notes that the current system in the United States might be best described as "dual-earner–marketized-carer." Both fathers and mothers are expected to be engaged fully in the workplace, and child care is largely left to the market. Crompton points out two drawbacks to these arrangements: parental time for care is limited, and leaving substitute child care to the market exacerbates gender inequality because paid care work is so poorly remunerated. As she observes, "Dual earning in combination with a marketized domestic economy has led to the expansion of 'junk jobs' and thus an increase in inequality (between men as a whole and women as a whole)" (Crompton 1999, 208). To that unsatisfactory result, we would add two other problematic aspects of the current situation in the United States. One is that the combination of unaffordable and poor-quality care forces many parents (in practice, mothers) to withdraw from the labor market more than they would otherwise prefer. The second is that low-quality care exposes children to worrisome risks.

As we adapt the earner-carer model to the American context, we make use of the main elements laid out by Crompton: gender symmetry, ample parental time for care, especially during the earliest years, and a limited market-based child care sector. We assume that the child care sector in the United States would also be transformed from a market-based to a largely public system, in which the state plays a major role in financing and delivery and sets a higher floor under quality and providers' wages.

This end vision resolves many of the schisms that have characterized both feminist welfare state scholarship and policy debates in the United States. It resolves the tension between "employment" and "care" feminists by valuing both market and caregiving work and distributing them equally between men and women. It helps to resolve conflicts between work and family by assuming that both mothers and fathers will reduce their employment hours when caregiving demands in the home are high. Finally, it balances support for parents' employment and children's well-being by assuming that parents combine temporary reductions in employment with the use of good-quality out-of-home child care, as appropriate to the changing needs of their children.

The realization of the earner-carer society, in the United States and abroad, would require at least three interdependent social transformations. First, by definition, it requires a radical transformation in gender relations—from the model of gendered partial specialization that characterizes most contemporary families to a model of full gender equality in the labor market and at home. The achievement of gender equality together with high levels of in-home care can come about only if men (on average) shift substantial portions of time from the labor market to the home. At the same time, it envisions a virtual end to full-time homemaking as it makes a place for all women in the world of employment. Second, the earner-carer society calls for a major alteration in the workplace, as it imagines substantial changes in employment time for the vast majority of fathers and for many mothers as well, at least when their children are young. As Crompton observes, "Full-time work as we know it might be superceded" (Crompton 1999, 208). Third, it calls for innovative new roles for the state in protecting parents' rights to secure time for care without undue economic sacrifice and in ensuring that families have access to affordable, high-quality substitute child care when appropriate.

These transformations would be mutually reinforcing. Many couples now reject equal sharing of paid and unpaid work because the shortage of institutional supports (such as paid leave for fathers, high-quality reduced-hour work, and affordable child care) makes that a costly choice. Expanded workplace supports and public programs would enable more couples to choose egalitarian divisions of labor. At the same time, an easing of gendered divisions of labor could further workplace and government reforms. If more women and men begin to share earning and caring, they may put more effective pressure on employers and policy makers for appropriate supports. Employer-initiated reforms could also hasten social policy expansions, and the reverse is also true: If more workplaces initiate work-family programs, employers are likely to ask government to assist through subsidies and tax breaks. New government services (such as public child care) could, in turn, catalyze employers to create complementary programs (such as information and referral services) to help their employees take advantage of public benefits. Transformations in gender relations, in workplace practices, and in social policies would reinforce one another.

TRANSFORMING GENDER ROLES AND LABOR MARKET ARRANGEMENTS: A THOUGHT EXPERIMENT

The realization of the earner-carer model would require a radical shift in the allocation of women's and men's time between the home and the workplace, especially during the earliest years of their children's lives. This raises many practical questions about how parents might reorganize their employment schedules to free up substantial and equal time for caregiving and what these changes would mean for total family labor supply. To understand what these reallocations might look like, it is helpful to imagine the time allocations within a hypothetical family in an earner-carer society and to compare those with the actual time allocations in contemporary American families (table 4.1).

It is easiest to begin this thought experiment by considering two-parent families. For the sake of illustration, we account for parents' and children's time during a continuous block of time that corresponds to the "normal" forty-hour week; we assume that outside of those forty hours, parents would be available to care for their own children.

During the first year of a child's life, parents in an earner-carer society would share time away from the market symmetrically to allow them to care for children at home. They might choose, for example, to work two half-time jobs at twenty hours a week each.

Parents with children aged one and two might reduce their working hours and stagger their schedules so that between them they could cover most of the caregiving time; they would supplement parental care with substitute child care to fit their children's needs. One possibility is that each parent works for pay twenty-five hours a week and cares for the child for fifteen hours a week. Assuming that parents can arrange some nonoverlapping employment hours, the child would spend about thirty hours in parental care and ten hours in substitute care (of the forty-hour workweek).

When their child turned three and was more able to benefit from group care, these same parents might increase their hours of paid work. If each worked for pay thirty-five hours a week, they

TABLE 4.1 Actual Weekly Work Hours in the United States, 2000, and Hypothetical Weekly Work Hours in an Earner-Carer Society

	Dual-Parent Families				Single Mothers	
Age of Youngest Child (Years)	Mothers' Hours	Fathers' Hours	Combined Hours	Hypothetical Hours Minus Actual Hours	Mothers' Hours	Hypothetical Hours Minus Actual Hours
Birth to two	(24) [20 to 25]	(44) [20 to 25]	(68) [40 to 50]	−18 to −28	(31) [15 to 20]	−16 to −11
Three to five	(24) [35]	(44) [35]	(68) [70]	2	(31) [30]	−1
Six to twelve	(28) [37.5]	(44) [44]	(72) [75]	3	(34) [32]	−2
Thirteen to seventeen	(31) [37.5]	(44) [37.5]	(75) [75]	0	(35) [32]	−3

Source: Authors' calculations based on the CPS.

Note: Numbers in parentheses indicate actual hours, using data from the 2000 CPS. Hours refer to usual hours worked per week, exclusive of commuting time and lunch breaks. Actual hours worked are also presented in the top panel of table 2.2.

Numbers in square brackets are hypothesized hours of market work in an earner-carer society in which fathers and mothers share market time equally and parents spend substantial time with children, especially during the first three years.

Average hours include persons spending zero hours in market work. Thus, for example, among mothers in dual-parent families with children aged three to five years, the difference between average weekly hours worked (twenty-four hours) and hypothesized hours in an earner-carer society (thirty-five hours) might be closed by more mothers entering the labor market and/or by some mothers in the labor market lengthening their hours. For fathers in these same families, average hours would fall if employed men shortened their hours and/or if some fathers left the labor market altogether.

could stagger their hours such that each week the child would spend about ten hours in parental care and thirty hours in a pre-school program. After the start of primary school, at the age of five or six, the parents might work full-time but stagger their schedules to remain available to their children. Assuming a future reduction in the standard full-time week, each parent might spend about thirty-seven and a half hours working for pay.

How does this thought experiment compare with contempo-rary reality in two-parent families? Employment hours for our hy-pothetical couple differ from the average hours worked by Ameri-can parents (in 2000) largely in the allocation of fathers' and mothers' time—not in the total time that couples jointly spend in the labor market.

This thought experiment suggests two conclusions about the changes in time allocations that would result if contemporary American couples with children shifted to this hypothetical earner-carer arrangement. First, during the first three years of a child's life, the average couple's combined hours of employment would be considerably less than the current average. Mothers' hours in the labor market would remain unchanged, but fathers' hours in paid work would decrease substantially. As shown in table 4.1, whereas American parents with children below the age of three now spend just under seventy hours a week in employ-ment, our hypothetical parents, as a couple, would work for pay about forty to fifty hours a week. Contemporary mothers' hours fall squarely in the range of the hypothesized earner-carer parent (twenty to twenty-five hours a week); in contrast, fathers' hours, presently at about forty-four, would have to decrease by about half (to twenty to twenty-five hours).

Second, after children reach the age of three, on average, mothers' hours in the labor market would increase and fathers' would decrease from the current average—with them meeting ap-proximately in the middle. There would be little to no reduction in total family (parental) labor supply. For parents with youngest children aged thirteen to seventeen, for example, both contempo-rary American parents and our hypothetical parents spend sev-enty-five hours a week (jointly) in paid work.

Thus for parents with children younger than age three, fathers would become—as Fraser suggests—"more like most women are now."[8] Among parents with children aged three and older, earner-carer couples would supply the same total hours of caregiving and employment as couples do now, but rather than specializing they would meet in the middle in their commitments to home and paid work. This surprising result means that for most families—families with infants and toddlers excepted—parents could provide the amount of caregiving time laid out in this thought experiment without a reduction in total hours spent in paid work.

Imagining a time allocation in an earner-carer society for single parents, about 95 percent of whom are mothers, is more difficult. Many single parents actually share caregiving with a second adult. Recent research suggests that a relatively large proportion of single mothers are either cohabiting or in a relationship with the father of their children, particularly during the years soon after birth. Others share residences and caregiving responsibilities with other adults—such as a grandparent or an aunt.[9] Parents in these nontraditional families might allocate their time, in an earner-carer society, in much the same way as parents with partners. Many other single mothers have no second caregiver, and that raises complex questions about the obligation of the welfare state to fill in for the missing parent.[10]

How might the time of single mothers be allocated in an earner-carer society? It is possible to imagine two scenarios based on norms of equality for children or for mothers. In the first, emphasizing equality for children, the children of single mothers would spend the same amount of time in substitute child care as the children of dual parents. Like their peers with two parents, children with a single parent could be cared for primarily by their parent until they were about three years old. This would be possible only if single mothers worked fewer hours for pay than either mothers or fathers in dual-parent families (for example, taking a full year of full-time leave in the first year after the birth of a child). The total hours of employment at the family level would be considerably lower than that of dual-parent families with children of this age. A second scenario, emphasizing equality of opportunities and responsibilities among parents, would assume that single mothers' employment hours would be about the same as those of mothers (and fathers) in dual-parent families. This would leave the children of single parents in substitute care for more hours of the week than their peers in dual-parent families. In either scenario, single mothers would need extra support—in the form of paid leave and other forms of income replacement during periods of reduced employment or more substitute child care (or both).

To compare employment hours for a hypothetical single parent in an earner-carer society with the actual hours of contemporary single mothers, we imagine a hybrid alternative in which single mothers work for pay slightly fewer hours a week than each parent in our hypothetical dual-parent family (table 4.1). During the first three years after the birth of a child, a single mother might work for pay about fifteen to twenty hours a week and use about twenty to twenty-five hours of substitute care. When her child reached the age that many children enter preschool, at about three years of age, she might increase her hours of paid work to thirty hours a week; when her child entered primary school around the age of six, she might increase her employment further, to thirty-two hours a week.

How does this compare with contemporary reality? Like our hypothetical dual-parent family, this single mother would spend less time in paid work during her child's first three years than single mothers now do. Beyond the first three years, however, our hypothetical single mother would work about the same number of hours for pay, on average, as single mothers do now.

TRANSFORMING THE ROLE OF GOVERNMENT: A POLICY PACKAGE

The realization of the earner-carer society in the United States would also require a transformation in the role of government— and this transformation is at the heart of this book. Families cannot reorganize their gender roles and labor market arrangements without the help of policies that allow them to reduce their employment hours during their children's earliest years without undue economic sacrifice, create incentives for men to assume a larger share of caregiving in the home, and provide substitute care for children while their parents are in the workplace.

Government policies alone cannot bring about these social

changes. However, they are a necessary, if not sufficient, condition for several reasons. Among all but the most privileged families, parents cannot realistically choose to reduce or reallocate employment hours in the absence of policies that protect their employment status and replace their wages; they cannot count on safe and affordable child care in the absence of policies that help defray costs and ensure quality care. By supporting individual families, government policies also serve a pivotal function in broader social change. Norms about work and family are socially constructed, and government policies send important signals about what society values. Policies that support parents' choice to reduce working hours when their children are very young, for example, signal the value of caregiving work; policies that support this choice by fathers and mothers signal the equal rights and responsibilities of men and women; policies that socialize the cost of substitute child care signal a shared commitment to the well-being of children. Beyond their symbolic function, policies that enable individual families to make new choices about employment and caring can help institutionalize these changes. In a society in which few men take time away from the workplace to care for their infants, for example, it can be difficult for any one father to do so; fathers' choices would be quite different in a society in which public policies helped establish paternal caregiving as the norm.

A review of current family policies in the United States provides few encouraging examples of policies that support earner-carer families. Policies that are consonant with these principles have, however, been partially or fully developed in several Continental and northern European countries. These policies can serve as models for the United States in three areas in particular: family leave, the regulation of working time, and child care in conjunction with school scheduling policies.

Family Leave

Family leave provisions grant parents the right to take time off to care for their children without losing their jobs and provide cash benefits (in the form of wage replacement) to offset wages lost during periods of leave. Leave policies in the countries that do the most to support earner-carer families grant short-term maternity leave rights and benefits, short-term paternity leave rights and benefits, longer-term parental leave for both parents, and temporary periods of paid leave—often referred to in Europe as "leave for family reasons"—that grant parents the option to take brief breaks from the workplace to respond to routine or unexpected caregiving demands.[11]

The question of gender equality raises vexing concerns in the design of leave policies. Women's disproportionate use of long leaves can result in extended absences from the workplace, exacerbating gender inequality in the home, and gender differentials in paid and unpaid work. Some of the countries with the most supportive policies for earner-carer families have developed models that include both gender neutrality in leave benefits and incentives to maximize the likelihood that men will take up the benefits to which they are entitled. Because men tend to have higher wages than women, for example, provisions for full or high wage replacement maximize fathers' propensity to take advantage of leave rights and benefits (Moss and Deven 1999). Men's incentives to take up leave also increase when fathers' rights are granted on an individual basis or are otherwise not "transferable" to their female partners. These benefits create "use-or-lose" provisions for fathers: leave time that is not taken by the father is lost to the family.

Regulation of Working Time

Labor market policies that enable parents to reduce and reallocate employment hours when their caregiving responsibilities are high are an essential form of support for earner-carer families, though they have been largely ignored in discussions of family policy in the United States. In countries that have policies consonant with an earner-carer society, working-time policies shorten the regular workweek for all workers to levels well below the standard forty-hour American week. Other working-time policies give workers somewhat more control over work schedules, including overtime hours and evening, night, and weekend shifts. Vacation policies in these same countries provide workers with blocks of uninterrupted time away from the workplace; for parents, this has the added benefit of freeing them to care for children during summer holidays.

Protections for reduced-hour and part-time workers are equally important—if not more so—for earner-carer families. In the absence of public policies that prohibit discrimination in wages and other employment conditions, workers are likely to pay high economic and career penalties in electing to reduce their working hours, even temporarily, to care for children. Countries that do the most to support earner-carer families protect parents' right to choose part-time work without undue economic and career sacrifice; some have taken active steps to encourage the creation of high-quality part-time jobs.

Early Childhood Education Care and School Scheduling

Education and care in early childhood and school schedules for older children constitute the third critical policy domain for an earner-carer society. Parents cannot fully engage in employment unless they can afford to make alternative arrangements for their children while they are at the workplace. In the countries that do the most to support earner-carer families, care for young children following periods of parental leave is provided through systems of extensive, publicly supported child care and early education (preschool). Access to care is guaranteed through parent- or child-based entitlements. Costs are socialized both to reduce the burden on parents and to equalize out-of-pocket expenditures across families at different income levels.

High-quality care is an essential form of support for children's healthy development and learning. It is also an essential form of support for gender equality. In the absence of high-quality options, parents—particularly mothers—face more difficult tradeoffs in their employment decisions. Moreover, in the absence of stringent standards for professional training and compensation, the highly feminized child care workforce will command very low pay, consigning many child care workers to poverty or near-poverty income levels. In the countries that have the most supportive policies for an earner-carer society, quality is ensured through standards that require that child care professionals be well trained, well supervised, and well compensated.

DISSOLVING GENDERED SPECIALIZATION: DO WOMEN AND MEN WANT TO SHARE AND SHARE ALIKE?

The earner-carer model of society assumes a radical transformation in gendered divisions of labor to achieve equal sharing between mothers and fathers. This raises at least two challenging questions. First, do women and men want to share earning and caring in a more egalitarian way? Second, would couples who share and share alike incur economic costs?

Many observers, both inside and outside of academia, argue that today's inegalitarian divisions of labor simply reflect the underlying preferences of women and men—both separately and as partners. At least two well-established schools of social-science theory support this point of view. The first perspective argues that mothers and fathers choose distinct time allocations because they have fundamentally different preferences, preferences that are essential and intrinsic. Naomi Gerstel characterizes the essentialist perspective as one that "suggests that differences in caregiving and nurturance are bound up with the biological make-up of women and men and are, by consequence, if not exactly invariant, at least deep and tenacious" (Gerstel 2000, 469).

This perspective suggests that women's disproportionate time spent in unpaid work in the home and consequent reduction in paid work and career advancement reflect the higher priority they give to caregiving work. The sociologist Catherine Hakim, for example, has argued that though some women are committed to careers in the labor market, a second group of women are qualitatively different. Women in this second group "give priority to their domestic roles and activities, do not invest in what economists term 'human capital' even if they acquire educational qualifications, transfer quickly and permanently to part-time work as soon as a breadwinner husband permits it, choose undemanding jobs 'with no worries or responsibilities' when they do work, and are hence found concentrated in lower paid and lower grade jobs which offer convenient working hours with which they say they are satisfied" (Hakim 1997, 43). In other words, men and women are simply different, and women who assume the majority of caregiving in their families are getting what they want. The second perspective, generally associated with the economist Gary Becker, argues that gender differences in work and family arrangements reflect rational, joint decision making (Becker 1981). This neoclassical economic perspective concludes that couples choose to specialize because of efficiency benefits afforded: comparative advantages and the opportunity for exchange raise family income. Although Becker originally argued that women have comparative advantage in the home sphere and men in the market sphere—due to differences in both biology and premarital investments in skills—specialization does not have to shape up along gender lines. Nevertheless, it is often taken as a given that women have the advantage in the home sphere, either because of their biological connections to children or their essential preferences for caregiving or because of existing labor market inequalities that benefit men. The overall conclusion is that specializing, especially along gender lines, makes economic sense for most families.

Although both essentialism and specialization deserve serious attention, both perspectives are flawed in important respects. Both assume that observed behavior reveals intrinsic preferences; they fail to acknowledge the extent to which those preferences, and the decisions that flow from them, are socially constructed. There is no question that current work and family arrangements reflect the individual and joint decisions of men and women. However, decisions about work and family life are made in a world with specific constraints and opportunities for women and men. Given current economic and social realities, it is impossible to know whether these decisions reflect underlying and enduring preferences or accommodations to inflexible working arrangements, limited options for nonparental child care, career penalties for allocating time to parenting, and the like. The meaningful question is not "What do men and women choose now?" but rather "In a much changed world—one in which women were valued as earners and men as carers and both could choose to engage in caregiving without costly employment penalties—how would men and women choose to allocate their time between the market and the home?" The situation posed is a classic counterfactual, and in today's socially constructed and highly constrained world, the question simply cannot be answered.

There are other reasons to question both essentialism and specialization as rationales for gendered divisions of labor. Arguments that claim that men and women are intrinsically different risk confusing difference with destiny and fail to recognize that women and men can decide to organize their partnerships in ways that overrule those differences. Despite substantial social and economic constraints, many couples are attempting to craft more egalitarian divisions of labor. As Susan Chira argues, "Whatever biological or cultural differences exist do not rule out the possibility that men can experience children just as intimately, or feel just as responsible for them, or simply take on more of the grinding work of caring for them" (Chira 1998, 232). Others point out that though men and women may have different psychological orientations toward children as a result of some evolutionary "hardwiring," social institutions can be structured to help counterbalance those differences. The anthropologist Melvin Konner argues eloquently that societies can and should commit to social institutions that support gender equality without first proving that "the sexes are psychologically equivalent" (Konner 1999).

In the case of specialization, the classical economic assumption that couples benefit economically fails to capture important tradeoffs. Although specialization may bring higher total income for some families, it also creates inequities within families (see Blau, Ferber, and Winkler 2002 for a review). Specialization is especially risky for full-time homemakers as it leaves them socially isolated in the home, lacking in bargaining power within the family, less able to exit the family in the event of domestic abuse or other serious problems, and in a precarious economic position if the family breaks up. These concerns also apply to partners who have some attachment to the labor market, but less than that of their spouses.

The net value of specialization depends on the magnitude of the gains in income relative to the losses on other dimensions, such as inequality with respect to the distribution of costs and benefits. A couple in which the man works for pay seventy hours a week and the woman provides full-time child care is likely to have greater disposable income than one in which each parent works for pay thirty-five hours a week and they purchase substitute child care. The relevant questions are these: How large is the income gap between these two families? Is the economic gain to the one-earner family worth the costs incurred by individual family members? For many families, the increased income may be accompanied by nonmonetary losses—such as inequality between partners in the assumption of economic risks and children's decreased access to their fathers. Focusing only on the benefits of specialization neglects its costs and its disproportionate impact on mothers and children.

There is a second reason to revisit the claim that specialization between partners is explained fully by utility-maximizing private choices. Gains to specialization are rooted in contemporary institutional realities, including the shortage of rewarding, reduced-hour work, the limited availability of high-quality affordable child care, and the persistent gender wage gap. If the couple described in the preceding paragraph could secure two well-paid jobs each at thirty-five hours a week (very difficult in the current labor market), if they had access to free or low-cost child care (currently unavailable to most families), and if her hourly earnings equaled his (not the case today, even if they have comparable skills), it is likely that the gains to specialization would be eliminated or greatly reduced. The magnitude of gains to specialization in a world with more workplace flexibility, gender equality, and state support are largely unknown.

SHOULD GOVERNMENT REDISTRIBUTE THE COSTS OF CARING?

The earner-carer model of society rests on another social transformation that is particularly foreign to American audiences: the redistribution of a portion of the costs of child rearing from the family to society through public policies for parental leave, regulation of working time, and early childhood education and care. Those who criticize drawing policy lessons from abroad often suggest that the heavy involvement of the European welfare states in social and workplace benefits is contrary to American preferences for market-based solutions. As Robert Kuttner observes in *Everything for Sale: The Virtues and Limits of Markets,* the United States has had a lifelong "romance with a utopian view of laissez-faire," albeit a romance that waxes and wanes over time (Kuttner 1999, 4). This raises significant normative questions about the role of the state in domains widely understood as private in the American context. Why should taxpayers, including those without their own children, contribute resources to families who are raising children? Why should employers be subjected to regulatory restrictions for the sake of helping workers with their caregiving needs?

In the European context, especially in the countries with social democratic political traditions, the case for government is much more straightforward. Many European conceptions of citizenship cast social benefits as social rights, and their legitimacy is taken as a given. In some countries, the case for social rights is integrated into, or bolstered by, a case for social inclusion. Yet most Americans reject social rights—Americans traditionally reject all positive rights—and the idea that states have an obligation to guarantee social inclusion holds little sway in American political discourse (Gornick 2002).[12] The case for a larger role for government, in supporting parents and children, needs to be considered within the American context.

One argument for greater public involvement in providing work-family supports is the demonstrated failure of our current arrangements. The results of the American experiment with market-based solutions have been calamitous for many American parents and children, as we report throughout this book. The granting of family leave has been left largely to employer markets, and a limited and regressive patchwork of provisions has been the result. Working-time arrangements have been left largely to employer-employee negotiations, with the result that Americans work unusually long hours, often around the clock, and pay a comparatively high penalty for reduced-hour work. The provision of child care has been left largely to consumer markets that produce services that strain working families' budgets, stint on quality, and impoverish many child care professionals.

It is possible that these largely market-based arrangements could work—but do not, in practice, due to various forms of market failure. For example, powerful information asymmetries may deter some employers from providing the optimal level of family-related benefits. Stephen Hardy and Nick Adnett argue that many workers are unwilling to reveal their preferences for more generous family leave options and shorter work hours because by doing so they risk being consigned to a "parent track," with its associated costs. As a result, "workers disguise themselves as having a low risk of requiring such leave or having a taste for long working hours" (Hardy and Adnett 2001, 13).

Markets for early childhood education and care are also likely to be hindered by various forms of market failure. Asymmetrical or incomplete information can lead some parents to make less-than-optimal investments in their children's care. For example, parents are often unable, in practice, to observe what transpires during the hours of care; others may lack knowledge about the short- and long-term consequences of their child care choices. In addition, capital-market imperfections may cause some parents—especially poor parents—to underinvest in their children's care during their early years. Credit markets rarely offer funds for early care or schooling, partly because the promise of future earnings is not accepted as collateral.

Some of these market failures might be alleviated through private or public efforts aimed at disseminating information, ensuring minimum quality standards, providing loans to poor parents, and the like. Even with well-functioning employer and consumer markets, however, the costs of child rearing would fall almost entirely on parents, particularly in children's earliest years. This is unlikely to produce optimal and equitable social and economic outcomes. The costs that parents incur on behalf of their children—including time, energy, forgone earnings, expenditures on children's consumer goods, and investments in child care and education—produce benefits that are widely dispersed. In other words, as Nancy Folbre and Paula England have argued, children are public goods—in the sense that their capabilities benefit society as a whole. In economic terms, children's capabilities are public goods in that others can reap the benefits without paying and one person's enjoyment does not diminish another's (Folbre 1994; England and Folbre 1999b).[13]

Although the conclusion that children are public goods derives from mainstream economic principles, this conceptualization of children is not readily familiar to most Americans, who view the bearing and rearing of children as a largely private concern. Most Americans think of children according to what England and Folbre call the "children-as-pets" reasoning (England and Folbre 1999a, 197). From this perspective, the decision to have children reflects the utility, or pleasure, that parents derive from the caregiving experience; the monetary, time, and other costs they incur are assumed to be offset by the happiness they derive and the future benefits they reap—for example, care that they hope to receive during their own later and more dependent years. Of course, parents do derive (or hope to derive) benefits from raising their children. Children are not pets, however; parents' reproductive and caregiving work, most of it performed by women, also contributes important benefits that other individuals and institutions reap and enjoy without paying a market price. All members of society benefit when parents invest more heavily in the "production" of well-nurtured children—children who are this generation's healthy playmates, creative peers, and well-behaved students and who become the next generation's productive workers, social insurance contributors, and civic participants.

We believe that the strongest argument for expanding government programs that enhance the care and education of children, especially very young children, is the recognition that children are public goods. To the extent that family caregivers pay the costs of "producing" children while others benefit, there are at least two persuasive arguments for using government mechanisms to socialize more of the costs of caregiving.

First, expanding public supports for child rearing would raise the likelihood of achieving economically efficient and socially optimal outcomes. Children who are well cared for generate positive externalities; and, absent government supports, goods that generate positive externalities generally receive levels of private investment that are suboptimal. As a result, society as a whole may eventually pay a collective price in the form of children who fail to achieve their full potential, at best, or become a drain on public programs, at worst. Although the United States has historically invested in public schooling for children starting at the age of five or six, public investments in younger children are limited. Government programs that help to ensure high-quality care for children below school age, such as paid family leave and high-caliber substitute care, constitute needed investments in today's children and tomorrow's adults. As the economists James Heckman and Lance Lochner argue, waiting until children reach school age before publicly investing in them is misguided: "We cannot afford to postpone investing in children until they become adults, nor can we wait until they reach school-age—a time when, for some, it may already be too late to intervene successfully" (Heckman and Lochner 2000, 78).

The second argument in favor of government support of the care of young children is a normative one, and it concerns equity. Extending government investments has implications for equity among children, especially among children from families at different points along the income distribution. To the extent that we rely on parents' private resources, children in low-income families receive far less than their affluent counterparts. Both the left and right in the United States call for equal opportunities for children; but without substantial new government supports for families, for many children that remains a hollow promise.

Programs that spread the costs of caregiving also have major implications for gender equity because women do most caregiving work. Because caregivers can neither exclude others from sharing the fruits of their labor nor recover the costs of their work—for example, by charging for the hours they invest in nurturing the health of their infants, socializing their toddlers, preparing their preschool children for school, and so on—others are able to free ride on their unpaid work. As Budig and England argue, "A general equity principle is that those who receive benefits should share in the costs. . . . Those who rear children deserve public support precisely because the benefits of child rearing diffuse to other members of society" (Budig and England 2001, 221). Policies that shift some of the costs of child caregiving from parents to taxpayers, and to employers, are equitable because they require that all who benefit make a contribution.[14]

CONCLUSION

European feminist and welfare state scholars have sought to imagine new divisions of labor, new conceptions of citizenship, and new social policy arrangements that would honor and reward both women's economic independence and family care work. Several have converged on the model of the dual-earner–dual-carer society and have suggested the outlines of a social protection system that would nurture and accommodate it.

We have taken that end vision as the organizing framework for the remainder of this book. Discussing social policy against the vision of an earner-carer society is admittedly idealistic. In fact, it is utopian. We situate our comparative analysis of family policy in this ideal because it offers a number of theoretical and analytic advantages. Conceptually, the earner-carer model has the potential to resolve many of the tensions that crosscut American and European debates about work and family, in that it both promotes gender equality and values caregiving. It especially holds promise for resolving the apparent tradeoff between gender equality and child well-being by strengthening mothers' labor market ties while securing fathers' time with their children. Analytically, it provides a blueprint for comparing and evaluating family and other policies across modern welfare states and for enlarging contemporary debates about family-policy development.

The achievement of an earner-carer society would require major transformations in gender relations, in labor market arrangements, and in the role of government. In the following three chapters, we take up the third of these transformations in more detail by describing work-family policies in various European countries. We focus on policies in countries that provide the greatest support for families in order to draw lessons for policy development in the United States.

—— Chapter 5 ——

Ensuring Time to Care During the Early Years: Family Leave Policy

THE MODEL OF an earner-carer society assumes that both mothers and fathers will have time for caregiving, intensively in the early weeks and months of their children's lives, and as needed during later childhood.[1] Public family leave policies are among the most important tools that many other countries use to ensure parents time for caregiving work.

Family leave policy refers to a package of benefits: maternity leave (granted to mothers for a limited period around the time of childbirth),[2] paternity leave (granted to fathers for a limited period around the time of childbirth), parental leave (granted to mothers and fathers for longer periods of time, typically following periods of maternity and paternity leave), and leave for family reasons (provided in brief increments to attend to children's unscheduled needs throughout childhood). The inclusiveness of these leave rights and the duration of benefits have implications for parents' time for caregiving. The availability and generosity of wage replacement have direct implications for families' economic well-being. Benefit levels and other design features are also consequential for gender equality because fathers are more likely to use leave benefits when replacement rates are high and granted on an individual "use or lose" basis.

A BRIEF OVERVIEW OF PUBLIC FAMILY LEAVE POLICIES IN THE UNITED STATES

Family leave provisions are limited in the United States. Federal law grants some but not all parents the right to brief periods of unpaid leave. Paid leave is uncommon, available only to parents who are covered by temporary disability insurance or private, employer-based provisions. The main components of public family leave policy in the United States are illustrated in figure 5.1.

Legal Rights and Benefits

Two government mechanisms regulate paid maternity leave benefits within the framework of disability: the federal Pregnancy Discrimination Act (PDA) of 1978 and five state-based Temporary Disability Insurance (TDI) programs. The PDA, an amendment to Title VII of the 1964 Civil Rights Act, mandates that public and private employers who offer disability benefits must extend them to employees for pregnancy, childbirth, and pregnancy-related medical conditions. The PDA regulates employers who do provide disability benefits, but it does not require them to do so.

In addition, five of the states have public TDI programs, which provide some wage replacement in the event of short-term disability; owing to the provisions of the PDA, pregnancy and a post-birth period are included. In the five TDI states (California, Hawaii, New Jersey, New York, and Rhode Island), average weekly benefits range from about $140 to $270, and average duration of receipt ranges from five to thirteen weeks (Wisensale 2001). For the most part, these state TDI programs do not pay paternity benefits, as disability is defined in relation to pregnancy. The exception is the state of California, which in 2002 became the first state in the nation to extend its disability-based benefits to fathers. The California law grants six weeks of leave to both mothers and fathers, paid at approximately 55 percent wage replacement, subject to an earnings cap.

Federal law grants the right to unpaid parental leave to a portion of all workers. Parental leave rights were established nationally in 1993 with the passage of the Family and Medical Leave Act

FIGURE 5.1 U.S. Family Leave Policy Provisions

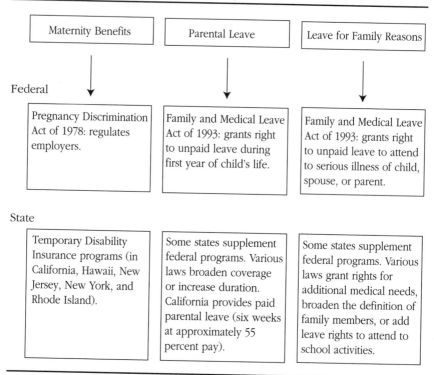

	Maternity Benefits	Parental Leave	Leave for Family Reasons
Federal	Pregnancy Discrimination Act of 1978: regulates employers.	Family and Medical Leave Act of 1993: grants right to unpaid leave during first year of child's life.	Family and Medical Leave Act of 1993: grants right to unpaid leave to attend to serious illness of child, spouse, or parent.
State	Temporary Disability Insurance programs (in California, Hawaii, New Jersey, New York, and Rhode Island).	Some states supplement federal programs. Various laws broaden coverage or increase duration. California provides paid parental leave (six weeks at approximately 55 percent pay).	Some states supplement federal programs. Various laws grant rights for additional medical needs, broaden the definition of family members, or add leave rights to attend to school activities.

Source: Authors' compilation.

(FMLA), the first piece of legislation signed by President Bill Clinton and the culmination of an eight-year political battle. The FMLA applies to all public employers and to private employers with fifty or more employees—which includes about 10 percent of private enterprises and nearly 60 percent of private-sector workers (DOL 2000). Within covered establishments, the FMLA applies to workers who have been employed for at least twelve months and worked a minimum of 1,250 hours in the prior year. Workers who are covered and eligible have the right to take up to twelve weeks of job-protected leave during the first year following the birth or adoption of a child. Both mothers and fathers, if individually eligible, may claim twelve weeks of leave during the first year (unless both parents have the same employer); partners may take those leaves simultaneously or sequentially. The FMLA does not address wage replacement, although it requires employers to continue contributions to workers' health insurance during covered leaves. Several of the states supplement the provisions of the FMLA.[3] About seventeen states have leave laws that are more generous than the FMLA. In particular, fifteen states extend the FMLA by including employers with fewer than fifty employees, and six provide periods of leave longer than twelve weeks or beyond the first year of infancy. Connecticut, for example, grants workers sixteen weeks of parental leave over a period of two years (Wisensale 2001).

Along with parental leave to care for newborns, the FMLA also grants some leave for family reasons. The FMLA provides eligible workers the right to twelve weeks a year to care for seriously ill family members—including children, spouses, and parents; nearly a third of FMLA leaves are taken to care for family members other than infants (DOL 2000). "Serious illness" refers to medical conditions requiring hospitalization or continuing treatment by a health-care provider. The FMLA allows workers to take these leaves in "chunks" when medically necessary—that is, a few hours, a half day, a day, a week, or some other increment.

As with parental leave, some states grant workers more generous rights to leave for family reasons. Steven Wisensale (2001) reports that three states extend the definition of "family member" beyond children, spouses, and parents to include relatives such as in-laws or grandparents. A few states extend medical leave to include illnesses that are less than "serious" or to cover routine doctor's visits; seven states grant workers leave to attend to their children's nonmedical needs, such as attendance at school activities. Massachusetts is an example of a state that extends leave rights for routine medical needs as well as school-related activities. The 1998 Massachusetts Small Necessities Leave Act requires employers with fifty or more employees to allow twenty-four hours a year of unpaid leave to eligible employees for certain family obligations. The law grants employees the right to

(1) participate in school activities directly related to the educational advancement of a son or daughter of the employee, such as parent-teacher conferences or interviewing for a new school; (2) accompany the son or daughter of the employee to routine medical or dental appointments, such

as check-ups or vaccinations; and (3) accompany an elderly relative of the employee to routine medical or dental appointments or appointments for other professional services related to the elder's care, such as interviewing at nursing or group homes. (State of Massachusetts 2003)

Collective Bargaining

With fewer than one-fifth of Americans unionized, organized labor has a limited reach in the United States. Nevertheless, unions have been able to use the bargaining process to extend family leave benefits for some covered workers. In some cases, unions have increased workers' rights to unpaid leave by negotiating supplements to the rights granted through the FMLA. For example, a union of public employees in California secured from a local school district a broader definition of eligible family members than that allowed under the FMLA; employees won permission to care for domestic partners as well as any relatives in their households. In another example, a flight attendants' union successfully negotiated for a reduction in the annual hours of services required by the FMLA—from 1,250 hours to less than 500 (Grundy, Bell, and Firestein 1999).

Other unions have made gains in securing wage replacement for workers on leave. An American Federation of State, County, and Municipal Employees council in Illinois, for example, negotiated two weeks of paid maternity or paternity leave for eligible state employees. A San Francisco local of the Hotel Employees and Restaurant Employees union secured from an employers group eight to twelve days of paid time off annually, to be used for any reason, including illness; these days were independent of allotted vacation time. In some cases, unions have bargained successfully for leave rights, paid or unpaid, so that workers can attend to small necessities. For example, a local of the Service Employees International Union negotiated an agreement with a local employer under which members have the right to take four hours of paid time off annually to attend parent-teacher conferences. Overall, although American unions protect only a small share of workers in the United States, they do play a role in extending the family leave provisions granted through public policy (Grundy, Bell, and Firestein 1999).

EVALUATING THE AMERICAN SYSTEM

Largely private, market-based maternity leave provisions, supplemented by limited disability-related public laws, do little to ensure that all American parents have access to paid maternity or paternity leave. Parental leave, though limited, is structured to allow both gender equality and flexibility in taking leave beyond the months immediately following childbirth. Without guaranteed wage replacement, however, these rights offer virtually no economic security and only the weakest of incentives for mothers and fathers to share caregiving responsibilities.

Access to Leave

One of the most important weaknesses of the family leave system in the United States is the lack of any paid leave for a substantial share of the workforce. The five states that pay maternity benefits through TDI programs include only about one-quarter of the nation's population. Mothers in the remaining forty-five states have to rely on paid leave granted voluntarily by their employers. As of the mid-1990s, only 43 percent of women who were employed during their pregnancies received any paid leave during the first twelve weeks after childbirth, through either public provisions or voluntarily provided employer benefits—including maternity pay, sick pay, and vacation pay (Smith, Downs, and O'Connell 2001). The rest received unpaid leave (40 percent), quit their jobs (27 percent), or were fired (4 percent).[4] As fathers are not eligible for the TDI-based programs (California is an exception since 2002), they have to rely solely on voluntary employer provisions for wage replacement. A recent survey of personnel managers revealed that only about 7 percent of employers offer paid paternity leave to their employees (U.S. Office of Personnel Management 2001).

Access to unpaid leave is also limited. Although the FMLA offers important protections, the law leaves many employed parents without the right to even unpaid leave at the time of childbirth or to care for seriously ill family members. A substantial share of workers are employed in establishments with fewer than fifty employees; almost forty-one million Americans, more than 40 percent of the private-sector workforce, are not covered by the FMLA.

Among those who do work in covered establishments, more than one-fifth fail to meet the work-history requirements and are thus ineligible. A minority of the establishments too small to be covered—only about 32 percent—offer workers any unpaid parental leave (DOL 2000). The FMLA is also limited in its provisions, with no allowances for parents who need to attend to routine or unexpected family needs such as medical appointments or school meetings.

Access to both maternity leave and parental leave is not only limited but is also sharply regressive; workers with greater needs and fewer resources are the least likely to have job-protected leaves or cash benefits. The likelihood that an employed mother has the right to paid maternity leave declines with her education, wages, and household income. For example, employed women who have not graduated from high school are half as likely to have paid maternity leave as women with high-school diplomas and only one-fourth as likely as women who have graduated from college (Smith, Downs, and O'Connell 2001). In her study of unequal access to paid leave and other workplace benefits, Jody Heymann (2000) reports that only 22 percent of poor families have access to four weeks of paid leave "some or all of the time," in comparison with 59 percent of nonpoor families. Access to unpaid leave is also regressive, as low-wage workers are disproportionately employed in the small enterprises that are exempt from the FMLA. Katherine Newman describes the millions of poor workers who are employed in workplaces too small for FMLA coverage as negotiating a "high-wire balancing act" (Newman 2000, 90).[5]

Economic Security

The absence of any guarantee of wage replacement under the FMLA leaves many families with no source of replacement income during leave periods and others unable to afford to take the leave to which they are entitled. Only about 25 percent of employers continue to pay workers their full salaries or wages during FMLA-covered leaves, and 25 percent offer partial pay or pay under certain circumstances; about 50 percent of employers provide no pay during parental leaves. About 10 percent of FMLA users who do not get their full pay go on public assistance during their leaves

(DOL 2000)—a striking indicator of the economic risk associated with unpaid leave.

The lack of cash benefits not only undermines the economic security of those who take parental leave, it also reduces the likelihood that parents will use the leave time to which they are entitled. Among those parents who take FMLA-covered leaves to care for newborns, more than two-thirds take fewer than half of their allowable days. Nearly 80 percent of employees who do not take FMLA leave when needed report that the reason is that they "could not afford to take leave" (DOL 2000). These FMLA survey data do not indicate what respondents mean by "could not afford"; some might be in low-income families, others might be higher earners who are deterred by the opportunity costs. Nevertheless, it is clear that the absence of wage replacement seriously disadvantages low-income families.

Gender Equality

The largely private system of leave rights and benefits in the United States does little to close gender gaps in paid and unpaid work. Limited job protections and the lack of wage replacement force many women to withdraw entirely from employment at childbirth, creating caregiving-related gender gaps in employment rates, hours, and pay. The provision of paid maternity leave as part of a disability framework (in the TDI states) is obviously gender inegalitarian as well, insofar as it creates no legal basis for men to claim paid leave benefits at the time of childbirth. Many fewer fathers than mothers have any paid leave during the first year of their children's lives, reinforcing gendered divisions in the care of young children.

Rights to unpaid leave granted through the FMLA are more gender egalitarian in structure. Women and men have exactly the same rights under the law, and they each have their own entitlements. A couple (together) gets six months of protected leave, but if the father does not take up his three months, that leave time is lost to the family—encouraging men to make use of their legal rights.

The potential for the FMLA to encourage greater equality in caregiving and market work is, however, severely compromised by the lack of wage replacement. Economists argue, and substantial empirical research confirms, that "economically rational," joint-decision-making couples choose to have the lower earner—in most families, the mother—withdraw from the labor market to care for children. Only with 100 percent wage replacement during the leave period would couples be "economically agnostic" as to which earner takes leave; the lower the level of wage replacement, the more severe the expected gender imbalance in take-up.[6] Not surprisingly, with a wage replacement rate of zero, fewer fathers than mothers take FMLA leaves to care for newborns; overall, workers who take family leaves under the provisions of the FMLA are 50 percent more likely to be women than men (DOL 2000).

Distribution of Costs

The care of young children necessarily imposes costs: costs on parents (if they withdraw from employment without replacement wages or continue employment and purchase private child care), on employers (if they provide wage replacement for their own workers), or on government (if tax revenues are used to provide wage replacement). The absence of comprehensive public leave policies in the United States results in these costs being over-whelmingly private. In the forty-five states without TDI programs, the majority of parents have no paid leave at the time of child-birth; they absorb the cost of caregiving directly through substitute child care costs or indirectly through forgone wages (and often, both). Employers in these states who provide paid leave typically finance leave directly through firm-based benefits. In the few states with contributory TDI programs, the direct costs of paid leave are shared between employers and employees.[7] Because the benefits paid through the public systems in the TDI states are so limited, however, most of the costs are still incurred privately.

The largely private financing of family leave in the United States imposes short-term costs on both employees and employers, and it may impose longer-term costs as well. Mothers who quit their jobs at childbirth and return to new employers—a common response to having no paid leave—often sacrifice wage growth and career opportunities for years to come. Employers may discriminate against parents, and those viewed as potential parents, in hiring and advancement to avoid the costs associated with privately financed leave. Employers find themselves squeezed between two alternatives: they can either finance paid leave out of their own pockets or provide no benefits and incur costs associated with high employee turnover.

FAMILY LEAVE POLICIES IN OTHER COUNTRIES

The United States does little to provide parents with time to care for their children or to distribute the costs of this caring time among parents, employers, and government. Our study of other industrialized countries provides models for family leave provisions that do much more to ensure that parents have time to care while also protecting families' economic security and promoting greater gender equality. These systems also provide models for distributing the costs of leave benefits more equitably through national social insurance funding schemes. These policy objectives are not all addressed equally well, even in the most well-developed leave systems. However, several countries exemplify generous approaches with a strong commitment to gender equality; others provide examples of less comprehensive, and less expensive, strategies.

Across our comparison countries, five features of family leave policy are especially important. First, maternity leave policies grant nearly all employed mothers job security and wage replacement around the time of childbirth. Second, maternity leave benefits are supplemented by parental leaves that provide both mothers and fathers paid leave during their children's preschool years. Third, leaves for family reasons grant both mothers and fathers time off throughout their children's lives. Fourth, leave policies promote gender equality by securing fathers' rights and benefits and encouraging fathers' usage. Finally, leave financing distributes the cost of time for caring across society and minimizes the burden on individual employers.

Maternity Leave Rights and Benefits

Maternity leave provisions protect mothers' jobs and grant wage replacement at the time of childbirth. They allow women to combine work in the market with caregiving work in the home without completely withdrawing from employment and sacrificing their families' economic security.

All of the countries in our study, with the exception of the United States, have national statutory programs that provide paid leave to mothers around the time of childbirth. In the countries with paid maternity leave, rates of coverage and eligibility are generally high. In most countries in Europe, high percentages of employed women who give birth are covered (including those employed in small enterprises) and individually eligible, and women's take-up rates are high (Kamerman 2000). Conditions are somewhat stricter in Canada, where only three-quarters of women with employment histories just before childbirth actually receive benefits (ten Cate 2000).

The Nordic countries—Norway, Sweden, Denmark, and (to a lesser extent) Finland—provide by far the most generous paid leave benefits for mothers. Figure 5.2 synthesizes the program rules presented in table 5.1 to report total weeks of full wage replacement available to mothers, assuming that mothers take all of the leave available to them through both maternity and parental leave.[8] Family leave policies in these countries offer mothers the equivalent of about thirty to forty-two weeks of leave with full pay, typically up to an earnings cap. These countries achieve high levels of provision through various mechanisms. In Norway and Sweden, maternity and parental leave are blended into a single program that grants couples an allocation of about a year to be shared between them; wage replacement is high for the whole period, at 80 to 100 percent. Finland and Denmark offer eighteen weeks of maternity pay (at about two-thirds pay, on average), followed by separate parental leave options that couples may allocate to the mother if they choose.[9] In Denmark, collective agreements compel many employers to "top up" public benefits so that, in practice, most workers receive their full pay.

Benefits are limited or capped for the highest-earning mothers. Finland, for example, reduces the replacement rate stringently as earnings rise. Norway and Sweden place caps on covered earnings, but the caps are set high—at about 1.9 and 2.2 times average earnings, respectively, among mothers of working age, including both part-time and full-time workers (authors' calculations, based on LIS data). High earnings caps result in a progressive benefit structure and restrain program expenditures while avoiding substantial losses in economic security for most mothers and their families.

More modest but still substantial public leave benefits are available to mothers in the five Continental countries, which grant employed mothers the equivalent of twelve to sixteen weeks of full pay. In these countries, maternity benefits are generally paid at high rates, 80 to 100 percent of wages, and for about three to four months. Again, some countries set caps on maximum covered earnings, and their levels vary widely; maternity pay in France is capped at about 1.2 times average mothers' earnings, whereas the Dutch cap is equivalent to nearly three times average earnings (authors' calculations, based on LIS data). Mothers' total leave rights and benefits lag behind those granted in the Nordic countries largely because the parental leave options are more limited.[10]

Although the English-speaking countries overall provide exceptionally little paid leave to mothers, Canada stands out as an exception. In terms of equivalent weeks of paid leave, Canadian mothers have access to benefits nearly as generous as those offered in Finland. Although the duration of paid leave is long by European standards (mothers may take fifty weeks of paid leave), Canadian family leave policy provides substantially less economic security to mothers and their families (wage replacement is 55 percent) than either the Nordic or Continental European systems. In addition, the benefit in Canada is capped at a substantially lower level than in the European countries. Canadian mothers with approximately average earnings receive the maximum benefit, and the effective replacement rate declines as earnings rise above that level (authors' calculations, based on LIS data).

How does the United States compare in cross-national terms? The United States stands out for its exceptionally meager public provisions. Neither national nor state laws provide job protections to all employed women at the time of childbirth. Moreover, though five of the states grant some employed mothers disability-related maternity benefits, the United States has no national law that ensures or funds maternity pay. This lack of legal protections for a large share of the female workforce is truly exceptional.

(Text continues on p. 128.)

TABLE 5.1 Family Leave—Maternity and Parental Leave Provisions, Approximately 2000

	Maternity Leave Benefits (Paid)	Parental Leave Benefits (Unpaid and Paid)
	Nordic Countries	
Denmark	Eighteen weeks. 100 percent of wages up to flat-rate ceiling of DKK2,758 (U.S.$321) per week, equal in practice to about 60 percent prior wages. Owing to collective agreements, many employers "top up," so 80 percent of parents receive 100 percent wage replacement.	Paid leave: Parents may share ten weeks of parental leave. Benefit level same as maternity leave. Extended to twelve weeks if father takes two weeks. As with maternity, 80 percent receive full wage. Following parental leave, each parent entitled to twenty-six weeks of additional child care leave (thirteen weeks if after first birthday). Benefit level is 60 percent of parental leave benefit level; sometimes supplemented by local authorities. Available until child's ninth birthday.[a]
Finland	Eighteen weeks (105 days). Benefit based on graduated replacement rate: approximately 70 percent at low income, 40 percent at medium income, 25 percent at high income (equal, on average, to approximately 66 percent).	Paid leave: Parents may share twenty-six weeks (158 days) of parental leave. Benefit level is 66 percent of earnings, flat rate if not employed. Following parental leave, family entitled to 108 weeks home care leave, on the condition that the child is not in public child care. Benefit paid at a low flat rate of approximately FIM2,900 (U.S.$475) per month. Available until child's third birthday.[b]
Norway	Paid leave: Parents may share fifty-two weeks of leave at 80 percent of wages or, alternatively, forty-two weeks at 100 percent of wages (nine weeks exclusively for the mother, four weeks exclusively for the father). Benefits subject to maximum income of NOK290,261 (U.S.$26,876) per year. Benefit can be paid while parent is employed at 50 to 90 percent time, and leave time is extended accordingly. Available until child's third birthday.[c,d]	

Sweden   Paid leave: Parents may share sixty-five weeks (fifteen months) of leave. Benefit level is 80 percent of earnings for fifty-two weeks (twelve months); flat rate for remaining thirteen weeks (three months) at approximately SEK1,800 (U.S.$187) per month. Earnings-related benefit subject to maximum income of approximately SEK270,000 (U.S.$28,000) per year. Benefit can be paid while parent is employed part-time, and leave is extended accordingly. Available until child's eighth birthday.[e]

Continental Countries

Belgium	Fifteen weeks. 82 percent of wages for first four weeks (one month), plus 75 percent of wages thereafter. Benefits during first month not subject to ceiling; thereafter, benefits subject to maximum income of approximately $95 per day.[f]
	Paid leave: Each parent entitled to thirteen weeks (three months) full-time leave or up to twenty-six weeks (6 months) of half-time leave. Parents taking leave receive flat-rate benefit payment of BF20,400 (U.S.$551) per month. Available until child's fourth birthday.
France	Sixteen weeks for first two children, twenty-six weeks for third and subsequent children. 100 percent of wages, up to maximum of FF387 (U.S.$59) per day.[g]
	Paid leave: Parents may share 156 weeks (three years) of leave. No benefit paid for first child; benefit level is flat rate FF3,024 (U.S.$462) per month for second and subsequent children. Benefit can be paid at reduced rate while parent is employed part-time. Available until child's third birthday.[b]
Germany	Fourteen weeks. 100 percent of wages.[i]
	Paid leave: Parents may share 156 weeks (three years) of leave. Benefit is flat rate of DM600 (U.S.$309) per month for two years or up to DM900 (U.S.$464) per month for one year. Benefits are income tested, but majority of families qualify (during the first six months, then the income limits are lower, and about half qualify). Benefits can be paid during part-time employment of up to thirty hours per week. Paid leave can be used until child's second birthday; third year of leave may be used until child is eight years old.[j]

(Table continues on p. 126.)

TABLE 5.1 *Continued*

	Maternity Leave Benefits (Paid)	Parental Leave Benefits (Unpaid and Paid)
Luxembourg	Sixteen weeks. 100 percent of wages.	Paid leave: Each parent entitled to twenty-six weeks (six months) full-time leave; one parent can receive flat rate of LF60,000 (U.S.$1,471) per month. Benefit can be paid at half rate if parent works part-time. One parent must take parental leave directly following maternity leave; other can take leave until child is five years old.
Netherlands	Sixteen weeks. 100 percent of wages, up to daily maximum of 310 guilders (U.S.$154) per day.[k]	Unpaid leave: Each parent entitled to leave of the equivalent of thirteen weeks (three months) at their usual hours of work per week. Standard take-up is twenty-six weeks (six months) at 50 percent working time. Available until child's eighth birthday.

English-Speaking Countries

Canada	Fifteen weeks. 55 percent of previous average insured earnings, up to a maximum benefit of C$413 (U.S.$350) a week. Family supplement for low-income earners (less than C$25,921 [U.S.$21,967] raises replacement rate to 80 percent.[l]	Paid leave: Parents may share thirty-five weeks of parental leave; combined maternity (fifteen weeks) and parental benefit cannot exceed fifty weeks. Benefit rate is same as for maternity (55 percent up to a maximum of $413 [U.S.$350] per week. Parents can continue to work, earning the greater of $50 (U.S.$42) per week or 25 percent of their weekly benefit rate without affecting their parental benefits. Available until child's first birthday.
United Kingdom	Statutory Maternity Pay (stricter eligibility): Six weeks at 90 percent of wages plus twelve weeks at flat rate (£60.20 [U.S.$92]) per week. Maternity Allowance (broader eligibility): eighteen weeks. Paid at lesser of 90 percent of wages or flat rate of £60.20 (U.S.$92)	Unpaid leave: Each parent entitled to thirteen weeks full-time leave per child. No more than four weeks can be taken in any given year. Available until child is five years old.

United States	No national policy of paid maternity leave. Some benefits paid under temporary disability insurance (TDI) laws in five states: California, Hawaii, New Jersey, New York, and Rhode Island. Approximately 23 percent of the U.S. population resides in these states. Maximum duration, twenty-six to fifty-two weeks; average duration, five to thirteen weeks. Maximum weekly benefits, $170 to $487; average weekly benefits, $142 to $273.	Unpaid leave: Each parent entitled to twelve weeks family and medical leave (if employer has 50 or more employees and work history requirements fulfilled). Available until child's first birthday. Several states extend federal leave; generally, state laws broaden coverage (including smaller employers) or increase duration or both. California enacted paid parental leave in 2002. Pays approximately 55 percent wage replacement for six weeks, subject to earnings cap.

Sources: Data from CAUT-ACPPU (2001); Clearinghouse on International Developments in Child, Youth, and Family Policies (2003); ISSA (2002); Moss and Deven (1999); OECD (2001a, 2001d); Wisensale (2001); country experts.

Note: All durations are expressed as weeks, to help with interpretation. Where authors converted from days, years, or months, original duration is given in parentheses. All currency amounts expressed as 2000 U.S. dollars, adjusted for purchasing-power parities.

[a] Danish parental leave reformed March 2002. Entitlement increased to thirty-two weeks (to be shared between the parents) at same pay as maternity; 80 percent of employers still top up. Other changes increased the flexibility of parents' take-up options.

[b] Finnish parents can replace home care leave payment with payment for private child care provider.

[c] Norwegian cap equivalent to approximately 1.9 times average annual earnings among working-age mothers (part-time and full-time combined).

[d] Norwegian parents can use cash benefit to pay for private child care (for children aged one or two) if child is not in a public slot. In addition to paid parental leave, each parent is entitled to one year of unpaid leave.

[e] Swedish cap equivalent to approximately 2.2 times average annual earnings among working-age mothers (part-time and full-time combined).

[f] Earnings ceiling in Belgium as of 2002.

[g] French replacement rate is 100 percent of net wages (after social insurance contributions are deducted).

[h] French parents working 50 percent time receive 66 percent of full benefit; parents working 50 to 80 percent time receive 50 percent of full benefit.

[i] German maternity leave is paid about 25 percent by health insurance and about 75 percent by employer.

[j] German parental leave law as of January 2001.

[k] As of January 2001, the Netherlands government offers subsidies to employers who provide paid leave, to defray some of the costs.

[l] Canadian maximum pertains to benefit level, not maximum covered earnings. Maximum benefit of U.S.$350 a week converts to approximately U.S.$17,500 per year, or equivalent to 55 percent of about U.S.$32,000 in earnings. Also, the national government pays benefits, but rights to take leave are established at the provincial level.

[m] As of 2003, both maternity leave benefits in the United Kingdom extended from eighteen to twenty-six weeks.

FIGURE 5.2 **Paid Leave Available to Mothers, Approximately 2000**

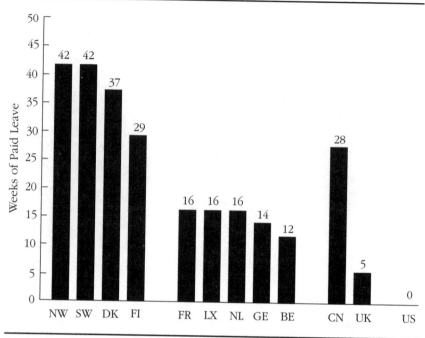

Sources: Data from CAUT-ACPPU (2001); Clearinghouse on International Developments in Child, Youth, and Family Policies (2003); ISSA (2000); Moss and Deven (1999); OECD (2001a, 2001d); Wisensale (2001); country experts.
Note: This indicator is calculated as the number of weeks of leave times the wage-replacement rate. Following these benefits, mothers can collect some additional low-paid benefits (generally at a flat rate) in Finland, Belgium, France, Germany, and Luxembourg.

Parental Leave Rights and Benefits

In an earner-carer society, parents would engage symmetrically in caregiving. Clearly, mothers' need for time at home is likely to exceed that of fathers' during the early postpartum period as they recover physically from the birth; their needs may be greater for longer periods if they breastfeed.[11] Nevertheless, couples could choose to share caregiving in any of a number of ways. They could postpone symmetrical engagement until after some initial period of time, or they could alternate spending time at home.[12] To enable these possibilities, supportive policies would include publicly financed parental leaves that provide substantial, flexible, and gender-egalitarian leave rights and benefits.[13]

Among our eleven comparison countries, nine countries provide some form of paid parental leave. As is true for maternity leave, coverage is very high, and most employed mothers and fathers qualify for benefits (Kamerman 2000).

The Nordic countries provide the most generous parental leave rights and benefits (table 5.1). Most employed parents have the right to take relatively long periods of leave—from one to three years—and, through social insurance funds, they receive about two-thirds or more of their wages during most or all of their leave periods (again, subject to caps for high earners). Parental leave policies in the Nordic countries also afford parents substantial flexibility; parental choice is valued and codified in the law. Denmark and Sweden allow parents to take their allotted paid leaves in increments until the child is eight years old. Norway and Sweden allow parents to combine prorated leaves with part-time employment, and Finland and Norway permit parents to use a portion of their leave benefits to purchase private child care instead.

Four of the five Continental countries also grant most employed parents paid parental leave, but provisions are less generous. Although leave periods are long in several of these countries—especially France and Germany, both of which pay portions of three-year leaves—wage-replacement rates are much lower than in the Nordic countries. In Belgium, France, Germany, and Luxembourg, for example, parents may claim relatively modest, flat-rate benefits, and in the Netherlands, parental leave is unpaid altogether.

Policy development at the European level—meaning within the policy-making bodies of the European Union (EU)—has played a role in standardizing and expanding parental leave programs across these countries. In 1996 the European Union enacted a Directive on Parental Leave and Leave for Family Reasons.[14] The 1995 directive required that member countries enact measures that provide men and women workers with at least three months of parental leave (paid or unpaid), as distinct from maternity leave, following the birth of a child until a given age of up to eight years. The directive also required that workers be protected against dismissal on the grounds of applying for or taking parental leave, that they have the right to return to the same or a similar job, and that they maintain previously acquired rights. Most of our comparison countries were already in line when the directive was enacted; a few needed to make marginal changes, and others (including Belgium, the Netherlands, and the United Kingdom) passed substantial new legislation.

How does the United States compare with other countries on parental leave policies? Under the FMLA, mothers and fathers who meet tenure requirements in covered firms may take up to twelve weeks of unpaid leave for childbirth. Many families lack even this minimal level of protection, however, and few have access to extended periods of paid leave through private employment agreements. The FMLA is limited in flexibility, as well, requiring parents to take the leave in the first year following the birth of their child.

Leave for Family Reasons

Public policies providing leave for family reasons provide mothers and fathers with time to attend to the routine and unexpected needs of their children; leaves with wage replacement also provide some economic security. Table 5.2 presents examples in one category of provisions—those designed to enable parents to care for sick children. Examples here include rights and benefits associated with caring for children with routine sicknesses as well as for children with more serious illnesses.[15]

The Nordic countries make the most generous provisions for parents to care for sick children, especially seriously ill children. In Denmark, for example, parents with seriously ill children may claim up to fifty-two weeks of leave with about two-thirds wage replacement. Swedish and Finnish parents may take twenty-four and twelve weeks, respectively, also with high levels of wage replacement. Sick-child benefits in Norway are paid for an unlimited length of time for the most seriously ill children and for shorter durations—typically, ten days—for children with routine illnesses. Although legal entitlements are long in these countries, in practice, benefits are drawn for much shorter periods of time. Swedish parents, for example, draw an average of about seven days a year, with just over 40 percent of days claimed by fathers.

As with other forms of leave, the Continental countries offer

TABLE 5.2 **Leave for Family Reasons, Example: "Sick Child" Provisions, Approximately 2000**

Country	Benefit
	Nordic Countries
Denmark	Paid benefit available: Parents entitled to paid time off to care for seriously ill child under age fourteen. Benefit is same as maternity benefit (in practice, about 60 percent wages) and is payable for fifty-two weeks within any eighteen-month period.
Finland	Paid benefit available: Parents entitled to paid time off to care for ill or disabled child up to age fifteen (with certification). Benefit is 66 percent of earnings for up to sixty working days per year.[a]
Norway	Paid benefit available: Parents entitled to paid time off to care for ill child under age twelve (age sixteen if a handicapped or chronically ill child). Benefit is 100 percent of covered earnings. Leave is ten days per child per year (for each parent), twenty or forty days if child is disabled or chronically ill, unlimited if very seriously ill. Leave duration doubled for single parents.
Sweden	Paid benefit available: Parents entitled to paid time off to care for sick child up to age twelve, or age sixteen in certain circumstances. Benefit is 80 percent of covered earnings. Parents may claim up to one hundred twenty days a year.[b]
	Continental Countries
Belgium	Paid benefit available: Parents entitled to paid time off to care for ill child or family member. Benefit is 100 percent of wages for ten days per year.
France	Paid benefit available: Parents entitled to paid time off to care for ill child under age sixteen. Benefit is 100 percent of wages, up to a ceiling. Generally, entitled to three days per year; for children less than age 1 or if parent has three children, entitlement is five days.[c]
Germany	Paid benefit available: Parents entitled to paid time off to care for ill child under age twelve. Benefit is 100 percent of earnings. Working adults in two-worker families may take ten days per year per child (up to maximum of twenty-five days); single parents may take twenty days per child (up to maximum of fifty days) per year.

(Table continues on p. 132.)

TABLE 5.2 *Continued*

Country	Benefit
Luxembourg	Paid benefit available: Parents entitled to paid time off in the event of a serious illness or accident affecting a child under fifteen. Benefit is 100 percent of earnings. Any working parent is entitled to two days' leave per year per child.
Netherlands	Paid benefit available: Workers entitled to paid time off to care for sick child or partner. Benefit is minimum wage or 70 percent of full-time wage, whichever is higher, for up to ten days per year.

English-Speaking Countries

Country	Benefit
Canada	Right to unpaid leave: Parents in some provinces entitled to "emergency leave." For example, Ontario allows employees in enterprises with at least fifty employees to take up to ten days of emergency leave per year to care for children (and other relations as well).
United Kingdom	Right to unpaid leave: Parents entitled to unpaid "time off for dependents," including sickness or a breakdown in care arrangement. Each parent allowed to take a "reasonable" number of days; usually limited to one or two days per year.
United States	Right to unpaid leave: Covered eligible workers may take twelve weeks of federal, job-protected leave during any twelve months to care for an immediate family member (spouse, child, parent) who has a "serious health condition." Leave may be taken in blocks of hours, a half day, a day, a week, a month, and so forth. A few states grant additional unpaid leave entitlements. For example, the Massachusetts Small Necessities Leave Act permits eligible employees to take up to twenty-four hours unpaid leave within a twelve-month period to attend child's school activity or accompany child or elderly relative to doctor's appointment.

Sources: Data from Clearinghouse on International Developments in Child, Youth, and Family Policies (2003); Equal Opportunities Commission (2002); European Commission Network (1994); ISSA (2000); Mallin (2000); Ministry of Health and Social Affairs (2002); National Partnership for Women and Families (1998); OECD (2002a); country experts.

Note: Examples in this table include provisions for caring for children with routine sicknesses as well as for children with longer-term or more serious illnesses.

[a]Finnish parents also have the right to unpaid leave for children's sicknesses, limited to four days per sickness. Some collective agreements provide full pay.

[b]An average of seven days per year are drawn, with just over 40 percent claimed by Swedish fathers.

[c]As of 2001, French parents can draw benefits at parental leave rate for four months to care for a seriously ill child. If working 50 percent of full-time, benefit paid at 66 percent of full benefit; if working 50 to 80 percent time, benefit paid at 50 percent of full benefit.

substantial but less-extensive leave for family reasons than the Nordic countries. Sick-child leaves generally provide generous wage replacement (100 percent of wages in Belgium, France, Germany, and Luxembourg) but are typically available for no more than ten days a year.

When considered in cross-national terms, the United States once again appears exceptional in its lack of support for employed parents. Through the FMLA, American parents may take up to twelve weeks of unpaid leave a year to care for seriously ill children. Although generous in duration and gender egalitarian in its provisions, FMLA benefits are severely weakened by the absence of wage replacement. Moreover, American parents have no rights at all, under national law, to paid time away from the workplace to attend to children's routine or emergency needs other than serious illnesses.

Gender Equality

The implications of generous family leave provisions for gender equality are complex and contradictory. Gender differentials are particularly critical in the case of extended parental leaves: if parental leave is taken up mostly or exclusively by women, mothers and children might benefit from extensive periods of maternal caregiving; these same arrangements, however, will weaken women's labor force attachment and exacerbate gender inequalities at home and in the workplace. To achieve the twin goals of supporting parents in their caregiving roles and promoting greater gender equality in both paid and unpaid work, government policies are needed that both enable and encourage fathers to share in family leave benefits.

None of the countries in our study have achieved the goal of gender equality in the usage of leave. Mothers' take-up of parental leave is high everywhere, but recent estimates suggest that fathers take well less than 10 percent of total days of paid parental leave in most Europe countries (Bruning and Plantenga 1999).[16] Peter Moss and Fred Deven describe the gendered effects of parental leave as a catch-22: "If parental leave were equally taken by women and men, it might promote or consolidate gender equality. But to be equally taken requires gender equality to be achieved already, or to be further advanced than at present. If gender equality is not already advanced, then parental leave may retard or even reverse progress towards its achievement" (Moss and Deven 1999, 13–14).

Although none of the countries in our study have achieved gender equality, several are taking steps to increase fathers' use of leave benefits. Three strategies appear particularly promising. High wage-replacement rates are the most straightforward instrument. Because men tend to have higher wages than women, in the absence of full wage replacement it often makes economic sense for couples to decide that the mother should withdraw from the labor market. High parental leave wage-replacement rates maximize fathers' propensity to take up leave rights and benefits; in practice, that means both a high rate and a high cap on covered earnings. Second, nontransferable rights can be created by granting individual rights to each parent for his or her own period of leave or by reserving for fathers some portion of a family-based entitlement. Both approaches create use-or-lose provisions that increase the incentives for fathers to make use of leave options; leave time that is not taken by the father is lost to the family. Third, public-education campaigns may reduce cultural and institutional resistance to leave taking by fathers by altering public and private discourse about fathers' engagement in caregiving.

The twelve countries in our study vary considerably in the extent to which they have actively incorporated these strategies. Table 5.3 provides institutional details, and figure 5.3 translates these into a quantified comparison. Figure 5.3 reports gender-egalitarian features of policy design, using a six-point index. We assigned countries one point on the "gender-equality scale" if they have any paid paternity leave, two points if fathers have nontransferable parental leave rights (either use-or-lose portions of shareable leave or individual entitlements), and up to three additional points for wage-replacement provisions (three points if benefits are wage related and at 80 percent or higher, two points if benefits are wage related but at less than 80 percent, and one point if benefits are paid but only at a flat rate).

Three of the Nordic countries—Sweden, Norway, and Denmark—stand out on multiple fronts. Fathers are eligible for more benefits, and incentives were added during the 1990s to encour-

TABLE 5.3 **Provisions for Fathers: Paternity Leave and Incentives for Take-Up of Parental Leave, Approximately 2000**

Country	Paternity Leave Benefits (Paid)	Incentives for Fathers' Take-Up of Parental Leave[a]
	Nordic Countries	
Denmark	Two weeks (ten days). Benefit is same as maternity pay, equal in practice to about 60 percent prior wages. Due to collective agreements, many employers "top up," so most parents receive 100 percent wage replacement.	"Use or lose": two weeks of leave added to the ten weeks of parental leave and designated for the father (for a total of twelve weeks); if he does not take them, they are lost to the family. Individual, nontransferable entitlement: The child care leave is granted to each parent and may not be transferred.
Finland	Three weeks (eighteen days). Benefit based on graduated replacement rate: approximately 70 percent at low income, 40 percent at medium income, 25 percent at high income (equal, on average, to approximately 66 percent).	—[b]
Norway	Four weeks as part of parental-leave scheme.	"Use or lose": Four weeks of leave are designated for the father; if he does not take them, they are lost to the family.
Sweden	Two weeks (ten days) paternity leave, paid at 80 percent.	"Use or lose": Four weeks of leave are designated for the father; if he does not take them, they are lost to the family.

(Table continues on p. 136.)

TABLE 5.3 *Continued*

Country	Paternity Leave Benefits (Paid)	Incentives for Fathers' Take-Up of Parental Leave[a]
	Continental Countries	
Belgium	Three to four days. 100 percent of wages.	Individual, nontransferable entitlement: Father has his own leave entitlement that may not be transferred. However, the low replacement rate is a disincentive to take-up.
France	No paid paternity leave.[c]	—
Germany	No paid paternity leave.	—
Luxembourg	Two days. 100 percent of wages.	Individual, nontransferable entitlement: Father has his own leave entitlement that may not be transferred. However, the low replacement rate is a disincentive to take-up.
Netherlands	Two days. 100 percent of wages.	Individual, nontransferable entitlement: Father has his own leave entitlement that may not be transferred. However, the absence of wage replacement is a disincentive to take-up.
	English-Speaking Countries	
Canada	No paid paternity leave.	—
United Kingdom	No paid paternity leave.[d]	Individual, nontransferable entitlement: Father has his own leave entitlement that may not be transferred. However, the absence of wage replacement is a disincentive to take-up.

TABLE 5.3 *Continued*

Country	Paternity Leave Benefits (Paid)	Incentives for Fathers' Take-Up of Parental Leave[a]
United States	No paid paternity leave.	Individual, nontransferable entitlement: Father has his own leave entitlement that may not be transferred. However, the absence of wage replacement is a disincentive to take-up.

Sources: Data from Clearinghouse on International Developments in Child, Youth, and Family Policies (2003); ISSA (2000); Moss and Deven (1999); OECD (2001d, 2002a); Work Life Research Center (2002); country experts.

[a]"Use-or-lose" days were implemented in Denmark in 1999; in Norway in 1993; and in Sweden in 1995.

[b]Finland introduced incentives for fathers' take-up in 2003.

[c]As of 2002, French fathers entitled to eleven working days (two weeks), paid at same rate as maternity benefit.

[d]As of 2003, fathers in the United Kingdom entitled to two weeks' paid paternity leave, paid at same rate as Statutory Maternity Pay.

age them to take up those benefits. In each of these countries, shareable parental leaves are lengthened if fathers take some portion—two weeks in Denmark and four in Norway and Sweden. If these weeks are not taken by the father, they are lost to the family. Although modest in duration, these so-called "daddy quotas" send a signal that paternal leave taking is valued and encouraged. After these provisions were introduced in Norway in 1993, fathers' take-up rate rose sharply (Ellingsaeter 1999). Incentives for Norwegian and Swedish fathers to take leave are further strengthened by the high wage-replacement rates and, for Danish fathers, by the fully individualized entitlement for the child care leave that follows parental leave. Finland lags behind its Nordic counterparts with the absence of parental leave "daddy days" but grants fathers a comparatively generous eighteen days of paternity leave.[17]

In some of the Nordic countries, gender-egalitarian policy designs are reinforced by public-education campaigns. The Swedish government, for example, launched public campaigns for employers and unions in the 1990s that emphasized the "benefits of fathers' taking parental leave for families, work organizations, chil-

FIGURE 5.3 **Index of Gender Equality in Family Leave Policy Designs, Approximately 2000**

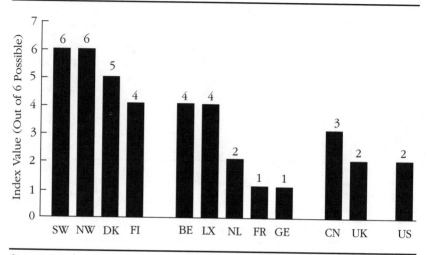

Sources: Data from Clearinghouse on International Developments in Child, Youth, and Family Policies (2003); ISSA (2000); Moss and Deven (1999); OECD (2001d, 2002a); Work Life Research Center (2002); country experts.

dren and society" (Haas and Hwang 1999, 62). Although take-up cannot be explained by any single factor, it has risen rapidly in recent years; in the mid-1990s, more than 40 percent of eligible Swedish fathers took some parental leave in their child's first year, up from 2 percent when parental leave was introduced in 1974 and nearly double the rate in the early 1980s (Kamerman 2000).[18] Ellingsaeter reports that in Norway, policy actors have also pushed fatherhood onto the political agenda: "While employment for women was the main issue of policies in the 1980s . . . the caring father, and thus the domestication of men, is the new issue of the 1990s" (Ellingsaeter 1999, 45).

Family leave provisions in the Continental countries have far less gender-egalitarian designs. Belgium and Luxembourg stand out for having paid paternity leave (although only two to four days) and some nontransferable paid parental leave. However, the low parental leave wage-replacement rate in both countries is a counterbalancing disincentive to fathers' take-up. The Netherlands also grants individual, nontransferable parental leave entitlement, but, again, the absence of wage replacement is a strong disincentive to fathers' take-up.

Although we have identified Canada's family leave provisions as generous relative to the other English-speaking countries, the Canadian system is weak in terms of egalitarian policy design. Leave benefits are equally available to both parents, but mothers in Canada may take 100 percent of the family's maximum allocation; there are no use-or-lose provisions to encourage fathers' use of benefits. This, combined with low wage-replacement rates (and low benefit caps), creates few incentives for mothers and fathers to share family leave entitlements.

On the dimension of supporting gender equality, the United States is relatively progressive in cross-national terms. Under the FMLA, fathers are granted their own leave rights, creating nontransferable entitlements for mothers and fathers. The potential to increase fathers' involvement at home is greatly diminished, however, by the absence of wage replacement. Parents' ability to take extended leave in the United States depends very much on their private resources, creating strong disincentives for fathers to take substantial periods of leave.

Distributing the Costs

Family leave rights are meaningful only when parents can afford to exercise them. Financing public leaves through social insurance schemes or general tax revenues has the potential to increase equality in access to leave for families of different income levels, ensure wage-replacement levels that create incentives for fathers and mothers to participate, and reduce the incentives for employers to discriminate against actual or potential leave takers.

When leave benefits are distributed across the employed (and tax-paying) population, the total cost is relatively modest. Figure 5.4 illustrates a comparison of average national expenditures, as of 1998, for family leave provisions (maternity and parental combined) for each employed woman.[19]

The Nordic countries, with the most extensive provisions, spend the most ($594 to $808), on average, for each employed woman. Moderate levels of spending in the Continental countries ($67 to $465 for each employed woman) reflect lower wage-re-

FIGURE 5.4 **Expenditures on Maternity and Parental Leave, per Employed Woman, 1998**

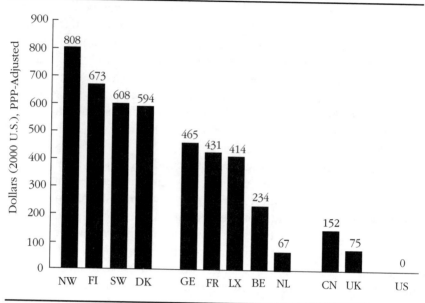

Source: Data from OECD (2001b).

placement rates; even France and Germany, with their long leave durations, spend far less than their Nordic neighbors, whose leaves are more generously remunerated. Canada spends at a moderate level ($152 for each employed woman in 1998), owing in part to the relatively low level of wage replacement.[20]

Although public expenditures are substantial for these family leave programs, the cost of paid leave is surprisingly modest when considered per capita. Even in the generous Nordic countries, public outlays for leave approximate only three or four dollars a day for each employed woman. When we consider expenditures as a share of GDP, the most generous Nordic programs cost no more than 0.5 to 0.7 percent of GDP. In the Continental countries, these programs capture from as little as .07 percent of GDP in the Netherlands to .35 and .39 percent in France and Germany, respectively. The Canadian program—often held up as a model for the United States—cost only .13 percent of Canadian GDP in 1998.

Although financing mechanisms vary, all eleven of the countries that provide paid leaves finance those benefits through social insurance schemes. That means that benefits are funded by employee and employer contributions, often supplemented by general tax revenues (table 5.4). Typically, maternity leave is paid out of social insurance funds designated for sickness or medical payments, although in some cases (Norway, Belgium, and the United Kingdom) it is paid out from funds that include other major social insurance programs (including retirement pensions). Canada uses a somewhat exceptional social insurance strategy, as it pays maternity leave out of unemployment insurance funds.[21] Parental leave, when paid, is usually financed out of the same funds as maternity benefits, although some countries finance parental leave entirely from general revenues.

The key observation we draw from table 5.4 is that none of our eleven countries with paid leave relies on individual families to finance leave nor on mandating employers to provide wage replacement for their own employees. Where social insurance financing does depend heavily on employer contributions, contributions are not "experience rated" at the firm level (as is the case with unemployment insurance in the United States), a mechanism that would increase costs for those employers whose workforce is more likely to use benefits (for example, employers who hire younger or female workers). Social insurance financing distributes the burden for employees and employers. The costs of caregiving are shared across employees' working years, among parents and nonparents, between those who take leaves and those who do not, and across enterprises as well. These financing mechanisms, especially when supplemented by substantial contributions from general tax revenues, reduce the risk for individual families and individual employers. They also reduce employers' resistance and lessen incentives to discriminate against potential leave takers.

The exceptionally meager provisions in the United States are thrown into sharp relief when we consider public expenditures: the United States is the only one of these countries that makes no public investments in paid leave at the national level. The direct costs of paid family leave are distributed narrowly among employers who provide paid leave as a firm-based benefit. Only state TDI programs approximate the social insurance financing devel-

TABLE 5.4 **Family Leave Financing, Late 1990s**

| Country | Maternity Leave | | Parental Leave |
	Contribution Framework	Contributors	
	Nordic Countries		
Denmark	Funded by employers and government.	Employers pay whole cost for first two weeks; local government whole cost from third week.	Parental leave: employer, employee, government. Child care leave: employee, government.
Finland	Funded through sickness-insurance fund.	Employers, employees, government; government pays substantial subsidy.	Same as maternity leave.
Norway	Funded through global social-insurance fund.	Employers, employees, government; government pays substantial subsidy.	Same as maternity leave.
Sweden	Funded through sickness-insurance fund.	Employers and government.	Same as maternity leave.
	Continental Countries		
Belgium	Funded through global social-insurance fund.	Employers, employees, government (paid from sickness and invalidity fund).	Employers, employees, government (paid from unemployment benefit fund).
France	Funded through health-care-insurance fund.	Employers, employees, government.	Same as maternity leave
Germany	Funded through health-care-insurance fund.	Employers, employees, government; employers pay a substantial share as they are required to "top up" public benefit.	Federal government pays whole cost.

TABLE 5.4 *Continued*

| Country | Maternity and Paternity Leave | | Parental Leave |
	Contribution Framework	Contributors	
Luxembourg	Funded through sickness-insurance fund.	Employers, employees, government.	Government pays whole cost.
Netherlands	Funded through general unemployment fund.	Employers, employees, government.	Unpaid (no financing).
English-Speaking Countries			
Canada	Funded through unemployment insurance fund.[a]	Employers, employees.	Same as maternity leave.
United Kingdom	Funded through global social insurance fund.	Employers, employees, government; government pays substantial subsidy.	Unpaid (no financing).
United States	In states with programs, funded through temporary disability insurance (TDI) funds.	In states with programs, various combinations of employer and employee contributions.	Unpaid (no financing).

Sources: Data from European Commission (2000); ISSA (2000); Jordan (1999); Rostgaard and Fridberg (1998); U.S. Office of Personnel Management (2001); country experts.
[a]In Canada, unemployment compensation program is called "Employment Insurance."

oped in the European countries and in Canada. Efforts in the United States to create more-extensive publicly funded leave—for example, proposals to "add wages to the FMLA"—often include employer mandates that would require firms to pay their own workers' wages during periods of leave. Justifiably, employers have resisted these reforms.

CONCLUSION

The family leave system in the United States ensures American working parents remarkably little time for caregiving during their children's earliest years and imposes the costs of caregiving on women, parents, and, to a lesser extent, employers. Access to both rights and cash benefits is not only limited, it is also highly regressive; the likelihood of having either unpaid or paid leave falls as parents' needs and resources fall. Many new parents end up choosing among unattractive alternatives: quitting their jobs altogether, returning to their jobs but doing so sooner than they would prefer, or returning after an adequate period of leave but having incurred substantial lost earnings.

Public family leave policies can do much more to support earner-carer families. Several of the European countries in this study—and Canada as well—have policies in place that grant parents time to care for their children, provide a reasonable level of economic security, and include incentives for equal sharing of caregiving between mothers and fathers. These comparative cases suggest lessons that might be used to guide the development in the United States of family leave policies that are consonant with the earner-carer framework.

First, maternity leave policies should grant employed mothers job security and publicly financed wage replacement around the time of childbirth or adoption. Mothers employed in small or large enterprises should be eligible for several months of job-protected leave with full, or nearly full, wage replacement. Benefit structures should be progressive, with benefits capped for high-earning mothers; caps should be set at levels that allow all but the highest earners to receive full benefits. Access to paid maternity leave would provide new mothers time for infant care and secure their ties to employment by reducing the likelihood that they quit their jobs following childbirth or change employers when they return to paid work. Wage replacement, in a social insurance framework, would reduce the costs of child rearing for mothers, provide short-term economic support for families, and make leave available to low- as well as high-earning families.

Second, following maternity leaves, parental leave rights and publicly financed benefits should grant both parents periods of paid leave during their children's earliest years. Parents should have the option, between them, to spend at least one full year at home, inclusive of the period of maternity leave. Parental leave policies would grant parents time to care for their children, with job security and some remuneration, beyond the first few months following birth or adoption. Flexible program designs would allow parents to choose among several options, depending on their employment status and preferences; for example, a one-year leave entitlement could be taken as full-time leave during an infant's first year, or as half-time leave for two years, or as intermittent periods of leave spread over the three years preceding preschool enrollment. Wage replacement would extend leave options to low-income families, who could not otherwise devote substantial time to caring for very young children.

Third, mothers and fathers should be entitled to some time off, with pay, to attend to short-term and unpredictable needs that arise throughout their children's lives, such as a child's routine illness, a disruption in child care, or a school-related emergency—without fear of job loss or lost pay. Publicly financed leave for family reasons would secure children's access to their parents when unpredictable needs arise and extend benefits to low-wage workers, whose jobs and employers typically grant the fewest options for parents who need to make short-term changes in work scheduling.

Fourth, eligibility and benefits should be designed to make gender equality a priority by securing provisions for fathers and including incentives for them to take up the rights and benefits to which they are entitled. To avoid encouraging gender differentials in caregiving, parental leaves ought to grant both parents the same entitlements and benefits, the wage-replacement rate (and caps) should be high, and program rules should disallow men from transferring their entitlements to their female partners. Designing family leave provisions requires grappling with real trade-offs. For example, government costs would be the same if workers were granted twelve months of full-time leave at 50 percent wage replacement or six months of full-time leave at 100 percent wage replacement. The former would allow a longer caregiving period for new parents but the latter would create stronger incentives for gender-egalitarian leave-taking. To take another example, policies could grant couples twelve months of paid leave, to be shared between them, or each partner six months of nontransferable leave. The former would increase parents' flexibility in allocating their benefits but the latter would increase fathers' participation.

Finally, leave financing should be designed to distribute the costs of time for caring across society and to minimize the burden placed on individual employers. Paid leave ought to be financed with revenues from employer and employee contributions. Social insurance financing would distribute the costs of temporary workplace absences across workers, firms, family types, and generations. Contributions from general tax revenues, typically designated for administrative costs, could further spread the fiscal burden. Financing designs should alleviate employers' responsibility to pay their own workers' wages during periods of leave; that would reduce employers' resistance and lessen their incentive to discriminate against potential leave takers.

Chapter 6

Strengthening Reduced-Hour Work: Regulation of Working Time

IN THE PARTIALLY transformed world in which most parents now live and work, time is scarce as they balance long hours in the workplace with the demands of caregiving at home. A central assumption of the earner-carer model is that parents—mothers and especially fathers—will have the option to reduce their hours of paid work, especially before their children reach school age and possibly throughout their children's lives. However, for many American workers, reductions in the workweek are impossible or entail great sacrifices in earnings, benefits, and career opportunities.

Working-time policies can help give parents time for caregiving.[1] Setting the standard workweek at below forty hours frees up caregiving time for those who are employed full-time. Part-time work regulations improve the compensation and quality of employment for those who choose to work for pay for less than thirty-five hours a week. Other regulatory measures can reduce the prevalence of involuntary nonstandard-hour work or raise its rewards. The establishment of minimum vacation rights could ensure all parents periods of unbroken time with their families.

A BRIEF OVERVIEW OF WORKING-TIME POLICIES IN THE UNITED STATES

Working time in the United States is regulated by several federal and state laws operating in conjunction with a limited collective-bargaining system. These are illustrated in figure 6.1.

147

FIGURE 6.1   U.S. Working-Time Policy Provisions

Federal

> Fair Labor Standards Act of 1938: regulates normal weekly working time by mandating overtime pay above a weekly threshold.
>
> Employee Retirement Income Security Act of 1974 and the Internal Revenue Code: regulate part-time workers' rights to employer-provided pension and health benefits.

State

> Some states supplement federal programs. Various laws apply overtime to daily hours (for example, above eight a day), restrict mandatory overtime, or require that workers receive a minimum numbers of days off each week.

Source: Authors' compilation.

The Fair Labor Standards Act and Related State Laws

The most important national law relating directly to working hours is the Fair Labor Standards Act (FLSA) of 1938, which covers federal, state, and local governments and private enterprises engaged in interstate commerce. Two goals motivated the passage of the FLSA: protecting the health and general well-being of workers and increasing employment by spreading out the available work (Costa 2000). The provisions of the FLSA reduced weekly working time for employees and mandated extra compensation for those who work more than the standard number of hours. The act and its subsequent amendments establish the standard workweek in the United States by requiring employers to pay time-and-a-half for each hour worked beyond forty hours in a seven-day week. The FLSA also places limits on working time for employees under the age of eighteen.

In contrast to the working-time regulations in place in many European countries, the FLSA is notable for what it does *not* address. First of all, the FLSA neither mandates maximum total hours nor prohibits mandatory overtime.[2] In the United States, employees who refuse overtime hours have no protection from job dismissals, demotions, or other repercussions. Lonnie Golden and Helene Jorgensen (2002) note that about one-third of overtime workers in the United States report being compelled by their employers to work overtime. With the exception of the minimum wage, the FLSA is also silent on issues of compensation and benefits for part-time and other reduced-hour workers, and it offers no extra compensation for workers in nonstandard shifts. Nor does it address daily or weekly rest breaks or annual vacation rights.

Nearly all of the individual states have overtime laws that conform to the FLSA, and a few provide additional protections. A small number of states establish overtime limits based on daily, rather than weekly, hours. Alaska and Nevada, for example, require that overtime be paid after eight daily hours under most circumstances (Wilson 1995). Some states also limit working time in specific industrial activities and sectors, such as transportation, partly for reasons of public safety (ILO 1995). Throughout the 1990s, several state legislatures debated prohibitions or limits on mandatory overtime (Golden and Jorgensen 2002), and seven states enacted legislation (American Nurses Association 2002). In most cases, however, these restrictions on compulsory overtime are limited to workers in health-care settings, motivated in part by concerns about patient safety. Finally, some states also regulate daily or weekly rest breaks, although none addresses the issue of paid vacation days. For example, seven states require that employees receive one day off out of every seven (Winning 2002).[3]

The Employee Retirement Income Security Act of 1974 and the U.S. Tax Code

Although not generally viewed as a component of working-time policy, regulations that govern employee benefits have important consequences for the relative quality of part-time work in the United States. Both the Employee Retirement Income Security Act (ERISA) of 1974 and the U.S. Internal Revenue Code set rules that give employers the right to offer different benefits to part-time and full-time workers.[4]

In the United States, this is especially consequential with regard to health insurance. Because the United States has no national health-insurance program, the overwhelming majority of working-age Americans rely on employers for coverage. A disproportionate share of part-time workers work for employers who offer no health insurance at all. One reason is that part-time workers are overrepresented among small employers, who are the least likely to offer health plans (GAO 2001).

Many part-time workers whose employers do provide health benefits are excluded due to their part-time status, in accord with federal regulations governing employee benefits. The U.S. Internal Revenue Code regulates "self-insured" health plans, referring to plans under which employees and employers pay into a fund that reimburses health claims. The tax code permits self-insured employers to exclude part-time workers from health coverage, with part-time defined as less than thirty-five hours of employment a week. Furthermore, self-insured employers are not permitted to discriminate on the basis of compensation levels, but they are permitted to exclude categories of workers—such as hourly workers or workers in selected job classifications—that, in practice, contain large numbers of part-time workers. Under the national tax code, employers with "fully insured" health plans (their carriers are external insurance companies) have even more leeway to treat part-time and full-time workers differently, as they face no non-discrimination requirements at all. In practice, these latter plans include two-thirds of all American workers with employer-based insurance (EBRI 1998).

A parallel situation exists with respect to the regulation of private pensions. The Employee Retirement Income Security Act, in combination with the Internal Revenue Code, allows employers to exclude from pension plans those workers who work fewer than one thousand hours annually—which translates to about half-time work. As with health insurance, employers are also permitted to exclude entire job classifications from pension coverage, albeit subject to Internal Revenue Service sanctions if they are found to be unfairly sorting workers into categories. To the extent that excluded job classifications are filled by part-time workers, substantial numbers will be de facto ineligible for pension coverage.

Collective Bargaining

Collective bargaining has played a circumscribed but important role in strengthening reduced-hour work in the United States. The

California-based Labor Project for Working Families archives "family-friendly" labor agreements, including several made in the 1990s that shortened weekly work hours, ended compulsory overtime, gained employees the right to work part-time, and secured benefits for part-time workers. For example, an Office and Professional Employees International Union local in California negotiated a thirty-two-hour workweek at several work sites, without loss of pay. In another example, the Washington-Baltimore Newspaper Guild secured an agreement with one large employer to ban compulsory overtime. A local of the Service Employees International Union negotiated an agreement with two county governments under which members may voluntarily reduce their working time by up to 20 percent, for up to six months, while retaining full-time benefits and seniority. A local of the International Brotherhood of Electrical Workers secured part-time workers' eligibility for benefits in a large utility company, including life and disability insurance, retirement and health benefits, and prorated vacation and holiday allowances (Labor Project for Working Families 2002).

Despite recent efforts and some impressive successes, American labor has been an inconsistent ally to advocates of shorter working hours and improved part-time work. Juliet Schor (1991) argues that, from the 1950s through the 1980s, American labor leaders largely abandoned earlier battles aimed at shortening standard full-time hours, partly because they perceived it to be a losing issue (especially during years of economic recovery) and partly because they concluded that most of their members—historically, mostly men—valued money over time. Unions largely neglected part-time workers as well during these years because their median voters were male workers who nearly all worked full-time. It is only in recent years, as unions have sought to increase their membership bases by organizing women and workers in the service sector, that many have started negotiating on working time and other "family-friendly" concerns.

EVALUATING THE AMERICAN SYSTEM

Given the federal and state legislation and the limited reach of labor unions, it is not surprising that American workers have few protections against working long and nonstandard hours. Labor law in the United States also does little to support—and in many cases actually creates barriers to—the availability of high-quality reduced-hour and part-time work options.

Limits on Weekly Work Hours

Although the FLSA establishes a legislative tool for limiting weekly working hours, its protections are weak in two respects. First, normal weekly hours set by the FLSA are high by cross-national standards. When the FLSA was enacted in 1938, it mandated that overtime be paid after forty-four hours as of 1938, after forty-two hours as of 1939, and after forty hours beginning in 1940 (Costa 2000). The forty-hour threshold, set more than sixty years ago, remains unchanged. In recent decades, proposals to reduce the threshold have received remarkably little attention.

Second, a large and growing share of workers are not covered by the FLSA's overtime provisions. More than a quarter of American full-time workers are exempt from the overtime requirements, generally because their job duties classify them as executives, managers, or professionals. To be exempt, workers must also be paid on a salaried basis and earn above a minimum level specified by the legislation; other categories of workers, such as computer-related employees paid at high hourly rates, are also exempt on this basis. According to the General Accounting Office (GAO 2000), as of 1998 as many as 26 million workers, or 27 percent of the full-time workforce, were exempt under these rules. The share of the labor market that is exempt has grown sharply in recent years, increasing by nine million workers during the 1980s and 1990s alone.

The percentage of American workers who are exempt has grown for several reasons, some more logical than others (GAO 2000). The general shift from manufacturing to services pushed up the number of exemptions, as service jobs are more likely to be classified as exempt. Employers have also reorganized their workplaces to create more supervisors and thus more exempt positions; for example, whereas in the past one exempt supervisor in a grocery store might supervise eight workers, now three exempt supervisors each supervise two workers. Compounding these occupational changes, the minimum salary levels for exempt positions have not been adjusted in more than twenty-five years. As a result of inflation, many more lower-earning workers are now classified as exempt. The U.S. Department of Labor (DOL 2002a) estimates that as many as seven million workers might be shifted from exempt back to nonexempt status were the salary thresholds adjusted for inflation.

Availability and Quality of Reduced-Hour Work

American workers who want to work for fewer than forty hours a week often face limited options. Whereas many European countries have shifted standard weekly work hours to the more family-friendly range of thirty-five to thirty-nine hours, few workplaces in the United States hire workers for hours in that range. In medium and large establishments, 86 percent of full-time employees (that is, working thirty-five hours or more) have weekly work schedules of forty hours or more (U.S. Bureau of Labor Statistics 1999). Among employed men and women aged twenty-five to fifty, only 3 percent of male workers and fewer than 9 percent of female workers work between thirty-five and thirty-nine hours a week (authors' calculations, based on 2000 CPS). Some share of those workers actually hold two part-time jobs.

Full-time workers in the United States who wish to reduce their work hours to fewer than forty hours a week typically have to accept employment at less than thirty-five weekly hours, meaning that they enter what is normally classified as part-time employment. In the absence of a right to shift to a part-time schedule in their current jobs, American workers who choose to drop below the forty-hour standard—either temporarily or permanently—usually have to change jobs and often occupations or industries as well.

The decision to work part-time usually carries substantial costs. In the United States, part-time jobs are disproportionately offered in a subset of occupations and industries that tend to be poorly paid.[5] Part-time jobs, on average, pay lower wages and grant fewer nonwage benefits than do full-time jobs; they also offer less job security and fewer promotional opportunities (Bassi 1995; EBRI 1993; Wenger 2001; Gornick and Jacobs 1996).

The wage losses associated with part-time work are substantial. As reported in chapter 3, women who work part-time in the United States earn about 20 percent less an hour than their full-time counterparts, after controlling for differences in human capital between the two groups of workers. Estimates vary as to what portion of that 20 percent gap is explained by differing mixes of occupation and industry. After controlling for occupation and industry, Elena Bardasi and Janet Gornick (2002) find a 17 percent part-time wage penalty, although other research finds a substantially smaller remaining differential (Wenger 2001).

At least some of the part-time pay penalty in the United States appears to be shaped by policy—or the absence of policy. The absence of a protected right to part-time work means that full-time workers who choose to reduce their hours are often forced to change jobs. This exacerbates segregation in the United States between part-time and full-time workers, increasing the pay differential. As Jeffrey Wenger observes about the United States, "Ultimately, choosing part-time work is almost always synonymous with choosing a lower-paying job" (Wenger 2001, 2).

Public policies also fail to prohibit employers from granting part-time workers lower wages than those paid to their full-time counterparts, even if the two have the same skills and responsibilities. Many employers do so—some to reduce their wage bill, others to recoup fixed costs, and still others because they perceive part-time workers to be less committed than comparable full-time workers.[6]

The absence of a national health-insurance policy and regulations that govern employee benefits result in extremely limited availability of health and pension benefits for part-time workers. Only 17 percent of part-time workers in the United States receive health insurance as a workplace benefit, compared with nearly two-thirds of full-time workers. Although another 60 percent of part-time workers have coverage through their spouses, about one-fourth of the part-time workforce have no health insurance at all. After controlling for worker and job characteristics, part-time workers in the United States have been found to be more than 85 percent less likely to receive health benefits than are comparable full-time workers. Part-time workers' lack of health coverage is compounded by their lack of pension coverage; only 21 percent of part-time workers are included in their employers' pension plans (see Wenger 2001 for a review of part-time workers' receipt of workplace benefits).

Gender Equality

For many working parents in the United States, a preference for working part-time is rendered infeasible by the prospect of substantial losses in pay and benefits. The paucity of attractive reduced-hour work has different effects on fathers and mothers, thus compounding gender inequalities at home and at work. For many men, the realistic choice between long hours on the job and no job at all pushes them to work longer hours that they might otherwise prefer. Women respond to the lack of quality reduced-hour work in several ways. Some work longer hours than they would otherwise choose, others choose part-time employment and incur the costs associated with that choice, while still others opt out of paid work altogether. As Marin Clarkberg and Phyllis Moen conclude in their study of couples' working-time preferences, "Where husbands apparently experience a relatively minor push in the direction of longer hours, wives frequently experience a fundamental displacement, forced to choose between the two extremes of non-work and 40 or more hours a week" (Clarkberg and Moen 1999, 25). The all-or-nothing structure of employment in the United States leaves a sizable proportion of women, especially mothers with young children, entirely disconnected from the labor market.

Nonstandard Hours and Vacation Time

Many American parents work nonstandard hours—that is, evenings, nights, and weekends—and a substantial share do so to accommodate caregiving needs at home. Whereas workers in some other countries are granted premium pay for nonstandard shifts, or compensatory time off, United States law guarantees neither. In a few countries, employers are restricted from requiring some parents to work nonstandard hours; again, American law is silent.

Finally, the absence of a national vacation policy in the United

States leaves vacation rights and benefits to the discretion of employers, and Americans are granted relatively little vacation time. Survey data indicate that, on average, workers in the United States take about eleven paid vacation days a year. The amount of annual vacation that workers take is unevenly distributed; professional and managerial workers spend, on average, one more week each year away from their jobs, with pay, than do their nonprofessional counterparts (Jacobs and Gerson forthcoming).

WORKING-TIME POLICIES IN OTHER COUNTRIES

Whereas the United States does little to protect workers from long hours or nonstandard-hour work, other industrialized countries have taken steps to help workers secure time away from the workplace without sacrificing economic security or career opportunities. Many of these measures have been adopted for reasons other than supporting parents. Once in place, however, they provide important support for parental caregiving time. From our study of twelve countries, we identify four features of working-time policies in countries that do the most to support parents' caregiving time and promote gender equality at home and in the labor market: First, working-time measures limit weekly employment hours, setting normal working time in the range of thirty-five to thirty-nine hours. Second, labor market measures improve the availability and quality of part-time work. Third, labor market measures limit or compensate nonstandard work schedules, without gendered protectionism. Finally, vacation policies ensure parents periods of unbroken time with their families.

Limits on Weekly Work Hours

An earner-carer society in which fathers and mothers balance work in the market with unpaid care work at home assumes that parents will be able to reduce their hours of paid work to below the current forty-hour standard, especially when caregiving demands are high. When the standard workweek is as long as forty hours—or longer, owing to compulsory overtime—parents lack meaningful choices about allocating their time between the labor market and caregiving work.

Public policies can play a role in protecting parents' time for caregiving by setting standard weekly working hours and by granting workers protections against long weekly hours. Table 6.1 describes a variety of measures that the countries in our study have used to establish working-time limits below forty hours. Working hours are shaped in these countries primarily through the setting of standards, or normal, working hours (above which overtime pay is required) and limits on maximum allowable hours (above which workers cannot be compelled to work).

The institutional context in most of our comparison countries is substantially different from the U.S. system. In particular, unions have much more influence on working time in all European countries than in the United States—partly because many European unions have placed working time high on their agendas and partly because union coverage is so much higher in Europe. In Canada and in the United Kingdom, 36 and 47 percent of workers, respectively, are covered by collective bargaining; in the remaining countries, union coverage ranges from about 70 to more than 90 percent of workers (Blau and Kahn 2002)—well higher than in the United States, where only one in seven workers is organized. In some countries (for example, France), the dominant mechanism for regulating working time is labor law, while in others (for example, Germany), it is collective bargaining; in still others (for example, Sweden), a strong statutory framework is supplemented at the bargaining table.[7] At the supranational level, diversity in policy mechanisms is fully supported; the EU directives that relate to working conditions allow member countries to implement the required practices through legislation or collective bargaining, or a combination of the two.

All across Europe, as of approximately 2000, normal full-time weekly hours are set at levels below the forty hours that is the legal norm in the United States—thirty-five hours in France and between thirty-seven and thirty-nine hours everywhere else (see table 6.1 and figure 6.2). The incidence of very long hours (for example, beyond fifty hours a week) is limited in Europe by the European Union–wide policy of setting maximum weekly hours at forty-eight hours a week. The 1993 EU Directive on Working

TABLE 6.1 Establishment of Normal Working Hours, Approximately 2000

| Country | Primary Mechanism for Regulation of Working Time | Normal Working Hours[a] | | Maximum Working Hours by Statute (Hours Worked Above Maximum May Not Be Compulsory) |
		By Statute	By Collective Agreement (Average)	
Nordic Countries				
Denmark	Primarily collective agreements.	Legislation sets maximum hours (forty-eight) but not normal working time.	37	48
Finland	Combination of collective agreements and labor law.	Forty hours, with possible reduction through collective agreement.	39.3[b]	40
Norway	Combination of collective agreements and labor law.	Forty hours, with possible reduction through collective agreement.	37.5	40
Sweden	Combination of collective agreements and labor law.	Forty hours, with possible reduction through collective agreement.	38.8	40
Continental Countries				
Belgium	Combination of collective agreements and labor law.	Thirty-nine hours, with possible reduction through collective agreements.[c]	39[d]	39

Country	Legal basis		Normal weekly hours	Maximum weekly hours
France	Primarily labor law.	Thirty-five hours, since national legislation in 2000 reduced statutory workweek to thirty-five hours (with no pay reduction). Law calls on collective bargaining "to negotiate the practicalities of actual reduction of working hours." Thirty-five-hour week applies to all workers, including skilled, salaried professions.	35	48
Germany	Primarily collective agreements.	Legislation sets maximum hours (forty-eight) but not normal working time.	37.7	48
Luxembourg	Combination of collective agreements and labor law.	Legislation sets maximum hours (forty-eight) but not normal working time.	39	48
Netherlands	Combination of collective agreements and labor law.	Legislation sets maximum hours (forty-eight) but not normal working time.	37	48
English-Speaking Countries				
Canada	Primarily national and provincial labor laws.	Varies across jurisdictions, from forty to forty-eight hours, with fewer than 50 percent of workers in forty-hour jurisdictions.	One-third of major collective agreements secure right to refuse overtime. Collective bargaining covers 35 percent of full-time jobs.	No limit.
United Kingdom	Primarily collective agreements.	Legislation sets maximum hours (forty-eight) but not normal working time.	37.5	48

(Table continues on p. 160.)

TABLE 6.1 *Continued*

Country	Primary Mechanism for Regulation of Working Time	Normal Working Hours[a]		Maximum Working Hours by Statute (Hours Worked Above Maximum May Not Be Compulsory)
		By Statute	By Collective Agreement (Average)	
United States	Primarily national labor law, with some supplementation by state laws.	Since 1938, normal workweek is forty hours. Approximately 27 percent of full-time workers are exempt.	Union coverage is low (15 percent of workers). Overall, in medium and large establishments, 86 percent of full-time employees have weekly work schedules of forty hours or more.	No limit.

Sources: Data from 32 hours (2003); Bilous (1998); Carley (2002); ECOTEC (2002); Evans, Lippoldt, and Marianna (2001); Fagnoni (2000); Global Labour Law (2002); ILO (1995); Incomes Data Services (2002); OECD (1998); Olmsted (1998); DOL (1999); White (2002).

Note: The 1993 EU Directive on Working Time stipulated a forty-eight-hour maximum working week. This affects the European countries, including Norway.

[a] Normal working hours refers to the threshold above which an overtime premium becomes payable.

[b] In 2002, in Finland, the range of collectively agreed-upon hours was thirty-five to thirty-eight.

[c] In Belgium, statutory normal hours is thirty-eight, as of 2003.

[d] In 2002, in Belgium, the range of collectively agreed-upon hours was thirty-five to thirty-eight.

FIGURE 6.2 **Normal Weekly Working Hours, Approximately 2000**

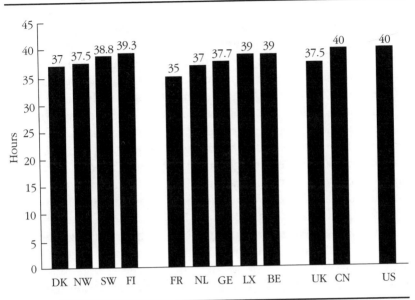

Sources: Data from 32 Hours (2003); Bilous (1998); Carley (2002); ECOTEC (2002); Evans, Lippoldt, and Marianna (2001); Fagnoni (2000); Global Labour Law (2002); ILO (1995); Incomes Data Services (2002); OECD (1998); Olmsted (1999); DOL (1999); White (2002).

Note: Normal weekly hours are the shorter of statutory or collectively bargained standard.

Time requires member states to "take the measures necessary to ensure that, in keeping with the need to protect the safety and health of workers . . . working time for each seven-day period, including overtime, does not exceed 48 hours." Countries are permitted to limit weekly hours "by means of laws, regulations or administrative provisions or by collective agreements or agreements between the two sides of industry" (see appendix B). The directive stipulates that employers may not compel workers to work longer hours nor subject them "to any detriment" for refusing longer hours, but workers may voluntarily work longer hours.[8]

How does the United States compare? Once again, the United States (along with Canada) stands out as an exceptional case. Whereas many other countries have pressed for normal hours below forty a week, the FLSA still sets normal working time at forty hours—and more than a quarter of American workers are exempt even from that limit. In addition, U.S. law does not set maximum hours for covered workers. Employers are free to schedule workers for very long weekly hours, and many choose to do so.

Given the regulatory framework in place in the United States, legislative strategies are especially germane, and two countries provide particularly useful models. In 1999 Belgian law reduced normal working hours (the overtime threshold) from 40 to 39 hours, with a reduction to 38 hours as of 2003. Collective bargaining has reduced hours still further for many workers; the main union federation has called for the gradual introduction of a four-day workweek. Several large employers have already agreed to shorten normal work hours. In 1999, for example, the Bayer chemicals plant in Antwerp signed an agreement that initiated a workweek of 33.6 hours (32 Hours 2003).

Legislative action to reduce working hours has been even more dramatic in France. In 2000 labor legislation reduced the statutory workweek to thirty-five hours. (The law requires that low-wage workers face no loss in weekly pay. Otherwise, pay negotiations are left to collective bargaining; for the vast majority of workers, weekly pay has been maintained, although some have agreed to moderated wage increases over a two- or three-year period in return.) According to the law, 25 percent premium pay must be paid for hours worked between thirty-six and forty-three and 50 percent premium pay for weekly hours above forty-three (Bilous 1999). What is perhaps most remarkable about the French case—a high-profile drama that is still unfolding—is that the French courts have ruled that the law applies to virtually all workers, including most highly skilled, salaried workers. Working-time inspectors visit workplaces, enforcing the law.

Movements to reduce working time even further remain active all across Europe. In both Belgium and Finland, for example, collectively bargained standard hours fell between 2000 and 2002, from about thirty-nine hours into the range of thirty-five to thirty-eight (see notes to table 6.1). Many European working-time advocates characterize the ongoing changes seen across these countries as indicative of an unfinished transformation, continent-wide, to a thirty-five-hour workweek.

In the 1970s and 1980s, reductions in working time were primarily aimed at lowering unemployment through work sharing. More recently, explicit objectives include the protection of family time and the promotion of gender equality. This is particularly the case in the Nordic countries. In Denmark, for example, which reports the lowest annual working hours among all of our countries, the government began talks in 1998 with business and labor to make working time more "family friendly." In Sweden, which also has low annual work hours, further working-time reductions remain at the top of the public-policy and collective-bargaining agendas. As in Denmark, the theme in Sweden is not job creation; rather, "shorter work time is seen mainly as a way to improve the well-being of workers and increase equality between men and women" (32 Hours 2003). France's thirty-five-hour law was enacted both to reduce unemployment (which has since declined) and to support work-family reconciliation. Recent evidence suggests that many French workers are spending their newfound time with their families. According to a 2001 survey, among parents with children under the age of twelve, 43 percent of French mothers and 35 percent of fathers say that the balance between work and family has improved since the enactment of the policy, and almost half report that they spend more time with their children (see Kamerman et al. forthcoming for a summary of recent French survey results).

Availability and Quality of Part-Time Work

When children are young, or otherwise in need of high levels of care, it may make sense for parents to reduce their employment commitments below the hours of the standard workweek (even if that was shortened to thirty-five hours). Government can play a role in supporting parents' choice to shift to shorter hours by granting workers the right to work part-time without changing jobs and by prohibiting discrimination against workers who choose part-time work.

Policies aimed at improving part-time work are widespread and expanding throughout Europe. The strength of this commitment is evident in the Directive on Part-Time Work, which was adopted by the European Union in 1997 (see appendix B). According to the official language in the directive, "The purpose of the agreement is to eliminate discrimination against part-time workers and to improve the quality of part-time work. It also aims to facilitate the development of part-time work on a voluntary basis and to contribute to the flexible organization of working time in a manner which takes into account the needs of employers and workers."

All ten of the European countries in our study have implemented the part-time directive through some mix of legislation and collective bargaining. The directive requires members to enact measures that prohibit employers from treating part-time workers less favorably than "comparable full-time workers." These measures address some combination of pay equity, social security and occupational benefits, training and promotion opportunities, and bargaining rights. The United Kingdom's new law, for example, grants part-time workers the same rights as full-time workers in terms of pay, holidays, training, parental leave and benefits (including access to pension schemes), and a right to equal treatment (Gilman 1998).

The EU Directive on Part-Time Work also urges, but does not require, member states to "eliminate obstacles" that limit opportunities for part-time work and instructs employers to "give consideration" to workers who request transfers between part-time and full-time work as their personal and family needs change. Examples of policies that protect workers' right to shift between part- and full-time employment are provided in table 6.2. These protections provide support for parents who choose to combine market and caregiving work in two important respects. First, they grant workers time for caring. Second, they have the potential to improve the quality of part-time work by reducing the segregation of part-time workers into a limited range of occupations and industries.

Prior to the directive, Sweden had already set the standard on the right to part-time work. Since 1978, Swedish parents have had the right to work six hours a day (at prorated pay) until their children reach the age of eight. Since the directive was issued in 1997, other European countries have instituted substantial new protections. Germany, for example, grants the right to work part-time to employees in enterprises with fifteen or more workers; the Netherlands has established a similar right for employees in enterprises of ten of more workers. Belgium grants employees the right to work 80 percent of full-time for five years. France has enacted a right to part-time work exclusively for parents. In most cases, these regulations give employers a safety valve; they can refuse a change on certain business grounds, but those grounds are often subject to judicial review.

The granting of rights to work part-time operate, in some European countries, in tandem with complementary family leave policies. As reported in chapter 5, a number of countries allow parents to collect prorated parental leave benefits while working part-time. Although the family leave policies are helpful to parents who do work part-time, they cannot secure parents the right to do so. These newly enacted measures strengthening workers' rights to work part-time are a crucial complement.

Some European countries have augmented measures that protect reduced-hour workers with policies that encourage or increase employer demand for part-time work. France, for example, offers employers reductions in social insurance contributions if they create part-time jobs. In the late 1990s Finnish localities established "six-plus-six" work hours, scheduling two six-hour shifts to offer reduced-hour work to public employees while increasing the public's hours of access to services. Some countries—including Norway and Sweden—have actively promoted the creation of part-time jobs in the public sector.

The Netherlands has designed what is probably the most comprehensive state effort to increase high-quality part-time work. The 2001 Work and Care Act includes several measures aimed at improving part-time work for Dutch women and, especially, for men. The new law allows Dutch workers to increase or decrease their work hours, unless employers demonstrate "specific conflicting business interests," and prohibits all forms of differential treatment based on working hours. These Dutch provisions on part-time work were folded in with a series of integrated reforms strengthening family leave legislation, child care provisions, and after-school programs.[9] The language of the authorizing legislation is remarkably consonant with the earner-carer framework. The stated intention of the law is to enable couples to hold "one and a half jobs" between them—with each holding a "three-quarter time

(Text continues on p. 171.)

TABLE 6.2 Measures Encouraging Development of Voluntary Part-Time Employment and Improvement of the Quality of Part-Time Work, Approximately 2000

		Examples of:	
Country	Measures that Improve the Quality of Part-Time Work[a]	Measures that Grant Parents or All Workers the Right to Work Part-Time[b]	Other Measures that Increase the Availability of Part-Time Work (Demand-Side)
Denmark	EU Directive on Part-Time Work implemented in 2001.		
Finland	EU Directive on Part-Time Work implemented in 2001.	Employees have the right to reduce working time 40 to 60 percent for one year, subject to employment agreement (an unemployed person must be hired for the same position).	During the 1990s, Finnish municipalities experimented with "six-plus-six" working-time arrangement, scheduling two six-hour shifts as a way to shorten employees' working hours and simultaneously lengthen service to the public.
Norway	EU Directive on Part-Time Work implemented voluntarily.	Employees have right to reduce working hours in response to "health, social or other weighty reasons of welfare" if this "can be arranged without particular inconvenience to the enterprise." Part-time workers who want to increase work hours are given priority if vacant position is available.	Government has actively sought to create part-time jobs in the public sector.

Sweden	EU Directive on Part-Time Work implemented in 2002.	Employed parents have right to work six-hour day instead of eight-hour day until children are eight years old or in the first grade. Workers have right to return to full-time work with advanced notice. Law enacted in 1978.	Government has actively sought to create part-time jobs in the public sector.

Continental Countries

Belgium	EU Directive on Part-Time work implemented in 2000.	Employees have the right to reduce their employment by one-fifth (one day or two half days per week) for a period of up to five years.	Administrative formalities are eased for part-time workers, and employers receive reductions in social security contributions.
France	EU Directive on Part-Time Work implemented in 2000.	Employees may request reduction of work hours for period of time for family reasons. Employees with at least a year's service may request to work part-time; request may be made during first three years after birth or adoption.	Employers receive reductions in social security contributions for employing part-time workers, if new jobs created.

(Table continues on p. 168.)

TABLE 6.2 *Continued*

Country	Measures that Improve the Quality of Part-Time Work[a]	Examples of: Measures that Grant Parents or All Workers the Right to Work Part-Time[b]	Examples of: Other Measures that Increase the Availability of Part-Time Work (Demand-Side)
Germany	EU Directive on Part-Time Work implemented in 2001.	Employers with fifteen or more employees must allow employees to reduce their hours (after six months of employment), unless there are justifiable "business reasons," as determined by the courts. Part-time workers may request increase to full-time and should generally be given preference over other applicants unless there are compelling business reasons otherwise.	
Luxembourg	EU Directive on Part-Time Work implemented in 1999.		

Netherlands	EU Directive on Part-Time Work implemented in 2000.	Employers with ten or more employees must allow employees to reduce their hours (after one year of employment), unless there are "serious business grounds." Part-time workers should be allowed to increase their hours unless the change "would create serious problems of a financial or organizational nature for the employer."	2001 Work and Care Act includes several measures aimed at promoting part-time work for women and, especially, men. The act is intended to encourage the adoption of a "three-quarters job model" whereby each partner in a couple works "three-quarters time" and the couple, jointly, hold "1.5" jobs. Government has actively sought to create part-time jobs in the public sector.

English-Speaking Countries

Canada	Some local provisions protect part-time workers. In Saskatchewan, for example, in enterprises with ten or more full-time-equivalent employees, workers employed fifteen to thirty hours a week are eligible for prorated benefits; workers employed more than thirty hours are eligible for full benefits.	During 1990s, the government of Quebec promoted part-time work in public and semipublic sectors, including for skilled and highly paid positions.	

(Table continues on p. 170.)

TABLE 6.2 *Continued*

Country	Measures that Improve the Quality of Part-Time Work[a]	Examples of: Measures that Grant Parents or All Workers the Right to Work Part-Time[b]	Examples of: Other Measures that Increase the Availability of Part-Time Work (Demand-Side)
United Kingdom	EU Directive on Part-Time Work implemented in 2000.		Government published "best-practice" guidelines for employers for making part-time work more available. They state, for example, that employers should periodically review whether full-time positions could be filled by part-time workers.
United States	FLSA guarantees part-time workers the minimum wage. No legal protections with regard to pay equity, benefits, or job conditions.	Some unions have won the right to reduced working time on a temporary basis so that workers can take care of family needs. For example, SEIU Local 715 (service employees) won a policy under which members may reduce working time by 1%, 2%, 5%, 10%, or 20%, for up to six months without loss of benefits and seniority.	

Sources: Data from 32 Hours (2003); AFL-CIO (2001); Bellemare and Simon (1994); Berg (2001a); Clauwaert (2002); Delbar (2002); Gilman (1998); Global Labour Law (2002); Government of Saskatchewan (2002); OECD (1998); "Part-Time Workers" (2001); Smith, Fagan, and Rubery (1998); DOL (2002c); Weber (1997).

[a]The 1997 EU Directive on Part-Time Work calls for (1) eliminating discrimination against part-time workers and improving the quality of part-time work and (2) facilitating the development of part-time work on a voluntary basis.

job"—thus achieving both time for care and gender equality (32 Hours 2003).

The United States stands out as a laggard, relative to Europe, in protecting workers' rights to part-time employment and in encouraging the creation of high-quality part-time alternatives. The only protection provided by the FLSA is the extension of the minimum wage to part-time workers. The law does nothing to discourage or prevent employers from granting their part-time employees lower wages and fewer benefits than their full-time counterparts. At least in part as a consequence of the poor remuneration, American workers are comparatively unlikely to work part-time; women workers in all of our study countries, Finland excepted, report higher rates of part-time work (Gornick 1999a).

The restricted part-time options in the United States have implications for gender equality, especially among parents, although the expected consequences are complex and contradictory. To the extent that limited part-time alternatives cause some American mothers to opt out of the labor force altogether, gaps in employment rates are exacerbated. To the extent that limited options for reduced-hour work propel some American mothers who would otherwise seek a part-time job into full-time employment, gender gaps in hours worked among the employed are lessened.

Current outcomes in the United States, in comparative perspective, suggest that both effects are operating. In the three Nordic countries (Denmark, Norway, and Sweden), for example, with strong protections for and higher rates of part-time work, employment rates for married mothers are higher than in the United States, and gender gaps in employment rates are substantially more favorable (see figure 3.6). At the same time, in the Netherlands and Germany, which also have strong protections and high rates of part-time work—especially part-time work at low hours—the gender gap in hours worked is much less favorable for women than it is in the United States (see figure 3.7).

Many feminist observers of the recent policy developments in Europe are beginning to track their impacts on gender equality (see, for example, Rubery, Smith, and Fagan 1998). Very much like generous family leave policy, policies that strengthen part-time work, even high-quality part-time work, will generate new forms of inequality if only or mostly women work part-time. Although strengthening part-time work holds the potential for breaking down gendered working-time patterns—more rights to work part-time and better remuneration are expected to pull more men into part-time employment—it is simply too soon to tell what the long-term consequences of the recent changes in Europe will be for gender differentials in engagement in paid and unpaid work.

Nonstandard Hours

The consequences of nonstandard work schedules may be mixed for parents. Staggered schedules may increase fathers' involvement in caregiving. The strain of nonstandard schedules, however, often has problematic social consequences. A number of public policies can reduce the prevalence or raise the rewards of nonstandard-hour work. These policies may operate directly, by limiting enterprise hours or restricting employers' options to schedule workers during nonstandard hours, or indirectly, by influencing the remuneration paid to employees who work these schedules. The countries in our comparison group have adopted a variety of such measures (see table 6.3).

Some countries directly regulate the demand for nonstandard-hour workers by limiting the opening or production hours of enterprises, thereby reducing the prevalence of workers' hours during evenings, nights, and weekends. Measures that directly restrict employers' hours of operation, although widespread in Europe, probably provide little guidance for the 24/7 economy of the United States. It is widely observed that Americans, perhaps more than most Europeans, want high levels of round-the-clock commerce. Even in Europe, pressures to uphold recent productivity gains are leading to the deregulation of enterprise hours in most countries (Skuterud 2001).

More-promising strategies are seen in countries that have adopted legislation that restricts employers' rights to schedule some categories of workers in nonstandard-hour shifts, including those with dependent-care responsibilities.[10] The lessons to be drawn, however, are complex. Policies such as these could support parents' ability to adapt their working schedules to their caregiving needs without fear of losing or greatly reducing the quality of their employment. These same policies could restrict parents' choices, however, if they eliminate employees' right to work non-standard hours rather than eliminating employers' right to compel workers to accept these schedules. They could also exacerbate gender inequality if they are applied exclusively to mothers. Several Continental European countries restrict employers' rights to employ certain categories of parents at night. Currently, these protections are all highly gendered. Typically, they disallow nighttime employment only for pregnant women or postpartum mothers. In Germany, an unusual law disallows nighttime work among women with dependent children under the age of fourteen who lack adequate care arrangements. These measures are consistent with an overall disposition in these countries toward emphasizing the family as the primary locus of caring, blended with elements of social conservatism.[11]

One European country that is not among our comparison cases—Italy—provides the single example that we found of gender-neutral legislation that disallows compulsory, but not voluntary, nighttime work among some groups of parents. Since 1999, Italian employers are not permitted to require male or female workers to work night shifts if they have a child under three years of age, if they are the single parent of a child under twelve, or if they are caring for a disabled person. The explicit intent of this law is to support caregiving time; the inclusion of fathers and mothers is also intended to promote equality in market and caregiving work. The law "recognizes the caring work of both parents and provides special protection to single-parent families. It also encourages the sharing of family responsibilities between women and men" (Governo Italiano 2002). At this point, the consequences of this law are not yet evident. Although it could both offer protection for parents and support gender equality, it could also cause employers to discriminate against parents during the hiring process.

Public policies and collective-bargaining agreements may also influence the choice and costs of working nonstandard hours by influencing its rewards. The Nordic countries award especially high pay premiums for work during nonstandard shifts. In both Finland and Denmark, for examples, many Sunday workers receive double pay, and one study of the European Union member countries finds that workers in Sweden are the most likely to re-

(Text continues on p. 178.)

TABLE 6.3 Measures Influencing Employment During Nonstandard Hours (Evenings, Nights, Weekends), Approximately 2000

Country	Examples of:	
	Measures that Reduce Work During Nonstandard Hours, for Parents or All Workers[a]	Measures that Compensate Employees for Working Nonstandard Hours
	Nordic Countries	
Denmark	By law, shop-opening prohibited after 8:00 p.m. Monday to Friday, after 2:00 p.m. Saturday, and on Sundays.	Nights: Employees who work night shifts tend to work fewer weekly hours than normal thirty-seven hours. Sundays: Under collective agreements, remuneration can be as much as 200 percent of the normal wage.
Finland	By law, shop-opening prohibited after 9:00 p.m. Monday to Friday, after 6:00 p.m. Saturday, and on many Sundays.	Sundays: Generally paid at 200 percent of normal pay rate.
Norway	By law, work between 9:00 p.m. and 6:00 a.m. considered "night work" and generally not permitted. Law provides for seventeen exceptions, including transport, health services, restaurants, and hotels. By law, Sunday work also prohibited, with many exceptions.	

Sweden	Legal regulation of shop-opening hours abolished, but collective bargaining regulates work during "inconvenient" hours, that is, hours outside normal business hours of 9:00 to 10:00 a.m. until 7:00 to 8:00 p.m. By law, workers have right to rest between midnight and 5:00 a.m. unless "conflicts with nature of work."	Nights: Employees working "unsocial" hours often receive premium pay.

Continental Countries

Belgium	By law, work between 8:00 p.m. and 6:00 a.m. prohibited, with several exceptions. Before 1998, women's night work was highly regulated. In 1998, legislation guaranteeing men and women equality with regards to night work came into force.	Nights: Workers are entitled to financial compensation. Sundays: "Working on Sunday entitles the worker to a full or half-day off, depending on whether more or less than four hours were worked. This time off is to be taken during the next six days."
France	By law, shops restricted to thirteen hours per day, six days per week. Retail establishments closed on Sunday, although small food shops may be open until 1:00 p.m.; other exceptions can be granted by administrative authorities. Before 2001, law banned night work for women under certain circumstances. In 2001, all bans concerning night work for women lifted.	Nights: Through collective agreements, night workers receive compensatory leave, higher pay, or a combination of the two. Sundays: Although legislation does not require higher pay for Sunday work, collective bargains often stipulate bonus pay.

(Table continues on p. 176.)

TABLE 6.3 *Continued*

Country	Examples of:	
	Measures that Reduce Work During Nonstandard Hours, for Parents or All Workers[a]	Measures that Compensate Employees for Working Nonstandard Hours
Germany	By law, Sunday work prohibited, although there are many exceptions including hospital work. By law, pregnant and breastfeeding women may not work at night, with the exception of some industries, including hotel work. Also, women may not "work between 10:00 p.m. and 6:00 a.m. if they have dependent child under fourteen years of age living with them, and if there is no way of ensuring that the child will be looked after."	Nights: Through collective agreements, night workers are normally given a pay supplement.
Luxembourg	By law, work on Sundays prohibited, with several exceptions, including restaurants and hospitals. By law, pregnant women cannot work between 10:00 p.m. and 6:00 a.m.	Sundays: Where authorized by law, Sunday work subject to compensatory leave. The break does not have to be given on a Sunday, but must equal one full day for Sunday work lasting more than four hours and at least half a day if it lasted less than four hours. Moreover, employees are entitled to a salary increase of 70 percent for each hour worked on a Sunday. Some Sunday workers, such as restaurant staff, entitled to two days paid holiday after twenty Sundays worked, instead of wage premium.

Netherlands	By law, work between 10:00 p.m. and 6:00 a.m. prohibited, with some exceptions. Law also restricts work on Sundays.	Nights: By law, night workers entitled to compensatory leave.

English-Speaking Countries

Canada	Federal and provincial law mandates twenty-four-hour rest period, preferably on Sundays. Generally, shops are to be closed on Sundays; trend has been to authorize shop-opening on Sundays, for example, for cross-border shopping.	Nights: Collective agreements can stipulate higher pay for night work. Sundays: Collective agreements can stipulate higher pay for weekend work.
United Kingdom		Nights: Through collective agreements, night workers generally receive pay premium. A survey of collective agreements found that the average night work premium to be 31 percent.
United States	Shop hours regulated locally; since 1960s, trend has been removal of Sunday restrictions. Twenty-two states restrict some Sunday shopping.	National law does not address overtime for evening, night, or weekend shifts. Empirical studies have found premiums for various types of shift work in range of 4 to 11 percent.

Sources: Data from Berg (2001b); CAW (2001); European Commission (1999); European Foundation for the Improvement of Working Conditions (2002); Global Labour Law (2002); ILO (1995); International Observatory of Labour Law (2001); Kajalo (2000); Krzeslo (1998); Lanfranchi, Ohlsson, and Skalli (2002); Skuterud (2001).

"A 1992 EU directive concerned the safety and health of pregnant workers. Under the directive, pregnant workers, workers who have just given birth, and women breastfeeding cannot be required to work at night if it would "compromise the health of the woman or her baby." However, the directive does not call for a ban on night work for these women; all bans that refer to women's work specifically are considered by the European Union to be in conflict with the 1976 Directive on Equal Treatment of Men and Women in Employment. Since 1960s, the trend in both North America and Europe has been toward deregulation of restrictions on Sunday shop openings.

ceive premium pay for Sunday hours (European Foundation 2001). Three of our comparison countries—Belgium, Luxembourg, and the Netherlands—have measures in place that grant workers compensatory time, rather than pay, as a reward for employment during nonstandard hours. In Belgium, for example, employees who work a Sunday shift are entitled to the equivalent time off (with pay) at some point during the subsequent week. This policy strategy overtly trades nonstandard hours for added time at home.

The implications of pay premiums and compensatory time are somewhat ambiguous with respect to the choices made by workers with caregiving responsibilities. By increasing the costs of employing nonstandard-hour workers, these policies could encourage some employers to shift some tasks (for example, taking inventory, stocking shelves) from evenings, nights, and weekends to standard hours, thus decreasing overall demand for workers during nonstandard hours. By increasing the rewards, they would provide parents working these hours more time or money to compensate for the added stress and inconvenience. At the same time, higher compensation could draw more parents into these shifts, with problematic implications for families.

In the United States, in contrast to some countries in Europe, public working-time measures rarely limit the demand for work during nonstandard hours, for parents or any other workers. There are no U.S. laws granting rewards to workers who work these shifts, although empirical studies have found that workers receive modest pay premiums (4 to 11 percent) associated with various types of nonstandard-hour work.

In the United States, would measures aimed at easing parents out of evening, night, and weekend work be misguided or futile, given high levels of consumer demand for round-the-clock access to products and services? Empirical results suggest that policy designs that would enable some parents to shift from nonstandard-hour work to daytime weekday employment are not necessarily at odds with the maintenance of the 24/7 economy. Although many parents are employed during nonstandard hours, only about 30 percent of all workers in nonstandard hours are parents, and only half of those have children who are not yet of school age.[12] If even half of all parents with nonstandard schedules were to shift to daytime weekday hours, the prevalence of nonstandard-hour workers would fall by about 15 percent—a substantial decline, but not one that would undermine the fundamentals of the round-the-clock economy.

Adopting gender-egalitarian protections that disallow employers from forcing parents into nonstandard shifts—in conjunction with extensive child care provisions—could enable parents who work nonstandard hours to switch out of those shifts if they want to do so. At the same time, increasing the rewards to nonstandard shifts could help employers fill these shifts—presumably, relying more on nonparents—if they choose to retain current levels of demand for nonstandard-hour work.

Vacation Time

Public policies that guarantee ample paid vacation time would provide all workers with respite from employment demands and lessen the need for out-of-home child care, especially during the summer. The European countries in our comparison group have uniformly adopted policies that provide extended periods of paid vacation to workers (see table 6.4). As it has with part-time work, the European Union has influenced policy development for member countries (and Norway). The 1993 EU Directive on Working Time stipulates that employees be granted not less than four weeks of paid vacation each year, an increase from the three weeks previously in place (see appendix B). All of the European countries have codified at least that much vacation in their laws, with about half requiring a fifth week (twenty-five days) (see figure 6.3). In several of these countries, collective agreements add even more vacation time; agreements in Denmark, Germany, and the Netherlands provide the most generous benefits—about thirty days a year. As with normal work hours, changes continue to unfold; after 2000, collectively bargained vacation rights increased in three of the Nordic countries and in France (see notes to table 6.4).

Workers in the United States have no similar rights. The FLSA sets no minimum standard for vacation time, nor does it address pay during vacation days.[13] In practice, American employees at medium and large enterprises are granted an average of about ten days a year during their first five years of service, rising to about

TABLE 6.4 **Regulation of Annual Paid Vacation Time, Approximately 2000**

Country	Vacation Time by Statute (Number of Days Required)[a]	Vacation Time by Collective Agreement (Number of Days, Average Across Awards)
Nordic Countries		
Denmark	25	32 employees with children under age 14 receive an additional day off
Finland	24 30 days after one year of service	25[b]
Norway	21	23[c]
Sweden	25	25[d]
Continental Countries		
Belgium	20	25[e]
France	25	25[f]
Germany	20	29.1
Luxembourg	25	27
Netherlands	20	31.5
English-Speaking Countries		
Canada	10 days (2 weeks) legally mandated. Since 1997, employees have right to third week, although employers are only required to pay for first 2 weeks.	Most agreements secure 15 days after one to five years, 20 days after six to ten years, 25 days after seventeen to twenty years. (Collective bargaining covers 35 percent of full-time jobs.)
United Kingdom	20	24.5
United States	Not addressed in national legislation.	Union coverage low (15 percent of workers). Overall, in medium and large establishments, average paid vacation days among full-time employees:

TABLE 6.4 *Continued*

Country	Vacation Time by Statute (Number of Days Required)[a]	Vacation Time by Collective Agreement (Number of Days, Average Across Awards)
		9.6 days after one year, 11.5 days after three years, 13.8 days after five years, 16.8 days after ten years.

Sources: Data from 32 Hours (2003); Carley (2002); ECOTEC (2002); European Union (2001); Grubb and Wells (1993); Human Resources Development Canada (1998); ILO (1995); Incomes Data Services (2002); DOL (1999).

[a]The 1993 EU Directive on Working Time stipulates not less than four weeks annual paid vacation. The deadline for implementation was 1996. This affects the European countries, including Norway.
[b]In 2002, in Finland, paid vacation under collective agreements ranged from five to six weeks.
[c]In Norway, average number of days under collective agreements twenty-five, as of 2003.
[d]In 2002, in Sweden, paid vacation under collective agreements ranged from twenty-five to thirty days.
[e]Data on collective agreements in Belgium is for 1993.
[f]In 2002, in France, paid vacation under collective agreements ranged from five to six weeks.

fourteen days after five years of service and about seventeen days after ten years (DOL 1999). Workers use about 93 percent of earned days, with slightly higher take-up reported by nonprofessionals and by women (Jacobs and Gerson forthcoming). Even with the high take-up, the United States has been dubbed "the most vacation-starved country in the industrialized world" (Woodward 2002).

CONCLUSION

Weak working-time regulations in the United States do little to help working parents secure time to care for their families; and collective bargaining does little to provide extra protections. The high overtime threshold set by national law (forty hours) and the extensive exemption of workers from working-time regulation leave many American parents with longer work hours than they would otherwise choose. The absence of rights to part-time work

FIGURE 6.3 **Minimum Annual Paid Vacation Days**

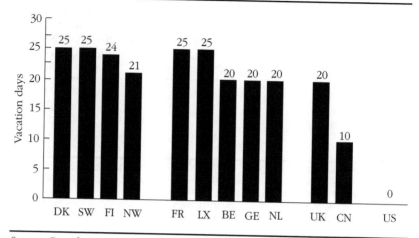

Sources: Data from 32 Hours (2003); Carley (2002); ECOTEC (2002); European Union (2001); Grubb and Wells (1993); Human Resources Development Canada (1998); ILO (1995); Incomes Data Services (2002); DOL (1999).
Note: The figure reports minimum number of paid vacation days required by statute.

means that employed parents who wish to reduce their working hours from full-time to less than forty hours a week are often forced to change employers, occupations, industries, or all three. The absence of protections for part-time workers further lowers the quality of part-time employment; this is exacerbated by the lack of universal public health insurance and by employee-benefit regulations that do not require employers to extend benefits to part-time workers. Raising the availability and quality of part-time work could have positive effects on gender equality in the United States. Gender gaps in paid work would narrow if women who would otherwise remain at home were pulled into the labor market and more men were enticed to work part-time.

The 24/7 economy and workers' lack of control over their working schedules—compounded by inadequate child care options—propel many parents into work during nonstandard hours. Parents' year-round time squeeze is exacerbated by the absence of a national vacation-time policy.

The European Union has taken an active role at the supranational level in the regulation of working time; there is now a relatively high and increasing degree of commonality in policies across countries. All ten of our European comparison countries—and EU policy itself—offer models for American working-time advocates and policy designers. Provisions in several of these countries offer lessons that could be used to guide policy reforms in the United States that would be most supportive of the goals of an earner-carer society.

First, working-time measures should limit weekly employment hours, setting normal full-time weekly hours in the range of thirty-five to thirty-nine hours a week. Limiting the standard full-time workweek to less than forty hours would grant parents more time for children on a daily basis. Limiting men's time in the labor market, in particular, would raise the likelihood of more gender-egalitarian time allocations between partners. Implementing reductions economy-wide would increase parents' opportunities to seek employment that is "full-time" but at less than forty hours across a broad range of enterprises, occupations, and industries. Overtime regulations should both offer compensation for those who work longer hours and protect workers against compulsory overtime at excessively long hours.

Second, labor market measures should aim to improve both the availability and quality of part-time work. Protections for part-time workers are an essential form of support for parents who choose to work for pay for fewer than thirty-five hours a week. Public measures should grant workers—or at least parents with young children—the right to shift temporarily to part-time work and to resume full-time employment later; workers should be refused only when employers can formally establish that granting the change in hours would create excessive hardship. Part-time workers should be granted equal pay relative to comparable full-time workers, as well as prorated benefits and equal treatment in working conditions; employers should not be allowed to exclude part-time workers from employee benefits such as health and pension plans. Allowing workers to move between part- and full-time employment without changing jobs would dramatically increase parents' employment options and reduce pay penalties associated with part-time employment. Improving the quality of part-time work would increase economic security for part-time workers and their families and provide incentives for more men to participate in part-time employment.

Third, labor market measures should aim to protect parents from being forced to work nonstandard-hour shifts and should offer premium pay or compensatory time for nonstandard-hour schedules. Public measures should grant parents hired for standard hours—both mothers and fathers—the right to refuse evening, night, or weekend schedules. If complemented with adequate child care provisions, many employees who currently work nonstandard hours involuntarily or because of child care constraints would be able to work daytime weekday schedules. Granting premium pay or time off in exchange for working nonstandard hours would encourage some employers to shift some tasks to standard hours while rewarding workers who do work these shifts for the added stress and lost family time. Premium pay would also make it easier for employers to fill nonstandard shifts with nonparents—and thus maintain round-the-clock production and commercial schedules—if substantial numbers of parents were to move to standard work hours.

Finally, vacation policies should ensure parents substantial periods of unbroken time with their families. Public measures should grant workers at least one month of paid vacation annually. In practice, that means that the normal work year would be defined as forty-eight weeks of work a year, rather than the fifty weeks that is now standard in the United States. Paid vacation rights of at least one month would alleviate some of the burden of arranging child care coverage during summer school breaks and would grant parents needed periods of uninterrupted family time.

Chapter 7

Providing Public Care: Child Care, Preschool, and Public Schooling

S UBSTITUTE CHILD CARE is an essential form of support for parents combining earning and caring roles; parents cannot commit to work outside the home without alternatives for the care of their children. Child care is an equally important factor influencing levels of gender equality in the labor market and in the home. Because it is mothers who usually reduce working time if they cannot find acceptable and affordable alternatives to full-time parental care, the availability and cost of child care are powerful predictors of women's labor market attachments. The financing of child care has other implications for the wages and working conditions of the overwhelmingly female child care workforce. Public school schedules also matter for parents, particularly the compatibility between children's school hours and days and parents' employment schedules.

A BRIEF OVERVIEW OF EARLY CHILDHOOD EDUCATION AND CARE AND SCHOOL SCHEDULING IN THE UNITED STATES

Most early childhood education and care is private in the United States. The government plays a role in financing some care through federal and state early education, subsidy, and tax policies. The quality of care is addressed largely post hoc through state-level licensing standards of some—but not all—private arrangements. Figure 7.1 illustrates the various elements of public policy for early childhood education and care in the United States.

185

FIGURE 7.1 U.S. Child Care Policy Provisions

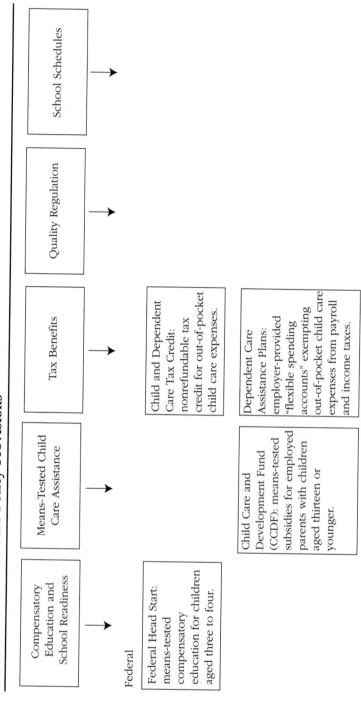

| Compensatory Education and School Readiness | Means-Tested Child Care Assistance | Tax Benefits | Quality Regulation | School Schedules |

Federal

Federal Head Start: means-tested compensatory education for children aged three to four.

Child Care and Development Fund (CCDF): means-tested subsidies for employed parents with children aged thirteen or younger.

Child and Dependent Care Tax Credit: nonrefundable tax credit for out-of-pocket child care expenses.

Dependent Care Assistance Plans: employer-provided "flexible spending accounts" exempting out-of-pocket child care expenses from payroll and income taxes.

Federal and State

Temporary Assistance for Needy Families (TANF): means-tested subsidies for employed parents in or leaving welfare system.

Social Services Block Grant (SSBG): means-tested subsidies for low-income parents.

State

State pre-kindergarten: targeted or universal preprimary education for four-year old children.

Child care tax credits: tax credits (usually nonrefundable) for out-of-pocket child care expenses.

State licensing and regulations: establish and enforce health, safety, and quality standards.

State and local

State and local regulations: set minimum number of pupil-teacher contact days and hours of school operation.

Source: Authors' compilation.

Compensatory Early Education Programs

Compensatory early education programs are the most public of the programs of early childhood education and care (ECEC) in the United States. Compensatory programs are explicitly designed to increase consumption of high-quality care among poor families and to reduce socioeconomic and human capital deficits in poor children. The single largest compensatory early education effort remains the federal Head Start program, which provides part-day educational services funded through federal grants to state and local providers. About one-half of states provide additional funding for Head Start or operate parallel state programs (Doherty 2002). The Head Start program provides high-quality developmentally oriented education services and health services to children along with educational, social, and mental health services for their parents. Recent federal initiatives have extended Head Start services in some locations both downward (to serve younger children) and outward (to provide full-day services).

In recent years, states have taken the lead in expanding early education programs. All states provide kindergarten services, and nearly all five-year-old children are now enrolled. In twenty-five states, these are provided for the full day, and in fourteen they are now compulsory (Doherty 2002). More recently, states have begun expanding early education (pre-kindergarten) programs designed to increase the school readiness of children, with particular benefits for children who are ill prepared to start school due to impoverished home environments or other forms of disadvantage. Thirty-six states now provide some funding for pre-kindergarten services (Doherty 2002). Most state pre-kindergarten programs target children at economic or educational risk; only three states, and the District of Columbia, have established pre-kindergarten as a universal right.[1]

Means-Tested Assistance with Child Care

Means-tested child care assistance is explicitly designed to reduce the cost of substitute care for low-income employed parents by contracting for direct child care provision, or, more commonly, by providing subsidies that increase the purchasing power of low-income families in the private child care market. Federal and state funding for means-tested assistance has grown sharply in recent years as part of welfare reform policies designed to require and support employment among welfare recipients. Since 1996, the federal government has provided funding for means-tested assistance through three block grants to the states.

The single largest source of funding for means-tested subsidies is the Child Care and Development Fund (CCDF), a federal block grant to the states. States are allowed to use CCDF funds to serve working families with incomes up to 85 percent of the state median, although many choose to set the threshold lower. Within general federal guidelines that require states to offer parents a choice of care type and provider, states are free to set other policies for the CCDF, including the level of parental co-payment, the level of provider reimbursement, and the procedures for establishing and recertifying eligibility.

The second major funding stream for means-tested assistance is the Temporary Assistance for Needy Families (TANF) block grant, which replaced the Aid to Families with Dependent Children program in 1996. States are authorized to transfer up to 30 percent of their TANF funds to the CCDF program, and about one-half of states commit at least some TANF funds to CCDF. States also use TANF funds directly to provide child care (largely through vouchers) for welfare-reliant families who are preparing for work and for current and former welfare recipients who are employed.[2] The Social Services Block Grant (SSBG) provides the third and smallest source of federal child care assistance for poor families. The SSBG provides federal funds for a wide range of services to the poor, and states have almost complete discretion in the allocation of these funds—including the decision whether to spend any funds on child care. As of 1999, an estimated 13 percent of all SSBG funds were used for child care services or vouchers.

Tax Benefits

Tax benefits (deductions and credits) constitute the third major form of child care assistance in the United States. The federal Child and Dependent Care Tax Credit (CDCTC) allows parents to deduct a portion (20 to 30 percent, depending on income) of their out-of-pocket child care expenses from their taxable earnings. More than half of states now provide additional child care tax credits, usually calculated as a portion of the federal benefit (Doherty 2002). Benefits under the federal tax credit are capped and decline in value for higher-income families, ranging from $480 to $720 for one child and $960 to $1,440 for two or more children. Families working for a participating employer may elect to use, instead, Dependent Care Assistance Plans (DCAP) to deduct child care expenses from their taxable income. Tax benefits are of greatest assistance to working parents with incomes sufficient to incur a tax liability; very low earners, who do not owe any income taxes, are unable to claim benefits through the nonrefundable CDCTC and unlikely to have access to DCAP programs.

Regulation of Quality

The consequences of substitute child care for children's safety, health, and intellectual and emotional development depend in large part on the quality of care they receive. Quality is a product of several factors: basic health and safety characteristics (such as the cleanliness and safety of the setting), structural factors (such as the number of children cared for and the number of adults providing supervision), and the characteristics of providers (including, especially, the type and quality of their interactions with children).

In the highly privatized U.S. system, the government provides largely post hoc control over the quality of care in private arrangements through licensing requirements and inspection of existing facilities. The licensing of ECEC services is left to state governments; outside of the federal Head Start program, there are no national standards for staffing, health and safety, or teaching curricula. State licensing requirements, standards, and rigor vary enormously from state to state. They vary in the share of the market that they regulate; many states exempt some forms of care—for example, small family child care homes in most states and centers in religious institutions in many—from any form of regulation. They also vary in the domains that they regulate. All states regulate basic health and safety standards, for those providers subject to regulation, and set maximums for group size and for the ratio of children to providers. Far fewer go beyond these basics to address, for example, education and training standards of providers.

School Schedules

School schedules are determined by state and local authorities, which legislate the minimum number of contact days between pupil and teacher each year, the annual schedule, and the hours of instruction and school operation. According to data from the Education Commission of the States (2000), the number of contact days varies by more than two weeks, from as few as 175 days a year in Alabama to 186 days in Kansas. (Most states require 180 contact days.) Particularly consequential local regulations set the hours of school opening—including hours of instruction and hours of supervised noninstructional activities. Hours of school operation often correspond closely to the usual six hours a day of instructional time. In part as a response to the demands of many families for longer hours of supervision, some states and local school districts have taken steps to lengthen the instructional day or to add supervised before- and after-school programs. More than 160 "extended-learning-opportunity" programs are operating in forty-four states, funded with a combination of federal, state, local, private, and parental contributions.

Collective Bargaining

Labor unions have played a minor role to date in influencing ECEC services. On behalf of their workers, some unions have advocated for greater public provision of ECEC; others have included child care benefits in contract negotiations (Grundy, Bell, and Firestein 1999). In 1989, for example, the Health and Human Services Employees Union, of the SEIU (1199), on behalf of its members in the health-care industry in New York City, successfully bargained for an employer-paid child care trust fund. Employers from 189 institutions now contribute to the fund, which provides benefits for more than eighty-five hundred children ranging from referral services to child care centers and vouchers for the purchase of private child care. In San Francisco, the Hotel Employees and Restaurant Employees Local 2 negotiated a mandatory fifteen-cent-an-hour employer contribution to a child care fund, which now benefits an estimated 25 percent of eligible workers. Although they are important for covered members, these successful efforts to obtain ECEC benefits have directly affected relatively few families overall. Labor unions' efforts to secure child care benefits have been limited by both low levels of unionization in the United States, particularly among workers in occupations that are dominated by women, and by the relatively low salience of these issues within many unions.

Labor unions have played a second, and potentially important, role in organizing the child care workforce and negotiating for higher salaries and improved benefits and working conditions. Professionals in the ECEC industry who work in public settings, most notably pre-kindergarten programs located in public schools, are often eligible for the same union representation and benefits afforded public school teachers. Efforts to organize child care workers in other settings have been constrained by their dispersion among many small employers and by limits in parents' resources for paying fees that fund wages. Child care workers have been successfully organized in a handful of locations (including Massachusetts, Philadelphia, and Seattle) in recent years. Fewer than 5 percent of child care workers in the United States currently belong to a union, however (Grundy, Bell, and Firestein 1999).

EVALUATING THE AMERICAN SYSTEM

The current patchwork of private ECEC arrangements and limited, targeted public assistance does little to ensure that care is accessible, affordable, or of high quality. Largely private, market-based arrangements do little to ensure reasonable wages and working conditions for the child care workforce. State and local policies for scheduling public school hours also fail to respond to many parents' working schedules.

Access

Although the child care problem in the United States is often described in terms of limited availability of care arrangements, the evidence suggests that private markets produce a sufficient supply of care in most areas for most children (Blau 2001). Although some specific forms of child care may be in short supply in the United States (for example, care for children with special needs), the problem of access is less one of supply than of constrained choice for many parents. For some, choice is constrained by working hours. Parents working nonstandard schedules, for example, are less likely to use formal modes of care than parents working regular hours (Han 2002). The heavy reliance of American parents on market-based arrangements and part-day preschools requires many to piece together multiple care arrangements for children. Among young children (under the age of five) with an employed mother, a large minority—38 percent—experience at least two different child care arrangements during the week; 8 percent experience three or more (Capizzano and Adams 2000). Among older children, care arrangements often change with the end of the school year as well, as parents increase their reliance on both care by relatives and formal care arrangements (Capizzano, Adelman, and Stagner 2002).

The choice to use more formal and presumably higher-quality care is also constrained by income. Enrollment of children into educationally-oriented preschool programs has increased dramatically during the past twenty years. Throughout this period, lower-income families have lagged behind their more affluent counterparts in the use of such care arrangements (Bainbridge et al. 2002). By a striking margin, low-income families are more likely than more affluent families to have children in informal care with relatives. According to analysts at the Urban Institute, 28 percent of employed families with incomes at or below 200 percent of the poverty line rely primarily on relative care for their children under the age of five, in contrast to 20 percent of families with higher income; only 26 percent of poor children are in more highly regulated, center-based settings, in contrast to 35 percent of their more affluent peers (Capizzano, Adams, and Sonenstein 2000). The greater reliance of low-income parents on informal forms of child care is sometimes interpreted as a reflection of distinct preferences, by, for example, race, ethnicity, education, or other characteristics. When analysts control for these factors, however, income-related differences in the use of more formal child care arrangements persist (Hofferth et al. 1993; NICHD 1997b; Bainbridge et al. 2002).[3]

Affordability

The heavily privatized ECEC system in the United States imposes steep financial costs on families. Among working families with children under the age of thirteen, about half (48 percent) pay for child care during their working hours. Across all families, these costs average $286, or 9 percent of family earnings, a month (Giannarelli and Barsimantov 2000; Giannarelli, Adelman, and Schmidt 2003). Child care costs are highest, as a share of income, for the poorest families.[4] Employed families with children under the age of thirteen and with earnings at or below 200 percent of the poverty level spend an estimated 14 percent of their earnings on child care; those at or below the poverty line spend an estimated 18 percent (Giannarelli, Adelman, and Schmidt 2003). If we restrict the analysis to the one-third of poor, employed families with young children who purchase care, child care costs consume nearly one-quarter of their earnings (Giannarelli and Barsimantov 2000).

Government programs to help low-income families defray the high costs of ECEC are limited. Despite the continuing popularity of the Head Start program, services are provided to only an estimated 36 percent of income-eligible four-year-old children and far fewer children below that age (OECD 2001d). Although federal and state funding for means-tested subsidies has grown in recent years, this assistance also reaches only a small fraction of income-eligible families. States have adopted various strategies for rationing assistance, from waiting lists to policies that control subsidy demand (such as high co-payments and low provider reimbursements). By one recent estimate, only about 15 percent of income-eligible families receive assistance—with levels varying from 6 to 25 percent across states (DHHS 2000). Researchers at the Urban Institute estimate that only about 12 percent of all American families with employed parents and children under the age of thirteen receive any (nontax) child care help from government (or private organizations); among low-income families (those with earnings below 200 percent of poverty), about 21 percent report receiving assistance (Giannarelli, Adelman, and Schmidt 2003).[5]

Quality

Although American families are paying a lot for child care, recent research suggests that the quality of much of that care may not be very good. Uneven and generally poor-quality care is attributable, in part, to the weakness of public quality oversight. Because informal babysitters and small family child care homes are exempt from regulation in most states, the majority of nonparental care for young children is provided in settings that have little or no public oversight. All states require that some child care centers be licensed, but many exempt some types of settings—for example, religious centers in twelve states and half-day nursery schools in twenty (Helburn and Bergmann 2002). Licensing of family child care centers is even more inconsistent. Only eleven states require that all family child care centers be licensed; others exempt providers who care for only a few children or do not receive any public funds. Because state resources for enforcing these requirements are limited, an unknown number of family child care homes operate illegally even in states that require licensing.

Centers and child care homes that are regulated are subject to minimal standards in most states. Most regulations address issues of health and safety, including, for example, minimum square footage, immunizations, and smoke detectors. Quality control regulations are much weaker. According to a recent survey by the Children's Foundation (2000), only twelve states require teachers in child care centers to have at least a high school education, and only twenty-nine require family child care providers to have any preservice or in-service training.

The care received by American children in this minimally regulated system is often of mediocre to poor quality. Observational studies of child care centers have concluded that the quality of care is "good" in only 15 percent of child care centers in the United States; in unregulated family child care and relative care, 50 to 69 percent is assessed as "inadequate" (Helburn et al. 1995; Galinsky et al. 1994). For children under the age of three, 61 percent of all forms of care are judged to be of "poor" to "fair" quality

(NICHD 1997a). Unfortunately, it is the children who are most developmentally vulnerable—those from poor communities and disadvantaged families—who are likely to receive the poorest-quality care (Helburn et al. 1995; NICHD 1997b).[6]

Compensation for the Child Care Workforce

Ironically, although child care costs are steep for many families, the overwhelmingly female child care workforce is poorly paid and usually works without either employment benefits or realistic opportunities for career advancement. The average child care center worker earns between $13,125 and $18,988 for full-time, full-year employment (Whitebook 1999). Women who work in other capacities—as assistant teachers and aides—earn even less. Among women providing unregulated family child care or relative care, between 50 and 65 percent have family incomes below $20,000 (Galinsky et al. 1994). Despite the substantial increase in demand for child care services in the 1980s and 1990s, wages for (nonhousehold) child care workers were an estimated one dollar an hour lower in 1997 than in 1977, adjusting for inflation (Blau 2001).[7]

School Schedules

The typical schedule in American public schools is poorly matched to the new realities of families in which all parents are employed. During the school year, the instructional school day is considerably shorter than the working day of employed parents, and schools vary widely in their capacity to provide supervised activities during noninstructional hours. By one estimate, the gap between parents' work schedules and their children's typical six-hour-a-day school schedules is as much as twenty to twenty-five hours a week (21st Century Community Learning Centers 2002). As a result, an estimated 39 million children between the ages of five and fourteen participate in no organized system of supervised activities when school is not in session (David and Lucille Packard Foundation 1999). School holidays, particularly long summer holidays, create even more vexing problems for parents who must organize alternative care arrangements for their children. The use of nonparental care increases when schools are out of session and the hours that children between the ages of six and twelve spend in self-care also increases by about six hours a week during the summer months (Capizzano, Adelman, and Stagner 2002).

EARLY CHILDHOOD EDUCATION AND CARE IN OTHER COUNTRIES

Our study of other industrialized countries suggests that it is possible for government to do much more to ensure that ECEC is accessible, affordable, and of high quality and that school schedules are more closely matched to parents' employment hours. Five policy features of ECEC and school scheduling are particularly significant in countries that do the most to support families, promote gender equality, and enhance child well-being: First, publicly supported care serves a large proportion of infants and toddlers while parents are at the workplace; full-day preschool programs enroll nearly all children from about the age of three until they start public school.[8] Second, government ensures that early childhood education and care is affordable. Third, government ensures high-quality ECEC services. Fourth, ECEC workers are well trained and well compensated. Finally, weekly preschool and public school hours conform to standard employment hours, and public programs and schools are in operation on many days of the year.

Access and Inclusiveness

Parents of young children cannot fulfill their responsibilities as earners and carers unless they have access to alternative care arrangements during their working hours. Access to substitute care is crucial for the achievement of gender equality in the home and in the market because in the absence of acceptable alternatives it is mothers and not fathers who loosen their ties to the labor market to care for children. Universality of access is crucial not only to ensure that all parents have equal employment opportunities but also to ensure that all children have equal opportunities to be cared for in arrangements that do not compromise their health and well-being.

The twelve countries in our cross-national comparison have developed varied systems for the provision of ECEC. Figure 7.2 illustrates the details of institutional arrangements and ages served, and table 7.1 provides information on institutional arrangements and service guarantees. Two systems stand out for their extension of nearly universal access to publicly supported care: the integrated systems in the Nordic countries and the dual systems of early child care and later preschool in France and Belgium.

Integrated ECEC systems in Denmark, Finland, and Sweden provide the most extensive access to publicly supported care.[9] Public systems under the authority of national social welfare or educational authorities serve children from the end of parental leave periods until the start of primary school at the relatively late age of six or seven. Younger children are cared for in centers or by supervised family child-minders; older children may spend all or part of their day in preschool programs.

These systems are most notable for extending a nearly universal entitlement for care (with a modest parental co-payment) during the years before the start of primary school and for the integration of care with early education services—sometimes termed "EduCare" to capture the dual focus on care and education. All children are entitled to a place in a public child care setting, and the regular use of fully private care is rare. In Sweden, for example, since 1995 all children have had an entitlement to public or private (and publicly subsidized) child care from age one to the age of twelve. Child care entitlements were initially linked to parents' employment status; they have recently been extended to children whose parents are unemployed, home on parental leave, or otherwise out of the labor force. In Finland and Denmark, all children have a right to care regardless of their parents' employment status.[10]

The countries of Continental Europe typically provide ECEC through dual systems of early child care and later preschool education. Of these, the systems in Belgium and France stand out for moderate provision of early child care and universal public preschool programs beginning at age of two and a half or three. Neither country provides child care as an entitlement before the start of public preschool. Subsidized spaces are available for some children in systems under the supervision of social welfare authorities—public crèches or supervised child-minder arrangements— with income-adjusted parental fees. Space is limited, however, and may be targeted to families with special economic or social needs. Child-based entitlements for care commences with enrollment in preschool—école maternelle in France and French-speaking Belgium and kleuterschool in Flemish-speaking Belgium.

How do these systems compare with the United States in ensuring accessible care to families? In terms of child enrollments in publicly supported ECEC programs, the Nordic countries that have established an entitlement for care from the end of the parental-leave period until the start of primary school provide the most support for families (table 7.2). In these countries, with generous maternity and parental leave policies, children are generally cared for at home during the first months of life.[11] Between one-quarter and three-quarters of children in the one- to two-year-old age group are in publicly supported care. (Cross-national variation for this age group reflects differences in the structure of parental leave and child care policies. In Finland, for example, child care enrollments are low, but the parents of an estimated 97 percent of children under the age of three receive some form of family support through leaves, a Home Care Allowance, or child care.) Among children in the three- to five-year-old age group, two thirds to 90 percent are in public care. In the last year before primary school, nearly all children are in public care.

The two Continental European countries with dual systems of early child care and universal preschool—Belgium and France— provide generous but less consistent support. By the age of two and a half or three, nearly all children are enrolled in preschool programs. Publicly supported care is available in crèches for only about 20 to 40 percent of children under three, however, and is highly targeted on needy families. As a result, families rely more heavily on private care arrangements for younger children.

How does the United States stack up in this comparison? In the extension of public ECEC services to children under the age of three, the United States ranks with the other English-speaking countries as among the lowest providers of care, serving only 6 percent of children through means-tested assistance programs. A much larger 53 percent of children in the three- to five-year age

(Text continues on p. 206.)

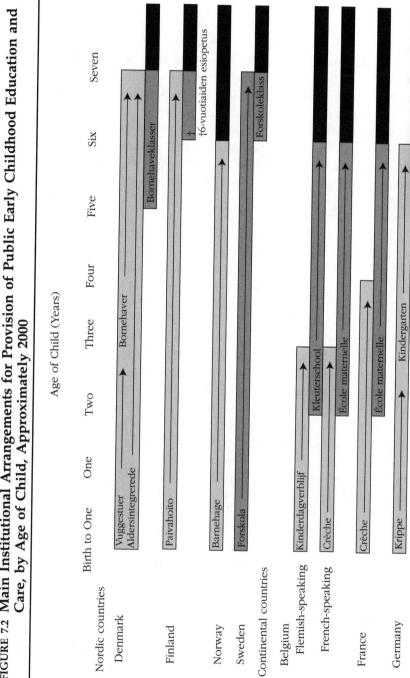

FIGURE 7.2 Main Institutional Arrangements for Provision of Public Early Childhood Education and Care, by Age of Child, Approximately 2000

Age of Child (Years)

| | Birth to One | One | Two | Three | Four | Five | Six | Seven |

Nordic countries

Denmark — Vuggestuer, Aldersintegrerede — Bornehaver — Bornehaveklasser

Finland — Paivahoito — †6-vuotiaiden esiopetus

Norway — Barnehage

Sweden — Forskola — Forskoleklass

Continental countries

Belgium

Flemish-speaking — Kinderdagverblijf — Kleuterschool

French-speaking — Crèche — École maternelle

France — Crèche — École maternelle

Germany — Krippe — Kindergarten

*compulsory at age six, but most attend at age five

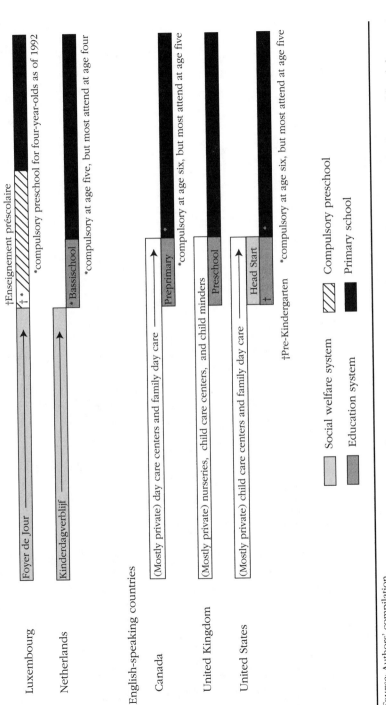

Luxembourg

†Enseignement préscolaire

Foyer de Jour

*compulsory preschool for four-year-olds as of 1992

Netherlands

Kinderdagverblijf

* Bassischool

*compulsory at age five, but most attend at age four

English-speaking countries

Canada

(Mostly private) day care centers and family day care

Preprimary

*compulsory at age six, but most attend at age five

United Kingdom

(Mostly private) nurseries, child care centers, and child minders

Preschool

United States

(Mostly private) child care centers and family day care

Head Start

†Pre-Kindergarten   *compulsory at age six, but most attend at age five

Social welfare system

Education system

Compulsory preschool

Primary school

Source: Authors' compilation.
Note: In three English-speaking countries, there is limited publicly provided or publicly subsidized care for children under the age of five (when most enter school-based programs). Public care for these young children is targeted on low-income families in Canada, and the United States, and, before the age of four, in the United Kingdom. Data for Germany are for the former West Germany only.

TABLE 7.1 Institutional Arrangements and Entitlements for Publicly Supported Early-Childhood Education and Care, Approximately 2000

Country	Primary Public ECEC Institutions	Entitlement for Children from Birth to the Age of Two	Entitlement for Children from Three Until School Age
	Nordic Countries		
Denmark	*Vuggestuer* for children age six to thirty-six months; *bornebaver* for children age three to six years; *aldersintegrerede institutioner* for children six months to six years; *bornebaveklasser* half-day preprimary through school system for children age six.	Yes, from age one or younger[a]	Yes
Finland	*Paivaboito* for children from birth to age six; *6-vuotiaiden esiopetus* (preschool) for six-year-olds.	Yes[b]	Yes
Norway	*Barnebage* for children from birth to age five.	No[c]	No
Sweden	*Forskola* for children from birth to age six; *forskoleklass:* preschool through school system for children age six.	Yes, from age one[d]	Yes
	Continental Countries		
Belgium	*Kinderdagverblijf* (Flemish) and *crèche* (French) for children from birth to age three; *kleuterschool* (Flemish) and *École maternelle* (French) for children aged two and a half to five years.	No	Yes, from thirty months
France	*Crèche* for children from birth to age three; *École maternelle* for children age two to five years.	No	Yes, from thirty to thirty-six months
Germany	*Krippe* for children from birth to age three; *kindergarten* for children age three to five years.	No	Yes, from age three (part-

Luxembourg	*Foyer de jour* includes *crèche* (birth to three years), *jardin d'enfants* (two to three years), and *groupes scolaires* (four to twelve years); *enseignement préscolaire*, compulsory preprimary for children age four; *education précoce*, optional preprimary for children age three.	No	Yes, from age four[e]
Netherlands	*Kinderopvang, gastouderopvang* and *peuterspeelzaal* for children age two months to three years, and sometimes older children as well. *Basisschool* for children age four to five.	No	Yes, from age four
English-Speaking Countries			
Canada	Market-based care main option for children below age five. Public pre-primary (usually part-day) available for four-year-olds in some provinces.	No	No
United Kingdom	Market-based care main option for children below age four. Part-day public nursery education for four- and some three-year-olds.	No	Yes, from age four (part-day)[f]
United States	Market-based care main option for children below age five. Public pre-kindergarten and Head Start for some children age four.	No	No

Sources: Data from OECD (2001d); European Commission Network (1996); Clearinghouse on International Developments in Child, Youth, and Family Policies (2002); Ministry of Education and Science in Sweden (1999); country experts.

[a] An estimated 87 percent of Danish municipalities guarantee places for all children between one and five years; national law mandates child care slots be provided within three months of parent request (or shorter, following parental leave); few children are on waiting lists.

[b] Every Finnish child under school age has an unconditional right to day care provided by the local authority once the mother or father's period of parental allowance comes to an end, irrespective of the parents' financial status or whether or not they are in work.

[c] In Norway, universal access is a political priority and access varies by location.

[d] Swedish municipalities required to provide spaces for all children age one to twelve whose parents work or are in school. Spots must be made available "without unreasonable delay"—defined as three to four months. An estimated 95 percent of municipalities are able to meet requirement. As of 2001, children of nonemployed parents also have right to services.

[e] In Luxembourg, preprimary school, *education précoce*, for three-year olds will be available in all communes by 2005.

[f] All four-year-olds have right to part-day preschool in United Kingdom; by 2004, part-day preschool is planned for all three-year-olds. Sure Start program provides comprehensive services for children from birth to three in deprived areas; goal is to extend services to one-third of poor families by 2004.

TABLE 7.2 Enrollment in Publicly Supported Early Childhood Education and Care, Approximately 2000 (Percentage)

	Share of Children Served in Publicly Financed Care, Under the Age of One	Share of Children Served in Publicly Financed Care, Ages One to Two years	Share of Children Served in Publicly Financed Care, Ages Three to Five years	Age Six Where the Start of Primary School Is at Age Seven
		Nordic Countries		
Denmark	15	74	90	98
Finland	few[a]	22	66	92
Norway	2	37	78	n.a.
Sweden	few	48[b]	82	93
		Continental Countries		
Belgium	15[c]	42[d]	99	n.a.
France	few[e]	20[e]	99	n.a.
Germany	few	5	77[f]	n.a.
Luxembourg	few	3[g]	67	n.a.
Netherlands		17[b]	71[i]	n.a.

English-Speaking Countries

Canada	few	5[j]	53[k]	n.a.
United Kingdom	few	2[l]	77[m]	n.a.
United States	few (153)	6	53[n]	n.a.

Sources: Data from OECD (1997, 2001d); Clearinghouse on International Developments in Child, Youth, and Family Policies (2002); National Association for the Education of Young Children (2002); Center for Urban and Community Studies (2000); DHHS (2001a, 2001b); Schumacher, Greenberg, and Duffy (2001); Doherty (2002); O'Hare (2001); Palme et al. (2002); Eurydice (1994b); Shulman, Blank, and Ewen (1999); country experts.

Note: Enrollments are for the year 2000 unless otherwise noted.

[a] Although few Finnish children under the age of one were in child care, as of 2000, 97 percent of children under the age of three received some form of family support, through leave, home care allowance, or child care.

[b] Does not include additional enrollments in family child care, which may be publicly subsidized and supervised for Sweden.

[c] Between ages three and thirty months, 30 percent of Belgian children are in care but only 20 percent in subsidized care; this estimate assumes no use of subsidized care from birth to three months and 20 percent between three and twelve months.

[d] Between ages three and thirty months, 30 percent of Belgian children are in care but only 20 percent in subsidized care; from age thirty months and older, 85 percent are in subsidized care.

[e] An estimated 9 percent of French children under age three are in *crèche* (mostly under the age of two) and 11 percent are in *école.*

[f] In Germany, approximately 80 percent part-time.

[g] As of approximately 1995; does not reflect expansion of preprimary services for three-year olds in Luxembourg beginning in 1998.

[h] Does not include playgroups, in the Netherlands.

[i] For the Netherlands, reflects average of 17 percent of three-year-olds in public care and 99 percent of four- and five-year-olds in preprimary or primary school.

[j] In Canada, as of approximately 1998.

[k] As of approximately 1998; based on estimates that approximately 5 percent of Canadian children are in subsidized arrangements and 48 percent of three to five-year-olds are in preprimary programs.

[l] As of approximately 1995. Does not reflect recent expansions of Sure Start and Neighborhood Nurseries in disadvantaged communities in the United Kingdom.

[m] Preschool part-day for four-year-olds and some three-year-olds in the United Kingdom.

[n] Based on estimates of approximately 6 percent of American children in subsidized arrangements and 47 percent of three- to five-year-olds in pre-k or kindergarten.

group are in some form of public care—due largely to the enrollment of nearly all five-year-old children in kindergarten. Even for this group, however, the United States lags well behind most of the European countries.

Affordability

Substitute care is not fully accessible if parents cannot afford it. A number of characteristics could be invoked to define affordability. Two are particularly relevant to policies in support of an earner-carer society. First, the out-of-pocket costs of child care should not impose an unreasonable burden on family budgets. Second, out-of-pocket child care costs should be proportionate to families' income. More affluent families may be expected to assume a larger share of the costs of their children's care than those with fewer resources.

The twelve countries in this comparison group have adopted various mechanisms for financing ECEC through the direct provision of public care, cost sharing with parents through co-payments, and the use of alternative financing mechanisms such as consumer subsidies and tax benefits. Table 7.3 presents the financing of ECEC programs in the twelve countries. These choices have important implications for the size and equitability of the cost burden on parents.

In the countries providing the most affordable ECEC for families—the integrated systems of the Nordic countries—the primary mechanism is direct provision, which is funded by a combination of national and municipal taxes and supplemented by parental co-payments. National tax revenues cover about one-quarter to one-third of the costs of ECEC, and municipal governments contribute about one-half. Parent fees cover a capped share of the costs. The parental share varies across countries and with the type of care, averaging about 20 percent or less.[12] Fees for individual families are calculated on a sliding fee scale and are often waived altogether for low-income families.

The Nordic countries make limited use of subsidies that allow parents to purchase care from private providers. In Denmark, municipal government may provide a cash grant to parents under the frit valgordningenof (free-choice) scheme to purchase private care for children between the ages of twenty-four weeks and three years. In both Finland and Norway, a cash benefit to parents with young children not in public care can be used for parental care or to purchase private child care. As in Denmark, these programs are relatively new and are much more limited than the fully public ECEC systems of care. Given the extensiveness of direct public provision, parents rarely purchase private child care in the Nordic countries. Of the four, only Norway provides tax benefits (deductions) for parents' out-of-pocket child care expenses.

The high-provision, dual systems of care in France and Belgium also use direct provision as their primary financing mechanism. Care for younger children is financed with a combination of national, regional, and municipal funds and parental fees. Parent fees cover about 17 to 25 percent of the cost of care for children under the age of three (depending on care arrangements), with parental co-payments set on sliding fee scales at around 8 to 11 percent of family income (in the crèche, fees are higher for other forms of care) (table 7.4). In both countries, employers also contribute: in Belgium, employers pay .05 percent of their wage bill for child care for children under the age of three; in France, compulsory employer contributions to the Caisse d'Allocation Familiales pay about one-quarter of the costs for services in the social welfare system (that includes child care for children under the age of three).[13] Care for children from about the age of three until the start of school, in école in France and French-speaking Belgium and kleuterschool in Flemish-speaking Belgium, is free to parents. Although public provisions are extensive for children beginning at the age of two and a half or three, parents do incur private child care costs for younger children and for hours of care outside école and kleuterschool. In both countries, parents can deduct a portion of these out-of-pocket child care expenses from income taxes.

The allocation of costs between the state and families is a function of both the size of the co-payments required of parents who use public care and the availability of publicly provided ECEC programs. When most ECEC is provided through public programs, the average co-payments provide a reasonable measure of this allocation.[14] In the integrated and largely public Nordic systems, income-adjusted co-payments represent the major out-of-pocket expenses for families; government funds cover approx-

(Text continues on p. 213.)

TABLE 7.3 Government Mechanisms for Financing Early Childhood Education and Care, Approximately 2000

Country	Financing Direct Provision of ECEC	Subsidies for Purchase of Private Care	Government Incentives or Support for Employer Contributions	Tax Relief for Purchase of Private Care
		Nordic Countries		
Denmark	Direct services financed by national and municipal governments and parent fees.	Local authorities can give a cash grant to parents with a child twenty-four weeks to three years; up to 70 percent of documented expenses, not to exceed 85 percent of least expensive municipal child care spot; average grants DKK30,800 to DKK36,400 annually (U.S.$3,586 to $4,327).		
Finland	Direct services financed by national (27 percent) and municipal (54 percent) governments and parent fees.	Since 1997, Private Care Allowance for purchase of private day care; basic flat-rate payment of FIM700 (U.S.$120) per child per month, with earnings supplements, paid directly to child minder or child care center.		
Norway	Direct services financed by national (36 percent) and municipal (28 percent) governments and parent fees.ᵃ	Cash Benefit Scheme may be used to pay for private child care; approximately NOK3,000 (U.S.$278) per		Documented child care expenses may be deducted from income of lowest-earning spouse;

(Table continues on p. 210.)

	month, roughly equivalent to state subsidy per child for preprimary services; may also be claimed by parents providing care in home.		two or more children) NOK23,325 (U.S.$2,884).
Sweden	Direct child care services financed by national and municipal governments (82 percent) and parent fees (18 percent); family child care financed by municipal government (82 percent) and parent fees (18 percent).		

Continental Countries

Belgium	Direct child care services financed by regional, municipal, and federal government and parent fees; preprimary services financed by national government.	Employers provide .05 percent of wage bill for development of services for children from birth to three.	Deduction to reduce taxable income by 80 percent of actual costs to maximum of BF450 (US$12) per day.
France	Direct child care services financed by national (24 percent), regional (12 percent) and municipal (34 percent) government and parent fees; preprimary services financed by national (56 percent) and municipal (34 percent) governments.	Means-tested subsidies for parents using registered family day carers of up to €197 (birth to three years) and €98 (for three- to six-year-olds) (U.S.$209 and $104) per month, and for social-security contribution for in-home providers up to €508 (U.S.$539).	Employers contribute to cost of service through compulsory contributions to the Family Allowance Funds (CAFs); employer contributions cover an estimated 25 percent of cost of services in social welfare system.	Tax reductions for employed parents of up to 25 percent of child care costs to a limit of €575 (U.S.$610) annually per child, and 50 percent of costs up to €3,450 (U.S.$3,662) annually for in-home care.

TABLE 7.3 *Continued*

Country	Financing Direct Provision of ECEC	Subsidies for Purchase of Private Care	Government Incentives or Support for Employer Contributions	Tax Relief for Purchase of Private Care
Germany[b]	Direct child care services financed by state and municipal governments and parent fees; preprimary financed by state (41 percent) and municipal (59 percent) governments.	Limited number of subsidies for low-income parents using private family day care services approved by local authorities, paid directly to the family day care or the center.		Families can deduct for employing in-home help to care for children under age ten.
Luxembourg	Direct child care services financed by national and municipal governments and parent fees; preprimary financed by national government.			Tax relief for the costs of (public or private) services for children under fourteen; reduce taxable income by documented costs or maximum of LF144,000 (U.S.$3,892) per child annually (with no documentation).
Netherlands	Playgroups funded by municipal government; other ECEC funded by national and municipal government (33 percent), employers (25 percent), and parental fees (42 percent). Goal is to divide costs evenly between municipalities, employers, and parents.		Stimulative Measure on Child Care to encourage employers to sponsor centers for children under age seven.	Deduction of portion of actual amount of private arrangement to maximum of NFL20,000 (U.S.$10,050) annually; employers can also deduct 30 percent of employer-provided care from taxable payroll.

English-Speaking Countries

Canada	Most ECEC is privately purchased. Provinces provide public kindergarten programs.	Limited number of means-tested subsidies provided with a combination of federal funding through Canada Health and Social Transfer block grant to provinces. Provinces vary in the extent to which they use these funds for child care and supplement with provisional funds.	Deduction (nonrefundable) of child care expenses for working parents to a maximum of CN$7,000 (U.S.$5,932) per child under age seven and CN$4,000 (U.S.$3,390) per child age seven to fourteen.
United Kingdom	Most ECEC for children under age four is privately purchased. Nursery school education for approximately a third of three-year-olds and most four-year-olds funded through grants to local authorities. Additional services for children from birth to three funded through national education and service programs (Sure Start) in disadvantaged communities.[c]		Tax credits for child care expenses up to 70 percent of costs up to £70 (U.S.$110) per week for one child or £105 (U.S.$165) for two or more children, available to low-income working parents. Credit decreases as family income rises.[a]

(*Table continues on p. 212.*)

TABLE 7.3 *Continued*

Country	Financing Direct Provision of ECEC	Subsidies for Purchase of Private Care	Government Incentives or Support for Employer Contributions	Tax Relief for Purchase of Private Care
United States	Most ECEC is privately purchased. Costs of public child care services and subsidies shared between federal and state governments and parents. Pre-primary programs financed by national government (Project Head Start) and state governments (pre-kindergarten).	Limited number of subsidies for low-income parents in welfare employment programs or employment through Child Care and Development and Temporary Assistance to Needy Families block grants; eligibility and maximum amount vary by state.	Employers can deduct portion of costs of child care from taxable payroll.	Nonrefundable tax credit for up to $2,400 (one child) to $4,800 (two or more children) in child care expenses for employed parents; maximum credit of $720 for one to $1,440 for two children. Flexible spending plans allow parents to set aside up to $5,000 pre-tax earning for child care expenses.

Sources: Moss (1990); Baker (1995); European Commission Network (1995, 1996); OECD (2000b, 2000d, 2001d); Rostgaard and Fridberg (1998); Lewis (1997); Friendly (2001); Doherty et al. (1995); Danish Ministry of Social Affairs (2000); Ministry of Health, Welfare, and Ministry of Education, Culture & Science (2000); Centre for Research in Early Childhood (n.d.); Clearinghouse on International Developments in Child, Youth, and Family Policies (2003); Michalopoulos and Robins (2000); Sure Start (2002); Palme et al. (2002); country experts.

Note: Currencies are expressed in national currency units for about 2000 (unless otherwise noted), followed, in square brackets, by the equivalent amount in 2000 U.S. dollars adjusted for purchasing power parity.

[a] For Norway, goal is 50 percent national and 30 percent municipal by 2005.

[b] Data for Germany are for the former West Germany only.

[c] Goal in United Kingdom is to extend part-day public nursery schools to all three-year-olds by 2004.

[d] Child Tax Credit will be combined with Child Credit as of 2003, which may change benefit levels in the United Kingdom.

imately 70 to 85 percent of the costs of ECEC (see table 7.4). In the dual systems in Belgium and France, parental costs include both co-payments and, for some parents, purchase of private care for younger children. Considering only co-payments, government assumes between 75 and 85 percent of the costs of care for younger children and 100 percent of the costs for children from the age of two and a half or three until the start of public school.

How does the United States compare? In contrast to these European models, most child care costs are private. By one recent estimate, household contributions accounted for 59 percent of all ECEC expenditures (including both private arrangements and co-payments) in 1999, with the federal government contributing 27 percent and states an additional 14 percent (OECD 2001d). This parental share of the child care burden is two to three times greater than the share assumed by parents in the countries with the most affordable ECEC systems.[15] Costs are also unequally distributed in the United States, where low-income families spend more of their income on child care than do more affluent families. In the heavily subsidized ECEC systems of many European countries, costs for parents are both lower overall and more equal (as a share of income) between low- and high-income families. Extensive public provisions with income-adjusted parent fees ensure that families with different means pay about the same share of their income for children's care.

To put the magnitude and distribution of costs in the U.S. into comparative context, we consider the likelihood that families incur private child care costs, and the amount of those costs if they do, at different income levels in the United States and France (table 7.5, column 1).[16] Among families with an employed mother and a child under the age of three, about one-half of families in both countries incur child care costs. In France, however, higher-income families are more likely to incur some costs than are lower-income families, who may be eligible for subsidized care from a crèche or child minder.[17] In the United States, in contrast, families at all income levels are about equally likely to be absorbing child care costs. Among families with somewhat older children—between the ages of three and five—those in France are considerably less likely than their counterparts in the United States to be paying anything for child care (table 7.5, column 3).[18] This

TABLE 7.4 Co-Payment Policies and Estimated Share of ECEC Costs Assumed by Government, Approximately 2000 (Percentage)

Country	Co-Payment Policies		Public Share of Costs[a]	
	Younger Children	Older Children	Younger Children	Older Children
Nordic Countries				
Denmark	Vary by type of provision; part-day preschools (bornehaveklasser) free.		75 to 84	
Finland	Vary with income and number of children; no fee for low-income families; part-day pre-schools (6-vuotiaiden esiopetus) free.		84	
Norway	Vary with family income.		55 to 72[b]	
Sweden	Vary with family income and number of children.		82[c]	
Continental Countries				
Belgium	Sliding scale based on income.	Free when children reach two and a half or three (école maternelle).	75 to 83	100
France	Vary with income and type of care.	Free when children reach two and half or three (école maternelle).	83[d]	100
Luxembourg	Vary with income and type of care.	Free when children reach the age of four (spielschoul, école maternelle).	75	100
English-Speaking Countries				
United States	Vary with income; rates vary by state and program.	Vary by region and type of care; some preprimary free.	41	

Sources: Data from OECD (1999a, 1999b, 2000c, 2001d); Danish Ministry of Social Affairs (2000); Palme et al. (2002); country experts.

[a] In all countries except the United States, public share refers to cost of public arrangements minus average parental copayments; in United States, public share is estimate of total ECEC expenditures that are assumed by government.

[b] For Norway, goal is that by 2005, parental share of costs will not exceed 20 percent.

[c] Since 2000 in Sweden parental fees have been capped. Average family costs have been reduced by more than half, to an estimated SEK1,100 per month (U.S.$112).

[d] Estimate based on parental co-payment for care in French crèche, assuming one child and more a famil

TABLE 7.5 Distribution of Parental Child Care Costs, Families with Employed Mother, Late 1990s (Percentage)

Country	Income Group[a]	Youngest Child Under the Age of Three — Percentage of Families with Any Out-of-Pocket Expenses for ECEC (1)	Youngest Child Under the Age of Three — Average Parental Payments Among Those with Any Expenses (Percentage of Total Household Income) (2)	Youngest Child Aged Three to Five Years — Percentage of Families with Any Out-of-Pocket Expenses for ECEC (3)	Youngest Child Aged Three to Five Years — Average Parental Payments Among Those with Any Expenses (Percentage of Total Household Income) (4)	Youngest Child Under the Age of Five — Average Parental Payments Among All Families with Employed Mothers (Percentage of Total Household Income) (5)
France	All	54	8	41	5	3
	Low income	32	8	23	5	2
	Middle income	53	8	41	5	3
	High income	65	7	50	3	4
United States	All	52	9	66	10	6
	Low income	59	22	65	21	12
	Middle income	48	9	58	9	4
	High income	52	6	75	6	3

Sources: Authors' calculations based on data from LIS (for France) and NSAF (Urban Institute 2002) (for the United States).

[a]Income groups are defined differently for the measures. For share of population with any parental costs (columns 1 and 3) and share of income paid by families with children under the age of six (column 5), low income is average for families in the second decile, middle income is average for fifth and sixth deciles, and high income is average for ninth decile. For estimated parental costs (columns 2 and 4), low income is average for families in the bottom quartile, middle income is average for families in the second and third quartiles, and high income is average for families in the top quartile.

is particularly true for lower-income families: fewer than one-quarter of low-income French families pay for any ECEC, in comparison with nearly two-thirds of low-income American families. The distribution of actual parental costs, among those who pay anything for child care, is even more dramatically unequal in the United States than in France. Among families whose youngest child is under the age of three, French families at all income levels who purchase care pay about 7 or 8 percent of their income for child care; the costs for lower-income American families—who pay 22 percent of income for child care—are about four times those of higher-income American families, who pay only 6 percent of their income (column 2). Among families with preschoolers (aged three to five), out-of-pocket costs for those who purchase any care are about twice as high in the United States (10 percent of income) as they are in France (5 percent) for most income groups. Once again, they are sharply higher for lower-income than for higher-income families in the United States (column 4).

The net result is that American parents have a heavier direct cost burden for child care than do French parents, on average, and a much heavier burden if their income is low (column 5). Considering all families with an employed mother and at least one child under the age of six, private child care costs in the United States consume about 6 percent of family income—twice the share of income devoted to ECEC in France. For lower-income families, these costs are six times greater (as a share of income) in the United States than in France.

Public expenditures provide another metric for comparing government support for ECEC. Because ECEC services are provided through various government agencies and levels of government, it is difficult to obtain comparable cross-national figures on total expenditures. Of our twelve countries, we were able to secure comparable expenditure data for only seven, as of the mid-1990s.[19] (Because expenditures for child care subsidies in the United States increased substantially in the late 1990s, we include comparable data for 2000 as well.) Table 7.6 presents data on total public investments through direct spending (subsidies and direct provision) as of approximately 1996, in 2000 U.S. dollars, per child in the population from birth to the usual starting age of public primary school.[20]

TABLE 7.6 **Public Spending on Early Childhood Education and Care, per Child (2000 US$ PPP-Adjusted), Mid-1990s**

Country	Spending on Services and Subsidies
Nordic Countries	
Denmark	$4,050
Finland	$3,189[a]
Sweden	$4,950
Continental Countries	
France	$3,161
Netherlands	$1,369
English-Speaking Countries	
United Kingdom	780[b]
United States	
1997	$ 548
2000	$ 679

Sources: Data from Adams and Sandfort (1992); Baker (1995); Child Care Resource and Research Unit (2000); Doherty et al. (1995); European Commission Network (1995); Hofferth (1998); Rostgaard and Fridberg (1998); Tietze and Cryer (1999); DHHS (1999); Shulman, Blank, and Ewen (1999); Gish (2002); Doherty (2002).

Note: Spending estimates are for approximately 1995 (unless otherwise noted), converted to 2000 U.S. dollars adjusted for purchasing power parity. Total spending calculated per child of relevant ages given country-specific institutions and available data: day care, nursery, and preprimary education for children from birth to four in United Kingdom; federal and state child care subsidies, Head Start, and state pre-kindergarten programs for children from birth to four in United States; *crèche* and *école maternelle* for children from birth to five in France; public child care for children from birth to four in the Netherlands; public care for children from birth to six in Sweden, Finland, Denmark.

[a]For Finland, does not include Private Care Allowance, received by an estimated 2 percent of children under the age of seven.

[b]For the United Kingdom, does not include expansions of Sure Start and public nursery schools since 1996.

As expected, the countries providing the most extensive access—the integrated systems of the Nordic countries—make the most substantial investments.[21] As of the mid-1990s, Denmark spent the equivalent of $4,050, and Sweden $4,950, for each child under school age. The less extensive coverage provided by the dual systems of France and Belgium is also less expensive. France spent the equivalent of $3,161 for each child under school age. Spending was less in France than in the Nordic countries, in large part, because enrollments were limited for children before the start of école.

How does the United States compare? As of the mid-1990s, the United States invested an average of only $548 for each child before the start of primary school—less than in any of our comparison countries. Both federal and state spending expanded substantially during the later 1990s as part of welfare-reform efforts and modest expansions of pre-kindergarten programs. Despite these expansions, average spending for each child under the age of five was only an estimated $679 by the end of the decade. The United States continued to invest only about 15 percent of the amount that the Nordic countries spent in child care and only about 20 percent of the amount spent in France. The United States provides additional funds to parents through provisions of the tax code. As of the mid-1990s, however, tax expenditures were, on average, only about $100 for each child under the age of seven.[22]

Quality and Workforce Standards

High-quality ECEC services are an essential form of support for an earner-carer society. Quality of care is important for parents, whose ability to engage in market work depends in large part on their trust in the care that their children are receiving while they are at the workplace, and is also essential for the health and development of children. Government has three principal mechanisms for ensuring quality ECEC: curriculum design, staffing structures, and staff preparation. Of these, staff preparation is arguably the most important. Care providers who have higher levels of education, more extensive training in ECEC, and longer tenure in the field provide higher-quality care for children.[23] Compensation plays an important indirect role: higher salaries attract and retain more qualified workers to ECEC settings. Compensation for ECEC is equally central to the achievement of gender equality in market opportunities and wages because the ECEC workforce is overwhelmingly female. The two systems that we have identified as models for accessibility and affordability also rank high in the quality of care they provide and in their levels of compensation for the ECEC workforce.

One of the fundamental dimensions on which countries vary is the share of all care arrangements that are subject to public oversight and the governing principles of that oversight. Not surprisingly, the highly integrated public ECEC systems of the Nordic countries have the most well-developed and consistently applied standards for the care of children. Nearly all care is overseen by public entities and regulated in reference to national standards for child welfare and educational development. In Finland, for example, ECEC is based on a national EduCare curriculum that is delivered and overseen by municipal authorities; in Sweden, oversight of ECEC services has been consolidated under the National Ministry of Education, and a national preschool curriculum was adopted in 1998.

Early childhood education and care provided in less formal settings, with child minders (family child care providers), is subject to less formal programmatic oversight. Providers in these settings, however, are typically linked together through child minder networks that are overseen and supported by the public sector. In Denmark, for example, child minders include both municipal employees and private providers and are supervised by child care professionals with advanced training. Municipal governments provide child minders with supports ranging from activity centers to government organization of substitutes and assistance with administrative tasks.

In the dual systems that characterize ECEC in France and Belgium, sharper institutional divisions separate public oversight of care for younger and older children and care within the public and private sectors. National educational ministries that set basic quality standards and curricular objectives oversee preschool programs; regional and municipal governments oversee specific curriculums and other program features. Regional and municipal variation is more pronounced in the structure and quality of care for children under the age of three who are cared for in public centers (crèches) and child minder (family child care) settings. Like the Nordic countries, many of these private providers have access to government programs of support. In Belgium, for example, child minders have access to specialized training and supportive networks under the supervision of trained social work advisers.

Within the sector of regulated ECEC providers, the most important dimensions of state oversight concern the preparation of child care workers (table 7.7). In all countries, national policies governing educational requirements generally require less training, and less-specialized training, for child care professionals than for teachers in compulsory education systems. Whereas primary

(Text continues on p. 224.)

TABLE 7.7 ECEC Quality Regulations, Approximately 2000

Country	Child-Staff Ratio for Children Under the Age of Three	Child-Staff Ratio for Children Aged Three to Five	Family Child Care Staff Qualifications	Center-Based Staff Qualifications	Preprimary Staff Qualifications
			Nordic Countries		
Denmark	Ranges from 3:1 in crèche to 6:1 in age-integrated centers and 5:1 for child minders.	Ranges from 7:1 in kindergarten to 6:1 in age-integrated facilities and 5:1 for child minders.	Municipal facility managers have specialized training; private child minders generally not required to have specific training.	Teachers complete three-and-one-half-year university program.	
Finland	Ranges from 4:1 or 5:1 in family child care to 4:1 in center based care.	Ranges from 4:1 or 5:1 in family child care to 7:1 in center-based care.	Most family child care supervisors are qualified as preprimary teachers; municipalities set training requirements for family child care providers.	Three-and-one-half-year training as "social educator" or three-year secondary vocational training as preprimary teacher.	Three to four and one-half years of university-level training.

Norway	Ranges from average of 3.6:1 to 4.8:1.	Ranges from average of 3.6:1 to 4.8:1.	For every thirty children in family day care, a trained preschool teacher is available to support care workers; private child minders generally not required to have specific training.	Three years of higher education for teachers; two-year apprenticeship for assistants.
Sweden	Varies locally; in practice, average 6:1.	Varies locally; in practice, average 5.4:1.	72 percent of family child minders completed certificate or municipal training program.	Three years of university training required; an estimated 60 percent of preschool teachers have completed university-level training.

Continental Countries

Belgium	7:1.	18:1 (Flemish) and 19:1 (French) preprimary.	Voluntary in-service training.	Flemish: one year training in addition to professional secondary education; French: three years beyond diploma (at age sixteen).	Three-year postsecondary degree.
France	Ranges from 3:1 in family day care to 8:1 for center-based toddler care.	Class size is 25:1, but in practice teachers have assistants, so ratio is 12.5:1.	Sixty hours of training, with ongoing supervision and in-service training.	Teachers have three-year college degree plus additional graduate professional degree in ECEC; assistants have secondary diploma plus additional year of vocational training in early care and education.	

(Table continues on p. 222.)

TABLE 7.7 *Continued*

Country	Child-Staff Ratio for Children Under the Age of Three	Child-Staff Ratio for Children Aged Three to Five	Family Child Care Staff Qualifications	Center-Based Staff Qualifications	Preprimary Staff Qualifications
Germany	Generally, 3:1.	Varies by *Lander*; range from twelve to twenty-five children with one teacher plus one assistant.	No requirements.	**	Three-year "upper-secondary" education, including two years of education and one-year apprenticeship in pre-school setting.
Luxembourg	6:1.	9:1 for two- to four-year-olds 10:1 for four- and twelve-year-olds.	**	Equivalent to secondary school diploma.	Three years of postsecondary training.
Netherlands	Varies by age from 4:1 for the youngest to 6:1 for two- to three-year-olds.	Varies by age from 8:1 for three- to four-year-olds to 10:1 for ages four and above in child care. Ratios are 20:1 in *bassiscbool*.	No national standards; family day care providers generally supervised by municipal-agency staff with postsecondary education.	Group leaders required to have three-years tertiary or four-year-years (nonuniversity) education.	Group leaders required to have three-or four-year professional education.

English-Speaking Countries

Canada	Varies by province and territory. For two-year-olds, range is 4:1 to 8:1.	Varies by province and territory. For four-year-olds, range is 7:1 to 10:1.	Varies by province and territory, from no provider requirements to sixty hours of training.	Provincial and territorial requirements vary from no training or experience to two-year degree; often, only a percentage of staff in a center must hold qualifications.	Generally, university degree.
United Kingdom	Varies by age from 3:1 for youngest to 4:1 for two- to three-year-olds.	Varies by type of care, from 3:1 for child minders to 10:1 for nursery school to 15:1 to 30:1 for reception classes for four- to five-year-olds.	No requirements.	Vary; more than half have no formal training.	Four-year university degree for teachers; two-year postsecondary degree for assistants.
United States	Varies by state, usually 4:1 to 6:1 for youngest, higher for two- to three-year-olds.	Varies by state and type of care, from 20:2 in Head Start to 8:1 to 15:1 for three-year-olds in child care centers.	Varies from none (eighteen states) to preservice plus at least six hours of in-service training a year (four states).	Vary from none (thirty states) to some specific ECEC training (nineteen states) to university degree (one state).	Varies from some specific ECEC training (eighteen states) to university degree (twenty states).

Sources: Data from Helburn and Bergmann (2002); OECD (1999a, 1999b, 2000a, 2000c, 2000d, 2001a); Ministry of Health, Welfare, and Sport and Ministry of Education, Culture and Science (2000); Centre for Research in Early Childhood (n.d.); Eurydice (1994a); Danish Ministry of Social Affairs (2000); Doherty (2002); Peer (2001); Palme et al. (2002); country experts.
**data unavailable.

school teachers are required to have university-level educational credentials, and in many countries completion of graduate-level education is required or encouraged, early childhood workers in both educational and care settings are not always required to have significant levels of training.

The integrated EduCare systems in the Nordic countries set the highest educational requirements for workers in both child care centers and preschool programs. All but Finland require bachelor-level university degrees for both child care workers and preschool teachers; Finland requires a university degree for preschool teachers and a three-year vocational or polytechnic degree for child care workers.

In the dual and early-school-enrollment systems in France and Belgium, variation in staff preparation is more pronounced across ECEC settings. Child minders often have little formal training. Staff in child care centers (who deal primarily with infants and toddlers younger than three) are typically required to complete one- or two-year postsecondary vocational programs. In contrast, teachers in preschool classrooms serving children from about the age of three until the start of school have the same levels of university training as teachers in the regular primary school system.

In contrast to generally high standards for professional training, standards for the ratio of adults to children—a structural indicator of child care quality—tend to be less rigorous. In all of the European countries, standards for the care of the youngest children (from the age of one to about three) generally limit the number of children cared for by a single adult to three or four, although the average is as high as six in Sweden. Cross-national variation is greater in preschool programs, which vary from relatively small classes of six or seven in the Nordic countries to large classes of eighteen or nineteen children in Belgian kleuterschool and French école maternelle. Relatively large class sizes in the Continental preschool programs are often described as a tradeoff: with higher levels of training and preparation, ECEC professionals in these systems are able to provide high-quality care to larger groups of children.

How does the United States compare on these quality dimensions? National articulation of quality standards and educational objectives has been extremely limited in the United States, and quality is overseen largely through local regulation of private child care arrangements. In comparison with the high-quality care provided in the integrated Nordic systems and the French and Belgian preschool programs, the United States has remarkably variable and generally weak oversight of ECEC, minimal standards for caregiver preparation, and extremely low wages for caregiving professionals.

An exceptionally large share of the ECEC market in the United States is entirely exempt from government oversight. Family child care providers (the primary care arrangement for an estimated 16 percent of children under the age of five) who care for as few as two to as many as six children are exempt from regulation in thirty-eight states; some child care centers (which care for about 32 percent of young children) may be exempt from oversight in thirteen states (Helburn and Bergmann 2002; Doherty 2002). These regulations are enforced by announced inspections, for both centers and family child care homes, in only seventeen states.[24]

Within regulated settings, public oversight is focused more heavily on health and safety issues than on quality or educational issues. With the exception of the Head Start program, the United States sets no national standards or curriculum requirements for early education programs. For example, though all states have standards for kindergarten, only sixteen have developed curricular or content standards for pre-kindergarten programs, and only six require their use (Doherty 2002).

Standards for professional training are also varied and are generally much weaker than those observed in many of the European ECEC systems. For example, though thirty-nine states require either a college education or specialized training in early education for pre-kindergarten teachers, fewer than half set any educational or training standards for workers in child care settings (Doherty 2002). Workers in regulated family child care homes have no education or training requirements in eighteen states and minimal hours of in-service or preservice training in the remainder (Helburn and Bergmann 2002).

One of the most important consequences of a market-based ECEC system with weak public oversight is that care is provided by a minimally educated and highly unstable workforce in the United States. An estimated 22 to 34 percent of teaching staff in regulated child care centers and family child care settings lack a high-school diploma, and only 18 to 22 percent have completed college. In unregulated family child care homes and relative child care settings, between 33 and 46 percent of caregivers have less than a high school education, and only 6 to 15 percent have completed college (Galinsky et al. 1994; Whitebook, Howes, and Phillips 1989). These minimally trained workers cycle in and out of low-paid child care positions. Some child care centers report an inability to hold staff in any position through even one year—resulting in rates of staff turnover in excess of 100 percent annually (Whitebook, Howes, and Phillips 1989).

Compensation for Child Care Workforce

Cross-national variation in required staff qualifications translates into substantial variation in compensation for child care workers (table 7.8). Early childhood workers tend to be relatively poorly paid in comparison with primary school teachers everywhere, although the gap is generally smaller for preschool teachers than for workers in other child care settings. Compensation also varies with the institutional framework for ECEC. Child care providers in private settings, particularly in the less formal sector of family child care provision (or child minders), earn substantially less than their counterparts in child care centers and preschool programs. Countries with relatively well developed infrastructure for public provision of child care and preschool provide the highest salaries for the largest share of their child care workforce.[25]

Variation across our comparison countries is substantial. To facilitate comparisons, we calculate the usual rate of pay (in original units) for the equivalent of a full-time worker: eight hours a day, five days a week, forty-eight weeks a year. Because usual wages vary across countries, we compare these annualized salaries to the average wage of all women workers in the country (including full- and part-time workers).[26] By this metric, the compensation for child care providers in two systems is notable. Workers in the integrated Nordic systems earn very close to the national average for all women workers, and in Denmark considerably more than the average. Workers in the dual systems of Belgium and France are also well compensated—particularly teachers in the école, who earn substantially more than the average.

Given the highly privatized and minimally regulated structure of ECEC in the United States, it is not surprising that child care workers in this country are among the worst paid in cross-national terms. Workers in child care centers in the United States earn barely half of the average wage for American working women. Those in preschool programs, which generally require much higher levels of education and training, earn only two-thirds of the average U.S. wage.

School Schedules

Although often overlooked in discussions of public support for earner-carer families, school schedules are an important component of family policy. From the perspective of children, the hours of instruction are a crucial input into learning and human capital development; the hours of supervision can be an equally important factor in children's safety, and their social and intellectual development. From the perspective of parents, the usual schedules of both preschool and primary schools determine the extent to which schools can function as supervised child care during their own hours of employment.

Countries vary substantially in both the usual hours and the usual days during which preschool and primary schools are in session (table 7.9). With respect to the hours of public care provision, Sweden and Denmark stand out from the remaining countries. Public child care during the preschool years is typically provided on a full-day, full-year basis. Primary schools are generally open for many hours beyond the instructional hours in both countries—as long as sixty hours a week in some parts of Sweden—and schools are open from 178 days in Sweden to 200 in Denmark. Before and after school hours, Denmark also provides for children in recreation centers, or skolefritidsordninger, and children in Sweden may be supervised in "leisure centers" located in or near the school.

The hours of preschool and school operation are much shorter in the Continental European countries of France and Belgium, and school years are short in both countries, in cross-national terms.

(Text continues on p. 232.)

TABLE 7.8 ECEC Staff Compensation, Approximately 2000

Country	Usual Wage			Equivalent Full-Year Full-Time Wage[a]		As Share of All Employed Women's Annual Wages[b]	
	Family Child Care Provider or Child Minder	Center-Based Child Care Worker (Wage of Highest-Trained Worker)	Preprimary Teacher	Center-Based Child Care Worker	Preprimary Teacher	Center-Based Child Care Worker	Preprimary Teacher
Nordic Countries							
Denmark	DKK17,200 per month	DKK20,700 to 25,900 per month	DKK22,300 to 25,900 per month	$28,917 to $36,182	$31,153 to $36,182	1.35 to 1.69	1.35 to 1.69
Finland	FIM7,740 per month	FIM8,857 per month	FIM9,385 per month	$17,424	$18,462	0.90	0.95
Norway	NOK190,000 per year	NOK160,700 to NOK227,300 per year		$17,485 to $24,730	$17,485 to $24,730	.88 to 1.20	.88 to 1.20
Sweden	SEK13,500 to 14,000 per month	SEK15,500 per month	SEK15,500 per month	$19,658	$19,658	1.02	1.02
Continental Countries							
Belgium	BF475 per child per day	BF50,694 per month	BF66,071 per month	$16,441	$21,428	1.12	1.45
France	Parents pay minimum of U.S.$20 per day and minders restricted to caring for three chil-	**	FF113,970 to 203,050 per year; average: FF176,850	**	$17,400 to $31,000; average $27,000	**	1.21 to 2.15; average 1.87

Germany	**	**	**	**	**	**	**
Luxembourg	**	Educateur gradué: €3,091 per month[c]	€2,956 per month[c]	$37,695	$36,049	1.84	1.76
Netherlands	**	2,488 to 2,847 guilder per month	2,488 to 3,803 guilder per month	$15,507 to $17,745	$17,745 to $22,704	.89 to 1.01	1.01 to 1.30
English-Speaking Countries							
Canada	CN$15,600 per year	CN$11.85 per hour	**	$18,907	**	0.85	**
United Kingdom	£1 to £3 per hour per child[a]	£10,000 to £13,000 per year	£17,000 to £18,000 per year	$15,361 to $19,969	$26,114 to $27,650	.83 to 1.03	1.42 to 1.50
United States	$4.04 per hour[e]	$6.98 per hour[e]	$8.79 per hour[e]	$13,401	$16,876	0.53	0.66

Sources: Data from OECD (1999a, 1999b, 2000c, 2001d); Danish Ministry of Social Affairs (2000); Centre for Research in Early Childhood (n.d.); Doherty (2002); Peer (2001); U.S. Center for the Child Care Workforce (2000); Beach, Bertrand, and Cleveland (1998); country experts.

[a]Annualized hours assume 1,920 paid hours annually (eight hours per day, five days per week, forty-eight weeks per year). Compensation expressed in $U.S. 2000, ppp-adjusted.

[b]Average wage for all women workers, full-time and part-time, calculated from Luxembourg Income Study (LIS).

[c]For civil servants in Luxembourg as of 2002.

[d]As of approximately 1997; by 2000, minimum wage in the United Kingdom raised to £3.70, which should set minimum per hour.

[e]As of 1996, in $U.S. 2000.

**data unavailable.

TABLE 7.9 Hours and Days of Supervised Care, Approximately 2000

Country	Usual Hours of Operation, Preprimary Programs[a]	Start of Compulsory Primary School	Hours of Primary-School Opening	Days of Primary-School Opening	Continuous School Day and Week
		Nordic Countries			
Denmark	7:00 a.m. to 6:00 p.m. all year	7	53	200	Yes
Finland	7:00 a.m. to 5:00 p.m. all year.[b]	7	25	190	Yes
Norway	Full day (forty-one or more hours per week).	6	21	190	Yes
Sweden	6:30 a.m. to 6:00 p.m. all year[c]	7	60	178	Yes
		Continental Countries			
Belgium	8:30 a.m. to 3:30 p.m. with after-school care available. Wednesday afternoon closed.	6	44	182	No; Wednesday afternoon closed.
France	8:40 a.m. to 4:30 p.m. during term time. Wednesday afternoon closed.	6	35	180	No; Wednesday afternoon closed.
Germany	Generally, morning or afternoon sessions during school year, without lunchtime.	6	28	198	Yes, although primary school is generally dismissed at lunch time.
Luxembourg	8:00 to 4:00 p.m. but usually closed for two-hour lunch each day and Tuesday and Thursday afternoons.	4	37	212	No; Tuesday and Thursday afternoon closed.

Netherlands	Child care full-day; preschool (for children four years and older during term time) 8:30 a.m. to 2:00 p.m.	5[d]	30	200	No; Wednesday afternoon closed.
English-Speaking Countries					
Canada	Part-day, part-year.	5 to 6[e]	varies, but 30 to 33 is typical	190	Yes
United Kingdom	Varies by type of program, from 2.5 to 6.5 hours per day.	5	33	190	Yes
United States	Usually part-day, part-year.	5 to 6[f]	33	179	Yes

Sources: Data from Eurydice (1994a, 1995a, 1995b, 2000); Clearinghouse on International Developments in Child, Youth, and Family Policies (2003); European Commission Network (1996); OECD (2001d); Tietze and Cryer (1999); country experts.

[a] In most countries child care centers and day care homes (child minders) available full time.
[b] In Finland, center-based and family day care available full-time. School-based *6-vuotiaiden esiopetus* is part-time.
[c] In Sweden, center-based *Forskola* and FDC (*Familiedagbem*) available full-time. *Forskoleklass* (preschool) is part-time.
[d] In the Netherlands, compulsory school begins at five but most children enrolled by age four.
[e] In Canada, compulsory at age six but most attend at age five; Junior Kindergarten available in Ontario at age four.
[f] In U.S., start of compulsory school set by state policy and begins as late as age eight in two states; in most states, school begins at five or six.

Preschool and primary school schedules can be particularly problematic in these countries because they are often discontinuous, owing to afternoon closings or unsupervised lunch breaks. Although école maternelle in France is provided full-day, for example, both école and primary schools are often closed on Wednesday afternoons and, in some regions, for a midday lunch break. Some, but not all, écoles and primary schools have "wraparound" or after-school care during these hours.

The United States fares poorly in cross-national terms in hours of preschool and primary school operation. Most pre-kindergarten, Head Start, and other preschool programs in the United States are operated only for part of the day. Public kindergartens are also part-day in one-half of all states (Doherty 2002). Once American children are enrolled in regular primary school, they are likely to have a continuous day-time school schedule—a more supportive daily schedule than that of many of the Continental European primary schools. Weekly hours of school operation are relatively short, however, in cross-national terms—at thirty-three hours a week, on average, schools in the United States are open for barely half the hours of their counterparts in Sweden. The usual days of school operation during the year are also lower in the United States than in all but one of our comparison countries. Schools are open anywhere from ten to twenty days longer each year in these countries; this corresponds to two to four weeks of additional supervision for young children provided through public school systems.

CONCLUSION

On nearly every dimension, the current patchwork in the United States of highly privatized ECEC arrangements and multiple federal, state, and local policies lags behind the most supportive countries of Europe. Families' access to care depends largely on their private resources and on what local private markets produce. Families often incur high costs when purchasing care. Despite this, quality is highly uneven and generally poor, due to weak public oversight and the minimal educational preparation of ECEC workers. Professionals in the ECEC field are among the most poorly paid workers in the country; as a consequence, they face few incentives to invest in their education or to accumulate experience in the field. The costs and uncertain quality of child care have implications for children, who may experience less-than-optimal or even neglectful care. It has implications for gender equality, as well. Child care increases the monetary and other costs of work for mothers; low wages contribute to a large, highly feminized and poorly paid child care workforce. In comparison with many of the countries in Europe, public schools also provide less support for employed parents—holding classes nearly one month less each year and providing supervision for children for relatively few hours each day.

Our comparative study suggests that government can do a lot more to support earner-carer families and to achieve gender equality through policies affecting child care, preschool services, and school schedules. In several European countries, government is already doing a great deal. Although the European Union has yet to adopt a binding directive in the area of ECEC, a 1992 Council of Ministers Recommendation on Childcare was adopted by all member-state governments. To "enable women and men to reconcile their occupational, family and upbringing responsibilities arising from the care of children," the recommendation urges adoption of ECEC policies that reflect the principles of the systems we have highlighted in our comparison: affordability, access for all children, a combination of reliable care with an educational (pedagogical) focus, professional training, and support for flexibility, diversity of arrangements, and parental choice (European Forum for Child Welfare 2003).

These systems suggest some lessons that could be used to develop ECEC and school scheduling policies in the United States that are more supportive of an earner-carer society. First, programs should be inclusive but provide differentiated services. Inclusive ECEC programs with universal entitlements spread the costs, create norms of participation that eliminate stigma, promote social integration, and build broad-based political support for government programs. National-level entitlements can be linked to individual- and local-level services using complementary strategies that differentiate services by children's ages: parental leaves greatly reduce the need for public provision of infant care; care for children aged one and two should be provided through a diversity of arrangements, including supervised child care homes and centers; full-day, universal preschool programs are particularly appropriate for children from the age of two and a half or three. Partnerships between national and local government can be used to tailor services to local concerns, while differentiated services help match services to the diversity of parents' and children's needs.

Second, most of the costs of early education and child care should be paid by the public sector, with parents paying income-scaled fees. The provision of good-quality child care is costly, and families, particularly those with young children, have limited resources. Public financing should be sufficient to provide the quality of care that children deserve without impoverishing the professionals who provide that care. Providing the majority of this funding at the national level would ensure adequate funding and reduce regional disparities. Rules for eligibility and parent fees should be standardized to decrease regional variation and support a progressive distribution of costs that relieves the lowest-income families from disproportionately heavy child care costs.

Third, the quality of care should be ensured through direct public provision or strong oversight and support of private providers. The regulation of quality through consumer choice and post hoc regulation of private providers is a challenging task. Parents have difficulty assessing quality, and regulators have difficulty specifying and enforcing features that ensure the best-quality services. The direct provision of ECEC programs would allow the public sector to devise and implement consistent standards for staffing, facilities, curriculum, and other features of care. Equivalent quality standards for private providers should be established at the national level, with oversight and support from well-trained professionals who can provide supportive rather than adversarial public oversight.

Fourth, child care professionals should be highly trained and well compensated. High levels of professional preparation are key to the provision of high-quality child care; adequate compensation is essential for both attracting and retaining skilled professionals and for reducing wage differentials between caring and other professionals.

Finally, school schedules should be matched to parents' working hours. Schools and ECEC meet the needs of children and parents only when they fit the working hours of employed parents. For parents working a standard-hour week, the hours of operation for child care centers and schools are crucial. For parents working nonstandard shifts, alternative forms of service delivery would be an essential component of a diverse delivery system, though children in these families would still benefit from participation in educationally oriented services provided during regular working hours.

—— Chapter 8 ——

Does Policy Matter?
Linking Policies
to Outcomes

IN THE PRECEDING chapters, we have described models for government policies that could help to reduce the time squeeze on employed parents, promote the well-being of children, and achieve greater gender equality in the labor market and the home. Our rationale has been largely conceptual: families in the United States are faring much worse, relative to these goals, than their counterparts in other countries in which policies are logically consistent with, and in some cases explicitly targeted on, their achievement. The policy lessons in the preceding chapters are based on more than logic, however. Substantial empirical research links many of these policies directly to outcomes relating to gender equality and to child and family well-being.

The associations between some of these policies and outcomes are direct and self-evident. For example, policies that grant maternity and paternity leave increase parents' time for caregiving; policies that provide wage replacement during periods of parental leave increase families' incomes; policies that increase vacation rights increase vacation time taken, as take-up is high everywhere; policies that subsidize child care reduce parents' out-of-pocket child care expenses. Other associations are less easily evaluated, due to the complexity of the behaviors involved. Family leave policies, for example, have ambiguous implications for gender equality in the labor market because short-term leaves may strengthen women's attachments to employment whereas longer leaves may weaken it. The net effect of most of these policies on children's

236

well-being can be understood only through carefully designed studies that control for other contributing factors.

Much is known about the association between the policies we have described and the goals that motivate our end vision of an earner-carer society. Because of their substantive relevance to the policy lessons presented in the preceding chapters, and because each has a reasonably large empirical literature,[1] we focus here on the following hypothesized policy effects:

- unpaid leave on maternal employment;
- the provision and length of paid leave on women's employment;
- leave design on men's take-up of benefits;
- parental time at home on child well-being;
- the regulation of weekly hours on actual working time;
- child care costs and availability on maternal employment;
- child care quality on children's well-being; and
- packages of policies on various outcomes.

There is remarkably little empirical literature on other policy associations of interest, including the effects of school schedules on maternal employment and the effects of working-time regulation on the prevalence of nonstandard work hours, the quality of part-time work, or on gender equality.

Much of the empirical research on these topics has been conducted in the United States. This reflects, at least in part, the particularly strong orientation of American policy makers and voters toward instrumental justifications and performance-based evaluations of public social programs. We cast a wide net to identify relevant studies. Because so much of the research has been conducted in the United States, where provisions of family leave and child care are largely market based, we include policy-relevant studies of private and market phenomena—such as the effects of employer-based leave and private child care arrangements. We also include research that considers policy-relevant intermediate factors. To evaluate the potential effects of family leave on child well-being, for example, we begin by reviewing the literature on the effects of parental time at home during the first year after childbirth.

Evaluating the effects of policy on individual and family-level outcomes is difficult. Many of the outcomes we care about—such as maternal employment and children's early development—result from complex interactions among individual and contextual factors; policy is likely to be only one of these factors. Additional complexity is introduced when we consider policy effects in different countries; similar policies may have quite different consequences in different social and economic contexts. In light of these challenges, we pay particular attention to studies that have the potential to rule out alternative explanations for the outcomes of interest by concentrating on those that have large samples, reliable research designs, and multivariate analyses. This is especially important in studies involving private behaviors—such as a parent's decision to reenter employment or to use a particular form of child care; such studies, if they improperly control for correlated family-level characteristics, can imply misleading conclusions about outcomes.

FAMILY LEAVE

The literature on the effects of family leave provisions is voluminous. Most of the research focuses on the impact of the availability or length of family leave on mothers' attachment to the labor market and, by extension, on gender equality at work. A subset of that literature directly addresses fathers' use of leave. A second, more limited literature assesses the effects of parental time at home on children's well-being, especially their health and cognitive development.

Family Leave, Women's Employment, and Gender Equality

Nearly all research on the employment effects of leave has focused on women, who are much more likely to use the leave to which they are entitled and to experience its effects. The employment effects of leave, paid and unpaid, short-term and long-term, are theoretically indeterminate. Employers' reluctance to hire workers who may take leave could diminish labor demand for women of childbearing age, whereas job protections and wage replacement could increase women's labor supply, both before and after childbirth. Because the potential for offsetting effects varies with leave characteristics, we consider the impacts of several different types of leave separately.

Leaves of Short to Moderate Duration   The consensus in the research literature is that unpaid leave—that is, job protection without pay—has a limited impact on women's labor market attachment, possibly because employer and worker responses balance each other out. Both Katherin Ross (1998) and Jane Waldfogel (1999) have concluded that the FMLA, which grants twelve weeks of leave to American families, has had little effect on women's aggregate (state-level) employment rates. In contrast, Kristen Smith, Barbara Downs, and Martin O'Connell find that maternity leave, unpaid as well as paid, raises new mothers' likelihood of returning to employment within three months. They note that "women who are let go or who quit obviously have greater difficulty securing employment after their child's birth" (Smith, Downs, and O'Connell 2001, 16). Sandra Hofferth (1996) also finds that having "liberal unpaid leave" provided by their employers raises women's likelihood of returning to employment, especially full-time, within a year after childbirth. Having job protection without pay appears to raise the likelihood that new mothers will return to employment after childbirth, but the impact seems to be too small to affect women's employment overall.

The evidence is clear that paid leaves of several months' to about a year's duration strengthen women's labor market attachment in a variety of ways (see OECD 2001a for a review). Several studies find that access to maternity leave raises the overall probability that women return to the labor force by the end of the first postpartum year and/or return to the same employer. In a comparison of employed women with and without access to paid leave, Jutta Joesch (1997) finds that women with access to paid leave worked later into their pregnancies but were less likely than women without such access to work during the month following the birth. Women with paid leave were also more likely than those without to return to employment in the second and subsequent months, with higher rates of employment lasting up to four years postpartum. Jennifer Glass and Lisa Riley (1998) find that the total length of childbearing leave exerted a strong positive effect on women's likelihood of remaining in the labor force postpartum and with the same employer. (Glass and Riley combine paid and unpaid leaves in their model, but they note that the vast majority of leaves counted in their study were paid.)

The positive effects of paid leave on women's employment are seen in the aggregate as well. Using a cross-national design, Christopher Ruhm (1998) finds that paid leave raises women's employment-to-population ratios by 3 to 4 percent, and with substantially larger effects for women of childbearing age. Ruhm attributes the increased employment to two factors: more women are motivated to enter the labor market before childbirth to gain future eligibility for paid leave (also reported by Baker 1997 and Rubery et al. 1998), and access to paid leave raises postpartum reentry rates. In a related study, Ruhm and Jackqueline Teague (1997) find that paid leaves of short to moderate duration are associated with statistically significant decreases in women's unemployment, as positive effects on employment are even larger than positive effects on participation rates. C. R. Winegarden and Paula Bracy (1995) also compare maternity leave policies across countries; they find that an added week of paid maternity leave raises the labor force participation rate of young women by .60 to .75 percentage points.

The beneficial effects of leaves of short to moderate length extend to mothers' wages. Waldfogel finds that American women who were covered by a maternity leave policy (paid or unpaid) and returned to their prebirth employer had higher wages, all else being equal, than other employed women with children. She concludes that "job-protected maternity leave could be an important remedy for the pay penalties associated with motherhood" (Waldfogel 1997, 122).

Leaves of Longer Duration   Whereas maternity leaves of up to about a year strengthen women's ties to the labor market, the effects of longer leaves—such as the two- or three-year leaves available in Finland, France, and Germany—are much less advantageous with respect to gender equality. Long-term leaves, paid or unpaid, are more problematic for two related reasons: they may erode human capital, and, even more than shorter-term leaves, they are overwhelmingly taken up by women.

The OECD, in reviewing the small literature on these two- to three-year leaves, concludes that "schemes to pay parents to look after their own children at home . . . may encourage labor market detachment if they continue over a long period of time" (OECD 2001a, 146). The OECD cites recent evidence from both Finland and France suggesting that these long leaves depress female employment rates. These researchers note that it is not yet clear at what duration leaves switch from being advantageous to disadvantageous to women's labor market attachment. They also conclude that, though leave duration is a key variable, other aspects of family leave policy design—such as the extent to which employers bear the brunt of the financing—may ultimately matter more. If employers are unduly burdened, reductions in demand for female labor may set in, with relatively shorter leaves.

In an assessment of the employment consequences of the French and German long-term leaves introduced in the mid-1980s, Kimberly Morgan and Kathrina Zippel (2002) find that, in both cases, take-up was more than 98 percent female and reduced the employment rates of women with children under the age of three. In France, eligibility was loosened in 1994, and in the subsequent five years mothers' labor force participation fell sharply, for the first time since the 1970s. The authors cite evidence from France estimating that "between 1994 and 1998, the extension of the childrearing benefit induced 100,000 French mothers to leave the labor market who otherwise would not have done so" (Morgan and Zippel 2002, 21). Morgan and Zippel underscore that these long leaves encourage labor market withdrawals among wives, in particular, adding to divisions of labor within families; few single mothers take them, as the benefit rates are well below family subsistence levels.

Fathers' Take-Up   Leaves have problematic implications for gender equality in the labor market because men's take-up of these benefits remains well below that of women in all countries. A small body of research addresses men's take-up of family leave. Several studies identify employer resistance, or workers' perceptions of employer resistance, as factors that depress take-up, especially in private employment (see OECD 2001a for a review). In addition to employer-related factors, at least two policy features have been found to affect men's take-up.

The first is the level of wage replacement, with higher benefit rates associated with higher male take-up (Moss and Deven 1999). The OECD (2001a) reports that the high-benefit Nordic countries have made the most gains with respect to male usage. The OECD researchers note, for example, that men's take-up is especially high among Danish public-sector employees, who are entitled to 100 percent of their wages during the period of leave.

Several researchers have concluded that men's take-up is raised by granting them use-or-lose leave rights and benefits that cannot be transferred to their female partners (Moss and Deven 1999). The implementation of use-or-lose leave in Norway has been associated with a sharp increase in fathers' take-up, from less than 5 percent to more than 70 percent following implementation (Ellingsaeter 1999; Leira 1999). Arnlaug Leira concludes that the use-or-lose days—what she calls "fatherhood by gentle force"—have encouraged men to take substantial amounts of leave that they would otherwise have transferred to their partners (Leira 2000, 165). The introduction of so-called daddy days in Sweden has had less effect (Haas and Hwang 1999), possibly because fathers' take-up in Sweden was already relatively high (Leira 1999).

Family Leave, Parental Time at Home, and Child Well-Being

Family leave policies have other implications for the well-being of children. Access to family leave increases parents' time at home, and that, in turn, seems to have some beneficial effects on infants and very young children. A number of studies focus on the effects of family leave on children's health outcomes, and a large literature assesses the effects of parental time at home on children's cognitive development during their earliest years.

Family leaves are expected to benefit child health indirectly by making more time available to parents, particularly during infancy, when caregiving demands are acute. Parental time at home during infancy is expected to influence child health because some health-promoting activities—such as breastfeeding—may be incompatible with employment. Research on this association, though limited, is generally supportive of the conclusion that parental time at home, especially during the first year, is advantageous for children. In a comparative study of sixteen European countries, Ruhm (2000) finds that rights to family leave are associated with substantial decreases in infant and early childhood mortality, with the strongest effects observed during the periods most plausibly affected by leave benefits. Winegarden and Bracy (1995) also find evidence linking longer leaves to lower rates of infant mortality.

Child-development research suggests that policies that increase parental time with children in the months following childbirth may have positive benefits for other aspects of child development as well, including children's cognitive development. We have found no studies that directly assess the effects of leave policy on cognitive development of children; indirect evidence is provided by studies of the effects of parental nonemployment (or time at home) on these outcomes. Unfortunately, although we are interested in the question of parental time with children, nearly all of the literature in this area has focused only on the role of maternal time.

The effect of having parents at home on early childhood development is difficult to estimate, in part because the same economic and personal characteristics that shape parents' decisions about employment and work hours may have direct effects on child development.[2] Some researchers have found that once family and maternal characteristics are controlled for, there is little or no relation between maternal employment during the first year and children's cognitive development (for example, Greenstein 1995; Moore and Driscoll 1997); others have found modest positive effects (Parcel and Menaghan 1994; Vandell and Ramanan 1992); still others document negative effects, particularly for full-time employment (Baydar and Brooks-Gunn 1991; Blau and Grossberg 1992; Desai, Chase-Landsdale, and Michael 1989; Leibowitz 1977; Mott 1991; Stafford 1987).

The ambiguous state of the literature is attributable, in part, to the sensitivity of results to model specification, subgroup differences, and variation in the timing and intensity of maternal employment. Ruhm (forthcoming), for example, finds that once a variety of parental and family characteristics are controlled for, lower levels of maternal employment during the first year of a child's life are associated with better outcomes on tests of both verbal and math achievement both in preschool and in the early school years. Research by Ruhm and others also suggests that the timing of parental time at home matters; though he finds negative outcomes for children associated with employment during the first year, these effects are partially (but not completely) offset by improvements in child outcomes associated with maternal employment in the subsequent two years. These results are most robust for two-parent families and for those in which the mother is a high earner. Waldfogel, Wen-Jui Han, and Jeanne Brooks-Gunn (2002); Han, Waldfogel, and Brooks-Gunn (2001) also find negative effects on cognitive development associated with extensive maternal employment during the first year, effects that persist until children reach the age of seven or eight; they find these effects, however, only among white non-Hispanic families and conclude that they are most robust for low-income families.

In related work, Jennifer Hill and her colleagues (Hill et al. 2001) find negative effects associated with full-time maternal employment during the first year, with stronger effects for higher-income families. Research that considers the intensity of early maternal employment suggests that children whose mothers work longer hours (twenty or more hours a week) fare worse than their counterparts (Brooks-Gunn, Han, and Waldfogel 2002; Han, Waldfogel, and Brooks-Gunn 2001; Waldfogel, Han, and Brooks-Gunn 2002). Working nonstandard hours has also been shown to have negative consequences for children's early cognitive development, with more serious compromises among children whose mothers worked thirty hours or more a week in nonstandard shifts (Han 2002).

The effects of maternal time at home are still uncertain, but many well-designed recent studies find evidence that children whose mothers are employed during the first year may fare worse than those with nonemployed mothers—particularly if that employment is full-time or during nonstandard hours. These studies also suggest that the strength of the association is mediated by a number of other risk and protective factors, including the quality of the parent-child relationship and the quality of substitute care that children receive. Waldfogel, Han, and Brooks-Gunn (2002), for example, find that the effects of early maternal employment vary with the type of child care setting, with children in "nonrelative care" (other than centers) most at risk (see also Brooks-Gunn, Han, and Waldfogel 2002). This suggests that some of the negative effects on children of not having time with their own parents may stem, in part, from the poor quality of the substitute care they receive. This finding is consistent with other research documenting the relatively poor quality of child care care services in the United States and the risk this poses for healthy child development.

Conclusions About the Effects of Family Leave

A large literature on family leave suggests five employment effects associated with access to family leaves of short to moderate duration; in nearly all cases, the effects are stronger if leaves are paid. First, access to employment-conditioned leave raises women's rates of labor force participation before the birth of their first child. Second, it raises the likelihood that new mothers take a break from employment during the month following the birth. Third, it raises women's likelihood of returning to employment by about the end of the first year. Fourth, it raises the likelihood that mothers reentering the workforce return to the same employer. Fifth, it seems to reduce the wage penalty associated with motherhood, that is, the gap between the wages of mothers and nonmothers. All of these contributions have the potential to reduce labor market inequalities between men and women by facilitating continuous employment and reducing the wage penalties associated with motherhood.

In contrast to the findings for short-term leaves, a few studies suggest that longer leaves may exacerbate gender inequalities by weakening women's employment ties; this is especially true for wives. Women's greater use of leaves in all countries remains problematic for gender equality. Several recent studies suggest that policies that offer high wage replacement and nontransferable rights could address this problem by inducing higher leave take-up among men.

A smaller body of research suggests that the availability of family leave has health benefits for children, reducing mortality during periods in which leaves are most likely to increase parental time with children. Evidence is mixed about the effects of early parental care on child development, but some recent studies suggest that high levels of maternal employment during a child's first year may be associated with worse outcomes for at least some groups of children and that these effects persist well into grade school. Effects of maternal employment during the second and third year of life appear to be negligible or positive. Although not definitive, this research suggests that leaves that provide parents with options to care for their children during the critical first year of life might contribute to the health and developmental well-being of children.

REGULATION OF WORKING TIME

There are theoretical reasons to believe that various working-time regulations can influence employment-related outcomes that would benefit many workers and their families. These outcomes include a decrease in weekly work hours, an increase in the availability of high-quality part-time jobs, a reduction in the percentage of parents working nonstandard hours, and a narrowing of labor market gender gaps.

Although a sizable social-science literature addresses the effects of regulation on actual hours worked, there is extremely little research assessing the effects of policy on these other outcomes of interest. Correlational findings link regulation to the availability or quality of part-time work (for example, more protective regulations are seen in countries with larger part-time labor markets and smaller pay penalties), but there is virtually no research that persuasively establishes a causal link. Several promising evaluations are under way in Europe that aim to assess the effects of the 1997 EU Directive on Part-Time Work. Because most of the national legislation was implemented in 2000 and 2001, currently available evaluations concern the processes of legislative development across the member countries; evaluations of labor market impacts are not yet available.[3]

With respect to the effect of regulations on nonstandard-hour work, the labor economist Daniel Hamermesh argues that "imposing penalties on evening/night and weekend work would clearly lead employers to substitute toward work at more conventional times" (Hamermesh 2002, 20) but notes that empirical literature on this question is virtually nonexistent.[4] Finally, though a large literature establishes that working-time patterns are themselves heavily gendered—nearly everywhere, part-time work is feminized whereas long (and overtime) hours are disproportionately worked by men— virtually no published research directly addresses the effects of working-time regulations on gender equality in working time.[5]

The Regulation of Weekly Working Time and Actual Hours Worked

As reported in chapter 6, weekly employment hours are limited in many countries through two mechanisms: the establishment of normal working hours and limits on maximum allowable hours. The effects on actual weekly hours of setting normal working time (the threshold for overtime pay) are actually theoretically indeterminate. Faced with a lower cutoff point (or a higher hourly premium), employers could reduce demand for overtime hours (thus reducing actual working time), or they could employ the same level of overtime labor and pay the differential—most likely, by adjusting straight-time (that is, nonovertime) wages downward. The effect of setting or reducing maximum hours is also theoretically indeterminate; maximum rules will have no (or little) effect if few workers actually reach the maximum or if a large share of those who do so volunteer to work beyond the maximum number of hours.

Several empirical studies assess the effects of standard-hour thresholds, and they all find evidence that lowering overtime-pay thresholds reduces actual working time among employees.[6] David Grubb and William Wells consider the effects of working-time regulations in eleven European countries. Using an index of restrictions on normal weekly hours (combining collectively bargained and legislated normal weekly hours), they find that regulations strongly (inversely) predicted usual weekly hours, defined as average hours per week usually worked by full-time employees (Grubb and Wells 1993). Jill Rubery, Mark Smith, and Colette Fagan also assess the effects of working-time regulations, using variation in statutory and bargained normal hours across Europe. They too conclude that "national working time regulations can be seen to have a major impact on usual working time" (Rubery, Smith, and Fagan 1998, 75).

Several empirical studies estimate the magnitude of the effect of reducing standard (regulated) hours on actual hours worked. Estimates of the magnitude of the effect range from about 75 to nearly 100 percent of the change in standard work hours. Researchers have reported the effect on actual hours to be about 77 percent in the United Kingdom, 85 to 100 percent in Germany, and close to 100 percent in France (see OECD 1998b and Costa 2000 for reviews). Another German study concludes that reductions in collectively agreed upon hours explain 70 percent of the two-and-a-half-hour drop in actual weekly hours seen between 1984 and 1997, with the remaining 25 percent attributable to the rising rate of part-time work (see Seifert 1998).

In addition, a study in the Netherlands has found that, after standard weekly working time was reduced to thirty-six hours, 90 to 95 percent of employees in medium-sized banks worked the agreed thirty-six hours (Plantenga and Dur 1998). In a study of working time in the United States, Dora Costa (2000) assesses the effect on work hours of lowering the FLSA overtime threshold from forty-two to forty hours (in 1940); she concludes that the 5 percent reduction in the standard workweek reduced by nearly one-fifth the share of American workers with actual weekly hours in excess of forty.

We found only one study that assesses the effects of setting maximum hours on actual working time. Grubb and Wells (1993) examine the effects of restrictions on overtime hours. They find that, across Europe, maximum limits on annual overtime hours—which ranged from less than one hundred to more than five hundred hours a year—are a strong negative predictor of the observed frequency of overtime work.

Conclusions About the Effect of Working-Time Regulation

Existing research on working-time regulations suggests that reducing the standard-hours threshold—now set at forty hours in the

United States—would, in fact, reduce average weekly work hours, and the magnitude of the effect could be three-quarters of an hour (or more) for each hour of change in the law. Much less is known about the effects of regulation on the quality of part-time work, especially regulations that mandate pay equity between comparable part-time and full-time workers—although evaluation research is now being conducted in Europe. The effects of other types of regulation, including restrictions on nonstandard hours or required pay premiums for nonstandard hours, have received little empirical attention. Researchers have not yet established a causal link between working-time regulation and gender differentials in working time.

EARLY CHILDHOOD EDUCATION AND CARE

Public ECEC policies have implications for many dimensions of family and child well-being. The availability and cost of ECEC affect gender equality through their effect on maternal employment. Policies that reduce the out-of-pocket costs of care directly reduce parents' cost burden and could increase children's access to formal, and potentially higher-quality, care. Child care quality has direct implications for children's well-being, and a substantial body of research has examined the link between child care quality and children's outcomes, in both private settings and high-quality public programs.

Maternal Employment and the Availability and Cost of Early Childhood Education and Care

The availability and cost of substitute child care arrangements are associated with gender equality in labor market outcomes through their effect on maternal employment. Both the availability and cost of substitute care are predicted to affect maternal employment by increasing (or decreasing) the relative attractiveness of time spent in the labor market as against time spent in the home. (As with family leaves, virtually all research in this area has concerned maternal behaviors.) Because the preponderance of research has been conducted in the United States, where private markets are expected to create an adequate supply of care in response to consumer demand, most have concentrated on the role of cost in decisions regarding maternal employment. In these models, child care costs are treated as the equivalent of a tax on maternal earnings; economic theory predicts that higher prices reduce maternal employment and that public policies that reduce these costs would thus increase the probability of employment among mothers with young children.

In an extensive review of the American literature, Patricia Anderson and Philip Levine conclude that "these studies . . . uniformly find a negative relationship between child care costs and maternal employment, regardless of econometric technique" (Anderson and Levine 1999, 18). Employment effects are typically modeled in terms of elasticities in the probability of employment with respect to a change in child care costs (that is, the increase in the probability of employment associated with a decrease in the cost of child care). Their review finds that although estimated employment elasticities vary across studies, the majority cluster between -0.3 and -0.4. This suggests that reducing the price of child care by 10 percent would lead to a 3 to 4 percent increase in the probability of maternal employment. Their own estimates suggest an overall elasticity in this range, with evidence of greater sensitivity to child care price among lower-skilled, unmarried, and low-income mothers. These findings are similar to those of the U.S. General Accounting Office (GAO 1994), with regard to the greater sensitivity of lower-earning mothers, and to Han and Waldfogel (2002) and Rachel Connelly and Jean Kimmel (1999), with regard to single mothers (but see also Kimmel 1998 and Michalopoulos, Robins, and Garfinkel 1992, who reach different conclusions with regard to marital status). Although the bulk of empirical research on child care and labor supply has been conducted in the United States, researchers using Canadian data (Cleveland, Gunderson, and Hyatt 1996; Michalopoulos and Robins 2000; Powell 2002) estimate similar overall elasticities.[7]

To link estimates of employment effects to policy, researchers often use their estimates to simulate the labor-supply response to a change in child care prices. Anderson and Levine (1999), for example, estimate that a fifty-cent per hour drop in the price of care increases labor force participation by nearly 8 percentage points overall (in comparison with an increase of 1 percentage point for an equivalent increase in wages). The predicted impact on relatively disadvantaged workers is even greater: they estimate that a similar subsidy could increase by more than one-third the labor force participation of unmarried women with children under the age of six with less than a high school education. Charles Michalopoulos and Philip Robins (2000) estimate the labor-supply effects of assistance through the tax system (child care tax deductions in Canada and nonrefundable credits in the United States) and conclude that increasing the tax-based subsidy by a hundred dollars would increase employment by just under 1 percentage point (estimated elasticity of .118), with stronger effects for full-time employment. Connelly and Kimmel (2001) extend these simulations to consider welfare receipt, estimating that a 50 percent subsidization of child care would reduce welfare receipt among single mothers by one-third and increase employment by about 50 percent.[8]

Child Care Policy, Child Care Quality, and Child Outcomes

Public child care policies have the potential to contribute to child well-being by increasing the quality of substitute care that children receive. A large research literature has considered the question of whether and how child care quality affects children. Much of this research has relied on natural experiments that include both private and public care arrangements, and its conclusiveness is somewhat limited by difficulties in measuring quality and the methodological challenge of estimating the marginal contribution of child care quality, given the nonrandom nature of families' child care choices (that is, the correlation between child care choices and other family characteristics that contribute to child outcomes). Similar conclusions are also supported, however, by evaluations using experimental designs to control for these family characteristics.

In an extensive recent review of the U.S. literature, Deborah Vandell and Barbara Wolfe (2000) conclude that both process quality (direct measures of the care environment, activities, and caregiver practices) and structural quality (for example, child-to-adult ratios, group size, and education and training of caregivers) are associated with children's cognitive development, emotional adjustment, and school readiness. Based on a separate review of the literature, Margaret Burchinal reaches a similar conclusion: "Most studies have indicated that children who receive higher-quality child care have better cognitive and language development, fewer behavioral problems, better social skills, and better relationships with peers" (Burchinal 1999, 11). Researchers have reached similar conclusions in studies of Swedish child care (Andersson 1992), nursery-school education in the United Kingdom (Feinstein, Robertson, and Symons 1999), and the French école (Jeantheau and Murat 1998; Jarousse, Mingat, and Richard 1992; Moisan and Simon 1997).[9] Other equally careful reviews of the literature in this area reach more cautious conclusions. Blau, in particular, has criticized the majority of U.S. research on the relation between child care quality and child outcomes as inconclusive because most studies lack sufficient rigor in sample selection, measurement, and estimation. Based on his own review of the literature, Blau does conclude, however, that the most carefully designed studies provide evidence of "modest but not inconsequential effects" of child care quality on child outcomes (Blau 2001, 145).

A general conclusion from these academic debates is that most studies suggest a positive association between child care quality and children's cognitive development and that the most carefully designed studies confirm that child care quality makes a significant contribution to child outcomes. The magnitude of this contribution is debated. Using data from a large longitudinal study of child care and child outcomes, Vandell and Wolfe find substantial effects of child care quality on child outcomes, after controlling for other parent and family characteristics. Their estimates indicate that, for example, a shift from the lowest to the highest rating of the caregiver's quality and language stimulation (a shift from one standard deviation below to one standard deviation above the mean) would result in "an improvement (relative to the mean) of about 50 percent in measures of children's school readiness, expressive language skill, and verbal comprehension" (Vandell and Wolfe 2000, 3). Blau (2001) reaches the more modest conclusion that two of the most carefully designed studies of quality imply elasticities of child development relative to child care quality of .03 to .09 for most measures and .07 to .27 for language skills relative to language stimulation.

Research linking child care quality to children's emotional well-being is more limited. The effects of child care on children's emotional and behavioral outcomes have been examined in studies of the effects of early maternal employment, reviewed earlier in this chapter, with ambiguous results. Studies that have included measures of child care mode and quality suggest that some of the negative effects may result from the experience of poor-quality care (for example, Han, Waldfogel, and Brooks-Gunn 2001). Among the most recent findings are those of the National Institute of Child Health and Human Development's Study of Early Child Care (forthcoming a, forthcoming b), a multisite study of the effects of early home and child care experiences. Recent results from this study suggest some evidence of increased behavior problems among four-and-a-half-year-old children who had early, and extensive, experience in child care. Among these children, however, those attending high-quality child care centers had fewer behavioral problems than those in poorer-quality care.

An important caveat in nearly all well-controlled studies is that family characteristics are far more predictive of child outcomes than is child care quality (Vandell and Wolfe 2000; Burchinal 1999).[10] Quality appears to makes a marginal, additional contribution to children's well-being. The effects of quality variation are particularly important, however, for more highly disadvantaged children. Children from low-income homes and those with less-educated mothers have been shown to benefit the most from high-quality care (and to suffer the most adverse outcomes from poor-quality care) in both experimental evaluations (Berlin et al. 1998; Ramey and Ramey 1998; Currie 2000; Karoly et al. 1998; Waldfogel 2002) and nonexperimental studies (Vandell and Corasaniti 1990; Baydar and Brooks-Gunn 1991; Bryant et al. 1994; Caughy, DiPietro, and Strobino 1994; Peisner-Feinberg and Burchinal 1997; and Burchinal et al. 2000).

The relatively greater importance of child care quality for disadvantaged children is underscored by the quite dramatically positive results of controlled evaluations of targeted, mostly public, early-intervention programs. Several decades' research on the federal Head Start program suggests that high-quality early education programs result in large initial cognitive gains for poor children and significant but more modest effects on later school achievement, grade completion, and high school graduation (see Barnett 1995 and Karoly et al. 1998 for reviews). The often-reported "fading" of early benefits is typically interpreted to mean that the developmental benefits of high-quality ECEC services are limited; it may be more appropriately understood, however, as an indictment of the quality of education that poor children receive after Head Start. A recent study by Janet Currie and Duncan Thomas (1995) finds that Head Start participation closes more than one-third of the gap in cognitive test scores between poor and more advantaged children and that this effect persists at least into adolescence for white children. White, but not African American, children who attend Head Start are also much less likely to have repeated a grade by the age of nine—more than closing the gap with their more affluent peers and reducing their risk of dropping out of high school by an estimated 5 percent. Although the authors are cautious in their interpretation, the size of the effects and racial differences suggest that high-quality ECEC may make a significant contribution to children's well-being but cannot serve as a life-long inoculation against other threats to the healthy development of poor children.

Conclusions About Early Childhood Education and Care

Substantial research establishes that high child care costs depress maternal employment. Simulations based on these estimates suggest that policies that reduce the cost of child care would increase the probability of employment and decrease the probability of public-assistance receipt, particularly among lower-income and less-skilled mothers, potentially closing employment and wage gaps between mothers and fathers with young children.

There is also substantial evidence suggesting that child care quality contributes to better child outcomes, particularly in the areas of cognitive development associated with school readiness. These contributions may be relatively modest for children from more advantaged backgrounds but are substantial for children from low-income families.

POLICY PACKAGES AND OUTCOMES ACROSS OUR TWELVE COMPARISON COUNTRIES

Although this review has concentrated on research linking individual policies to family and child outcomes, families and workers experience policies not singly and distinctly but as combinations or packages of policies. Family leave policies, working-time regulations, and early childhood education and care are bundled together within countries, along with income transfers, housing assistance, income-tax rules, and so on. Several researchers in comparative work and family policy have considered these national packages and related them to the outcomes reviewed here. The usual methodology is to quantify and combine several policy indicators into an index that can be associated with measures of outcomes such as women's attachment to paid work and gender equality at work and at home. Most of these studies are cross-sectional and limited to the industrialized countries or to the European welfare states. Constrained by small sample sizes (that is, the number of countries), most use simple correlations or one-variable regressions to assess the links between policy packages and outcomes.

Janet Gornick, Marcia Meyers, and Katherin Ross (1997) have constructed indexes of support for maternal employment across fourteen countries as of the mid-1980s; these policy indexes combine eleven elements of child care and (short-term) family leave policy. They assess the relation between the generosity of these policy packages and the likelihood that married mothers of young children were employed, relative to otherwise similar mothers in the same country whose children were older. They found strong positive associations between the policy-index values and the continuity of mothers' employment.

Haya Stier and Noah Lewin-Epstein (2001) assess the three-way relation between welfare state regime type (using the Esping-Andersen framework), specific policy provisions (using the Gornick, Meyers, Ross index), and the costs of interruptions in maternal employment on lifetime earnings. They estimate a series of logistic regression models and find that both the type of welfare-state regime and the generosity of the specific policy package are associated with women's employment patterns. They conclude that "welfare regime and female employment policies go a long way to explain the differential patterns of women's employment along the family life course" (Stier and Lewin-Epstein 2001, 1750). Specifically, generous child care and family leave provisions, in tandem, reduce the extent to which employment interruptions (when children are young) penalize wages later in life.

Janneke Plantenga and Johan Hansen (1999) have studied gender-equality outcomes in sixteen European countries. They constructed a composite indicator of gender equality in paid and unpaid work and classified these countries into four groups (from low to high) with reference to equality outcomes. They then scored the countries on six factors capturing "equal opportunities": economic growth, attitudes toward women's employment, family-taxation rules, working-time regulations, child care facilities, and leave arrangements. In a third step, the authors related the outcomes to the policy configurations. Acknowledging the methodological limits, they find a strong correlation between policy elements and gender-equality outcomes. In particular, the two countries with the most egalitarian outcomes—Denmark and Sweden—were also those with the strongest equal-opportunity factors across dimensions, with few exceptions.

Researchers for the OECD constructed a composite index of "work/family reconciliation policies and relevant flexible work arrangements" (OECD 2001a, 152). The index included five elements: child care coverage for children under three years of age, maternity-pay entitlements, voluntary family leave in firms (weighted down to reflect the lesser importance of extrastatutory provisions), flextime working, and voluntary part-time working. Using variation across eighteen countries, they correlated both the individual elements and the composite index scores with the employment rates of women aged thirty to thirty-four. They find that the composite index had a fairly high correlation, of just under 0.7, with the employment rate. The OECD researchers conclude that "this suggests the importance of work/family reconciliation measures of this type and also the importance of taking account of a range of such policies—this correlation is higher than that with any of the individual indicators" (OECD 2001a, 153).

Correlational studies such as these cannot establish a causal link between policies and outcomes. They cannot rule out reverse causation (for example, the possibility that high levels of female employment create demand for supportive policies) or the influence of other, unmeasured national characteristics (for example, the possibility that cultural values favoring gender equality explain both high levels of female labor force participation and the provision of supportive public policies). When interpreted in conjunction with the more methodologically rigorous studies described earlier in this chapter, many of which correct for these problems, research that combines indicators of several policy dimensions does provide useful illustrations of the association between total policy packages and outcomes.

We close this chapter by engaging in a similar exercise. Using a subset of the policy indicators reported in the tables in chapters 5 through 7, we construct several indexes of relative policy performance in our comparison countries. Given differences in the packages of policies available to families with children of different ages, we consider policies in two groups: those potentially affecting families with children from birth to the age of five and those affecting families with school-age children (aged six and above in most countries). (Details of the index construction are provided in appendix C.)

Figure 8.1 illustrates a comparison of country performance on each of these indexes and on a combined index that sums the two. Index A, for the younger children, includes indicators of public ECEC provision (entitlements, levels of provision, cost burden assumed by government, tax provisions, and quality features), family leave policy (length of leave, provisions for fathers, generosity of benefits, and provisions for sick-child leave), and working-time regulation (affecting weekly hours and vacation time).

With regard to provisions to families with children under the age of six, the Nordic countries of Denmark, Sweden, and Norway provide the most supportive total package of policies. In the highest-ranked country, Denmark, this package includes eighteen weeks of maternity leave at a high wage-replacement level, followed by paid parental leave with incentives for fathers' take-up,

FIGURE 8.1 **Index of Performance of Policies Regulating Family Leave, Working Time, Early Childhood Education and Care, and School Scheduling**

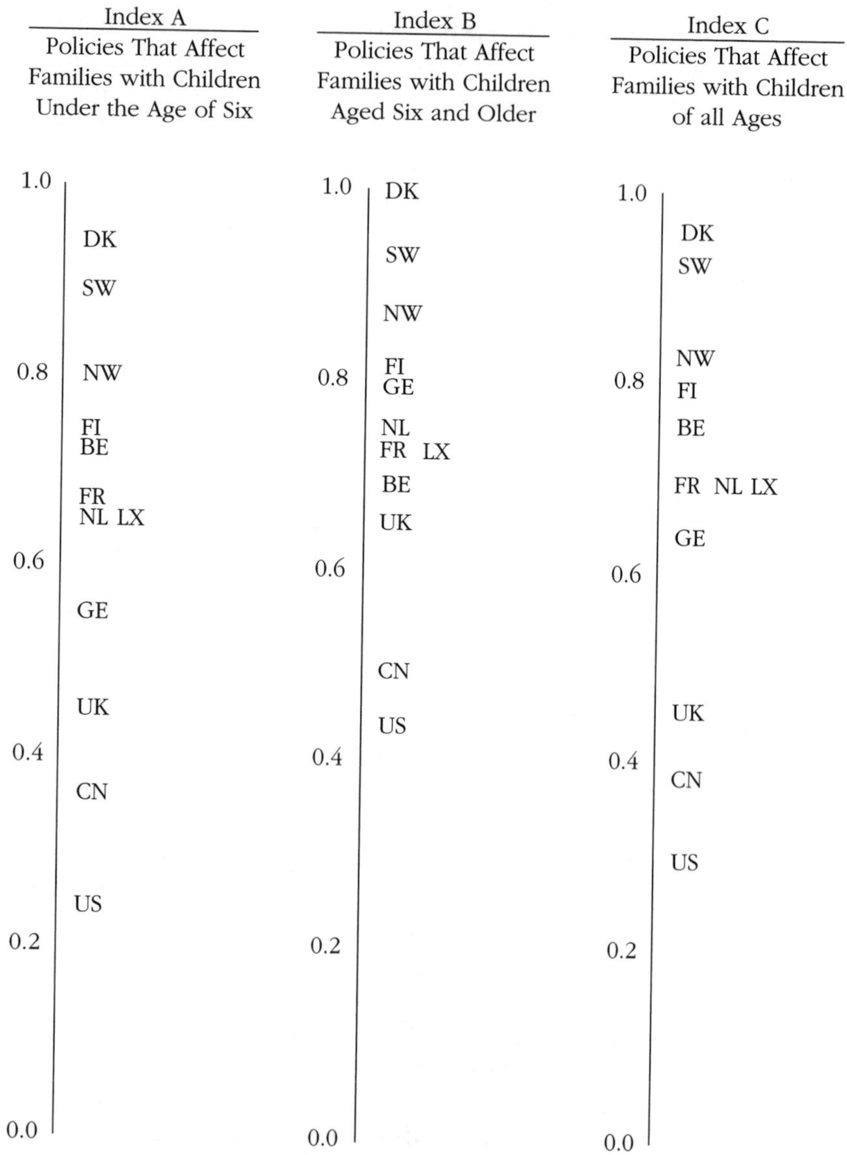

Index A	Index B	Index C
Policies That Affect Families with Children Under the Age of Six	Policies That Affect Families with Children Aged Six and Older	Policies That Affect Families with Children of all Ages

Index A

1.0

DK
SW

0.8 NW

FI
BE

FR
NL LX

0.6

GE

UK

0.4

CN

US

0.2

0.0

Index B

1.0 DK

SW

NW

FI
0.8 GE

NL
FR LX

BE

UK

0.6

CN

US

0.4

0.2

0.0

Index C

1.0

DK
SW

NW
0.8 FI

BE

FR NL LX

GE

0.6

UK

0.4 CN

US

0.2

0.0

Source: Authors' compilation.
Note: For index values, see appendix table C.3.

and the option to take fifty-two weeks of leave within any eighteen-month period to care for a seriously ill child; a thirty-seven-hour standard workweek and twenty-five days of paid vacation annually; and an integrated EduCare system that extends child-based entitlements to ECEC following parental leave periods, absorbs 75 percent or more of ECEC costs through income-adjusted parental fees, and employs highly trained providers who earn more, on average, than other female workers in the country.

The Continental European countries occupy a second tier. France and Belgium, for example, provide fifteen to sixteen weeks of well-paid maternity leave, followed by parental leave paid at a flat-rate (which means weak incentives for fathers' take-up), and five to ten days a year of paid sick-child leave; and a standard workweek of less than forty hours and twenty to twenty-five days of paid vacation. In terms of ECEC, these countries extend child-based entitlements to high-quality care provided by highly trained and well-compensated staff, but these entitlements extend only to children aged two and a half or three and older, and the hours of preschool services are often short or noncontinuous.

The United States and the other English-speaking countries fare poorly in this comparison. These countries provide much more limited paid family leave (with the exception of Canada, which provides parents access to long, but only moderately well-paid, leave) and no rights to paid sick-child days. Working-time protections are generally weak, especially in the United States and Canada, in both of which the standard workweek remains forty hours and vacation days lag behind those granted all across Europe. On ECEC policies, their highly privatized systems fail to guarantee either child care or preschool enrollment, leave families with a high cost burden, and they rely on markets to set staff qualification and compensation levels, which are generally low.

Our index of policies affecting older children (index B in figure 8.1) includes indicators of school schedules (primary-school starting age, hours and weeks of school operation, and continuity of the school day), relevant leave policies (sick-child leave), and working-time regulation (regulation of weekly hours and vacation time). On this package of policies, the Nordic countries of Denmark, Sweden, and Norway again rank the highest among our comparison countries, reflecting their generous entitlements to sick-child leave; standard workweeks in the range of thirty-seven to thirty-nine hours and twenty-one to twenty-five days of paid vacation annually; and school schedules that keep schools open many hours a week and many weeks a year. Most of the Continental European countries cluster together at a lower rank, despite strong working-time regulations, primarily because school schedules provide supervision for relatively few hours of the day and fewer weeks of the year, often with lunchtime breaks and part-day sessions.

The English-speaking countries lag behind the European countries on this index as well, although the gap is not so great. Provisions for sick-child leave are weak, as are working-time protections, especially in the United States and Canada; school schedules are continuous and moderately long in terms of weekly hours but average to short in weeks of the school year, particularly in the United States.

To illustrate the relation between these policies and outcomes, we make use of several of the comparative outcome indicators reported in chapter 3. We select indicators of the main goals that have defined our end vision of an earner-carer society: gender equality in the labor market, gender equality in the home, child well-being, and family economic security. Outcome indicators are constructed from a variety of multicountry data sets (measurement details are provided in chapter 3 unless otherwise noted). We associate these indicators to indexes reflecting packages of policies to which they are plausibly associated, theoretically or empirically.

Figure 8.2 associates national ECEC policies targeted on children in the three- to five-year-old age group with an indicator of the strength of maternal employment. The indicator of maternal employment is the effect of having a child aged three to five on mothers' likelihood of employment, relative to mothers in the same country whose youngest child is aged thirteen to seventeen, holding other maternal and family characteristics constant. Comparing intracountry differences rather than simple maternal-employment rates helps us to net out country-level factors that influence overall employment levels, and it allows us to isolate the effect of having young children specifically. (This is the same indicator presented in figure 3.5, except that here the differentials are net of control variables.)[11] As expected, this maternal-employment

FIGURE 8.2 **Association Between ECEC Policies and the Preschooler Effect on Mothers' Employment, Mid-1990s**

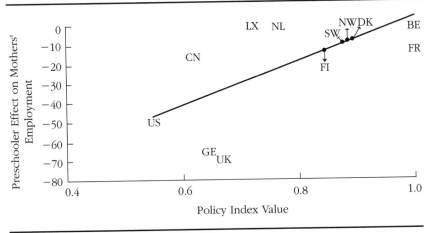

Source: Outcome data from LIS.
Note: Variable on vertical axis compares mothers with three- to five-year-olds to mothers with thirteen- to seventeen-year-olds, controlling for mother's age and education, total number of children, and other household income. Policy index refers to ECEC for children aged three-to-five.

outcome (the "preschooler effect") is negatively associated with ECEC policy packages. Mothers in the countries with the strongest ECEC policy packages are less likely to report sizable employment effects of having young children; mothers in the United States have access to the least adequate package of policies, and they report relatively large effects on employment of having young children.

Figure 8.3 illustrates the association between policies that regulate working time (specifically standard working hours) and long joint hours of employment.[12] The association is strongly negative. The United States does the least to regulate working time, and couples in the United States are the most likely—by a wide margin—to work a combined total of eighty hours a week or more. Parents in countries that do more to set limits on working time cluster together with much lower average rates of long weekly working hours.

FIGURE 8.3 **Association Between Working-Time Regulation and the Prevalence of Long Joint Weekly Work Hours Among Dual-Earner Couples with Children, Mid-1990s**

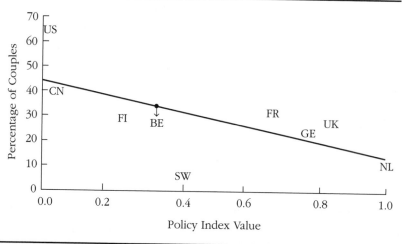

Source: Outcome data from LIS.
Note: Policy index captures regulation of normal weekly hours.

To consider the association between public policies and the prevalence of nonstandard-hour work, we use an index that reflects all the policies that are expected to affect parents' choice or necessity to work during evenings, nights, or weekends in response to the lack of alternative care arrangements for young children (index A). Figure 8.4 illustrates a negative association: countries with the least-supportive policies have the highest shares of parents working nonstandard hours. Once again, the United States stands out for having the least-supportive policies and the highest rate of nonstandard-hour work.

Figure 8.5 compares this same package of policies (index A) with an indicator of gender equality in the home: the ratio of fathers' to mothers' hours of child caregiving. On this outcome, the association with policy is inconsistent. Whereas the overall association is weak, the figure also suggests that within the clusters of countries—in particular, within the English-speaking and Nordic clusters—fathers' relative contribution to family child care rises with the strengths of family leave, child care, and working time

FIGURE 8.4 **Association Between Index A Policies and the Prevalence of Evening or Nighttime Work Among Employed Parents, 1997**

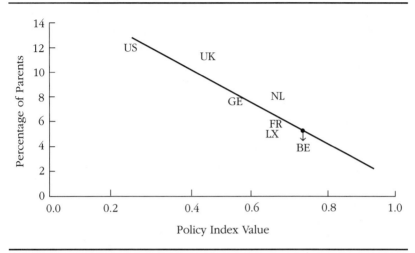

Source: Outcome data from European LFS and U.S. CPS.

FIGURE 8.5 **Association Between Index A Policies and Gender Equality in Mean Daily Hours Spent in Child Care at Home, 1985 to 1992.**

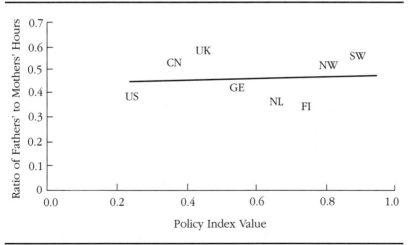

Source: Outcome data from MTUS.

provisions. Nevertheless, this policy package is not correlated in any straightforward way with gender differentials in caregiving at home.

Figures 8.6 and 8.7 link age-specific policy packages to indicators of child well-being. Child mortality (within five years of birth) has a reasonably strong negative association with the package of policies (index A) that are expected to provide parents with more time for caregiving and more-adequate alternatives to parental caregiving through public ECEC (figure 8.6). A strong negative association is also observed between an indicator of long hours (four hours or more) of television watching among eleven-year-old children and the package of policies (index B) reflecting public-school supervision for school-age children during parents' working hours combined with other measures that free up parents' time for caregiving (figure 8.7).

In our final illustration, we expand our comprehensive policy package to include expenditures on cash benefits for families, because family poverty is clearly shaped by both sets of policies. In figure 8.8, the horizontal axis reflects our comprehensive package of policies (index C, which relates to children of all ages)—policies governing the duration, benefits, and gender equality of leaves; policies that shape working time; policies affecting the availability, cost, and quality of ECEC; and policies affecting the supervision provided by public schools—combined with government cash benefits for families (reported in table 2.1).[13] The vertical axis indicates family poverty, measured as the percentage of families with income at or below 50 percent of country-specific median income. The policies in index C are expected to affect families' income security through various routes, for example, by facilitating continuous maternal employment and ensuring income during family leave and vacation periods. The cash-benefit policies have direct antipoverty effects through transferring income to families.

Figure 8.8 indicates that the association between the larger policy package and family poverty is strong and negative: countries that do more for families on these dimensions have sharply lower levels of family poverty. Additional analyses suggest that the work-family policies (captured in index C) may be responsible for a substantial share of the link. The correlation between family poverty and the larger policy package—work-family policies

FIGURE 8.6 **Association Between Index A Policies and Child Mortality Rates, 1999**

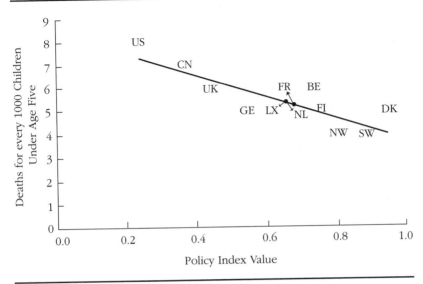

Source: Outcome data from UNICEF (2001).

FIGURE 8.7 **Association Between Index B Policies and the Prevalence of Television Watching Among Eleven-Year-Olds, 1997 to 1998**

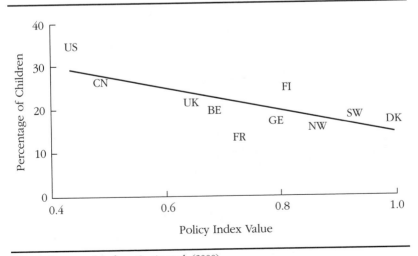

Source: Outcome data from Currie et al. (2000).
Note: Outcome is television watching for four or more hours per day.

FIGURE 8.8 **Association Between Index C Policies Combined with Index of Cash Benefits and the Poverty Rate Among Families with Children, Mid-1990s**

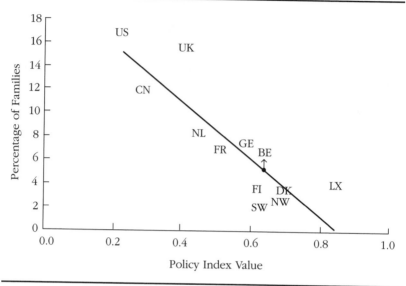

Source: Outcome data from LIS.

combined with benefits—is considerably stronger ($r = .87$) than the association with cash benefits alone ($r = .53$). This suggests that the policies described in this book may moderate family poverty by facilitating employment and employment-related income.

What can we learn from these analyses? Without more extensive controls for other country-level characteristics associated with these outcomes—from demographic characteristics to labor market structures and cultural values—we cannot interpret these associations to mean that these policies fully explain the outcomes. They illustrate, rather than prove, many of the associations that have been established in more fully controlled studies reviewed earlier in this chapter. They demonstrate that the pattern of cross-national variation in policy provisions is in many cases quite similar to the pattern of variation in the outcomes that concern us. They also suggest that progress toward the goals of an earner-carer society—greater gender equality, child well-being, and family economic security—has been best achieved in countries that have developed the most supportive packages of leave, working-time policies, ECEC, and school scheduling. They also suggest an important caution. Some goals may be more policy sensitive, and thus more readily achieved, than others. Shortening employment hours, for example, may be easier than changing complex, private behaviors such as the division of child caregiving responsibilities in the home.

—— Chapter 9 ——

Developing Earner-Carer Policies in the United States

O UR SURVEY OF policy in other industrialized countries suggests that government policies that support parents in their earning and caring roles are institutionally and economically feasible. The empirical literature is encouraging regarding the potential of these policies to grant parents time for caregiving, to promote gender equality, and to enhance child well-being. Cross-national comparisons also reveal the exceptionalism of the United States, however, particularly in the paucity of contemporary policy provisions. This raises questions about whether and how we might develop more-supportive family leave, working-time, child care, and school scheduling policies in this country.

The United States is exceptional, in cross-national terms, not only in the absence of social policy but also in the diversity of the population, the extent of single parenthood and poverty, the structure of labor markets, and the decentralization of policy-making authority. Political culture also sets the United States apart from our European counterparts. Americans are unusually enthusiastic about private-market solutions and dubious about using government, especially the national government, to allocate resources. These contextual differences raise important questions about the value of looking abroad for policy models, but they do not rule out possibilities for policy development. We close this volume by posing and then addressing some of the most salient of these objections. In the latter part of this chapter we reflect on two other objections voiced by those who are skeptical about the possibilities for change in gender roles and workplace practices more generally.

"THE UNITED STATES IS TOO DIVERSE TO SUPPORT INCLUSIVE POLICIES"

Under the right conditions, it is possible and fruitful to draw policy lessons across national borders. Many critics argue, however, that contextual differences are simply too great to allow fruitful lessons to be drawn for the United States from the welfare states of Europe and even from Canada. The extent of racial, ethnic, and national diversity strikes many as the most important dimension on which the United States differs from other wealthy industrialized countries. The population of the United States is remarkably diverse in terms of race and ethnicity; nearly 10 percent of residents are foreign born, and just over one-quarter are African American, Hispanic, Asian or Pacific Islander, or Native American. Critics often portray this as an insurmountable barrier to lesson-drawing from abroad, arguing that the generosity of the European welfare states, in particular, is possible only because the populations of these countries are so homogeneous.

This caution deserves to be taken seriously. Our comparative study of policies in other countries suggests that the most successful and resilient policies are broadly inclusive, providing similar options to all families and creating strong and broad-based support for their continuation. The United States does not have a similar history of inclusive social provision. Welfare state scholars have frequently explained this exceptionalism in terms of deep racial and ethnic cleavages and resistance to policies that redistribute across these divides (Quadagno 1994; Gilens 1999). In recent years, fissures have grown particularly wide when social programs are seen to benefit recent immigrants.

Racism and other social cleavages are formidable problems in the United States, and they are likely to fuel resistance to redistributive family policies. The policy designs described in the chapters of this book do not target provisions along race, ethnic, nativity, or other lines; one of the most consistent features of the European models is inclusiveness. These policies are redistributive, however, from families without to families with children, from older to younger workers, and from more- to less-advantaged families. Political resistance to such policies in the United States has so far centered on transfers from nonparents to parents (see, for example, Burkett 2000); with more extensive provisions and a larger price tag, opposition that is explicitly or implicitly tied to race, class, and other divides is more likely.

Although these cleavages are formidable, there are also compelling reasons to believe that they do not have to be an insurmountable barrier to the development of more supportive family policies. The history of U.S. social policy itself provides some encouragement. Policies that benefit all earner-carer families are not "welfare" in the traditional sense. Indeed, policies that support parents in their dual roles are deeply consonant with the traditional American values of personal responsibility to both paid work and the family. They are a logical complement to the welfare "reform" efforts of the 1990s that have emphasized parental employment and reductions in welfare reliance. History suggests that it is possible to mobilize broad support for social policies that fall outside of the welfare context. Social Security—which includes old-age, survivors, and disability benefits—is the most striking example of the political resiliency of universal programs. These programs have become more inclusive over time, and the redistributive structure of benefits has survived years of heated debate and efforts to restructure and privatize the basic provisions.

The European experience provides further encouragement. Although generous social welfare provisions in Europe are often credited to the homogeneity of the population, most European countries have levels of immigration that are as high as or higher than those of the United States. Nearly 10 percent of residents across Europe as a whole are foreign born, about the same share as in the United States. The immigrant share of the population is nearly twice that high in Canada and even higher in some European countries; in Luxembourg, for example, nearly one of every three residents is foreign born (OECD 2001c).

Nearly all of Europe grapples with complex ethnic and linguistic diversity, but this diversity has not prevented these countries from maintaining inclusive social welfare programs that cover legal immigrants as well as racial and ethnic minorities. Rather than dividing the population, the extension of social rights to all residents is intended to promote inclusion. Universal preschool programs are particularly notable in this regard. An OECD survey of public ECEC policies in Europe notes, for example, that several countries—including Belgium, Denmark, Finland, the Netherlands, Norway, Sweden—have adopted policies explicitly aimed at "increasing access to early childhood services for immigrant and ethnic minority groups in order to expose children and families to the language and traditions of mainstream society, and provide opportunities for parents to establish social contacts and networks" (OECD 2001d, 25). Some American observers have reported with amusement that the école in France provides children with lessons on French culture—including the distinctions among French cheeses. These lessons reflect, in part, the commitment to extend preschool to all children in France in the interest of promoting social solidarity. Nearly all immigrant parents in France choose to enroll their children in preschool.

Immigration is growing all across Europe (OECD 2001c). Both large and small welfare states are grappling with the arrival of ever greater numbers of immigrants, refugees, asylum seekers, and economic migrants. As populations are becoming more heterogeneous, there are clear signs of political strain and polarization along ethnic and nativity lines. These strains are most evident in the rise of anti-immigrant and other explicitly racist political movements in many of the European democracies. To date, however, this political polarization has not translated into either wholesale or selective reductions in social benefits in these countries. The countries from which we have drawn our lessons continue to provide generous social benefits and continue to provide them inclusively. Although some European countries have trimmed some social programs—most notably, old-age pensions, unemployment insurance, and disability pensions—these restructurings have not had the effect of replicating racial, ethnic, or class divides through social welfare policies. The basic structures and functions of the social welfare states remain strong in the face of growing population diversity in part because their inclusive structures create broad political support.

"AMERICAN PARENTS WANT TO
MAKE THEIR OWN CHOICES"

Issues of parental choice are also particularly salient in U.S. policy debates. In cross-national terms, Americans do appear to be deeply concerned about the protection of individual choice and freedom from government interference. Critics often suggest that the highly centralized and standardized policy approaches of Europe would be a poor fit to a society in which individuals expect to exercise choice in the consumption of everything from athletic shoes to their children's education.

In the area of family policy, these concerns are often related to issues of diversity. It is all well and good, some argue, for all French children to attend the same preschool program and learn about national cheeses, but American parents want to be free to choose the type of care their children receive. The political pollster Ed Goeas, for example, observes that "people do believe that 'It takes a village to raise a child,' but they want a village that expresses the values and beliefs they have" (Sylvester 2001, 9). In "The Advancing Nanny State," Darcy Olsen, of the conservative Cato Institute, argues even more pointedly that the creativity of private and community solutions "should not be replaced with a set of rigid standards, which run roughshod over the individual needs of parents and children. As parents know, every child has unique needs that cannot be met by a uniform code" (Olsen 1997, 16).

Americans are justifiably sensitive about their right to preserve their own beliefs and cultural practices, and this sensitivity is particularly acute on family issues. As our data in chapter 2 suggest, however, families also share a number of common challenges, dilemmas, and problems. Problems of balancing work and family are often portrayed as the concern of high-achieving, two-career families. In reality, the time squeeze on parents, the difficulty of finding high-quality child care, and the social and economic penalties that parents incur by assuming most of the responsibility of caring for children are not unique to affluent or poor, white or black, native-born or immigrant, gay or straight families. They cut across the lines of class, race, ethnicity, and sexual preference.

Policies that would reduce these dilemmas can and should be equally inclusive, without violating the rights of families and communities to determine the precise shape of policy provisions. Casting European-style social policies as inconsistent with these goals is misleading for at least two reasons.

First, although the policies we have described are generally national in terms of authorizing legislation and financing, they are flexible enough to allow individuals and communities to tailor them to their own preferences. In the case of family leave, for example, parents in several of the Nordic countries have a nationally established and financed entitlement to a set period of leave. They have enormous flexibility, however, in scheduling their use of that leave. Parents may elect to use all their benefits within the first months after childbirth, or they may stretch their leave out over a period of several years, combining part-time employment with part-time leave. In some countries, such as Finland, they may even elect to take their benefits in the form of leave or subsidized child care. Choice is protected in ECEC provisions as well; the EduCare systems in the Nordic countries, for example, set overarching objectives at the national level but tailor specific program designs at the community level. Flexibility and parental choice are guiding principles in the expansion of ECEC throughout Europe. The 1992 Council of Ministers Recommendation on Childcare for the European Union notes, for example, that principles for the development of services for young children should include "close and responsive relations between services and parents and local communities, diversity and flexibility of services, and increased choice for parents" (European Forum for Child Welfare 2003).

A second and more compelling reason to question the claim that European systems provide less choice is the reality that the "choices" of many American parents are profoundly constrained by economic and other circumstances. In many respects, American parents have fewer choices than their European and Canadian counterparts because minimal and fragmented social provisions do not extend parental choice so much as they force parents to choose among undesirable alternatives. The lack of strong working-time regulations, for example, may leave employers with a great deal of choice about working hours. American workers, however, are more likely than their European counterparts to face a choice between forty-hour-a-week employment and no employment, or between working mandatory overtime and losing their jobs. The lack of paid family leave and subsidized child care forces equally difficult choices on many families. In the absence of leave entitlements, most parents face the choice of returning to work twelve weeks after childbirth or quitting their jobs. In the absence of affordable child care, they must choose between reducing their working hours to care for their own children and reducing their effective earnings by purchasing substitute child care.

Issues of parental choice have particular salience in U.S. debates about subsidized child care. Substitute child care arrangements are far more diverse in the United States than in most of the European countries we have examined. Promotion of "parental choice" in care arrangements has been a central feature of public child care policy in the United States and is formally incorporated in federal child care subsidy programs (Hofferth 1999). It is possible that more American parents than French parents "choose" to rely on relative babysitters for their three- and four-year-old children because they believe that their children are better off with relatives. It is equally plausible, however, that for many this "choice" is an accommodation to the lack of alternatives that are both affordable and of acceptable quality. The empirical research reviewed in chapter 8 suggests that parents' child care choices are highly sensitive to price. Given the choice, many if not most, might well choose to enroll their children in free or minimal-cost child care and public preschool programs.

"AMERICAN FAMILIES HAVE GREATER NEEDS: SINGLE PARENTS"

Crafting policies for earner-carer families with two parents is challenging. Adapting these policies to the needs of single-parent families is even more difficult. These challenges may be particularly great in the United States, where the rate of single parenthood is high in comparative terms (Bradbury and Jantti 1999). Given the prevalence of single parenthood in the United States, some critics argue that it is impossible to design family policies that meet the needs of both two- and one-parent families. The European experience suggests otherwise. Policies that support both earning and caring can provide an important first tier of support that actually reduces the need for targeted, welfare-based assistance.

Although the proportion of families headed by single parents is higher in the United States than in most of our comparison countries, the challenge of fitting social policies to the needs of lone parents is not uniquely American. The needs of these parents may be greater in the United States, however, because current social policies marginalize them from the labor market and from mainstream society through residual assistance that is available only to the most highly disadvantaged. What is often termed the "social safety net" provides American families with little in the way of direct government help unless they are poor enough to qualify for means-tested public assistance (welfare), health insurance, housing, or child care. This system of residual assistance virtually guarantees that those receiving assistance are single, highly disadvantaged in terms of education and human capital, and among the most socially and economically marginalized members of society. Recent welfare "reforms" have been designed to increase the labor market attachments of those receiving assistance. These policies do little, however, to increase the human capital of recipients, and they have been only marginally successful in providing the types of supportive assistance—such as health insurance and child care—that could decrease the social and economic isolation of parents and children.

The other industrialized countries from which we have drawn our lessons premise most family policies on a fundamentally different conception of the role of government. By structuring family leave benefits as social insurance, they distribute the costs of child rearing across families and across the life span. By regulating working time, they protect the rights of all workers, often with special considerations for parents of young children. By providing ECEC as a child- or parent-based entitlement, they ensure widespread access to affordable, high-quality substitute care. By providing other forms of basic support—for example, health care and housing assistance—they relieve families of financial burdens that may be particularly unmanageable for single parents. Although each of these countries also provides means-tested cash assistance to the poorest families, far fewer of their families fall through the cracks in these social protections to land in the "social safety net" targeted on the most disadvantaged.

These institutional arrangements are important because they reduce the challenge of providing extra support for lone parents in an earner-carer society. Policies granting leave, regulating working time, and ensuring ECEC provide a first tier of support for single parents. These policies also facilitate employment as a first line of economic support within the family. Not surprisingly, as of 1996 the percentage of lone mothers who are in paid employment was substantially higher in nearly all of our comparison countries than in the United States (Bradshaw et al. 1996).

The absence of this first tier of support makes the challenge of assisting single mothers particularly daunting in the United States.[1] Single mothers in the United States are likely to face even more acute financial dilemmas than their married counterparts when they lose a job at the time of childbirth, pay a wage penalty for electing part-time work, or rely on their earnings to purchase child care. Extension of paid leave, working-time, and ECEC benefits would have particularly positive consequences for these families and could substantially reduce the need for extra forms of assistance.

Although policies that support earner-carer families are important, we would not argue that they are all that is needed to help single parents. Even with these programs in place, lone mothers in Europe are seen as needing extra support. This extra support comes in the form of universal family allowances supplemented by special lone-parent allowances and systems for assured child support. The expansion of similar forms of support would be a necessary adjunct to ensure the economic security of single parents in the United States as well. Given exceptionally high rates of single parenthood in the United States, these benefits are likely to be costly. The key lessons from the experiences of these other countries is that this combination of benefits can be effective in ensuring the economic security of single-parent families and that they can be provided in ways that foster employment and social inclusion.

"AMERICAN FAMILIES HAVE GREATER NEEDS II: LOW WAGES AND POVERTY"

The United States differs from most European countries in another important respect that has implications for the adoption of European-style family policies: far more of our workers are employed in low-wage jobs. Some critics argue that earner-carer policies, and issues of gender equality in the home and market, are largely irrelevant for families who are struggling to make ends meet on low earnings. The problem of low-wage employment is a serious one in the United States and poses challenges for the achievement of an earner-carer society. The policies we have described would not, in isolation, ensure the economic security of these families or allow them to make more gender-egalitarian choices about their division of work. They would, however, provide important assistance and could help reduce existing disparities in families' burdens and support.

About 25 percent of American full-time workers earn less than 65 percent of national median earnings, compared with fewer than 15 percent of workers in France, Germany, and the Netherlands and about 5 percent in the rest of our comparison countries (Smeeding 2002). Low-wage employment is a major factor underlying the exceptionally high rates of family poverty seen in the United States; the cross-country correlation between the child-poverty rate and the percentage of low-wage workers is about 0.9 (Smeeding 2002).

Low-wage employment may also create serious barriers to the promotion of gender equality. Our "thought experiment" about working time (in chapter 4) suggests that given leaves with adequate wage replacement, mothers and fathers would be able to devote substantial time to caregiving in the first months after childbirth without a major loss of income; beyond this period, mothers and fathers could reallocate their employment hours to achieve greater gender equality without a net reduction in family labor supply. Even with these policies, however, low-earning parents would have trouble making ends meet. Low-wage work, even when supplemented by the Earned Income Tax Credit, leaves many fully employed families living at or near poverty; even full wage replacement during family leave periods would leave them at the margins of self-sufficiency. Few parents working for low wages would be able to benefit from working-time regulations that allowed them to reduce their standard workweek, shift temporarily to part-time schedules, or forgo the extra compensation afforded by working nonstandard-hour schedules. Moreover, fathers are generally the higher earners, so a reallocation of market time "from him to her" is likely to be infeasible in low-income families.

The precarious financial circumstances of many American families are a challenge to the development of an earner-carer society. They are also a compelling justification for the initiation and expansion of policies that support parents' ability to care, and care equally, for their children. Policies that support earner-carer families could make a particularly significant contribution to the economic security of families headed by a low-wage worker—relieving these families of the costs of financing their own absences from the workplace at the time of childbirth, lost wages when they take time off from work to care for a sick child, and the costs of purchasing child care.

These policies could also greatly increase equality across families that vary in economic resources. A recent study of work-family conflict in low-income families concludes that in comparison with more affluent families, working-poor families have both significantly higher caregiving demands—for example, for disabled and chronically ill family members—and fewer resources in the form of job benefits, flexibility, and supportive assistance from the workplace (Heymann et al. 2002). In the absence of inclusive public family leave, working-time, and ECEC policies, options for earner-carer parents are in fact highly regressive: the lowest earners have the least access to paid leave and vacation time and also have the poorest-quality child care arrangements.

Even the most generous earner-carer policies alone, however, cannot ensure the economic security of low-earning families or provide them with realistic options for choosing more gender-equal allocations of time between the market and the home. To support parents' time for caregiving without sacrificing gender equality, government would have to do more to help low-earning families. In cross-national terms, the United States does relatively little to shore up the income of low earners. It spends far less than all of our comparison countries on active labor market policies that could increase employment options and market wages or improve human capital and earnings potential.[2] Although the Earned Income Tax Credit provides crucial wage supplementation for some families, it is not sufficient to ensure economic security for families in which adults work at the lowest-wage jobs; the United States provides no universal income transfers for families (for example, family allowances); and unemployment insurance is meager (especially for low-earning mothers).

As is the case with single parents, the United States faces a greater challenge than its European counterparts and Canada in ensuring economic security for families headed by a low-wage worker. There is no simple or inexpensive solution to this problem. The exceptionally large proportion of families who earn too little to allow self-sufficiency will not diminish unless government does more to help raise wages or supplement market income. Even with substantial improvements in earned income, these families will have trouble making ends meet without more help with health-care and housing expenses.

The issues that arise in designing policies to support low-wage workers, and the costs and benefits of alternative designs, are well beyond the scope of this volume. The policies we have described do not offer a complete solution. Nevertheless, implementation of these policies would contribute to a solution by relieving families of a portion of the direct and indirect costs of child rearing. Moreover, they would provide this assistance in a form that resonates with American values of work and family responsibility by supporting parents in both their earning and caregiving roles.

"THESE PROGRAMS HAVE UNINTENDED CONSEQUENCES FOR FERTILITY"

Policies that provide assistance specifically to families with children raise questions, in the minds of many, about collateral effects on fertility and family formation. In the European context, these questions arise from concerns about declining fertility and the possibility that work-family policies are actually contributing to falling birthrates. In the United States, critics suggest that generous social welfare policies could increase birthrates and decrease marriage rates, particularly among nonemployed mothers. Given these concerns, many observers question the wisdom of borrowing European social policy models that have had a "pronatalist" orientation.

The European debate about family formation has been motivated largely by the problem of declining fertility. In most of the European countries, as in nearly all high-income countries, rising childlessness and shrinking family size have pushed the total fertility rate (TFR) below the replacement level of 2.1 births, on average, for each woman.[3] Although fertility remains relatively near replacement level (1.7 or higher) in a number of European countries—including Denmark, Finland, France, and Norway—in others, the TFR has dropped to below 1.5. Particularly worrisome cases include Germany, where the TFR is 1.3, and Italy, where it has fallen to 1.2 (Bureau of the Census 2002a). If current patterns are not reversed, countries with very low fertility rates will face serious social, economic, and cultural dislocations in the future. In Italy, for example, if 1995 fertility and longevity are projected forward one hundred years, the country's population would drop to 14 percent of its current level, and in Germany, to 17 percent (McDonald 2000b). The effects of population declines of these magnitudes would be enormous. In the absence of extreme levels of immigration, there would simply be too few workers to sustain economic growth—much less the security of retirees and other social welfare recipients.

These trends have prompted some observers to argue that policies such as those described in this book may have contributed to the destabilization of the European family by pushing or pulling women into the labor market and away from childbearing. In fact, variation within Europe suggests that the policy story, if it exists, is more complex. The Australian demographer Peter McDonald (2000a, 2000b) argues that two distinct fertility scenarios are possible in countries that provide women with substantial opportunities in both education and labor market entry. In countries in which it is feasible to blend employment and childbearing, without major losses in labor market status and earnings, many women will choose both paid work and parenting. In countries in which it is more difficult to combine motherhood and employment, because of conservative family cultures combined with weak social policies, large numbers of women will forgo childbearing. Although other factors are influential as well, these predictions are consistent with variation across the countries in this study. Moreover, there is some evidence that recent policy expansions may be nudging fertility back toward optimal levels in some countries (see, for example, INSEE 2002). Countries with the most generous work-family programs and high levels of employment—including the Nordic countries and France—are among those experiencing the least decline in fertility; fertility crises are most severe in countries with less fully developed work-family policies.

Although it is tempting to draw a causal inference, this finding is correlational, and causality could run in any of a number of directions. A large body of research has failed to find substantial or consistent effects of policy on fertility outcomes (see, for example, Gauthier and Hatzius 1997). As McDonald notes, "The generally held wisdom is that past and present pronatalist policies have been largely ineffective" (McDonald 2000b, 3). What appears certain is that generous work-family programs are consistent with high levels of fertility in conjunction with high rates of maternal employment, and no meaningful evidence suggests that these programs are harmful in this regard.

Although there is limited evidence that European family policies have had either a positive or negative effect on fertility, these policies have often been framed in pronatalist terms in European policy debates. In the wake of two world wars that devastated their populations, several countries enacted or expanded family policies—including cash benefits, family leave programs, and public child care—in the hopes of encouraging women to bear more children. In recent years, pronatalism has experienced a revival as a motivation for family policy in Europe (McDonald 2000b). Although important, pronatalism has been only one justification for these policies. Family policies have been expanded to address a number of different goals over the years, from achieving social rights and strengthening social inclusion to increasing gender equality and protecting family time (OECD 2001c).

Although pronatalism is only one of several motivations for European family policy, it raises particularly grave concerns about policy borrowing in the minds of some American observers. Whereas Europeans have worried that generous social programs are contributing to fertility declines, many Americans have been preoccupied with the possibility that generous social programs might raise fertility among certain vulnerable populations. In the United States, where rates of single parenthood are exceptionally high, many of the most vocal critics of social policy aimed at families with children have argued that generous social benefits available to single parents create incentives for (or at least increase the economic feasibility of) nonmarital childbearing. Some worry about public benefits provided to high-income single parents, but the most pressing concerns are raised about single women with no ties, or limited ties, to paid work.

Although the employment disincentives of cash-assistance programs are well established, particularly for mothers, the empirical evidence linking social policies to nonmarital childbearing is at best inconsistent (for reviews, see Moffitt 1990; Acs 1995; Peters, Plotnick, and Jeong 2001). Policy effects, where they have been found, appear to operate through choices about marriage and living arrangements rather than through choices about childbearing. Virtually all of this research has examined the effects of cash assistance to the nonemployed (that is, welfare) and, more recently, of child-support enforcement, and it has concentrated on women with weak ties to the labor market.

These studies offer no persuasive theoretical reason or empirical evidence to suggest that the policies described here would increase childbearing among single women who are not attached to employment. Policies that support women who combine employment and child rearing have the potential to increase employment among single women who are already mothers. Because they are predicated on employment, they are unlikely to have the contrary effect of encouraging single women with little or no attachment to employment to have children.

Although work-family policies would not be expected to encourage single women to have children, the possibility remains that they could enable women with children to live outside of marriage by contributing to the economic feasibility of that choice. American critics of European-style family policies often point to the increase in nonmarital childbearing in Europe, particularly in the Nordic countries that have notably generous packages of cash benefits and work-family policies. This criticism is largely unwarranted, however, because the majority of unmarried parents in most European countries are in stable, cohabiting relationships. As Kathleen Kiernan observes, "The increases in nonmarital childbearing in the majority of European countries are attributable to women having babies within a cohabiting union. . . . With the notable exception of Great Britain, there is little evidence of a movement to solo motherhood" (Kiernan 2001, 107).

The extent to which supportive work-family policies would contribute to the formation of single-parent households in the United States remains unknown. Although there is some evidence linking traditional forms of welfare assistance targeted on single mothers to the formation of single-parent households, the effects of universal family leave, working-time regulations, and ECEC on marital decisions have received virtually no theoretical or empirical study. Policies that support women in combining earning and caring could make single parenthood more economically feasible. It is equally possible, however, that these policies—by extending support to married as well as single parents and by extending benefits equally to mothers and to fathers—would increase the attractiveness of marital childbearing and create new incentives for fathers to remain connected to their children.

"THESE PROGRAMS ARE HARMFUL TO THE MACROECONOMY: LOOK AT UNEMPLOYMENT IN EUROPE"

Throughout the 1980s and much of the 1990s, unemployment rates across Europe were much higher than those in the United States; some European countries experienced double-digit unemployment rates. Many Americans, especially in the business world, argue that the United States should not borrow policy ideas from Europe because these social policies and labor market regulations have actually caused Europe's unemployment woes. As the argument goes, high social insurance taxes raise labor costs, which lower the demand for labor; demand is further depressed by labor market regulations that, for example, restrict employers' options to fire workers when consumer demand takes a downturn.

The claim that social welfare provisions weaken the economy has been aimed broadly at everything from old-age pensions to unemployment insurance to work-family programs. The conservative Employment Policy Foundation, for example, argues that "the United States should not emulate the work-family policies of Europe unless America is willing to endure double-digit unemployment and other European economic problems" (Employment Policy Foundation 2000). This line of thinking has filtered into popular discourse, in part because it has been widely reported in the American press. Seth Ackerman (1999) reports that American news outlets published six hundred articles between the mid-1980s and the late 1990s on the unhealthy effects of European social protection—dubbed "Eurosclerosis" by *Time* magazine.[4]

It is true that the United States experienced a remarkable period of job growth in the 1990s. A more sober read of the evidence provides little support, however, for the conclusion that Europe lagged behind the United States during this period because of its social and labor market policies (Blank and Freeman 1994; Blanchard and Wolfers 1999; Nickell 1997; Siebert 1997). In a *Journal of Economic Perspectives* review of the literature, Stephen Nickell (1997) concludes that some features of the welfare state do seem to drive up unemployment rates—in particular, unemployment benefits paid for extremely long duration, coupled with weak active labor market policies. Other welfare state and labor market features, however—such as high payroll taxes, high overall taxes, strict employment-protection legislation, high unionization, and high benefit-replacement rates—have been no less common in high-employment than in low-employment countries. The economists Rebecca Blank and Richard Freeman, in a review of "the case against social protection" and "the case against the case against social protection," conclude that "there is little empirical evidence for large trade-offs between labor market flexibility and social protection programs in general. At the present state of knowledge, the best attitude toward the trade-off hypothesis is one of open-minded skepticism" (Blank and Freeman 1994, 36).[5]

The argument that European-style social policies and labor

market regulations are incompatible with strong economic performance has been rendered nearly moot by recent rebounds in most of the European economies. During the 1990s, most of the European countries entered periods of recovery; as of 2002, the average unemployment rate was less than 8 percent across Europe and less than 5 percent in some of the most extensive welfare states, including Denmark, Sweden, and the Netherlands. Unemployment in about half of the European countries was still higher than in the United States, but not substantially so.

Of particular relevance for the issues in this volume, the recent economic recoveries in Europe have been achieved without major reversals in public spending on family policy. Labor market deregulation and welfare state restructuring have been prominent issues on political agendas across Europe in recent decades. Several European countries have substantially loosened labor market regulations that, for example, restricted employers from hiring temporary workers or from opening during nonstandard hours. Some social programs have been scaled back in some countries; restructuring has been most common in old-age pensions, in response to worries about rapidly rising old-age dependency ratios, and in programs that economists identified as harmful to (male) labor supply, including long-term unemployment compensation and disability benefits. Although important, these adjustments were relatively modest and did little to weaken the basic structures of social provision. (For a review of European welfare state restructuring, see Pierson 2001; for a review of expenditure trends, see Gornick forthcoming.)

Restructuring of the European welfare states has been, contrary to American press accounts, quite modest in general. In the midst of these changes, the policies at the heart of this book were singled out for protection and expansion in nearly every European country.[6] Between 1980 and 1995, average public spending on cash transfers to families (for each child) increased by more than 50 percent in Europe. Bolstered by decision making at the EU level, provisions for family leave were expanded in several countries, and entirely new programs were introduced in others; public investments in early childhood education grew nearly everywhere during this period (Gornick and Meyers 2001). In our view, the European experience provides encouraging evidence that these family policies are economically feasible, even in fiscal hard times.

"THESE PROGRAMS ARE NATIONAL, AND MOST CURRENT POLICY EFFORTS IN THE UNITED STATES ARE STATE-BASED"

Most of the European and Canadian social policies described in this volume are national in scope. With a few exceptions, family leave rights are established at the national level, and benefits are financed through national or nationally mandated social insurance funds; working-time conditions are set in national legislation or through nationally coordinated collective-bargaining schemes; and ECEC services are financed by national and regional or local funding and subject to national quality standards and oversight. Even the federalist countries among our comparison cases—Germany, Belgium, and Canada—have, for the most part, built their family policy systems at the national level.

In contrast, most social policy and many of the most promising new initiatives in work-family policy in the United States are state-based. A critic of drawing lessons from the European experience may well ask whether the national systems of Europe provide any useful guidance for the more federalist U.S. system. We believe that they do and that we should look to our own history of successful efforts to create comprehensive national approaches.

State-level control over many aspects of social and family policies is a legacy of both the federalist structure of U.S. government and the early traditions of localized assistance to the poor. States are also the locus of many of the current efforts to expand family policy. Legislatures in several states are considering paid family leave bills that would extend unemployment insurance or temporary disability insurance benefits to parents during periods of family leave; a smaller number of states are considering allowing low-income parents to cash out their child care subsidies so that they can provide their own infant care at home. State legislators in a few states are weighing proposals to prohibit compulsory overtime or establish daily-overtime pay premiums. States have historically set policy for public child care subsidies and quality control; many are currently expanding public pre-kindergarten programs and initiating new quality-enhancement programs such as tiered subsidy-reimbursement structures and wage supplements for child care professionals.

These state initiatives are important, but they are unlikely to provide the comprehensive and inclusive support that American families need and deserve. One of the important lessons from Europe is that family policies are most equitable when they combine national entitlements and funding with flexibility for families and communities. Although state-based initiatives are important, they are unlikely to produce a coherent national family policy in the United States. In the most optimistic scenario, a subset of states would develop comprehensive packages of family policies; another subset would pass a patchwork of improvements; and the remaining states—in all likelihood, the poorest states—would make little progress at all. Until state efforts "go to scale" as national policies, however, their reach will remain limited. States have far more restricted revenue bases than the federal government. Nearly all are legally required to balance their budgets, limiting the magnitude of the investments they can make and forcing direct tradeoffs when state revenues fall. Given these limitations, states are unlikely to provide substantial benefits or to extend benefits to all potentially eligible families.

Policies that are supportive of an earner-carer society will require more than incremental state-by-state tinkering with existing social policy institutions. Many of our current policies are not working for earner-carer families precisely because they are provided across uncoordinated and overlapping government jurisdictions, localized in financing and delivery, and supported by fragmented constituencies. A meaningful and effective expansion will require a retooling of the system to create new institutions and financing mechanisms at the national level, along with appropriate delivery systems at the state and local levels.

Is there reason for optimism about policy development at the national level? We see at least two possible avenues. First, the United States has a history of state-level social welfare initiatives "trickling up" to become either fully national programs (as happened with retirement pensions) or federal-state programs that create incentives for state participation (as happened with unemployment insurance). Policy developments in the most progressive of the states may be laying a foundation and developing models for national-level policies of the future. Second, American history also provides examples of "big bangs" in the development of national policy. Major national policies have been adopted under both Democratic and Republican administrations, both in times of crisis (for example, the New Deal) and in times of economic prosperity (for example, the War on Poverty).

Although most family policy in the United States is controlled at the state level, some mechanisms are already in place for an expansion of the federal role. The Family and Medical Leave Act provides a base for the enactment of paid family leave. Social-insurance-based wage replacement could be added to the FMLA and financed through Federal Insurance Contributions Act (FICA) payroll taxes, the national scheme that funds old-age, survivors, and disability pensions as well as health insurance for the elderly. The Fair Labor Standards Act provides a ready regulatory framework for shortening working time, prohibiting compulsory overtime, enacting minimum vacation-leave requirements, and requiring enterprises with benefits to extend them, prorated, to reduced-hour workers. The federal government currently provides most of the funds for ECEC through various block grants, tax credits, and the Head Start program. Head Start serves as a particularly interesting model for a national preschool program with local flexibility. Head Start is financed primarily with federal funds, services are provided by local community entities who are closely monitored against national performance standards, and eligibility rules are standard across the states. It is not clear that the Head Start program itself would be the optimal vehicle for developing a national program of universal preschool education in the United States, but the program provides one model for national funding and oversight of locally tailored services.

"THESE POLICIES WON'T PLAY IN THE AMERICAN HEARTLAND"

The exceptionalism of political culture in the United States suggests a final, and some would argue particularly insurmountable, barrier to the adoption of European-style family policy. Translating European policies to the United States would require an exercise of political will and the mobilization of political support. These policies may be widely valued in Europe, but many would argue that there is little hope in this country for a major expansion of government into the historically private domain of the family.

We have argued that the United States is exceptional in the extent to which individual and family needs are constructed as private problems. American families are forced to rely far more heavily than their counterparts in other high-employment economies on private solutions to the dilemmas of caring for dependents. The paucity of government support for working families in the United States is often ascribed to political tastes. Americans are accurately characterized as suspicious of government intrusions into private life. In public-opinion surveys, Americans tend to express less support for social welfare programs than their European counterparts, even when asked about relatively popular programs such as retirement benefits and health insurance (Shapiro and Young 1989).

American attitudes are more nuanced than this characterization would suggest, however. Americans are particularly negative in their assessments of programs that are considered to provide "welfare" to the nonworking poor (Shapiro and Young 1989; Gilens 1999). They are far more supportive of government programs that are construed as enhancing opportunities or providing support to those who are gainfully employed. When asked directly, most American parents say they believe that government should be doing more to support working families. In this, they are more alike than different from parents in other industrialized countries. According to data from the 1994 International Social Survey Programme (ISSP), fully 85 percent of American parents in working families believe that employed women should receive paid maternity leave—close to the 90 to 98 percent who express similar views in our comparison countries. Sixty-three percent of American parents also believe that working parents should get financial benefits for child care, a share that is similar to that in most of our comparison countries (authors' calculations, based on ISSP data).[7]

The desires of Americans for additional government support are echoed in recent public-opinion polls conducted for research and public-interest groups. A number of polls, which asked specifically about ways in which government can help families, suggest that American parents believe government is not doing enough to support working families. Large majorities of respondents support paid family leave, and they want it to be publicly financed (Zero to Three 2000; National Parenting Association 1998); substantial majorities of Americans also say that they support amendments to working-time regulation that would extend workers' options to trade salary for reduced working time (Hewlett and West 1998). Americans also express support for government assistance with child care (Lake Sosin Snell Perry 1998; Wall Street Journal–NBC 1998), after-school programs (Mott Foundation 1998), and longer school days and school years (Hewlett and West 1998).

Changes in social policy initiated in the 1990s may have, paradoxically, bolstered public support for government aid to working families. The past decade and a half has seen reductions in public assistance, culminating in the 1996 passage of the Personal Responsibility and Work Opportunity Reconciliation Act, which reversed the sixty-one-year-old entitlement to public assistance for families with children and drastically reduced access to cash benefits. This shift in social policy might suggest that Americans' support for government aid for families is at a particularly low ebb. In fact, the social policy reforms of the 1990s did not only cut cash assistance; they also increased public spending on supports for poor employed parents. In conjunction with the cutbacks in cash assistance, Congress authorized a large expansion in child care subsidies for the working poor. Other recent federal policies have also been directed toward helping poor working families, including expansions of the Earned Income Tax Credit and health insurance for children through Medicaid and the Child Health Insurance Program. Many states have followed suit with state-level programs or supplements to the federal policies. The expansion of employment supports for poor parents may signal new political opportunities for the development of more universal work-family policies.

"MEN DON'T WANT TO 'HALVE IT ALL'"

Whereas some argue that the earner-carer policy package could not play in the American heartland, others dismiss the prospects for gender-egalitarian divisions of labor within families. These latter critics argue that most men—in Europe or the United States—will never agree to engage more deeply in caregiving at home. Some argue that it is self-evident that most men do not want to share caregiving equally; if they did, they would have done so by now. Men's unwillingness, they claim, will constitute an insurmountable barrier for those women who do want change.

These concerns are serious ones. As men choose to spend more time with their children, they will have to relinquish some labor market time or attachment; they will need to trade economic and political advantages for closer ties at home. Although some men will doubtless be unwilling to make these changes, we believe that there are also reasons for optimism. Considerable evidence suggests that many men want a different work-family balance but feel constrained by external factors. Women may also have more opportunities to influence their partners' engagement at home than is generally realized.

A large literature on contemporary fatherhood suggests that a sizable and apparently growing number of fathers are dissatisfied with carrying disproportionate economic responsibility for their families and unhappy about their limited involvement in their children's daily lives (see, for example, Barnett and Rivers 1996; Braun Levine 2000; Coltrane 1996; Deutsch 1999; Levine and Pittinsky 1997; Malin 1994). In a 1997 survey by the Families and Work Institute, 70 percent of fathers reported feeling that they do not have enough time with their children. In another recent survey by the institute, one-third of men under the age of forty reported that they would be willing to trade raises and advancement for a better home life—twice the percentage who gave a similar response in a survey conducted five years earlier (Barnett and Rivers 1996). Several studies in the United States have documented increases in employed fathers' requests for parental leave and working-time arrangements in order to spend time with their children (Thornthwaite 2002). Michael Kimmel, a leading scholar of fatherhood and masculinity, argues that more-active fatherhood is on the horizon, catalyzed by wives' increasing commitment to their own employment, new notions of masculinity, and wage declines that have caused many to evaluate the importance of paid work in a harsh new light. Kimmel concludes, optimistically, "The most dramatic shift in family life in the twenty-first century will surely be the changing roles of men, just as the dramatic demographic shift in the workplace in the twentieth century was the dramatic entry of women" (Kimmel 2000, 148).

A resounding theme in the literature on fatherhood is that many fathers already want more time at home but those desires are frustrated, at least in part, by resistance from unsupportive co-workers and employers. In a review article on fathers and parental leave, Martin Malin (1994) concludes that two factors inhibit many fathers from taking time off from the workplace during their children's early years: the lack of paid family leave and employer hostility. Malin cites survey data indicating that about two-thirds of large employers say that it is inappropriate for men to take any parental leave; nearly another one-fifth think that the only reasonable length for men's leaves is two weeks or less. Much research has demonstrated the powerful influence of supervisors' attitudes and company culture on workers' use of leaves and flexible work arrangements (for example, Schwartz 1994). If workplaces change, it is quite possible that many men's behavior will change as well. When flextime was introduced in two federal agencies, for example, half of the male employees with children changed their work hours in order to spend more time with their partners and children (Barnett and Rivers 1996).

It is nearly impossible to estimate how many fathers would want and agree to "halve it all" with their female partners, given the appropriate contextual supports. Many of the existing studies are qualitative; others have sampled subjects with prior commitments to active fatherhood or to equal sharing. Self-reported preferences are also a notoriously poor proxy for actual behavior; it is easier to report a desire to be an active father than it is to actually reorganize one's work and family life. Research on contemporary work and family arrangements cannot tell us what men would prefer and how they would behave if they lived in a world that truly valued caregiving, worked in a transformed workplace, and had access to more support from government. What we do know, however, is that men in the United States who do desire to be more active caregivers face considerable workplace constraints that could be lessened by new and expanded government policies.

Other recent research suggests that women may have more power to influence these changes than we typically recognize.

Women's influx into paid work in recent decades has been accompanied by increases in men's domestic and caregiving work at home, although not to the point of parity. Women who want equal sharing in their own partnerships, however, can do much more than simply working for pay and hoping that their partners will respond by committing more to caregiving.

Rhona Mahony (1995) argues that as young women are simultaneously preparing for paid work and seeking partners, many of them make decisions—largely inadvertently—that raise the likelihood that earning and caring will be gendered in their future families. Mahony argues that, even today, substantial numbers of women "train down" by underinvesting in their own skills relative to their capabilities, in part owing to expectations that they will be able to rely on male partners for additional economic support. In addition, many young women still seek to "marry up"—meaning that they are drawn to men whose expected earnings are higher than their own. The reasons underlying women's inclination to marry up (in that narrow sense of the term) are complex. Some women want a conventionally gendered family; others may hope for an egalitarian partnership but are influenced by social norms about masculinity and male success; still others may seek economic security. Mahony argues that to the extent that women "train down and marry up," they will forfeit possibilities for more egalitarian patterns of earning and caring.

Perhaps paradoxically, Mahony's conclusions are encouraging. They suggest that if more women make decisions that raise their own potential earnings, and if more women come to accept men whose earnings are not higher (or not much higher) than their own, divisions of labor at home will be lessened. By all accounts, it is logical for couples to allocate the larger share of unpaid work to the lower earner. To the extent that women can reduce the likelihood of being the lower earner, they hold considerable power over the process of changing gendered divisions of labor at home. Current wage structures surely lower women's chances of finding male partners whose earnings do not exceed their own, but the likelihood that women will find compatible men whose earnings are close to their own will increase if gender wage gaps narrow.

Recent empirical research on caregiving behaviors also suggests that in some families, women could increase the probability that their male partners share the care work. Even as they negotiate for more equal caregiving arrangements with their partners, some women inadvertently engage in "gatekeeping"—that is, setting rigid rules about caregiving practices or criticizing or redoing tasks completed by their male partners. One large study of dual-earning couples with children found that approximately 20 to 25 percent of mothers engaged in some kind of gatekeeping behavior (Allen and Hawkins 1999). In response, the researchers conclude, their partners retreat from caregiving, assuming the role of helper, at best. According to study author Sarah Allen, many mothers who "believe they need more support in family work . . . don't even realize their actions may be placing obstacles in the way" (Brigham Young University Family Studies Center 1999).

In at least some families, fathers may want to do more daily caregiving than their partners will allow. Although the claim that women push men out of caregiving is overstated—it seems to be only about a quarter of mothers—these mothers in particular have important opportunities to influence change. Gendered divisions of labor will dissolve more readily if and when mothers who want to share caregiving refrain from exclusionary behaviors that inhibit this very outcome.

"EMPLOYERS WILL RESIST"

Some argue that large numbers of fathers will simply refuse to change; others make similar predictions about employers. We often hear that American employers will not accept the kinds of public programs laid out in this book—such as paid family leave and regulations that grant workers the right to work part-time with pay and benefit equity—because they are harmful for productivity and profits. The concern is that American employers will resist compliance with these new public policies and find ways to undermine their implementation. Some argue that employers' opposition to work-family programs is clear from their behavior: employers have not initiated these programs precisely because the often-repeated claim that they are "good for the bottom line" is not defensible.

There is reason to worry about employers' willingness to co-operate with new and potentially costly public policies. We are not starry-eyed about the ease with which employers can be convinced to accept and fully implement these policies. The reality is that employers and employees have different interests; that is true in the United States and in all of our comparison countries. Employers are not in business to support workers and their families; for the most part, owners' and managers' priorities are efficiency, productivity, and profitability.

On the other hand, it is also true that millions of employers have implemented these policies in other countries, and we believe that there are reasons to expect that American employers will do the same. The argument that employers will resist because these programs are not profitable misses the point that the earner-carer policy framework neither asks nor expects that employers will initiate or directly finance most family programs. It does not rest on the hope that individual employers will provide these benefits because they are economically advantageous for their enterprises. Crucially, the earner-carer model does not advance, or rely on, making "the business case" for work-family benefits.

Research evidence suggests that some work-family programs—for example, allowing workers to take time off to care for sick family members—are good for profits and that others, such as flextime and compressed workweeks, seem at least not to be harmful (Meyer, Mukerjee, and Sestero 2001).[8] Shorter workweeks might also raise productivity; though the United States ranks first among the industrialized countries in productivity when it is calculated as the output per worker, it drops in rank when productivity is calculated per hour worked, presumably due to diminishing returns from our long hours (ILO 1999). Other programs, if entirely private, really are not "good for the bottom line." That is apparently the case, for example, with on-site child care. High-quality child care is simply too expensive for most employers to finance out of the added productivity of their own workers (Meyer, Mukerjee, and Sestero 2001). Although conclusions about the profitability of family leave are more mixed, there is no compelling evidence that suggests that generous paid-leave programs would be economically feasible for most employers, if financed individually for their own workers.

Imposing the costs of these programs on individual employers is both infeasible and inequitable. As we have argued throughout this volume, the cost of caring for children should be spread widely—across employers, workers, and taxpayers. The earner-carer model does not call upon employers to pay the bulk of the direct costs, certainly not for universal child care and paid family leave. It does require that all employers share some of the costs through payroll contributions and by accommodating workers taking temporary leaves or working reduced hours. However, it is important to note that the regulatory and financing mechanisms we have suggested impose these costs on all employers equally. This reduces collective-action problems that might discourage any one employer from taking voluntary action. When all employers face the same constraints and costs, no single employer risks competitive disadvantage.

The 1993 passage of the FMLA provides a recent test of the success with which work-family requirements could be imposed on American employers. Employers have reacted much more positively than many expected. For example, in a recent evaluation of the act, 81 percent of covered employers reported that workers taking intermittent family and medical leave had no effect on workplace productivity, and 94 percent reported no effect on profitability; fully 90 percent of covered establishments reported that the FMLA overall has had either no effect or a positive effect on growth (DOL 2000).

Work-family advocates and policy makers can also increase the likelihood of employer cooperation by designing policies that do not place undue burdens on employers. If financing mechanisms and program rules are designed to balance workers' and employers' needs, employers will be more likely to acquiesce to, and possibly even welcome, programs that reduce work-family conflicts for their employees. We illustrate this with an example about paid family leave policy. A recent cross-national study concludes that what employers find especially difficult is not long leaves but unpredictability in the duration of leaves.[9] Many employers place a premium on the right to have substantial advance notice of the beginning and end of leave periods (Alewell and Pull 2001). In a telling example from Canada, a provincial employers' association recently praised Canada's parental leave law but noted that two policy changes would help employers manage workers' absences: first, a requirement that employees give three months' notice before leaving and returning to work and, second, government assistance in locating qualified replacement workers from among the unemployed (Mississauga Board of Trade 2002).

As knowledge and experience accumulate, work-family advocates and policy makers can learn what employers find most useful and what they find most disruptive. To the extent that policy designers balance employers' and workers' needs, they can hope to blunt employers' resistance and encourage cooperation. We are not convinced that the enactment and implementation of work-family programs has to be characterized by adversarial relations between policy makers and employers, nor between employers and employees.

CONCLUSION: THE QUESTIONS OF COST AND POLITICAL DEMAND

American families are struggling with a shared dilemma: if everyone is at the workplace, who will care for the children? Academic, public, and political conversations in this country have addressed the dilemma of balancing earning and caregiving piecemeal, in terms of child well-being, work-family conflict, or gender equality. These conversations usually arrive at equally piecemeal solutions that require fundamental tradeoffs in the interests of women, men, and children.

When the dilemma is placed in the historical context of changes in the organization of economic and family life, the most pressing conflicts of interest are seen to arise not among women, men, and children but from current divisions of labor, workplace practices, and social policies. The dominant contemporary pattern of family organization in the United States—partial specialization between fathers and mothers—remains highly gendered. Employers and all of society benefit from the unpaid caregiving provided by families and by women, in particular. These arrangements are imposing high costs on families, however: women pay a high price for loosening their ties to the labor market to care for children, fathers spend far less time than mothers with their children, and children have less of their parents' time and attention than may be optimal, particularly during the developmentally sensitive first year of life. Although these arrangements are not uniquely American, they seem to be particularly problematic in this country because the United States does much less than other rich industrialized countries to distribute the costs of caregiving among all those who benefit. Other countries provide models for public policies that give parents more time with their children without undue economic sacrifice, encourage fathers as well as mothers to adjust employment hours to accommodate their caregiving needs, and ensure that all families can afford high-quality substitute care for their children.

None of the countries in our study has achieved a fully gender-egalitarian earner-carer society—and we would not expect that these policies alone could bring about fundamental transformations in gender relations or in workplace practices. However, these policies do provide important support for earner-carer families now and, by supporting private changes, may encourage even greater social and workplace transformations over time.

Although they may be idealistic, we do not believe that similar policies are unrealistic in the American context. They are likely to be expensive; but their costs, relative to resources and current expenditures on public education in the United States, are more modest than we might expect. They also represent a departure from the traditional neglect of family policies in the American welfare state. Here, too, we believe that the prospects are brighter than might be expected.

Many observers argue that enacting leave and ECEC programs on the scale of our European counterparts, or even Canada, would simply be too expensive. It is true that comprehensive family leave and ECEC would require substantial public outlays. It is also true that even the highest-providing countries in our study devote a surprisingly small share of their GDP to these programs. Sweden, with arguably the most extensive benefits, spends about 2.5 percent of its GDP on family leave and ECEC; Denmark and Finland each spend just under 2 percent of GDP; France, with somewhat less extensive leave benefits, spends about 1.3 percent.[10] The United States currently spends about one-tenth of these amounts: approximately 0.2 percent of its GDP on publicly financed child care and a negligible amount on publicly financed leave.[11]

These comparisons suggest that there is considerable room for growth in the United States. Given the size and strength of the economy of the United States, the question of whether work-family benefits are too costly is not a question of whether we can afford to make these investments. It is a normative question of whether we should. One concrete way to pose the question is to ask whether the United States should extend its established commitment to older children—through public education—to children below school age. Although the United States is a laggard in many areas of social welfare spending, it was one of the early leaders in extending public education to all children. It continues to invest heavily in the education of its children, spending about 3.4 percent of GDP on primary and secondary public education (OECD 2002b).

Relative to what the United States currently spends on public education, what would it cost to extend the generous Swedish package of family leaves and ECEC to families with younger children in the United States? If the package of benefits costs the same amount in real per capita dollars in the United States, providing generous family leaves would require about 0.4 percent of GDP; extending ECEC to the levels of provision in Sweden would translate into another approximately 1.0 percent of GDP (assuming the 0.2 percent we already spend). Together, these benefits would require an investment that is equivalent to 1.7 percent of the U.S. GDP; that is about one-half of what we now commit to public primary and secondary education as a share of GDP.[12]

Extending work-family benefits to American families would require substantial new public spending. The normative question remains, Are these expenditures justified? We would argue that they are. Because children are "public goods," private investments are likely to be too low to produce socially optimal results. The most common rationale for investments in public education is that children's education and accumulation of human capital provide important shared benefits to society. We currently make less than one-tenth of the investment in early childhood education and care that we make in primary and secondary education. As a result, many of our youngest children receive child care that is mediocre, at best, or even neglectful. Increasing public spending for ECEC and family leave programs is warranted both as protection for the well-being of children now and as an investment in the citizens and workers of the future.

Increased investments are also warranted on equity grounds. The care and nurture of children demands an investment of time, money, and attention. In the absence of public policies that distribute these costs, these investments are made by families—and particularly by women—for the benefit of all society. We currently spend next to nothing in public funds for parental leave, provide minimal assistance with child care, and do little to require employers to accommodate the needs of employed parents. Instead, women pay most of these costs in the form of employment interruptions, forgone wages, and diminished career opportunities; families pay these costs in the form of out-of-pocket child care expenditures, long hours at the workplace, and often stressful adjustments to work schedules. Increasing public investments that socialize a portion of these costs represents a more equitable distribution of the costs of caring.

However well justified such policies might be, the United States will not undertake an expensive expansion of family policies, or potentially intrusive increases in workplace regulations, unless the demand for these changes is mobilized and communicated to government. We have argued that many of the political forces that have limited the size of the welfare state in the United States—from racial cleavages to suspicion of big government and hostility toward traditional welfare programs—may pose less serious barriers in the case of policies that support families in their earning and caring roles. Moving these policies onto the policy agenda, however, will take more than innovative analyses of parenting. For a new approach to family policy to become a reality, the private dilemmas of contemporary families will need to be translated into political demands.

Although interest-group advocates, labor unions, and political actors have had some recent successes in advancing work-family policies, parents have yet to mobilize broadly in support of more-extensive family policies. One of the most important reasons for the failure to mobilize strong demands for family policy in the

United States is the fragmentation of interests—child advocates have concerned themselves largely with services for the most needy families, often ignoring the interests of a broader constituency of families; work-family advocates have focused on the problems facing women who are balancing employment and family demands, largely ignoring feminists' concerns about gender equality; feminists have split into separate camps on issues related to support for caregiving in the home and have too often ignored issues of child well-being.

By predicating policies on the principles of gender equality and greater socialization of the costs of caregiving work, the earner-carer policies outlined in this volume have the potential to bridge a number of the cleavages that have thus far weakened political demands for government support. By extending benefits to all families, earner-carer policies could garner broad support across income and other social divides while avoiding the controversies associated with means-tested welfare benefits for the most needy. By looking to government to create programs that provide inclusive benefits and distribute costs broadly—that is, by "enlarging the pie" rather than redistributing the slices—earner-carer policies could resonate broadly without forcing political tradeoffs between those who benefit and those who pay.

Addressing issues of gender equality in family policy has the potential to close other political cleavages as well. As long as family issues are viewed as women's domain, they are likely to remain marginalized from larger political interests. Formulating leave, child care, and labor market policies that extend benefits to fathers has the potential to engage men's support. Designing these policies as supports for equal sharing of employment and caring may also close schisms between feminists oriented to reducing gender differentials in the labor market and those focused on rewarding caregiving in the home and between advocates for gender equality and those primarily concerned with children's well-being.

For issues of gender inequality in caregiving to become a more central concern, they will need to taken more seriously by stakeholders—including feminists, work-family activists, and children's advocates—who influence public and political agendas. Issues of the division of unpaid care work have fallen off feminists' political agendas to a remarkable degree. When the second wave of the women's movement emerged in the late 1960s, American feminists vigorously critiqued housewifery and identified it as a locus of women's oppression. As more married women entered the labor market in the following decades, however, feminists' attention to gendered divisions at home were largely eclipsed by concerns about gender equality in the labor market. Eventually, a substantial number of feminists recast the sexual division of household labor as a middle-class and heterosexual concern, not worthy of concentrated activist energy. Ironically, feminists' lack of focus on the involvement of fathers with their children has aroused the ire of some conservatives. One conservative columnist, writing in the *National Review,* has complained that "hardly anybody is talking about Dad. . . . Other than occasional lip service, groups like the National Organization for Women and the Feminist Majority don't actively exhort fathers to get more involved. Nor do they ever expound upon the benefits of father involvement for moms and kids" (Sylvester 2002). That criticism is not unfounded.

Gendered divisions in care work have also received little attention from activists and researchers concerned about work-family conflict. Men's limited engagement with children, particularly young children, is widely assumed, and issues of work-family conflict are located almost entirely in women's lives. The resulting public and academic discourse casts earning and caring narrowly as a "women's issue"—from the expansion of maternity (but not paternity) leave to concerns about the effects of mothers' employment on children and the costs of women's (but not men's) lost childbearing opportunities. It is equally difficult to find examples of research and advocacy on child well-being that pay serious attention to issues of gender equality. Many child advocates have accepted the inevitability of tradeoffs between women's equality and children's well-being, glorifying women's sacrifices for the sake of their children.[13]

Moving a family-policy agenda forward in the United States will require pulling together the currently fragmented constituencies that care about children's well-being, the balance between work and family, and gender equality. Reframing these same issues through the lens of an earner-carer society, and building on the lessons of our counterparts abroad, has the potential to catalyze policy developments in the short term and even greater long-term transformations in gender relations, workplace arrangements, and the role of the state. We do not expect to see the realization of an earner-carer society in the near term, or even in our lifetimes. Nevertheless, by focusing on the principles of gender equality, time for children, and greater sharing of the costs of caregiving, we can hope to see progressive social change that does not force tradeoffs among the interests of women, men, and children.

—— Appendix A ——

Description of Cross-National Data Sets Used

C ROSS-NATIONAL DATA in chapters 3 and 8 come from four main sources. Each is described here, along with information on sampling and variable definition. The data source for figures 3.1 to 3.8, 3.12, 3.13, 8.2, 8.3, and 8.8 is the Luxembourg Income Study (LIS) (for general information, see: *www.lisproject.org*). (Detailed information on the original surveys, including sample sizes, is available at: *www.lisproject.org/techdoc/surveys.htm*.) The Multinational Time Use Study (MTUS) is the source for figures 3.9, 3.10, and 8.5 (for general information, see: *www.iser.essex.ac.uk/mtus*). (Detailed information on the original surveys, including sample sizes, is available at: *www.iser.essex.ac.uk/mtus/structure.php #notes*.) Eurostat's European Labor Force Surveys (LFS) are the data source for the European countries in figures 3.11 and 8.4 (for general information, see: *europa.eu.int/comm/eurostat*). Data on the United States in figures 3.11 and 8.4 are from the 1997 Current Population Survey (CPS); the U.S. results were provided by Harriet Presser. The International Social Survey Programme (ISSP) is the data source for figure 3.19 (available at: *www.issp.org*). (Detailed information on the surveys and modules is available at: *www.gesis.org/en/data—service/issp/index.htm*.)

LUXEMBOURG INCOME STUDY

The Luxembourg Income Study is a public-access archive of microdata sets from approximately twenty-five industrialized countries, with data available for up to five points in time, depending on the country. The LIS data include demographic, income, and labor market indicators; data are available at the person and household level, and records can be linked.

Most of our comparisons based on the LIS data include all twelve comparison countries and cover the time period from 1992 to 1997. An exception are analyses related to working time; weekly hours are available for only nine of these countries (and including Finland necessitated using data on weekly hours in Finland from 1991, as the Finnish data exclude hours worked in 1995). A second exception is the analysis of the part-time wage penalty, in which we were able to locate data for only five of the twelve countries. In addition, though later Danish data are available through the LIS, we used the 1992 data set because of missing or problematic variables in later data sets.

In the LIS-based analyses, we selected persons aged twenty-five to fifty or couples in which either partner was aged twenty-five to fifty. Couples include both married and cohabiting persons, wherever possible. When reporting employment rates, we exclude workers in the agricultural and military sectors; when reporting weekly hours, we further exclude the self-employed. In the German data set, we include the western Lander (states) only, and in the U.K. data set we include only England, Scotland, and Wales—in both cases to raise the comparability with both available policy data and the ISSP data.

Employment status (yes or no) is coded from labor-force-status variables generally referring to the prior week (where "no" includes those out of the labor force and the unemployed), and weekly hours refer to hours usually worked each week. Labor-market earnings are gross (pretax) earnings with one exception—France—where they are net (posttax). Poverty is defined as having income below 50 percent of the national median posttax and posttransfer income, with an adjustment for family size. Details on coding of specific variables are available from the first author (Janet Gornick) on request.

MULTINATIONAL TIME USE STUDY

The Multinational Time Use Study (MTUS) compiles comparable time-use-diary data from a number of countries. The MTUS data were available for only eight of our twelve comparison countries; the time period used is 1985 to 1992.

In the MTUS-based analyses, the sample is restricted to married (or cohabiting, where available) couples in which the adults are between the ages of twenty-five and fifty with at least one child under the age of five living in the household. Measures of unpaid work in the home include time spent in routine housework (cooking, cleaning up, and housework), in nonroutine housework (other domestic work, gardening, shopping, domestic travel), and care for children. Only primary activities are recorded. Time is recorded daily and averaged (in minutes) across the seven days of week.

Results based on the MTUS data were provided to us by Anne H. Gauthier. All computations are our own, and our interpretations do not necessarily reflect those of the MTUS and its statistical partners. We gratefully acknowledge Anne Gauthier's assistance and that of her research staff.

EUROPEAN LABOR FORCE SURVEYS (LFS)

Eurostat, the statistical arm of the European Union, conducts annual Labor Force Surveys in its member countries. Cross-national tables are published annually in *European Social Statistics: Labour Force Survey Results*. As we needed the LFS data reconfigured to match the available data on the United States, we commissioned special extracts from the Eurostat staff.

In the analyses presented in this volume, we include the six European countries among our cases in which Eurostat could identify parents. The data pertain to 1997. The European samples include persons aged eighteen and over in nonagricultural occupations who are wage and salary earners, and the work shifts refer to the worker's principal job. Parents are defined as heads of household or partners of heads of households with children under the age of fifteen. Nationals and nonnationals are included.

Extracts of LFS data were prepared for us by Larus Blondal and Sylvain Jouhette, and we gratefully acknowledge their assistance. We also thank Harriet Presser, with whom we collaborated on this cross-national inquiry.

The U.S. Comparison in Figures 3.11 and 8.4

The CPS sample matches the European samples, except that children are defined as under the age of sixteen. More substantially, the U.S. definition of evening and night employment is somewhat more restrictive, meaning that the prevalence of evening and night work in the Eurostat results is likely to be overstated.

INTERNATIONAL SOCIAL SURVEY PROGRAMME (ISSP)

The ISSP is a public-access archive of microdata sets coordinated across approximately twenty industrialized countries. There is an annual core survey, and each year a module includes a series of additional questions. We used the 1997 *Work Orientations II* module. We included the seven countries, from among our group of twelve, for which comparable data were available. We selected persons aged twenty-five to fifty who resided in households with children in them.

Appendix B

Summary of Selected European Union Directives

A s REPORTED IN chapters 5 and 6, three European Union (EU) directives passed in the 1990s have influenced family leave and working-time policy in Europe. Such directives, which are binding for member countries, are supranational laws that take precedence over the laws of individual member states. In most cases, individual countries are permitted to bring provisions into line through either national legislation or formalized agreements among the social partners (groups representing employers and workers) or through some combination of the two. The European Union's directives also apply to Norway, which, although not a member, implements EU directives. Our ten European cases include nine member countries and Norway.

What follows is some of the key language from these directives. The directives are available in their entirety at *Europa*, the official EU web site, at: *europa.eu.int/eur-lex/en/index.htm.*

DIRECTIVE ON WORKING TIME: COUNCIL DIRECTIVE 93/104/EC OF 23 NOVEMBER 1993

Objective: To adopt minimum requirements covering certain aspects of the organization of working time connected with workers' health and safety.

Contents:

3. Member States shall take measures to ensure that workers enjoy:

- the minimum daily rest period of 11 consecutive hours per period of 24 hours;
- the minimum period of one rest day on average immediately following the daily rest period in every seven-day period; for a daily period of work of more than six hours, a break as defined by the provisions of collective agreements, agreements concluded between social partners or national legislation;
- not less than four weeks' annual paid holiday, qualification for which shall be determined by reference to national practice/legislation;
- an average weekly working period of not more than 48 hours, including the overtime for each seven-day period.

Deadline for implementation of the legislation in the member states: 23 November 1996.

DIRECTIVE ON PARENTAL LEAVE AND LEAVE FOR FAMILY REASONS: COUNCIL DIRECTIVE 96/34/EC OF 3 JUNE 1996

Objective: To establish minimum requirements in respect of parental leave and unforeseeable absence from work, as an important means of reconciling professional and family responsibilities and promoting equal opportunities and treatment for women and men.

Contents:

2. The framework agreement provides for: male and female workers to have individual entitlement to parental leave on the grounds of the birth or adoption of a child, enabling them to take care of the child for at least three months; the conditions of access to, and procedures for applying, parental leave to be defined by law and/or collective agreement in the Member States, subject to compliance with the minimum requirements of the agreement; the Member States and/or social partners to take the necessary measures to

protect workers against dismissal on the grounds of an application for, or the taking of, parental leave; workers to have the right to return to the same job at the end of parental leave or, if that is not possible, to an equivalent or similar job consistent with their employment contract or relationship; the maintenance of rights acquired or in the process of being acquired by the worker on the date on which parental leave starts; at the end of the period of leave, those rights will apply; the Member States and/or the social partners to take the necessary measures to allow workers to take time off from work, in accordance with national legislation, collective agreements and/or practice, for unforeseeable reasons arising from a family emergency in the event of sickness or accident making the immediate presence of the worker indispensable.

3. The Member States may introduce more favourable provisions than those laid down in the Directive.

4. Implementation of the provisions of the Directive will not in any way constitute sufficient grounds to justify a reduction in the general level of protection afforded to workers in the field covered.

5. The Member States are to determine the range of penalties applicable for infringements of national provisions pursuant to the Directive, and are to take all the necessary steps to ensure their implementation. The penalties applied must be effective and commensurate with the infringement, and must constitute a sufficient deterrent.

Deadline for implementation of the legislation in the member states: 3 June 1998 (15 December 1999 in the U.K.).

DIRECTIVE ON PART-TIME WORK: COUNCIL DIRECTIVE 97/81/EC OF 15 DECEMBER 1997

Objective: To ensure that workers concerned by the new forms of flexible working receive comparable treatment to full-time staff on open-ended contracts.

Contents:

2.1. The purpose of the agreement is to eliminate discrimination against part-time workers and to improve the quality of part-time work. It also aims to facilitate the development of part-time work on a voluntary basis and to contribute to the flexible organization of working time in a manner which takes into account the needs of employers and workers.

2.2. The agreement applies to part-time workers who have an employment contract or employment relationship as defined by the laws, collective agreements or practices in force in each Member State.

2.3. Definitions: "part-time worker": an employee whose normal hours of work, calculated on a weekly basis or on average over a period of employment of up to one year, are less than the normal hours of work of a comparable full-time worker; "comparable full-time worker": a full-time worker in the same establishment having the same type of employment contract or relationship, who is engaged in the same or a similar work/occupation.

2.4. In respect of employment conditions, part-time workers shall not be treated in a less favourable manner than comparable full-time workers solely because they work part-time, unless different treatment is justified on objective grounds.

2.5. Member States after consultation of the social partners and/or social partners may, where appropriate, make access to particular conditions of employment subject to a period of service, time worked or earnings qualifications.

2.6. Member States after consultation of the social partners and/or social partners should identify and review obstacles which may limit the opportunities for part-time work and, where appropriate, eliminate them.

2.7. A worker's refusal to transfer from full-time to part-time work or vice versa should not in itself constitute a valid reason for dismissal.

2.8. Wherever possible, employers should give consideration to: requests by workers to transfer from full-time to part-time work that becomes available in the establishment; requests by workers to transfer from part-time to full-time work or to increase their working time should the opportunity arise; the provision of timely information on the availability of part-time and full-time jobs in the establishment; measures to facilitate access to part-time work at all levels of the enterprise; the provision of appropriate information to workers' representatives about part-time working in the enterprise.

2.9. Member States and/or social partners can maintain or introduce more favourable provisions than set out in the agreement. Implementation of the provisions of the agreement does not constitute valid grounds for reducing the general level of protection afforded to workers in the field of the agreement.

3. Member States must bring into force the laws, regulations and administrative provisions necessary to comply with the Directive within two years of its entry into force, or ensure that the social partners have, by that date, introduced the necessary measures by agreement. The Member States may have a maximum of one more year, if this is necessary to take account of special difficulties or implementation by a collective agreement. They must inform the Commission forthwith in such circumstances.

Deadline for implementation of the legislation in the member states: 20 January 2000 (7 April in the U.K.).

Appendix C

Construction of Policy Indexes

T HE INDEXES PRESENTED in chapter 8 were constructed as follows: First, we converted the policy data presented in chapters 5, 6, and 7 to twenty-two indicators. We entered quantified data (for example, ECEC enrollment rates) numerically, and we coded qualitative data (for example, ECEC quality) into categories (high, medium, low).

We included all of our major policy measures, with the exception of those that regulate part-time work, as nearly all current policies governing part-time work in Europe were enacted after our most recent data on labor market outcomes. For all twenty-two policy indicators, coded data correspond to the data in chapters 5, 6, and 7, with one exception: Because the current regulated workweek in France (thirty-five hours) was implemented after our outcome data on working time, we used the value that was current in France in the mid-1990s. The twenty-two indicators (with units) are as follows:

EARLY CHILDHOOD EDUCATION AND CARE

- v1 guaranteed slot for some children 0-1-2 (yes, no)
- v2 enrollment in public care < age 1 (percent of age group)
- v3 enrollment in public care age 1–2 (percent of age group)
- v4 cost to parents if children in public care age 1–2 (percent of total cost)
- v5 enrollment in public care age 3-4-5 (percent of age group)
- v6 cost to parents if children in public care age 3-4-5 (percent of total cost)

- v7 typical hours age 3-4-5 (full-day, mixed, part-day)
- v8 enrollment age 6 (percent of age group)
- v9 quality (low, medium, high)
- v10 tax relief for ECEC (yes, no)

SCHOOL SCHEDULING

- v11 starting age (age)
- v12 hours per day (hours)
- v13 days per year (days)
- v14 continuity of school day (yes, no, sometimes)

FAMILY LEAVE

- v15 weeks of full-pay available to mothers (weeks)
- v16 paid paternity leave (yes, no)
- v17 gender equality scale / incentives for fathers (see chapter 6)
- v18 some paid leave after third birthday (yes, no, some)
- v19 paid sick-child leave (yes, no)
- v20 expenditures on leave (2000 $U.S. per employed woman)

WORKING TIME

- v21 normal weekly hours (hours)
- v22 normal vacation time (days)

The raw data on these twenty-two indicators are presented in tables C.1 and C.2.

Second, we converted all qualitative values to quantitative values (for example, high, medium, and low were coded as 1.0, .66, and .33). We then rescaled all indicators such that a higher value signified more policy support. For example, cost to parents if children in public care was converted to cost to government (for children in public care), with a higher value signifying more government support. School starting age and normal weekly hours were converted such that higher values signify an earlier starting age and shorter weekly hours.

Third, we rescaled all indicators again so that values fall between 0 to 1. We did that using one of three methods: for percentages the original value was used (for example, enrollment rates); other values were divided by the observed maximum (for example, weekly school hours) or by the theoretical maximum (for example, the gender-equality scale).

Fourth, we created seven subindexes by combining the rescaled indicators. We weighted some items, based on our expectation of the share of the families affected by individual components or based on their relative importance. The subindexes were constructed as follows:

- sA. ECEC, youngest child under the age of three: v1 + [.33 × v2] + [.66 × v3] + v4 + v9 + [.25 × v10]
- sB. Family leave, youngest child under the age of three: v15 + v16 + v17 + v19 + v20
- sC. ECEC, youngest child aged three to five: v5 + v6 + [1.5 × v7] + v9 + [.25 × v10]
- sD. Family leave, youngest child aged three to five: v17 + v18 + v19
- sE. Family leave, youngest child six or older: v19
- sF. School schedules: [.10 × v8] + [.10 × v11] + v12 + v13 + v14
- sG. Working time: v21 + v22

We then rescaled these subindexes to values of 0 to 1 by dividing each by the observed maximum.

Next, we converted the subindexes into Indexes A, B, and C as follows:

- Index A = all policies that affect families with children under the age of six = sA + sB + sC + sD + sG
- Index B = all policies that affect families with children ages six and older = sE + sF + sG (weighted to give school schedules [sF] 50 percent)
- Index C = all policies that affect families with children of all ages = sA + sB + sC + sD + sE + sF + sG

Finally, we rescaled Indexes A, B, and C to values of 0 to 1 by dividing each by the theoretical maximum (5, 3, and 7, respectively). These index values are presented in appendix table C.3.

TABLE C.1 Raw Data for Indexes Presented in Figure 8.1

Country	Guaranteed Slot for Some Children 0-1-2	Enrollment in Public Care < 1	Enrollment in Public Care 1-2	Cost to Parents if Children in Public Care 1-2	Enrollment in Public Care 3-4-5	Cost to Parents if Children in Public Care 3-4-5	Hours 3-4-5	Enrollment at 6	Quality	Tax Relief
Belgium	no	0.15	0.42	0.21	0.99	0	full	100	high	yes
Canada	no	few	0.05	0.10	0.53	.10 subsidy care; 0 prek or k	part	100	med	yes
Denmark	yes	0.15	0.74	0.205	0.90	0.205	full	98	high	no
Finland	yes	few	0.22	0.16	0.66	0.16	full	92	high	no
France	no	few	0.20	0.17	0.99	0	full	100	high	yes
Germany	no	few	0.05	0.15*	0.77	0	part	100	med	some
Luxembourg	no	few	0.03	0.25	0.67	0	part	100	med	yes
Netherlands	no	0.17	0.17	0.15*	0.71	0	mix of part and full	100	med	yes
Norway	no	0.02	0.37	0.37	0.78	0.37	full	100	high	yes
Sweden	yes	few	0.48	0.18	0.82	0.18	full	93	high	no
United Kingdom	no	few	0.02	0.15*	0.77	.10 subsidy care; 0 prek or k	part	100	med	yes
United States	no	few	0.06	0.10	0.53	.10 subsidy care; 0 prek or k	part	100	low	yes

ECEC Indicators

Source: Authors' compilation.

TABLE C.2 Raw Data for Indexes Presented in Figure 8.1

School Schedule Indicators

Country	Starting Age	Hours	Days	Continuity
Belgium	6	44	182	no
Canada	5.5	33*	190	yes
Denmark	7	53	200	yes
Finland	7	25	190	yes
France	6	35	180	no
Germany	6	28	198	sometimes
Luxembourg	4	37	212	no
Netherlands	5	30	200	no
Norway	6	21	190	yes
Sweden	7	60	178	yes
United Kingdom	5	33	190	yes
United States	5.5	33	179	yes

Family Leave Indicators

Country	Weeks of Full-Pay Available to Mothers	Paid Paternity Leave	Gender Equality Scale/ Incentives for Fathers	Paid Leave After Third Birthday	Paid Sick-Child Leave	Expenditures on Maternity and Parental
Belgium	12	yes	4	some	yes	234
Canada	28	no	3	no	no	152
Denmark	37	yes	5	yes	yes	594
Finland	29	yes	4	no	yes	673
France	16	no	1	no	yes	431
Germany	14	no	1	no	yes	465
Luxembourg	16	yes	4	some	yes	414
Netherlands	16	yes	2	no	yes	67
Norway	42	yes	6	no	yes	808
Sweden	42	yes	6	yes	yes	608
United Kingdom	5	no	2	no	no	75
United States	0	no	2	no	no	0

TABLE C.2 *Continued*

	Working-Time Indicators	
Country	Normal Weekly Hours	Normal Vacation Time
Belgium	39	20
Canada	40	10
Denmark	37	25
Finland	39.3	24
France	38	25
Germany	37.7	20
Luxembourg	39	25
Netherlands	37	20
Norway	37.5	21
Sweden	38.8	25
United Kingdom	37.5	20
United States	40	0

Source: Authors' compilation.
Note: French normal weekly hours are for the mid-1990s, prior to the 2000 reduction to 35 hours. Values marked with asterisks are estimates.

TABLE C.3 Index Values in Figure 8.1

Country	Index A		Index B		Index C
Denmark	.94	Denmark	1.00	Denmark	.96
Sweden	.89	Sweden	.93	Sweden	.92
Norway	.80	Norway	.86	Norway	.83
Finland	.74	Finland	.81	Finland	.79
Belgium	.73	Germany	.79	Belgium	.75
France	.66	Netherlands	.75	France	.69
Netherlands	.65	France	.73	Netherlands	.69
Luxembourg	.65	Luxembourg	.72	Luxembourg	.69
Germany	.55	Belgium	.69	Germany	.63
United Kingdom	.45	United Kingdom	.65	United Kingdom	.45
Canada	.36	Canada	.49	Canada	.38
United States	.24	United States	.43	United States	.29

Source: Authors' compilation.

—— Notes ——

1. In the case of poor families, ironically, many of these same pro-family advocates support greater parental work effort—laying the blame for parental unavailability on childbearing outside of marriage and on marital disruptions.
2. Following the convention in cross-national research, we refer to Canada as "English-Speaking," although it is officially bilingual, part Anglophone and part Francophone. All of the European countries in this study, with the exception of Norway, are members of the European Union.

Chapter Two

1. In the nineteenth century, married women had more pregnancies and bore more children than their counterparts do today. These high levels of fertility undoubtedly bolstered the logic for such a rigid gendered division of labor.
2. For an excellent summary of the effects of industrialization on gendered divisions of labor and the genesis of the traditional breadwinner-homemaker family, see Blau, Ferber, and Winkler (2002).
3. Substantial racial differences in women's employment patterns were still evident in 2000. The labor force participation rate of married mothers (with husbands present) was even higher for black mothers than for white mothers—81 and 70 percent respectively.
4. The 1963 Pay Equity Act and Title VII of the 1964 Civil Rights Act outlawed discrimination on the basis of sex in virtually all aspects of employment, and two executive orders in the late 1960s introduced affirmative action for employers with federal contracts.
5. Wives' earnings were particularly crucial for lower-income families. Between 1979 and 1989, average income for families in the bottom

fifth of the income distribution fell by 6 percent; without wives' increased earnings, it would have fallen by more than 10 percent. During the next decade (1989 to 1999), incomes for this group rose by 5 percent but would have risen by only half as much without an increase in wives' earnings (Mishel, Bernstein, and Schmitt 2001).

6. How much of the increase in women's engagement in paid work has been pull and how much has been push remains an open question. In one empirical study, Philip Cohen and Suzanne Bianchi (1999) address the question of whether women's labor market involvement has increased more because of rising opportunities or declining constraints. They analyze women's employment between 1978 and 1998, focusing on changes in the effects of a series of predictor variables, including women's own educational attainment and their spouses' earnings. They find that the largest increase in participation was among the most educated women and that, though spousal earnings continued to influence wives' labor supply—low earnings raising wives' participation in paid work—the income effect diminished over time. They conclude that the rise in women's employment during these years is more consistent with an opportunities than with a constraints interpretation.

7. The small increase in hours was partly driven by falling wages, which caused some workers, both male and female, to elect to increase their overtime hours (ILO 1995).

8. In addition to time at the job, American workers spend an average of 3.7 hours a week commuting to and from the job (Bureau of Labor Statistics 1999).

9. Jacobs and Gerson (2001) note that many women are counted as part-year workers when, in fact, they are beginning long spells of employment and just happen to start a spell in the middle of the survey year. Thus part-year work is falling, and average total weeks rising, principally because fewer women are entering the labor market in any given year as more and more are continuously employed. Leete-Guy and Schor's work (1992) suggests that the increase in weeks worked per year is real—not simply a measurement artifact, as Jacobs and Gerson conclude. It is likely that both findings are correct. Jacobs and Gerson analyze weeks worked per year using data from the Census Bureau's Current Population Survey (CPS), and in the CPS, paid time off—vacations, holidays, and so forth—is generally counted as working time. Thus the increase in weeks worked due to decreases in paid time off (as reported by Leete-Guy and Schor) would not even be captured in the CPS. If those increased weeks were counted, the rise in annual weeks (and days) worked would most likely be even larger.

10. Mishel and colleagues also report that increases in working time in recent decades have taken place among diverse groups of workers: "Some critics have argued that the increase in income inequality has been generated simply by those with higher incomes working longer and harder while other less well-off families did not increase their work effort. But the data on weeks and hours worked belie this claim: the increases in hours and weeks occurred throughout the income distribution. . . . In a similar vein, work hours have increased about as quickly among families headed by someone with more ('at least some college') as with less ('high school degree or less') education. . . . Hours of work have grown especially quickly among black families" (Mishel, Bernstein, and Schmitt 2001, 24–25).

11. Women's work hours lag behind those of men on the high end of the hours distribution as well. Whereas a third of professional men and nearly 40 percent of male college graduates work fifty or more hours a week, only 17 percent of professional women and 20 percent of female college graduates do so (Jacobs and Gerson forthcoming).

12. Sanjiv Gupta (1999) reaches the slightly different conclusion that married men spend an average of 3.5 fewer hours each week on housework than single men and that additional children have no effect on men's weekly housework time (excluding child care), whereas each additional child adds more than three hours a week to women's housework.

13. Time-use studies typically distinguish three types of time that adults spend with children: time in which child care is a primary activity (for example, direct physical care, medical care, transportation, talking or reading, indoor or outdoor play); time in which the adult is involved in another primary activity and child care is mentioned as a secondary activity; and time doing any activity "with children present."

14. Married fathers spend an average of 3.8 hours a day with children, in contrast to 5.5 hours by mothers, and only 1 hour a day in primary child care, in contrast to 1.7 hours by mothers (Bianchi 2000). Bianchi estimates that between 1965 and 1998, mothers' time in child care actually increased slightly—from 5.3 to 5.5 hours a day in contact of any kind and 1.5 to 1.7 hours in child care as a primary activity.

15. Prominent explanations focus on historical factors that diminished working-class concerns and impeded the development of a broad-based workers' movement, including the absence of a feudal tradition, a relatively inclusive form of capitalism, early public education and voting rights, the development of a two-party political system

and the absence of a labor party, and the high level of ethnic and racial diversity (Wheeler 1989).

16. The rules that govern the processes of worker representation, union organizing, and collective bargaining for most private-sector workers are established in the National Labor Relations Act (NLRA) and enforced through the regulatory agency that it created, the National Labor Relations Board. In addition, state labor laws oversee collective bargaining in sectors not covered by the NLRA, which include state and local government workers, agricultural workers, and supervisors. The NLRA also permits states to pass so-called right-to-work laws, and twenty-three states have done so (DOL 2002b); these laws restrict unions by disallowing them from requiring workers in unionized enterprises to join the union or pay dues. These national and state laws have very likely played a major role in reducing union coverage. Many scholars and union activists have argued that the NLRA ultimately grants the balance of power to employers, inadequately protecting workers' rights to organize (see, for example, Rose and Chaison 1996). Others find that right-to-work laws have depressed union density in the states that have enacted them and, in turn, nationwide (see, for example, Palley 2001).

17. As of 2000, 70 percent of mothers with children under the age of six were employed, in contrast to 85 percent of working-age women without children and nearly 95 percent of working-age men (authors' calculations, based on 2000 CPS). Rates of part-time employment were also high among women with young children: only 56 percent of married women with children under the age of six worked the equivalent of full time, in contrast to 75 percent of women without children and 90 percent of men (authors' calculations, based on 2000 CPS).

18. Note that the results in tables 2.2 and 2.3 are consistent with findings that we reported earlier in this chapter—that long hours spent in paid work are not simply the province of highly educated workers or workers in high-income families. Average joint labor market time in the middle two quartiles (about seventy-three hours a week) is similar to that reported in the top income quartile (about seventy-seven hours a week, on average). Time spent in paid work clearly lags at the bottom (the lowest quartile), consistent with Mishel, Bernstein, and Schmitt's (2001) finding that married males' hours lagged only in the bottom quintile. It is also important to note that the comparisons presented in tables 2.2 and 2.3 use a different indicator. For the purpose of this comparison—about gender inequality—average hours include adults with zero hours. That conflates

variation in employment rates with variation in hours, rendering this comparison across income and education groups somewhat different from those presented by Jacobs and Gerson (forthcoming) and Mishel, Bernstein, and Schmitt (2001).

19. This is especially true in families in which women have left the labor market altogether (or never entered it). As Nancy Folbre observes, homemaker wives remain dependent on their husband's largess. Folbre argues that married women who divorce gain rights to joint property, but in most of the American states, "within marriage a person who specializes in nonmarket work has no legal right to any more than the partner earning a wage or salary chooses to give them" (Folbre 2001, 92).

20. Gender inequalities in paid work are mirrored in the structure of many public social-welfare provisions. The primary forms of government income replacement in the United States—old-age, disability, and unemployment insurance—are largely predicated on formal labor force attachment. In general, a woman's unpaid work history, in caregiving and other domestic work at home, entitles her to no compensation or social insurance of her own. At the same time, many women caregivers are eligible for public benefits, not specifically as caregivers but as the wives of breadwinners who are unable to support them owing to death, disability, or work-related injury. Eligible widows, married for at least ten years, can receive survivors' benefits if their breadwinning spouses die; benefits are paid to elderly widows and to those of any age raising dependent children. In addition, some social-insurance programs—including the national Old-Age and Disability Insurance programs and, in some states, Workers' Compensation—add a "dependents' supplement" to the recipients' benefits, on behalf of an eligible spouse. Yet for the most part, women's uncompensated work does not grant them their own benefits; the entitlements they do have are not based on the value of their work.

21. Men in dual-earner couples also devote more time to housework when their schedules do not overlap with those of their wives (Presser 1994).

22. Presser's research suggests that the increased tendency for marital instability does not result from spouses in troubled marriages seeking nonstandard hours; the causality seems to run the other way.

Chapter Three

1. In each cross-national comparison presented in this chapter, we include the maximum number of countries from among our group

of twelve; countries are omitted from individual figures only when sufficiently comparable data were not available. In all of the figures, to facilitate comparison we cluster our countries into the three groups introduced in chapter 1: the Nordic European countries of Denmark (DK), Finland (FI), Norway (NW), and Sweden (SW); the Continental European countries of Belgium (BE), France (FR), Germany (GE), Luxembourg (LX), and the Netherlands (NL); and two English-speaking countries, Canada (CN), and the United Kingdom (UK).

2. Throughout this book, when we refer to "work," we generally distinguish "unpaid work" from "paid work." In this chapter, in the discussions of labor market hours and gender equality in the labor market, when we use the term "work" unmodified, we mean paid work. Maintaining that distinction seems unnecessarily cumbersome in this context.

3. The data presented in figures 3.1 to 3.8, 3.12, and 3.13 are from the Luxembourg Income Study (LIS). For a description of the LIS data, including a discussion of the years to which they pertain, see appendix A.

   Throughout this chapter, all results that pertain to adults, couples, or families refer to adults aged twenty-five to fifty or to families in which either the head or the partner of the head was aged twenty-five to fifty. The lower-end cutoff allows us to avoid variation across countries in educational enrollments, and the upper-end cutoff enables us to avoid the potentially confounding issue of early retirement, which also varies markedly across countries. The one exception is in figure 3.11 (evening, night, and weekend work), which refers to workers aged eighteen or older.

4. There is some ambiguity in these employment comparisons because some percentage of "employed" women are on family-related leave, and we cannot reliably identify them using our data. This might be problematic for our comparisons because the percentage of women on leave is likely to be larger in some of the high-employment countries (the Nordic countries), due to the cross-country correlation between women's employment and the generosity of family leave provisions. Thus more women may be officially employed in the Nordic countries than in the United States, but it is possible that on any given day the percentage of women who are "on the job" might not be appreciably higher.

   Three factors suggest that the results in figure 3.1 are meaningful. First, these refer to mothers with children up through the age of eighteen; a relatively small share are mothers with children in the first year of life, the intensive time for leave take-up. (In Denmark, where an estimate is available, country experts report that about 3 percent of women counted as employed are on maternity or parental leave; that includes women with and without children [OECD 2002a].) Second, we code women as employed based on survey items that ask respondents about their current labor market status. Some share of women out on extended leaves will describe themselves as not employed; that should include all mothers on child-rearing leaves that are not conditioned on employment (see chapter 5 of this volume). Third, and most important, the employment status of women on paid leave, especially the short-term well-paid leaves that are common across much of Europe, is in fact ambiguous, and "employed" is arguably the best description. In most cases, women on leave maintain their labor contracts, they receive a cash benefit that replaces most or all their wages, and they typically return to the same employer. Thus, we argue, it is more reasonable to describe women who are on leave as employed than to count them among those not employed.

5. We collaborated with Jerry Jacobs on the analysis of couples' work hours across countries. For more details on couples' labor market hours across countries, see Jacobs and Gornick (2002). In other work with Kathleen Gerson, Jacobs has introduced the measure of couples' joint hours into American scholarship on working time, broadening the earlier focus on the work hours of individuals (Jacobs and Gerson forthcoming).

6. The comparatively long working hours of American parents are driven upward by both mothers' and fathers' weekly hours. Across the twelve countries studied, employed American mothers work the longest hours, on average—with only one exception, Finnish mothers. Employed American fathers log the longest hours among these countries, tied only with Belgium.

7. We find that about 10 percent of American dual-earner couples with children work for pay one hundred or more hours a week. This is a slightly lower figure than the 13 percent reported by Jacobs and Gerson (2001), using the same data. The discrepancy derives from small differences in sample definitions.

8. We collaborated with Elena Bardasi on the analysis of part-time pay penalties across countries. For more details on part-time–full-time wage differentials across countries, see Bardasi and Gornick (2002). Note that we were able to calculate part-time–full-time differentials in only five of our twelve countries, due to limitations in the LIS data on weeks worked each year. These differentials refer to cash compensation; they take no account of benefits.

9. To capture the effects of having young children on employment, we compare parents with young children with parents with older children, rather than with nonparents, because restricting the universe to parents nets out the effects of traits associated with both the propensity to have children and the propensity to be employed. We chose parents with children aged thirteen to seventeen as our comparison group because they face relatively minimal caregiving constraints; their employment rates approximate a sort of "natural parental employment rate" in each country.

10. We limit these comparisons to married or cohabiting parents (with children under the age of eighteen) because we are primarily interested in differentials between women with child-rearing responsibilities and their male counterparts. Because single mothers have so few male counterparts (that is, single fathers), we omit single mothers from these comparisons.

11. Because of the high degree of uniformity in men's employment rates, there is a strong correlation across these countries between female-to-male employment ratios and women's employment rates. In contrast, there is extensive variation in the female employment rate, and that variation, standardized against the men's rates, is captured in the ratio measure.

12. For an analysis of measurement issues that arise in cross-national comparisons of gender inequality in paid work, see Gornick (1999a). Note that throughout this book, we equate "gender inequality in the labor market" with any observed gender differentials in labor market activity or outcomes. This definition does not take into account gender differences in tastes or preferences, nor does it address questions of equity.

13. Because we are interested in gross gender differentials (rather than discrimination), the ratios in this figure are not adjusted for gender differences in human capital or job-related differences.

These hourly wage differentials are estimates in that, due to data limitations, they do not take into account differences between mothers and fathers in average weeks worked per year. The gender ratio in hourly wages is calculated as follows: (mothers' annual earnings / mothers' average weekly hours) / (fathers' annual earnings / fathers' average weekly hours). Fortunately, the accuracy of these estimates is supported by other published findings on gender wage ratios, using different data, which produce similar results as to cross-country rankings. The Organisation for Economic Co-operation and Development (OECD) reports gender wage differentials across countries, from the middle to late 1990s, estimated as the difference between women's and men's median full-time earnings (OECD 2001c).

In most countries, the gender gaps reported by the OECD are smaller than what we find; that is not surprising because the OECD estimates are not limited to parents, as ours are. However, the cross-country ranking is very similar across the two studies. In both cases, the United States has a larger gender wage gap than do Finland, Sweden, Belgium, France, and the Netherlands; and in both cases, the United States has a smaller gender wage gap than do Germany and the United Kingdom. The one discrepancy is with Canada; where we find that Canada has a smaller gender wage differential than does the United States, this OECD study reports the reverse. Note also that in our French data set, wages are net of taxes. Because of the progressivity of taxation, the use of net wages would be expected to reduce the gender differential (overestimating women's relative wages), compared with the other countries for which we report gross wages. The resulting bias seems to be limited, however, as the OECD study reports a wage gap in France that is ten points smaller than the U.S. gap, which is also in line with our findings.

14. Multiple factors underlie variation across countries in the gender wage gap. First, some portion of the cross-country variation is explained by variation across countries in gender differences in human capital and job-related factors, and some by variation in differences in the returns to these factors; the latter is generally defined as discrimination. Second, some portion of the cross-country variation—as with the wage gaps between part-time and full-time employment—derives from variation across these countries in overall levels of wage dispersion. As Francine Blau and Lawrence Kahn (1992) have established, gender wage gaps are larger where wage inequality is more extensive, because the two groups' distributions fall further from one another.

Although our data do not allow a full analysis of the underlying factors, we know from the literature (Blau and Kahn 1992, using the ISSP data) and from our earlier research (Gornick 1999a, using the LIS data) that the gender wage gap in the United States lags cross-nationally primarily because the United States has such a high level of overall wage inequality. The median female earner in the United States falls at about the same place in the male wage distribution as her counterpart in countries with smaller gender wage gaps. The U.S. gap is larger, however, because wage dispersion pushes that median female worker further from the middle of the male distribution. In other words, relative to their counterparts elsewhere, American mothers fare relatively poorly in terms of gender equality in wages, but their poor outcome is explained more by general wage structures than by gender-specific factors.

Ideally, we would also include a fourth indicator, one that captures the extent to which women and men work in different jobs, occupations, or industries. Accurate measures of gender segregation at work require virtually identical job or sectoral data across countries, and sufficiently comparable data (that include the United States) were not available. The main reason that labor market scholars are concerned about gender segregation is that feminized jobs and sectors tend to pay low wages, and we do capture gender differentials in pay in our wage and earnings comparisons.

15. We also calculated women's shares of total labor market earnings for the entire working-age population, that is, including workers without children. Not surprisingly, in all countries, women's share of overall earnings is higher than mothers' shares of parental earnings. American women command 36 percent of all labor market earnings; that places the United States near the middle of these countries. The United States' rank among all working-age adults is somewhat higher than its rank among parents, underscoring the role that caregiving plays in shaping American women's labor market attachment, in comparative perspective.

16. In addition, in the Nordic countries, though occupational segregation tends to be high, that segregation does not have the strong adverse affect on women's pay that it does in the United States. See, for example, Rosenfeld and Kalleberg (1991).

17. We gratefully acknowledge the assistance of Anne H. Gauthier with the preparation of data from the Multinational Time Use Study. See appendix A for further information about the MTUS data. Note that unpaid work includes time spent in routine housework (cooking, cleaning, and housework), in nonroutine housework (other domestic work, gardening, shopping, domestic travel), and in care for children.

Although these MTUS data are among the highest-quality time-use data in existence, time-use data are subject to considerable measurement problems. Time-use researchers raise concerns about the representativeness of the time surveyed (generally, a single day) and about recall accuracy, even in relation to time spent earlier the same day. Respondents sometimes find it difficult to categorize their activities, especially if they are engaging in multiple tasks simultaneously. Respondents' time assessments may also be biased by their judgments about the social acceptability of various activities (such as caring for children). For the purposes of cross-national comparisons, however, the most relevant question is whether the errors introduced by these measurement problems are likely to vary systematically across countries. There is no convincing evidence to suggest that they do. Finally, these particular comparisons are also somewhat weakened by the fact that the data span seven years and the timeframe is somewhat earlier than that of the other microdata sets that we use in this chapter.

18. No existing surveys that include both the United States and Europe collect information on employment during nonstandard hours. These comparative results are based on the 1997 European Labor Force Surveys (LFS), for the European countries, and a working-time supplement to the 1997 CPS for the United States. The Nordic countries are excluded, as the surveys in those countries do not allow the identification of parents. For this comparison, Eurostat (the statistical office of the European Union) adopted definitions that matched those used in the CPS as closely as possible. Unfortunately, some incomparability remains, and the result is that the European rates of evening and night work may be somewhat overstated, as the threshold for what constitutes "usually working" during these hours is lower. We are grateful to Harriet Presser, with whom we collaborated on this inquiry. For further information on the Labor Force Survey data, see appendix A.

19. Family income is adjusted for family size; the adjustment assumes that family income needs are proportional to the square root of family size. Note that in the United States, income includes the Earned Income Tax Credit.

20. We thank author Stacy Kim for this tabulation.

21. For example, a highly publicized study by Arlie Hochschild (1997) reaches the provocative conclusion that many workers actually elect to spend long hours at work. Hochschild finds that most workers in the large Fortune 500 company that she studied failed to take advantage of benefits that would have reduced their hours. She concludes that the rewards of home and work have been reversed and that many workers flee home for more time at work; they feel more effective and successful on the job. Although Hochschild's research raises crucial concerns—especially about the devalued state of caring work at home—several critiques have cast doubt on the generalizability of her results (see, for example, Landy

1998). Others argue that she fails to appreciate fully the subtle messages that employees receive in the workplace discouraging them from taking up the "family-friendly" benefits that are offered.

22. Linda Bell and Richard Freeman (2001) attribute American workers' longer hours to structural factors, specifically to wage inequality, and not to an inherent preference for long hours or other cultural factors. They conclude that "inequality of pay contributes to hours worked. In sum, in the United States we work hard because we face a good 'carrot' for putting out time and effort, and because we also face a substantial 'stick" if we do not'" (Bell and Freeman 2001, 96).

23. For a description of the ISSP data, see appendix A.

Chapter Four

1. There are actually several versions of the "sameness" versus "difference" debate. As Joan Williams argues, what is known as the sameness-difference debate often conflates two issues: whether men and women are "really" the same or different and whether men and women should receive the same treatment under the law. For a comprehensive analysis, see her book *Unbending Gender: Why Work-Family Conflict and What to Do About It* (Williams 2000).

2. Although we prefer the full label—the "dual-earner–dual-carer" society—because it stresses time allocation between family members, we use the shorthand "earner-carer" for the remainder of this book. In either case, our intention is to suggest social and policy reforms that support single parents as well as coupled parents. Providing this support to single mothers raises additional challenges, which we address more fully in chapter 9.

3. Marshall's observations were rooted in time and place—in postwar England, where the British Labour Party was implementing a social democratic welfare state during a time of considerable optimism. Nevertheless, Marshall intended to tell a generalized historical story about the expansion of citizenship rights and the development of the modern welfare state.

4. In the citizenship literature, the terms "social rights" and "social and economic rights" are generally used interchangeably. Americans tend to refer to both as "economic rights."

5. Knijn and Kremer do argue that, in addition to granting "rights to time for care," welfare states can also secure a "right to receive care," but by that they refer to out-of-home care. They conclude that rights related to informal care have to be established through

the caregiver, as informal care is conditional on the relationship between the giver and the receiver of that care. See Knijn and Kremer (1997, 332).

6. American scholars have, however, addressed a number of related concerns. There are large and excellent literatures on the "costs of motherhood" (Crittenden 2001; England and Folbre 1999a, 1999b; Waldfogel 1998), on the determinants of gender differences in unpaid work in the home (Brines 1994; Greenstein 2000; Presser 1994), and on "gendered time" (Mutari and Figart 2001). There is also a growing literature on factors that strengthen fathers' engagement with child caregiving (see Marsiglio et al. 2000 for a review). Nevertheless, American scholars, on the whole, have not granted the dual-earner–dual-carer model the centrality in social theory or in policy analysis that European feminists have.

7. For example, Anne-Lise Ellingsaeter, writing about the Norwegian "worker/carer model," describes the core policy package, which includes gender-egalitarian family leave and the right to reduced-hour work. To that, she adds "access to high-quality public childcare. Public day care plays an important part in the everyday life of parents" (Ellingsaeter 1999, 44).

8. If American families were to shift toward the working time suggested in this thought experiment, there would also be a substantial redistribution of working time among women, as many stay-at-home mothers would enter the labor force and others would reduce their hours in paid work. Although the average employment hours of mothers in the labor force are longer than the averages presented in table 4.1 (which include those with zero hours), average hours among employed mothers are still well less than those of their partners. In 2000, for example, employed married mothers spent an average of thirty-six hours a week in employment, about ten hours fewer than did their husbands (authors' calculations, based on 2000 CPS).

9. Presser (1989b, 1995a) reports that single mothers and grandmothers, jointly raising children, often work split shifts, very much like dual-earner couples.

10. As Majella Kilkey and Jonathan Bradshaw (1999) observe, "A welfare state can really claim to provide women's social rights only if lone mothers are enabled to live independently of men, out of poverty, and also are not forced to choose between paid work or full-time care to avoid poverty" (Kilkey and Bradshaw 1999, 176).

11. Several countries also have leave provisions that support and remunerate time spent caring for other family members—including, for

example, disabled and elderly adults—but for the purposes of this study, we focus on child-related provisions.

12. Americans tend to be skeptical of positive rights, which imply a right to have one's needs met, in particular, by the state. In contrast, American political culture prizes negative rights, which are rights that guarantee freedom from government interference.

13. In economic language, when others can reap the benefits without paying, the public good is nonexcludable; when one person's enjoyment does not diminish that of another, it is characterized by nonrivalness.

14. England and Folbre (1999a) stress that parents are not the only producers of children's capabilities. Many who are employed in caring occupations, such as child care and teaching, contribute to the nurturing of children but receive remuneration that is incommensurate with the benefits they produce. Although these care workers are paid, they are systematically underpaid, partly because caring occupations are so heavily feminized and partly because care work itself tends to exact a wage penalty (for an empirical treatment, see England, Budig, and Folbre 2002). The case for government provision of benefits and services targeted on children, as a means to lessening free riding or caregivers' labor, extends beyond unpaid parental caregivers to waged but underpaid caregivers as well.

Chapter Five

1. Nearly all family leave programs extend the same benefits to parents who adopt as to those who bear children. Throughout this chapter, when we refer to childbirth, in nearly all cases we mean childbirth or adoption; repeating the distinction throughout seems unnecessarily cumbersome.

2. In this chapter, we focus on maternity leave policies that grant some cash benefits.

3. Before the passage of the FMLA, thirty-two states had leave legislation in place. Laws in ten states granted rights that were fairly similar to what would be extended nationally by the FMLA; the rest provided less protection (Wisensale 2001).

4. Percentages do not sum to 100 due to multiple responses.

5. The lack of both paid and unpaid leave available to workers in small enterprises is compounded by their limited access to other workplace benefits. The 1997 *National Study of the Changing Workforce* reveals that "employed parents who work . . . for

smaller organizations have [less] access to family health insurance from their employer, health insurance for their children from some source, paid vacations, paid holidays, child care resource and referral, on- or near-site child care, financial assistance for child care, and dependent care assistance plans" (Galinsky and Bond 2000, 109).

6. For example, imagine a couple that decides that only one parent will take leave; his salary is $200, and hers is $100. If the wage-replacement rate during parental leave were 100 percent, their combined earnings would remain $300, regardless of who took the leave. If the wage-replacement rate were 50 percent of earnings, it would be in their economic interest for her to take the leave. If she were to take leave, their earnings would be $250 (200 + 50), whereas if he does, their earnings would be only $200 (100 + 100). With a wage replacement of zero (as under the FMLA), if she took the leave, their earnings would be $200; if he were to take the leave, their earnings would fall to $100. The incentives to assign the leave to the lower earner rise as the wage-replacement rate falls.

7. The five state TDI programs are financed through social insurance, with varying contributions from employers and employees. One state (Rhode Island) finances its TDI entirely through employee contributions. In the other four states, the balance of employer and employee contributions varies extensively both across and within states, depending on which financing scheme or insurance option employers choose (Wisensale 2001).

8. Figure 5.2 excludes the United States's TDI programs because they are available in only five states. In the remaining countries, the figure includes only the earnings-related components of family leave (and assumes earnings below the cap). About half of our comparison countries supplement the benefits captured in figure 5.2 with additional periods of leave paid at a low flat rate—most substantially in Finland, France, and Germany. We exclude these low-paid benefits here because in some cases (Finland and Germany) the benefits are not conditioned on employment, so characterizing them as wage replacement is not fully accurate. In addition, the program in France is payable only for second and subsequent children. Furthermore, take-up is much lower than in the earnings-related programs, so including them distorts the level of provision upward.

Note that countries could reach equivalent levels of generosity on this indicator in different ways. For example, in Finland, twenty-nine weeks results from forty-four weeks at about two-thirds pay, whereas in Canada the twenty-eight weeks corresponds to fifty weeks at 55 percent.

9. Mothers in Finland may also collect a low flat-rate benefit (a "home care" benefit) for about two years following the end of maternity and parental leave, that is, until the child's third birthday. The benefit is allowed only if the child is not in public child care. Parents may also choose to use that payment to purchase care from a private child care provider. See table 5.1.

10. As in Finland, mothers in France (starting with the second child) and in Germany (subject to a means test) may also collect low flat-rate benefits for additional periods of time—three and two years, respectively. See table 5.1.

11. Few women in the United States, or in Europe, breastfeed for more than one year ("Breast Cancer Risk Reduced by Breastfeeding" 2001), and that is true of both employed and stay-at-home mothers (Ross Products Division 2001).

12. Ellingsaeter underscores the difference between the early and later years of motherhood by distinguishing "biological motherhood," which lasts about one year, from "political motherhood," which includes "all the other care work mothers do in connection with children (including economic provision, physical and psychological care), and its content is defined politically and socially, by prevailing practices and ideas" (Ellingsaeter 1999, 45). There is no universal point in a child's life cycle after which mothers' and fathers' time spent in caregiving could easily be arranged symmetrically, but the consensus is that it takes place sometime during the first year of life.

13. Longer leaves are sometimes further divided into "parental leave," typically conditioned on employment, versus "child-rearing" (or "child care") leave, which is typically available to parents regardless of employment history; child-rearing leaves are generally paid at a lower rate and for a longer duration. We use the general term "parental leave" to encompass both. Examples of child-rearing leaves are the flat-rate programs available in Finland, France, and Germany.

14. European Union directives are binding for member countries. Norway, the one nonmember among our European countries, voluntarily implements EU directives. See appendix B for a summary of the directive.

15. Some countries provide leave rights and wage replacement for a range of family reasons. For example, Swedish parents may take short-term leaves (with 80 percent pay) to visit children at child

care centers or at school, to take a parent-education class, or to stand in for a regular child care provider who is ill (Haas and Hwang 1999). Dutch parents have the right to short periods of paid "emergency leave," and Belgian parents are granted paid time off for brief periods to attend to child-related needs (Bettio and Prechal 1998). Table 5.2 is confined to sick-child leave because it is the most widespread form and because comparable information is available for all twelve countries.

16. Across Europe, mothers' take-up of paid leave, both maternity and parental, is high. However, many well-educated and highly paid women take up the benefits offered for less than the full duration of available parental leave (Kamerman 2000).

17. In figure 5.3 we credited Finland with having a use-or-lose component. Although it is not part of parental leave (for which the term is generally used), the eighteen-day paternity benefit is, in effect, a "use-or-lose" benefit, as fathers cannot transfer those days to their partners. Moreover, its duration approaches that of the use-or-lose quotas in Norway and Sweden.

18. In Sweden, fathers who take up the most parental leave are public-sector workers (who usually get 100 percent wage replacement), highly educated white-collar workers, or men with well-educated and highly paid female partners (Kamerman 2000).

19. Expenditures reflect more than program rules; aggregate spending is influenced by employment rates, wage levels, take-up, and the mix of beneficiaries. Nevertheless, expenditures offer a powerful metric for comparing policy effort across countries in that they capture multiple dimensions of program duration, benefit rates, and policy elements that affect take-up.

Expenditure data are from the OECD's Social Expenditure Database (OECD 2001b). These data include expenditures on "maternity and parental leave" as a single line item; unfortunately, expenditures on "leave for family reasons" are not included. Totals include public and mandated private spending; thus expenditures in Germany include both the social insurance payments and the mandated employer "top up" (reported in table 5.4). These expenditure data pertain to 1998—except for Luxembourg (1990) and the Netherlands (1989), where later data are not available.

We standardized expenditures across countries by dividing total spending in each country by the number of employed women in that country at that time. Expenditures are then expressed in 2000 U.S. dollars, PPP-adjusted. We standardized using women, rather than all workers, because men take a small share of total leave time everywhere and because female employment varies much more markedly across countries. Ideally, we would be able to calculate average expenditures for each leave taker, but comparable data on take-up are not available across countries.

20. Unfortunately, this Canadian expenditure figure probably underestimates the costs of the program as it is described in table 5.1. Cross-nationally comparable spending data are available only through 1998, whereas the rules that we report reflect 2000. Between these two dates, the duration of the shared parental leave benefit was increased from ten to thirty-five weeks.

21. Most countries finance maternity from a combination of employer and employee contributions. Although the balance between the two contributions varies widely, the larger direct contribution usually comes from employers. In France, for example, the employer contributes more than 90 percent of the combined contribution; in the Netherlands, about 80 percent, and in Belgium, about two-thirds (European Commission 2001). In a few cases—for example, Luxembourg—the employer and employee contribute matching amounts.

Chapter Six

1. We use the terms "working-time policies" and "regulating working time" broadly to refer to national and local legislation, public labor market regulations, and collective agreements that affect a large share of the workforce. We use the term "reduced-hour work" to refer to paid work at less than forty hours a week, and the term "part-time work" to mean paid work at less than approximately thirty-five hours a week. Across our comparison countries, definitions of part-time work vary. In the United States and in several other countries, part-time work is usually defined as less than thirty-five hours a week, in others, less than thirty hours a week.

2. In other words, U.S. labor law sets a monetary deterrent on overtime but not a statutory limit, as is common in Europe. In the European Union countries, employers who compel or pressure workers to work beyond set weekly limits can be prosecuted.

3. These states are California, Illinois, Maryland, New York, North Dakota, Rhode Island, and Virginia.

4. The rules covering self-insured health plans can be found in section 105(h) of the Internal Revenue Code, and the regulations can be found at 26 CFR 1.105–11. The standards related to pensions can be found in section 202 of ERISA and section 410 of the code. The regulations

under ERISA can be found at 29 CFR 2530.202-1 and 2530.202-2, and the regulations under the code can be found at 26 CFR 1.410(a)-3 and 1.410(a)-3T. We thank Deborah Forbes at the Pension Benefits Guaranty Corporation for providing this information.

5. For example, 50 percent of women working part-time in the United States are employed in just 10 out of 236 industries—including eating and drinking establishments, grocery stores, department stores, and hospitals, child day care, nursing and personal, and private household services. The weighted average hourly wage in these 10 industries is $8.27, which is 20 percent below the median wage for all workers (Wenger 2001).

6. For a review of the economics literature on the gap between part-time and full-time wages, see Bardasi and Gornick (2003).

7. Although industrial-relations systems are extremely varied across countries, labor-management relations and the bargaining process are highly regulated everywhere. In some countries—for example, France—union membership is much lower than rates of coverage, as collective agreements set the working conditions of workers who are not union members. In most of our comparison countries, including the United States, membership and coverage are approximately the same.

8. Ellen Mutari and Deborah Figart (2001) note that there was much in the 1993 Working-Time Directive that benefited employers—in particular, the option to calculate maximum hours using a reference period of as long as four months. They argue that, ultimately, employers may have gained more flexibility in scheduling than workers gained in shortened hours, especially because several European countries had maximum hours in place before adoption of the directive. Mutari and Figart make the larger point that reforms that increase working-time "flexibility" and those that reduce working time are by no means equivalent. Although increasing flexibility for employers may also extend employees' options, the consequences can be problematic for workers—if, for example, employers shift toward a greater use of nonstandard hours. The consequences of increasing employers' flexibility could also further weaken gender equality. That would be the case if new workplace practices—such as a greater reliance on part-time work, overtime, shift work, or "on-call" working—exacerbated gender gaps in working patterns.

9. Surveys in the Netherlands reveal that "that 30% of couples would like to shift their schedules, with women wanting more hours and men wanting less, [and the act was] designed to accommodate these wishes" (32 Hours 2003).

10. There is some concern among working-time scholars that nonstandard hours in Europe will rise in the future, perhaps—ironically—as the flip side to the reduction in total working time and the strengthening of part-time work now under way. Some scholars speculate that the price European workers will have to pay for shorter total hours and more part-time work, ultimately, will be increased freedom ("flexibility") for employers to schedule workers around the clock (see, for example, Rubery et al. 1998).

11. Despite a 1991 European court ruling that all bans on women's nighttime work violate the 1976 EU Directive on Equal Treatment, the issue of women's nighttime work remains contested. During the 1990s, at least two of these countries—Germany and Luxembourg—were advised by the European Union that their bans on nighttime work for pregnant women and women with newborns breached the EU Directive on Equal Treatment; negotiations are still under way.

12. We thank Harriet Presser for these results, tabulated for us, based on the 1997 CPS.

13. In addition, although the U.S. Congress establishes several federal holidays throughout the year, they actually apply only to federal establishments. Although many private employers observe them, they are not obligated to do so.

Chapter Seven

1. Of these, only Georgia is approaching full coverage. Oklahoma currently serves about 50 percent of four-year-olds. Although universal access is a goal in New York, the state currently lacks both the funding and service delivery capacity to realize it.

2. The TANF block grant assumed increasing importance in the late 1990s. As of 2000, states were spending more TANF than CCDF funds for child care (Schumacher, Greenberg, and Duffy 2001). These commitments are vulnerable to changes in welfare caseloads, however, and states began limiting TANF investments as welfare caseloads grew in 2001 and 2002.

3. Empirical studies also suggest that a reduction in the price of formal care leads parents to substitute market forms of care for more informal arrangements (Michalopoulos and Robins 2000; Michalopoulos, Robins, and Garfinkel 1992). David Blau, for example, finds that both maternal wage and family income elasticities are positive for center care and negative for other forms of care; this suggests that as wages and family income rise, families tend to switch from less

formal to more formal care arrangements. He simulates the effect of reducing the cost of all forms of child care from $1.50 to $0 (for all households) as increasing the use of child care centers by 11.8 percent and family child care homes by 22.6 percent while decreasing the use of parental and other forms of nonparental care (such as babysitters). He suggests that "parents feel most 'priced out' of center and family day care and would prefer these types over other nonparental care and parental care if they were equally as cheap" (Blau 2001, 74).

4. Poor and near-poor families are less likely to purchase care because they rely more heavily on free care from relatives or fully subsidized arrangements. Lower-income families are also more likely than more affluent families, however, to pay the relatives who care for their children, which may reflect greater financial needs among those relatives (Anderson and Levine 1999).

5. Although the number of families getting help from government rose between 1997 and 1999, as federal and state governments increased expenditures for child care subsidies, the number of employed families with children also increased—leaving the share of families assisted unchanged.

6. The association between income and child care quality is slightly curvilinear for children in center care because some of the poorest children receive high-quality care through Head Start and other subsidized programs.

7. The reasons underlying the low wages of child care and other care workers are complex and much debated (see, for example, Blau 2001; England, Budig, and Folbre 2002). England and Folbre (1999a) summarize five possible explanations for why care work is so poorly paid: (1) care work is devalued specifically because it is so heavily performed by women; (2) care work offers intrinsic rewards, so employers feel they can lower the pay ("compensating differentials"); (3) care work produces public goods, so there is no practical way to set a price that reflects its full value; (4) care services in the public sector often serve poor clientele, and political factors depress the workers' wages; and (5) caring labor is viewed, somewhat ironically, as "sacred," and we as a society are ambivalent about fully commodifying it, which reduces the pay.

8. Educationally oriented care for children between the ages of three and the start of primary school is usually referred to as preprimary in Europe. We use the more familiar term "preschool" (unless we are referring specifically to state pre-kindergarten programs in the United States), but it should be kept in mind that these programs

are largely public in Europe, whereas in the United States they are a mix of public and private provisions.

9. Although Norway also provides extensive public ECEC, the costs of this care fall much more heavily on parents (because of high co-payments), and supply shortages have contributed to the growth of a "black market" in private, unregulated care arrangements.

10. Since 1997, an agreement between the national government and the National Association of Local Authorities in Denmark has guaranteed a place in public child care for all children from the age of one year through school age, and most municipalities now guarantee a place for children within three months of parents' requests. Child care is also provided as a right in Finland; every child under compulsory school age has an unconditional right to early care and education from the end of parental leave. There is considerable disagreement about where the youngest children should be cared for, however, and Finnish parents may choose instead to receive a Home Care Allowance for parental care. Of the Nordic countries, only Norway has failed to extend a legal child care entitlement for care during the preschool years. However, "it is a political priority [in Norway] to achieve universal access for all children under 6 years," and that goal has been reached for children aged three and older (OECD 2001d, 171).

11. In Sweden, parents have a right to a place in an ECEC program for children aged one and older; about three hundred children under that age are enrolled in public care. In Finland, all children have a right to public ECEC, but there is little demand for care while parents are on leave; child care during the parental leave period is usually used by entrepreneurs, students, or parents with some sudden difficulty or illness. In Denmark, most municipalities guarantee a place for children starting between nine and twelve months of age. There are some shortages of care for children under nine months of age, and employed parents may have priority for those places (Michelle Neuman, Columbia University, personal communication, September 16, 2002).

12. Parental co-payments covered a much higher share of the costs in Norway as of the late 1990s. National policy has set as a goal, however, capping parental fees at 20 percent of costs.

13. The most aggressive scheme for encouraging employer involvement has been adopted in the Netherlands. The 1990 Stimulative Measure on Child Care encourages employers to subsidize care for their employees' children under the age of seven (Rostgaard and

Fridberg 1998). The country has set as a goal the equal division of ECEC costs among municipalities, employers, and parents.

14. We do not report data for systems that have limited public provisions (other than the United States) because the co-payments do not capture the costs to parents of purchasing private alternatives and would severely underestimate the total costs to parents. The measure of government and family shares of ECEC costs in the United States includes both private expenditures and family co-payments for public care.

15. Another estimate of the direct financial effect of ECEC policies is provided by researchers at the European Observatory on National Family Policies (Bradshaw et al. 1996). They use estimates of the "average costs of the most prevalent form of formal day care" to calculate child care costs as a percentage of the average earnings (PPP-adjusted) for a single parent with one child in different ECEC policy regimes. In the Nordic countries, with extensive provisions from birth to the start of school, child care costs are estimated to be between 7 and 13 percent of the average earnings of a single parent; in France and Belgium, costs are estimated as zero for families with children enrolled in école; in the highly privatized American system a lone parent would pay an estimated 22 percent of his or her earnings for care for a single child.

16. Cross-national comparisons of actual parental costs are extremely constrained by data limitations—in the mostly public systems by the lack of survey data on parental costs and in the mostly private systems by the lack of data on public subsidies. For this analysis we make use of measures of reported household-level expenditures on all forms of child care for all children in the family, from the Luxembourg Income Study (France) and the National Survey of America's Families (United States), a nationally representative survey conducted by the Urban Institute (2002). Note that in each country we assume that these are costs net of any direct government assistance received through subsidies or the use of a public program (such as école in France or pre-kindergarten in the United States). Family expenditures are not adjusted for tax credits.

17. It is important to remember that these child care costs are for all children in the family, not only the youngest child. A family with a child under the age of three may be purchasing care for that child and for an older child or only for the older child.

18. Although nearly all three- to five-year-old children in France are enrolled in free école programs, these classes are often offered for

less than forty hours a week. Many parents purchase private child care to cover the remaining hours of the workweek.

19. Most expenditure data for five of the seven countries were collected by Tine Rostgaard and Torben Fridberg (1998), appendix table A1. Data for Canada and the United States were obtained by the authors from various country-specific sources.

20. Due to data limitations, these figures do not include tax benefits for the purchase of private care, available in three of the comparison countries (France, the Netherlands, and the United States) as of the mid-1990s.

21. Because spending for the direct provision of care is calculated as the average for each child of the relevant age group, average totals reflect both the cost of care and the levels of enrollment. Totals will not correspond directly to the cost of providing specific forms of care. In a country such as France, for example, total expenditures are the average of the higher-cost services in the écoles, provided to nearly all children aged three to five, and the less expensive services in crèches, which are provided to only about one-quarter of children under the age of three.

22. The figure for each child is calculated as the total tax expenditure relative to the total population of children under the age of seven, including those whose families did not make use of the credit. Actual benefits of the credit were obviously higher for those families able to make use of it, whereas low-income families are likely to receive no benefits.

23. There is considerable debate in the child care field about how best to define and measure the quality of care. Researchers have sometimes noted that parents and child care experts consider different attributes of care when they evaluate quality. Studies that have examined the link between child care characteristics and child outcomes suggest that structural characteristics, particularly group size and staff preparation, predict higher process quality and better child outcomes (for example, NICHD 2002). See chapter 8 of this volume for a more detailed review.

24. There is evidence that regulation of public care settings is also becoming weaker. For example, as states have expanded pre-kindergarten programs, many have also "privatized" these programs by situating services in existing private child care centers. As a recent review of child care in the United States concludes, these programs display extreme diversity in the "goals, administrative structures and funding, the types of agencies operating programmes, the eligi-

bility criteria, the quality standards, and the scope of supports provided to children and families" (OECD 2001d, 19).

25. In an interesting comparative study, Debby Cryer and her colleagues find that teacher and director wages contributed to child care quality in four industrialized countries and had the strongest positive association with quality in the United States (Cryer et al. 1999).

26. The average wage for women workers is calculated using data on annual earnings from the Luxembourg Income Study (LIS).

Chapter Eight

1. A very large and related literature examines the association between poverty and child well-being. For a comprehensive review, see Gershoff, Aber, and Raver (forthcoming).

2. For example, parents who work many hours during their child's first year may do so out of economic necessity, and constrained family income may directly compromise children's well-being; alternatively, parents who work long hours may have unusually high levels of education and other human-capital characteristics that directly support children's healthy development. For a discussion of these and other estimation issues, see Ruhm (forthcoming).

3. To the best of our knowledge, there are no rigorous assessments of the effects on either labor market or family outcomes of the 1978 Swedish law that grants parents the right to work six hours a day. Some researchers, however, note that take-up is heavily female and suggest that some women might shift to the part-time option and to more feminized workplaces as well—so that their working hours resemble the workplace norm. That would suggest that the Swedish law may increase job-level or occupational segregation (see Lewis and Astrom 1992).

4. One study (Grubb and Wells 1993) assesses the effect, across Europe, of regulations on evening and weekend work on the actual prevalence of evening and weekend work. The authors find a weak relation with evening work—in the expected direction—but no relation with weekend work. They note that their measures of regulation were crude.

5. Ellen Mutari and Deborah Figart (2001) consider the correspondence across countries between regulatory approaches and working-time outcomes. They conclude that countries with shorter standard workweeks and limited overtime rank highest on gender-egalitar-

ian outcomes, noting that "the alternative to policies that accommodate work hours to the gendered divisions of labor are policies that change the male model of full-time employment. Reductions in the standard work week are a long-term solution for achieving gender equity in the labor market and the redistribution of domestic labor. . . . A shorter work work can enable both men and women to participate in the labor market on an equal basis" (Mutari and Figart 2001, 40–41). The authors identify four countries among our comparison countries as having "made strides toward gender equity by changing social norms concerning working time," Denmark, Finland, Belgium, and France (Mutari and Figart 2001, 40). For other analyses of working time, state regulatory approaches, and gender, see Rubery, Smith, and Fagan (1998) and Figart and Mutari (1998).

6. We are assessing here the effects of overtime regulations on workers' actual hours worked. A different—and important—literature addresses the effect of reducing workers' weekly hours on aggregate employment levels. The literature suggests that the impact is likely to depend on the mechanism used. If hours are directly restricted (as they are in France), new jobs may be created as employers hire new workers to supply the needed hours. If hours are restricted by lowering the threshold above which overtime must be paid or by raising overtime rates (the more commonly used mechanisms), employers might shed workers to compensate for the extra costs associated with paying the workers already employed. The empirical findings are mixed (see Hamermesh 2002 for a review).

7. A few researchers have extended the research by considering other dimensions of maternal labor supply. David Blau and Philip Robins (1989) and Sandra Hofferth and Nancy Collins (2000) demonstrate the role of child care costs (and, in the Hofferth and Collins study, availability) on employment stability. Charles Baum (2002) and Lisa Powell (2002) both extend their analyses to show the impact of child care costs on hours worked among those who are employed.

8. Although useful, simulations of changes in child care prices are highly sensitive to estimation methods. Examining the issue of subsidy receipt more directly using a variety of natural experiments, Mark Berger and Dan Black (1992), Marcia Meyers et al. (2002), Jonah Gelbach (1999), Bruce Meyer and Dan Rosenbaum (2001), Jay Bainbridge et al. (2002), and Magaly Queralt, Ann Dryden Witte, and Harriet Griesinger (2000) have all demonstrated that the expansion of child care subsidies (during the 1980s and 1990s) explains a portion of the increase in employment among single mothers during this period.

9. For a recent review of U.S. and European research on the effects of ECEC, see Kamerman et al. (forthcoming).

10. Burchinal (1999) argues that the observed ratio between the contribution of parental and child care characteristics should be interpreted cautiously, given the difficulty of distinguishing between them in nonrandomized studies. As she points out, failure to control for parental characteristics will lead to an overestimate of the contribution of child care (because those with strong parenting skills also select high-quality care), but inclusion of these controls may lead to an underestimate of the contribution of child care features that are correlated with these family characteristics.

11. The indicator is the estimated effect of the presence of a preschool-age child on employment, based on logistic regression analysis that controls for mothers' age and education, total number of children, and other household income.

12. Due to incompatibilities in the time periods for the policy and outcome data, we are unable to include provisions affecting the availability and quality of part-time work in this index.

13. To construct the horizontal axis of figure 8.8, we created a new policy index that includes all of the elements of index C (weighted at 50 percent) and expenditures on cash benefits for families (weighted at 50 percent). Cash benefits were measured as the average spent per child (table 2.1, right-hand column) and rescaled to values of 0 and 1.

Chapter Nine

1. In the absence of family leave, for example, public assistance has been the only form of paid leave available to many low-skilled workers at the time of childbirth.

2. The United States spends about .25 percent of GDP on active labor market measures—including public-service employment, labor market training, youth measures, subsidized employment, and programs for disabled workers. Canada spends more than twice that share, and these European countries spend, on average, four times that share (Gornick (1999b).

3. The total fertility rate is defined as the average number of births each woman would have if she were to live through her reproductive years and bear children at each age at the rates observed in the current period (OECD 2001c).

4. It is not clear exactly what has driven this anti-European-social-policy drumbeat, although Ackerman concludes that cozy relations

between major media companies and American big business have been a major culprit. "The 'sick man of Europe' is in truth a straw man of American capitalism," he writes, "a cautionary fairy tale as widely believed by our journalists as it is beloved by the businessmen who sign their checks" (Ackerman 1999, 66). What is clear is that these stories satisfy those who oppose public solutions to market-generated risks and inequalities.

5.   Proponents of the Eurosclerosis theory frequently fail to take account of other crucial factors. Many European economists have pointed to the increased demand for technical skills across industries and occupations—which pushed large numbers of less-skilled workers out of jobs; others have considered the effects of growing competition from low-cost producers in eastern Europe and Southeast Asia. Other economists, including Robert Solow, argue that persistently high real interest rates run by Europe's central bankers kept millions out of work (Modigliani et al. 1998).

6.   As Europe expanded paid family leave, so did Canada. The duration of maternity and parental leave benefits in Canada was doubled in 2000.

7.   There has been relatively little cross-national comparative research on public attitudes toward these benefits in particular. For a recent review of comparative research on attitudes toward the welfare state more generally, see Shapiro and Young (1989).

8.   Nancy Johnson and Keith Provan (1995) have studied the relation across firms between wages and four types of benefits—child care (mostly information and referral services), flextime, sick-child leave, and maternity leave. Overall, they find that none of these exerted a significant negative impact on wages. They conclude that the productivity-enhancing effects of these benefits may be substantial enough that employers do not need to reduce wages to pay for them.

9.   This study concludes that, contrary to popular perceptions, longer leaves (financed through social insurance) do not necessarily create more severe challenges for employers. In fact, leaves of moderate length (say, three to five months) may be harder on employers because they are too long for work sharing and too short to make hiring a substitute efficient (Alewell and Pull 2001).

10.   These cost estimates are based on the family leave expenditures reported in figure 5.4 and the ECEC expenditures reported in table 7.5. Across these countries, total ECEC expenditures are generally three to five times higher than expenditures on family leave.

11. The United States now spends about 15 percent of GDP on social policy, by far the lowest percentage among our comparison countries. Relative to these other countries, the percentage of total social expenditures allocated to work-family programs is also exceptionally low in the United States (Gornick and Meyers 2001). In other words, in comparative perspective, the United States allocates a small slice of a small pie to policies that help families to reconcile employment and caregiving.

12. We calculated this as follows: We converted Swedish per capita spending on leave and ECEC into U.S. dollars (adjusting for differences in purchasing parity). We multiplied per capita spending by the total U.S. population to arrive at estimated total spending and then converted that to a share of U.S. GDP. That procedure is equivalent to estimating these expenditures as the share of GDP that they capture in Sweden (2.5 percent) and adjusting that 2.5 percent downward to account for the differences in GPD per capita—that is, multiplying 2.5 by (Sweden's per capita GDP / the United States's per capita GDP). In fact, the two methods produce exactly the same result: these programs would cost about 1.7 percent of U.S. GDP.

13. By failing to locate this tradeoff in the larger context of gender inequalities, these advocates risk undermining the power of their own efforts to improve the lives of America's children. As Mahony argues, "Part of children's troubles does come from the sexual division of labor in the home. Some observers think it has been hard to build a social movement to advocate for children because children are seen as women's work and women lack status" (Mahony 1995, 25).

References

Ackerman, Seth. 1999. "Supply-Side Journalism: An All-American Prescription for German Unemployment." *Harper's Magazine* (October): 66–67.

Acs, Gregory. 1995. "Does Welfare Promote Out-of-Wedlock Childbearing?" In *Welfare Reform: Analysis of the Issues*, edited by Isabel V. Sawhill. Washington, D.C.: Urban Institute.

Adams, Gina, and Jodi R. Sandfort. 1992. "State Investments in Child Care and Early Childhood Education." Washington, D.C.: Children's Defense Fund.

Alewell, Dorothea, and Kirsten Pull. 2001. "An International Comparison and Assessment of Maternity Leave Regulation." Accessed August 18, 2002, at: *www.wiwi.unijena.de/Personal/Diskussionspapier—Maternity—Leave.pdf*.

Allen, Sarah, and Alan Hawkins. 1999. "Maternal Gatekeeping: Mothers' Beliefs and Behaviors That Inhibit Greater Father Involvement in Family Work." *Journal of Marriage and the Family* 61(1): 199–212.

American Federation of Labor and Congress of Industrial Organizations (AFL-CIO). 2001. "Bargaining Alternative Work Schedules." Accessed January 1, 2001, at: *www.aflcio.org/women/f—altwrk.htm*.

American Nurses Association. 2002. "Legislation: Prohibition of Mandatory Overtime." Accessed July 8, 2002, at: *www.nursingworld.org/gova/state/2002/gaovtime.htm*.

Anderson, Patricia M., and Philip Levine. 1999. "Child Care and Mother's Employment Decisions." Working paper W7058. Cambridge, Mass.: National Bureau of Economic Research.

Andersson, Bengt-Erik. 1992. "Effects of Day-Care on Cognitive and Socioemotional Competence of Thirteen-Year-Old Swedish Schoolchildren." *Child Development* 63(1): 20–36.

Bainbridge, Jay, Marcia K. Meyers, Sakiko Tanako, and Jane Waldfogel. 2002. "Who Gets an Early Education?" Unpublished paper. Columbia University.

Baker, Maureen. 1995. *Canadian Family Policies: Cross-National Comparisons.* Toronto: University of Toronto Press.

———. 1997. "Parental Benefits Policies and the Gendered Division of Labor." *Social Service Review* 71(1): 51–71.

Bardasi, Elena, and Janet C. Gornick. 2002. "Explaining Cross-National Variation in Part-Time/Full-Time Wage Differentials Among Women." Paper presented at the Workshop on Comparative Political Economy of Inequality. Cornell University, Ithaca, New York (April 5–7).

———. 2003. "Women's Part-Time Employment Across Countries: Workers' 'Choices' and Wage Penalties." In *Women in the Labour Market in Changing Economies: Demographic Consequences,* edited by Brigida Garcia, Richard Anker, and Antonella Pinnelli. OUP Studies in Demography Series. Oxford: Oxford University Press.

Barnett, Rosalind C., and Caryl Rivers. 1996. *He Works, She Works: How Two-Income Families Are Happier, Healthier, and Better Off.* New York: HarperCollins.

Barnett, W. Steven. 1995. "Long-Term Effects of Early Childhood Programs on Cognitive and School Outcomes." *Future of Children* 5(3): 25–50.

Bassi, Laurie J. 1995. "Policy Implications of Part-Time Employment." *Journal of Labor Research* 16(3): 315–18.

Baum Charles L., II. 2002. "A Dynamic Analysis of the Effect of Child Care Costs on the Work Decisions of Low-Income Mothers and Infants." *Demography* 39(1): 139–64.

Baydar, Nazli, and Jeanne Brooks-Gunn. 1991. "The Effects of Maternal Employment and Child-Care Arrangements on Preschoolers' Cognitive and Behavioral Outcomes: Evidence from the Children of the National Longitudinal Survey of Youth." *Developmental Psychology* 27(6): 932–45.

Beach, Jane, Jane Bertrand, and Gordon Cleveland. 1998. *Our Child Care Workforce: From Recognition to Remuneration.* Ottawa: Child Care Human Resources Steering Committee.

Becker, Gary. 1981. *A Treatise on the Family.* Cambridge, Mass.: Harvard University Press.

Bell, Linda, and Richard B. Freeman. 2001. "The Incentive for Working Hard: Explaining Hours Worked Differences in the U.S. and Germany." *Labour Economics* 8(2): 181–202.

Bellemare, Diana, and Lise Poulin Simon. 1994. "Canada." In *Times Are Changing: Working Time in 14 Industrialized Countries,* edited by Gerald Bosch, Peter Dawkins, and Francois Michon. Geneva: International Institute for Labour Studies.

Berg, Annika. 2001a. "Government Proposes Legislation to Implement

EU Directives on Part-time and Fixed-term Work." Accessed June 4, 2002, at: *www.eiro.eurofound.ie/about/2001/06/inbrief/se0106104n. html.*

———. 2001b. "Train Drivers Strike for Own Pay Agreement." Accessed June 5, 2002, at: *www.eiro.eurofound.ie/about/2001/11/inbrief/ se0111102n.html.*

Berger, Mark C., and Dan A. Black. 1992. "Child Care Subsidies, Quality of Care, and the Labor Supply of Low-Income, Single Mothers." *Review of Economics and Statistics* 74(4): 635–42.

Berlin, Lisa J., Jeanne Brooks-Gunn, Cecelia McCarton, and Marie C. Mc-Cormick. 1998. "The Effectiveness of Early Intervention: Examining Risk Factors and Pathways to Enhanced Development." *Preventive Medicine* 27(2): 238–45.

Bettio, Francesca, and Sacha Prechal. 1998. *Care in Europe.* Brussels: European Commission.

Bianchi, Suzanne M. 2000. "Maternal Employment and Time with Children: Dramatic Change or Surprising Continuity?" *Demography* 37(4): 401–14.

Bianchi, Suzanne M., Melissa A. Milkie, Liana C. Sayer, and John P. Robinson. 2000. "Is Anyone Doing the Housework? Trends in the Gender Division of Household Labor." *Social Forces* 79(1): 191–228.

Bilous, Alexandre. 1998. "35-Hour Working Week Law Adopted." Accessed February 6, 2003, at: *www.eiro.eurofound.ie/about/1998/06/ feature/FR9806113F.html.*

———. 1999. "National Assembly Passes 35-Hour Week Bill." Accessed April 21, 2003, at: *www.eiro.eurofound.ie/about/1999/10/inbrief/ FR0010197N.html.*

Blanchard, Olivier, and Justin Wolfers. 1999. "The Role of Shocks and Institutions in the Rise of European Unemployment: The Aggregate Evidence." Accessed December 4, 2001, at: *www.mit.edu/blanchar/ www/articles.html.*

Blank, Rebecca, and Richard B. Freeman. 1994. "Evaluating the Connection Between Social Protection and Economic Flexibility." In *Social Protection and Economic Flexibility: Is There a Trade-Off?*, edited by Rebecca Blank. Chicago: University of Chicago Press.

Blau, David M. 2001. *The Child Care Problem.* New York: Russell Sage Foundation.

Blau, David M., and Philip K. Robins. 1989. "Fertility, Employment, and Child Care Costs." *Demography* 26(2): 287–99.

Blau, Francine D., Marianne A. Ferber, and Anne E. Winkler. 2002. *The Economics of Women, Men, and Work.* Upper Saddle River, New Jersey: Prentice-Hall.

Blau, Francine D., and Adam J. Grossberg. 1992. "Maternal Labor Supply and Children's Cognitive Development." *Review of Economics and Statistics* 74(3): 474–81.

Blau, Francine D., and Lawrence M. Kahn. 1992. "The Gender Earnings Gap: Learning from International Comparisons." *American Economic Review* 82(2): 533–38.

———. 2002. *At Home and Abroad: U.S. Labor Market Performance in International Perspective.* New York: Russell Sage Foundation.

Boushey, Heather, Chauna Brocht, Bethney Gunderson, and Jared Bernstein. 2001. *Hardships in America: The Real Story of Working Families.* Washington, D.C.: Economic Policy Institute.

Bradbury, Bruce, and Markus Jantti. 1999. "Child Poverty across Industrialized Nations." Innocenti Occasional Papers. Economic and Social Policy Series no. 71. Florence, Italy: UNICEF.

Bradshaw, Jonathan, Steven Kennedy, Majella Kilkey, Sandra Hutton, Anne Corden, Tony Eardley, Hilary Holmes, and Joanne Neale. 1996. *Policy and the Employment of Lone Parents in 20 Countries: The EU Report.* York, England: University of York.

Braun Levine, Suzanne. 2000. *Father Courage: What Happens When Men Put Family First.* New York: Harcourt, Brace and Jovanovich.

Brayfield, April. 1995. "Juggling Jobs and Kids: The Impact of Employment Schedules on Fathers: Caring For Children." *Journal of Marriage and the Family* 57(2): 321–32.

"Breast Cancer Risk Reduced by Breastfeeding for Two or More Years." 2001. Yale University press release, February 2, 2001. Accessed August 20, 2002, at: *www.yale.edu/opa/v29.n17/story2.html*.

Brigham Young University Family Studies Center (BYU). 1999. "Women May Be Inhibiting Greater Father Involvement in Family Work." Accessed April 21, 2003, at: *www.byu.edu/news/releases/archive99*.

Brines, Julie. 1994. "Economic Dependency, Gender, and the Division of Labor at Home." *American Journal of Sociology* 100(3): 652–88.

Brooks-Gunn, Jeanne, Greg J. Duncan, and Lawrence J. Aber, eds. 1997. *Neighborhood Poverty: Context and Consequences for Children.* New York: Russell Sage Foundation.

Brooks-Gunn, Jeanne, Wen-Jui Han, and Jane Waldfogel. 2002. "Maternal Employment and Child Cognitive Outcomes in the First Three Years of Life: The NICHD Study of Early Child Care." *Child Development* 73(4): 1052–72.

Bruning, Gwennaele, and Janneke Plantenga. 1999. *Journal of European Social Policy* 9(3): 195–209.

Bryant, Donna M., Margaret Burchinal, Lisa B. Lau, and Joseph J. Sparling. 1994. "Family and Classroom Correlates of Head Start Children's Developmental Outcomes." *Early Childhood Research Quarterly* 9(3–4): 289–309.

Budig, Michelle J., and Paula England. 2001. "The Wage Penalty for Motherhood." *American Sociological Review* 66(2): 204–25.

Burchinal, Margaret. 1999. "Child Care Experiences and Developmental Outcomes." *Annals of the American Academy of Political and Social Science* 563(May): 73–97.

Burchinal, Margaret, Ellen Peisner-Feinsberg, Donna M. Bryant, and Richard Clifford. 2000. "Children's Social and Cognitive Development and Child-Care Quality: Testing for Differential Associations Related to Poverty, Gender, or Ethnicity." *Applied Developmental Science* 4(3): 149–65.

Burkett, Elinor. 2000. *The Baby Boon: How Family-Friendly America Cheats the Childless*. New York: The Free Press.

Burtless, Gary. 1999. "Political Consequences of an Improved Poverty Measure." *LaFollette Policy Report* 10(1): 1–24.

Bussemaker, Jet, and Kees van Kersbergen. 1994. "Gender and Welfare States: Some Theoretical Reflections." In *Gendering Welfare States*, edited by Diane Sainsbury. London: Sage Publications.

Caiazza, Amy B., and Heidi I. Hartmann. 2001. "Gender and Civic Participation." Paper presented at the Work, Family, and Democracy Conference. Racine, Wisconsin (June 11–13).

Canadian Association of University Teachers–Association canadienne des professeures et professeurs d'université. (CAUT-ACPPU). 2001. "Feds Up Time for Parental Leave." Accessed May 11, 2002, at: *www.caut.ca/english/bulletin/2001—jan/news—parentlv.asp*.

Canadian Auto Workers (CAW), Canada Local 504. 2001. "Ratification Highlights Between Camco Inc. (Hourly) and CAW-Canada and Its Local 504." Accessed February 6, 2003, at: *www.geworkersunited.org/uploads/Camco2001Highlights/pdf*.

Capizzano, Jeffrey, and Gina Adams. 2000. "The Hours that Children Under Five Spend in Child Care: Variation Across States." Washington, D.C.: Urban Institute.

Capizzano, Jeffrey, Gina Adams, and Freya Sonenstein. 2000. "Child Care Arrangements for Children Under Five: Variation Across States." Washington, D.C.: Urban Institute.

Capizzano, Jeffrey, Sarah Adelman, and Matthew Stagner. 2002. "What Happens When the School Year is Over? The Use and Costs of Child Care for School-Age Children during the Summer Months." Washington, D.C.: Urban Institute.

Capizzano, Jeffrey, Kathryn Tout, and Gina Adams. 2000. "Child Care Patterns of School-Age Children with Employed Mothers." Washington, D.C.: Urban Institute.

Carley, Mark. 2002. "Working Time Developments: Annual Update 2001." Accessed June 4, 2002, at: *www.eiro.eurofound.ie/2002/02/update/tn0202103u.html.*

Caughy, Margaret O'Brien, Janet A. DiPietro, and Donna M. Strobino. 1994. "Day-Care Participation as a Protective Factor in the Cognitive Development of Low-Income Children." *Child Development* 65:457–71.

Center for Urban and Community Studies. 2000. *Early Childhood Care and Education in Canada: Provinces and Territories, 1998.* Toronto: University of Toronto Press.

Centre for Research in Early Childhood. n.d. *The OECD Thematic Review of Early Childhood Education and Care: Background Report for the United Kingdom.* Accessed April 3, 2002, at: *www1/oecd.org/els/pdfs/EDSECECDOCA009.pdf.*

Child Care Resource and Research Unit. 2000. "Early Childhood Care and Education in Canada: Provinces and Territories 1998." Accessed September 14, 2002, at: *www.childcarecanada.org/pt98/pdf/Prov&Terr98.pdf.*

Children's Foundation. 2000. *Child Care Licensing Study.* Washington, D.C.: Children's Foundation.

Chira, Susan. 1998. *A Mother's Place: Choosing Work and Family Without Guilt or Blame.* New York: Harper Perennial.

Chun, Hyunbae, and Injae Lee. 2001. "Why Do Married Men Earn More: Productivity or Marriage Selection?" *Economic Inquiry* 39(2): 307–19.

Clarkberg, Marin, and Phyllis Moen. 1999. "The Time-Squeeze: The Mismatch Between Work-Hours Patterns and Preferences Among Married Couples." Paper presented at the meetings of the American Association for the Advancement of Science. Anaheim, California (January 21–26).

Clauwaert, Stefan. 2002. *Survey on the Implementation of the Part-time Work Directive/Agreement in the EU Member States and Selected Applicant Countries.* Brussels: European Trade Union Institute.

Clearinghouse on International Developments in Child, Youth, and Family Policies. 2002. "Table 1.23: Main Institutional Day Care for Children in 7 European Countries." Accessed February 13, 2003, at: *www.childpolicyintl.org/index.html.*

———. 2003. "Comparative Policies: Countries Database." New York: Columbia University. Accessed February 8, 2003, at: *www.childpolicy.org.*

Cleveland, Gordon, Morley Gunderson, and Douglas Hyatt. 1996. "Child Care Costs and the Employment Decision of Women: Canadian Evidence." *Canadian Journal of Economics* 29(1): 132–51.

Cohen, Philip, and Suzanne Bianchi. 1999. "Marriage, Children, and Women's Employment: What Do We Know?" *Monthly Labor Review* 122(12): 22–31.

Coltrane, Scott. 1996. *Family Man: Fatherhood, Housework, and Gender Equity.* Oxford: Oxford University Press.

Connelly, Rachel, and Jean Kimmel. 1999. "Marital Status and Full-time/Part-time Work Status in Child Care Choices: Changing the Rules of the Game." Paper presented to the 1998–1999 ASPE–Census Bureau Small Grants Sponsored Research Conference. Washington, D.C. (May 17–18).

————. 2001. "The Effect of Child Care Costs on the Labor Force Participation and Welfare Recipiency of Single Mothers: Implications for Welfare Reform." Upjohn Institute Staff working paper 01–69. Brunswick, Maine: Bowdoin College.

Costa, Dora. 2000. "Hours of Work and the Fair Labor Standard Act: A Study of Retail and Wholesale Trade, 1938–1950." *Industrial and Labor Relations Review* 53(4): 648–64.

Crittenden, Ann. 2001. *The Price of Motherhood: Why the Most Important Job in the World Is Still the Least Valued.* New York: Metropolitan Books.

Crompton, Rosemary, ed. 1999. *Restructuring Gender Relations and Employment: The Decline of the Male Breadwinner.* Oxford: Oxford University Press.

Cryer, Debby, Wolfgang Tietze, Margaret Burchinal, Teresa Leal, and Jesus Palacios. 1999. "Predicting Process Quality from Structural Quality in Preschool Programs: A Cross-Country Comparison." *Early Childhood Research Quarterly* 14(3): 339–61.

Currie, Candace, Klaus Hurrelmann, Wolfgang Settertobulte, Rebecca Smith, and Joanna Todd, eds. 2000. *Health and Health Behavior Among Young People.* Copenhagen: World Health Organization Regional Office for Europe.

Currie, Janet. 2000. "Early Childhood Intervention Programs: What Do We Know?" Working paper no. 169. Chicago: Joint Center for Poverty Research.

Currie, Janet, and Duncan Thomas. 1995. "Does Head Start Make a Difference?" *American Economic Review* 85(3): 341–64.

Danish Ministry of Social Affairs. 2000. "Early Childhood Education and Care Policy in Denmark: Background Report Prepared for the OECD Thematic Review of Early Childhood Education and Care Policy." Accessed April 3, 2002, at: *www1.oecd.org/els/pdfs/EDSECECDOCA015. pdf.*

Danziger, Sheldon, and Jane Waldfogel, eds. 2000. *Securing the Future: Investing in Children from Birth to College.* New York: Russell Sage Foundation.

David and Lucile Packard Foundation. 1999. "When School Is Out." *Future of Children* 9(2): 4–20.

Delbar, Catherine. 2002. "2001 Annual Review for Belgium." Accessed July 13, 2002, at: *www.eiro.eurofound.ie/2002/01/feature/BE0201196F. html.*

Desai, Sonalde, P. Lindsay Chase-Landsdale, and Robert T. Michael. 1989. "Mother or Market? Effects of Maternal Employment on the Intellectual Ability of 4-Year-Old Children." *Demography* 26(4): 545–61.

Deutsch, Francine D. 1999. *Halving It All: How Equally Shared Parenting Really Works.* Cambridge, Mass.: Harvard University Press.

Doherty, Gillian, Ruth Rose, Martha Friendly, Donna Lero, and Sharon Hope Irwin. 1995. "Childcare: Canada Can't Work Without It." Occasional paper 5. Accessed April 3, 2002, at: *www.childcarecanada.org/ resources/CRRUpubs/op5/5optoc.html*

Doherty, Kathryn M. 2002. "Early Learning." *Education Week* 17(January 10): 54–68.

ECOTEC Research and Consulting. 2002. "Legal and Contractual Limitations on Working Time." Accessed May 7, 2002, at: *www.ecotec.com/ eco/tdb/en97/2—1—2—1.htm.*

Education Commission of the States. 2000. "ECS State Notes: Scheduling/ School Calendar." Accessed September 1, 2002, at: *www.ecs.org/clearinghouse/14/28/1428.htm.*

Ehrle, Jennifer, Gina Adams, and Kathryn Tout. 2001. "Who's Caring for Our Youngest Children? Child Care Patterns of Infants and Toddlers." Washington, D.C.: Urban Institute.

Ellingsaeter, Anne Lise. 1999. "Dual Breadwinners Between State and Market." In *Restructuring Gender Relations and Employment: The Decline of the Male Breadwinner,* edited by Rosemary Crompton. Oxford: Oxford University Press.

Employee Benefit Research Institute (EBRI). 1993. "Part-Time Work: Characteristics of the Part-Time Work Force: Analysis of the March 1992 Current Population Survey." Working paper P-55. Washington: U.S. Government Printing Office.

———. 1998. *Employment-Based Health Care Benefits and Self-Funded Employment-Based Plan: An Overview.* Washington: Employee Benefits Research Institute.

Employment Policy Foundation. 2000. "Should the U.S. Follow Europe's

Work-Family Policies? Paid Family Leave Mandates Will Be Costly in U.S., Book Finds." News release, April 24. Accessed December 5, 2002, at: *www.epf.org/media/newsreleases/2000/nr20000424.pdf.*

England, Paula, Michelle J. Budig, and Nancy Folbre. 2002. "Wages of Virtue: The Relative Pay of Care Work." *Social Problems* 49(4): 455–73.

England, Paula, and Nancy Folbre. 1999a. "The Cost of Caring." *Annals of the American Academy of Political and Social Science* 561(January): 39–51.

———. 1999b. "Who Should Pay for the Kids?" *Annals of the American Academy of Political and Social Science* 563(May): 194–207.

Equal Opportunities Commission. 2002. "Family Friendly Working: What the Law Says." Accessed May 23, 2002, at: *www.eoc.org.uk/cseng/advice/family—friendly——law.asp.*

Esping-Andersen, Gosta. 1990. *The Three Worlds of Welfare Capitalism.* Princeton, New Jersey: Princeton University Press.

European Commission. 1999. *Report from the Commission on the Implementation of Council Directive 92/85/EEC of 19 October 1992 on the Introduction of Measures to Encourage Improvements in the Health and Safety at Work of Pregnant Workers and Workers Who Have Recently Given Birth or Who Are Breastfeeding.* Brussels: European Commission.

———. 2000. *Social Protection in the Member States of the European Union (MISSOC).* Brussels: Directorate General V: Employment, Industrial Relations, and Social Affairs.

———. 2001. *Social Protection in the Member States of the European Union (MISSOC).* Brussels: Directorate General V: Employment, Industrial Relations, and Social Affairs.

European Commission Network on Childcare and Other Measures to Reconcile Employment and Family Responsibilities. 1994. *Leave Arrangements For Workers With Children: A Review of Leave Arrangements in the Member States of the European Union and Austria, Finland, Norway, and Sweden.* Brussels: European Commission.

———. 1995. *The Costs and Funding of Services for Young Children.* Brussels: European Commission.

———. 1996. *A Review of Services for Young Children in the European Union 1990–1995.* Brussels: European Commission.

European Forum for Child Welfare. 2003. "Policies and Programmes on Reconciliation and Family Responsibilities." Fact sheet. Accessed February 3, 2003, at: *www.efcw.org/ChildcareEN.html.*

European Foundation. 2001. "Third European Working Conditions Survey: Data." Accessed January 5, 2003, at: *www.eurofound.ie/working/3wc/3wc20.htm.*

European Foundation for the Improvement of Living and Working Conditions. 2002. "Germany." Accessed May 31, 2002, at: *www.eurofound.eu.int/emire/germany/nightwork-de.html.*

European Union. 2001. "Encouraging Higher Labor Standards: Organisation of Working Time." Accessed April 19, 2002, at: *www.europa.eu.int/scadplus/leg/en/cha/c10405.htm.*

Eurydice. 1994a. "Pre-School Education in the European Union: Current Thinking and Provision." Accessed August 30, 2002, at: *www.eurydice.org/documents/preschool/en/FrameSet.htm.*

———. 1994b. "Provision for Pupils in Primary Schools Out of School Hours." In "Pre-School and Primary Education in the European Union." Accessed August 30, 2002, at: *www.eurydice.org/documents/preschool—n—primary/en/c32pe1en.htm.*

———. 1995a. "Length of the School Day (Primary Education)." Table IX in "Organisation of School Time in the European Union." Accessed September 7, 2002, at: *www.eurydice.org/documents/time1/en/tableIX.HTM.*

———. 1995b. "Opening Hours of Schools (Primary Education)." Table X in "Organisation of School Time in the European Union." Accessed August 30, 2002, at: *www.eurydice.org/documents/time1/en/table—x.htm.*

———. 2000. "Starting Dates of the School Year in 2000/2001." Table II in "Organisation of School Time in Europe." Accessed September 6, 2002, at: *www.eurydice.org/documents/time3/en/table2.htm.*

Evans, John M., Douglas C. Lippoldt, and Pascal Marianna. 2001. "Labor Market and Social Policy: Trends in Working Hours in OECD Countries." Occasional paper 45. Paris: Organisation for Economic Co-operation and Development, Employment, Labour, and Social Affairs Committee.

Fagnoni, Cynthia M. 2000. "Fair Labor Standards Act: White-Collar Exemptions Need Adjustments for Today's Workplace." Press release, May 3, 2000. Washington: U.S. General Accounting Office.

Feinstein, Leon, Donald Robertson, and James Symons. 1999. "Preschool Education and Attainment in the National Child Development Study and British Cohort Study." *Education Economics* 7(3): 209–34.

Figart, Deborah M., and Lonnie Golden. 1998. "The Social Economics of Work Time: An Introduction." *Review of Social Economy* 56(4): 411–24.

Figart, Deborah, and Ellen Mutari. 1998. "Degendering Work Time in Comparative Perspective: Alternative Policy Frameworks." *Review of Social Economy* 4(winter): 460–80.

Folbre, Nancy. 1994. "Children as Public Goods." *American Economic Review* 84(2): 86–90.

————. 2001. *The Invisible Heart: Economics and Family Values.* New York: New Press.

Fraser, Nancy. 1994. "After the Family Wage: Gender Equity and the Welfare State." *Political Theory* 22(4): 591–618.

Freeman, Richard B., ed. 1994. *Working Under Different Rules.* New York: Russell Sage Foundation.

Friendly, Martha. 2001. "Early Childhood Education and Care in Canada 2001." Briefing notes. Canadian Resource and Research Unit. Accessed February 13, 2003, at: *www.childcarecanada.org/pubs/bn/ECEC2001 summary.html.*

Fuligni, Allison Sidle, and Jeanne Brooks-Gunn. 2001. "What is Shared in Caring for Young Children? Parental Perceptions and Time Use in Two-Parent Families." Paper presented at the Biennial Meetings of the Society for Research in Child Development, Minneapolis, Minn. (April 9).

Galinsky, Ellen, and James T. Bond. 2000. "Helping Families with Young Children Navigate Work and Family Life." In *Balancing Acts: Easing the Burdens and Improving the Options for Working Families*, edited by Eileen Appelbaum. Washington, D.C.: Economic Policy Institute.

Galinsky, Ellen, James T. Bond, and Stacy S. Kim. 2001. *Feeling Overworked: When Work Becomes Too Much.* New York: Families and Work Institute.

Galinsky, Ellen, Carollee Howes, Susan Kontos, and Marybeth Shinn. 1994. *The Study of Children in Family Child Care and Relative Care: Highlights of Findings.* New York: Families and Work Institute.

Gauthier, Anne Helene, and Jan Hatzius. 1997. "Family Benefits and Fertility: An Econometric Analysis." *Population Studies* 51(3): 295–306.

Gelbach, Jonah. 1999. "How Large an Effect Do Child Care Costs Have on Single Mothers' Labor Supply? Evidence Using Access to Free Public Schooling." Working paper. Department of Economics, University of Maryland, College Park.

Gershoff, Elizabeth Thompson, J. Lawrence Aber, and C. Cybele Raver. Forthcoming. "Child Poverty in the U.S.: An Evidence-Based Conceptual Framework for Programs and Policies." In *Promoting Positive Child, Adolescent, and Family Development: A Handbook of Program and Policy Innovations*, edited by Richard M Lerner, Francine Jacobs, and David Wertleib.

Gershuny, Jonathan. 2000. *Changing Times: Work and Leisure in Post-Industrial Society.* Oxford: Oxford University Press.

Gershuny, Jonathan, and John P. Robinson. 1998. "Historical Changes in the Household Division of Labor." *Demography* 25(4): 537–52.

Gerstel, Naomi. 2000. "The Third Shift: Gender and Care Work Outside the Home." *Qualitative Sociology* 23(4): 467–83.

Giannarelli, Linda, and James Barsimantov. 2000. "Child Care Expenses of America's Families." Washington, D.C.: Urban Institute, Human Development Report Office.

Giannarelli, Linda, Sarah Adelman, and Stefanie Schmidt. 2003. "Getting Help with Child Care Expenses." Occasional paper 62. Washington, D.C.: Urban Institute.

Giannarelli, Linda, and James Barsimantov. 2000. "Child Care Expenses of American Families." Washington, D.C.: Urban Institute.

Gilens, Martin. 1999. *Why Americans Hate Welfare: Race, Media, and the Politics of Antipoverty Policy*. Chicago: University of Chicago Press.

Gilman, M. W. 1998. "Working Time Directive Implemented in the UK." Accessed May 14, 2002, at: *www.eiro.eurofound.ie/1998/10/inbrief/uk9810155N.html*.

Gish, Melinda. 2002. "Child Care: Funding and Spending under Federal Block Grants." Congressional Research Service Report. Washington: Library of Congress.

Glass, Jennifer, and Lisa Riley. 1998. "Family Responsive Policies and Employee Retention Following Childbirth." *Social Forces* 76(4): 1401–35.

Global Labour Law. 2002. "National Labour Law Database: Dialogue With Citizens." Accessed September 10, 2002, at: *www.globallabourlaw.com*.

Golden, Lonnie, and Helene Jorgensen. 2002. "Time After Time: Mandatory Overtime in the U.S. Economy." Briefing paper. Washington, D.C.: Economic Policy Institute.

Goldscheider, Frances. 2002. "Non-Domestic Employment and Women's Lives: Revisiting the Roles of Supply and Demand." Paper presented at the 2002 annual meeting of the Population Association of America. Atlanta, Georgia (May 9–11).

Goldschmidt-Clermont, Luisella, and Elisabetta Pagnossin-Aligisakis. 2001. "Measures of Unrecorded Economic Activities in Fourteen Countries." New York: United Nations Development Programme, Human Development Report Office.

Gornick, Janet C. 1999a. "Gender Equality in the Labor Market." In *Gender and Welfare State Regimes*, edited by Diane Sainsbury. Oxford: Oxford University Press.

———. 1999b. "Income Maintenance and Employment Supports for Former Welfare Recipients: The United States in Cross-National Perspective." In *Rethinking Income Support for the Working Poor: Perspectives on Unemployment Insurance, Welfare, and Work,* edited by Evelyn Ganzglass and Karen Glass. Washington, D.C.: National Governors' Association Center for Best Practices.

———. 2002. "Against the Grain: 'Social Exclusion' and American Political Culture." In *Beyond Child Poverty: The Social Exclusion of Children*, edited by Alfred J. Kahn and Sheila B. Kamerman. New York: Columbia Institute for Child and Family Policy.

———. Forthcoming. "Social Expenditures on Children and the Elderly, 1980–1995: Shifting Allocations, Changing Needs." In *The Allocation of Private and Public Resources Across Generations*, edited by Anne Helene Gauthier, Cyrus Chu, and Shripad Tuljapurkar. Unpublished manuscript.

Gornick, Janet C., and Jerry A. Jacobs. 1996. "A Cross-National Analysis of the Wages of Part-Time Workers: Evidence from the United States, the United Kingdom, Canada, and Australia." *Work, Employment, and Society* 10(1): 1–27.

Gornick, Janet C., and Marcia K. Meyers. 2001. "Support for Working Families." *American Prospect* 12(1): 3–7.

Gornick, Janet C., Marcia K. Meyers, and Katherin E. Ross. 1997. "Supporting the Employment of Mothers: Policy Variation Across Fourteen Welfare States." *Journal of European Social Policy* 7(1): 45–70.

Government of Saskatchewan. 2002. "Benefits for Part-Time Employees." Accessed June 7, 2002, at: *www.labour.gov.sk.ca/standards/guide/benefits.htm*.

Governo Italiano. 2002. "Women and the Economy: New Regulations on Night-Time Work." Accessed July 16, 2002, at: *www.palazzochigi.it/parioportunita/cosa/sett—intern/pechino/pechino8/english.hmt*.

Greenstein, Theodore N. 1995. "Are the 'Most Advantaged' Children Truly Disadvantaged by Early Maternal Employment? Effects on Child Cognitive Outcomes." *Journal of Family Issues* 16(2): 149–69.

———. 2000. "Economic Dependence, Gender, and the Division of Labour in the Home: A Replication and Extension." *Journal of Marriage and the Family* 62(2): 322–35.

Grubb, David, and William Wells. 1993. "Employment Regulation and Patterns of Work in EC Countries." *OECD Economic Studies* 21(winter): 7–58.

Grundy, Lea, Lissa Bell, and Netsy Firestein. 1999. "Labor's Role in Addressing the Child Care Crisis." New York: Foundation for Child Development.

Gupta, Sanjiv. 1999. "The Effects of Transitions in Marital Status on Men's Performance of Housework." *Journal of Marriage and the Family* 61(3): 700–11.

Haas, Linda, and Philip Hwang. 1999. "Parental Leave in Sweden." In *Parental Leave: Progress or Pitfall*, edited by Peter Moss and Fred Devens. Brussels: NIDI CBGS Publications.

Hakim, Catherine. 1997. "Sociological Perspectives on Part-Time Work." In *Between Equalization and Marginalization: Women Working Part-Time in Europe and the United States of America*, edited by Hans-Peter Blossfeld and Catherine Hakim. Oxford: Oxford University Press.

Hamermesh, Daniel S. 2002. "Overtime Laws and the Margins of Work Timing." Paper prepared for the Conference on Work Intensification. Paris (November 21–22).

Han, Wen-Jui. 2002. "Nonstandard Work Schedules and Child Cognitive Outcomes." Paper prepared for the Family and Work Policies Committee of the National Research Council and the Institute of Medicine's Board on Children, Youth, and Families.

Han, Wen-Jui, and Jane Waldfogel. 2002. "The Effect of Child Care Costs on the Employment of Single and Married Mothers." *Social Science Quarterly* 82(3): 552–68.

Han, Wen-Jui, Jane Waldfogel, and Jeanne Brooks-Gunn. 2001. "The Effects of Early Maternal Employment on Later Cognitive and Behavorial Outcomes." *Journal of Marriage and Family* 63(2): 336–54.

Hardy, Stephen, and Nick Adnett. 2001. "The Parental Leave Directive: Towards a 'Family Friendly' Social Europe." Unpublished paper. Staffordshire, England: Staffordshire University Business School.

Heckman, James J., and Lance Lochner. 2000. "Rethinking Education and Training Policy: Understanding the Sources of Skill Formation in a Modern Economy." In *Securing the Future: Investing in Children from Birth to College*, edited by Sheldon Danziger and Jane Waldfogel. New York: Russell Sage Foundation.

Helburn, Susan W., and Barbara Bergmann. 2002. *America's Child Care Problem*. New York: St. Martin's Press.

Helburn, Suzanne, Mary L. Culkin, Carollee Howes, Donna Bryant, Richard Clifford, Debby Cryer, Ellen Peisner-Feinsberg, and Sharon Lynn Kagan, eds. 1995. *Cost, Quality, and Child Outcomes in Child Care Centers*. Denver: Department of Economics, Center for Research in Economic and Social Policy, University of Colorado at Denver.

Hernandez, Donald. 1994. "Children's Changing Access to Resources: A Historical Perspective," *Social Policy Report, Society for Research in Child Development*, VIII(1): 1–23.

Hernes, Helga. 1987. *The State and Working Women*. Oslo, Norway: Norwegian University Press.

Hewlett, Sylvia, and Cornel West. 1998. *The War Against Parents: What We Can Do for Americas' Beleaguered Moms and Dads*. New York: Houghton Mifflin.

Heymann, Jody. 2000. *The Widening Gap: Why America's Working*

Families Are in Jeopardy—and What Can Be Done About It. New York: Basic Books.

Heymann, Jody, Renee Boynton-Jarrett, Patricia Carter, James T. Bond, and Ellen Galinsky. 2002. *Work-Family Issues and Low-Income Families.* Milwaukee, Wis.: 9 to 5, National Association of Working Women.

Hicks, Alexander. 1999. *Social Democracy and Welfare Capitalism: A Century of Income Security Politics.* Ithaca, New York: Cornell University Press.

Hill, Jennifer, Jane Waldfogel, Jeanne Brooks-Gunn, and Wen-Jui Han. 2001. *Towards a Better Estimate of Causal Links in Child Policy: The Case of Maternal Employment and Child Outcomes.* New York: Columbia University School of Social Work.

Hochschild, Arlie Russell. 1997. *The Time Bind: When Work Becomes Home and Home Becomes Work.* New York: Henry Holt.

Hofferth, Sandra L. 1996. "Effects of Public and Private Policies on Working After Childbirth." *Work and Occupations* 23(4): 378–404.

———. 1998. "Child Care and Women's Employment in the United States." Paper presented at the Women's Employment in a Comparative Perspective Conference. Utrecht, The Netherlands (May 13–14).

———. 1999. "Child Care, Maternal Employment, and Public Policy." *Annals of the American Academy of Political and Social Science* 563(May): 20–38.

Hofferth, Sandra, and Nancy Collins. 2000. "Child Care and Employment Turnover." *Population Research and Policy Review* 19(4): 357–95.

Hofferth, Sandra L., Jerry West, Robin Henke, and Phillip Kaufman. 1993. *Access to Early Childhood Programs for Children at Risk.* Washington: Department of Education, Office of Educational Research and Improvement.

Human Resources Development Canada. 1998. "Working Time and Related Provisions." *Workplace Gazette* 1(1): 90–102.

Incomes Data Services. 2002. "Working Hours and Holidays in the European Union." Accessed December 28, 2002, at: *www.incomesdata.co.uk/infotime/eucomparisons.htm.*

Institut National de la Statistique et des Etudes Economiques (INSEE). 2002. "The French Population in 2001: Births and Marriages Are Still on the Rise." Accessed January 17, 2003, at: *www.insee.fr/en/ffc/pop—age4.htm.*

International Labour Organization (ILO). 1995. *Conditions of Work Digest: Working Time Around the World.* Geneva: International Labour Office.

———. 1999. "Maternity Protection at Work" Report V(2). Geneva: International Labour Office.

————. 2001. "New ILO Study Shows U.S. Workers Put in the Longest Hours." Press release, August 31, 2001. Accessed December 26, 2002, at: *us.ilo.org/new/prslrs/200010831—kilm.html.*

International Observatory of Labour Law. 2001. "Labor Law News." Accessed May 29, 2002, at: *ilo.org/public/english/dialogue/govlab/ioll/news.htm.*

International Social Security Association (ISSA). 2000. *Social Security Worldwide.* (CD-ROM). 2d ed. Geneva: International Social Security Association.

Jacobs, Jerry A., and Kathleen Gerson. 2001. "Overworked Individuals or Overworked Families?" *Work and Occupations* 28(1): 40–63.

————. Forthcoming. *The Time Divide: Work, Family, and Social Policy in the 21st Century.* Cambridge, Mass.: Harvard University Press.

Jacobs, Jerry A., and Janet C. Gornick. 2002. "Hours of Paid Work in Dual-Earner Couples: The United States in Cross-National Perspective." *Sociological Focus* 35(2): 169–87.

Jarousse, Jean-Pierre, Alain Mingat, and Marc Richard. 1992. *La scolarisation maternelle à deux ans: Effets pedagogiques et sociaux: Education et formation.* Paris: Ministère de l'Education Nationale et de la Culture (April–June).

Jeantheau, Jean-Pierre, and Fabrice Murat. 1998. *Observation à l'entrée au CP des élèves du "panel 1997": Note d'information de la DPD.* Paris: Ministère de l'Education Nationale.

Joesch, Jutta M. 1997. "Paid Leave and the Timing of Women's Employment Before and After Birth." *Journal of Marriage and the Family* 59(4): 1008–21.

Johnson, Nancy, and Keith G. Provan. 1995. "The Relationship Between Work/Family Benefits and Earnings: A Test of Competing Predictions." *Journal of Socio-Economics* 24(5): 571–84.

Jordan, Laura. 1999. "Background Information on European and Canadian Parental Leave Laws." Accessed February 11, 2002, at: *www.cga.state.ct.us/ps99/rpt/01r/htm/99-r-1214.htm.*

Kajalo, Sami. 2000. "Review of Shop Opening Regulations in Several Countries." Accessed June 6, 2002, at: *hkkk.fi/talsos.internet.htm.*

Kamerman, Sheila. 2000. "Parental Leave Policy: An Essential Ingredient in Early Childhood Education and Care Policies." *Social Policy Report* 14(2): 3–19.

Kamerman, Sheila B., Michelle J. Neuman, Jane Waldfogel, and Jeanne Brooks-Gunn. Forthcoming. *Social Policies, Family Types, and Child Outcomes in Selected OECD Countries.* Paris: Organisation for Economic Co-operation and Development.

Karoly, Lynn A., Peter W. Greenwood, Susan S. Everingham, Jill Hoube, M. Rebecca Kilburn, C. Peter Rydell, Matthew Sanders, and James Chiesa. 1998. *Investing in Our Children: What We Do and Don't Know About the Costs and Benefits of Early Childhood Interventions.* Santa Monica, Calif.: RAND Corporation.

Katz, Lawrence F., and David H. Autor. 1999. "Changes in the Wage Structure and Earnings Inequality." In *Handbook of Labor Economics (Volume 3A),* edited by Orley Ashenfelter and David Card. Amsterdam: Elsevier Science.

Katz, Michael B. 1986. *In the Shadow of the Poorhouse: A Social History of Welfare in America.* New York: Basic Books.

———. 1989. *The Undeserving Poor: From the War on Poverty to the War on Welfare.* New York: Pantheon Books.

Kauppinen, Timo. 2001. "The 24-hour Society and Industrial Relations Strategies." Accessed April 20, 2003, at: *www.eurofound.ie/industrial/24hr.doc.*

Kiernan, Kathleen. 2001. "European Perspectives on Nonmarital Childbearing." In *Out of Wedlock: Causes and Consequences of Nonmarital Fertility,* edited by Lawrence L. Wu and Barbara Wolfe. New York: Russell Sage Foundation.

Kilkey, Majella, and Jonathan Bradshaw. 1999. "Lone Mothers, Economic Well-Being, and Policies." In *Gender and Welfare State Regimes,* edited by Diane Sainsbury. Oxford: Oxford University Press.

Kimmel, Jean. 1998. "Child Care Costs as a Barrier to Employment for Single and Married Mothers." *Review of Economics and Statistics* 80(2): 287–99.

Kimmel, Jean, and Lisa M. Powell. 2001. "Nonstandard Work and Child Care Choice: Implications for Welfare Reform." Paper presented at the conference, From Welfare to Child Care: What Happens to Infants and Toddlers When Single Mothers Exchange Welfare for Work? Washington, D.C. (May 17–18).

Kimmel, Michael. 2000. "What Do Men Want?" In *Harvard Business Review on Work and Life Balance.* Boston, Mass.: Harvard Business School Press.

Knijn, Trudie, and Monique Kremer. 1997. "Gender and the Caring Dimension of Welfare States: Towards Inclusive Citizenship." *Social Politics* 4(3): 328–62.

Konner, Melvin. 1999. "Darwin's Truth, Jefferson's Vision." *American Prospect* 10(45). Accessed December 10, 2001, at: *www.prospect.org/print/V10/45/konner-m.html.*

Krzeslo, Dryon. 1998. "Normalising Night Work in Belgium: Legislation Establishes Equality of Men and Women." Accessed May 31, 2002, at: *www.eiro.eurofound.ie/1998/05/Feature/be9805143f.html.*

Kuttner, Robert. 1999. *Everything for Sale: The Virtues and Limits of Markets.* New York: Alfred A. Knopf.

Labor Project for Working Families. 2002. "Bargaining for Alternative Work Schedules." Accessed August 21, 2002, at: *www.newecon.org/ AlternativeSchedules—AFLCIOwomen.html.*

Lake Sosin Snell Perry. 1998. "Polls Indicate Widespread Support for Increased Investment in Child Care." Accessed January 18, 2002, at: *cdfweb.vwh.net/childcare/cc—polls.html.*

Landy, Joanne. 1998. "Family Values and the Shorter Work Week." *New Politics* 6(4). Accessed August 7, 2001, at: *www.wpunj.edu/~newpol/ issue24/landy24.htm.*

Lanfranchi, Joseph, Henry Ohlsson, and Ali Skalli. 2002. "Compensating Wage Differentials and Shift Work Preferences." *Economic Letters* 74(3): 393–98.

Leete-Guy, Laura, and Juliet B. Schor. 1992. "The Great American Time Squeeze: 1969–1989." Briefing paper 28. Washington, D.C.: Economic Policy Institute.

Leibowitz, Arleen. 1977. "Parental Inputs and Children's Achievement." *Journal of Human Resources* 12(2): 242–51.

Leira, Arnlaug. 1999. "Cash for Child Care and Daddy Leave." In *Parental Leave: Progress or Pitfall,* edited by Peter Moss and Fred Deven. Brussels: NIDI CBGS Publications.

———. 2000. "Combining Work and Family: Nordic Policy Reforms in the 1990s." In *Gender, Welfare State, and the Market: Towards a New Division of Labor,* edited by Thomas P. Boje and Arnlaug Leira. New York: Routledge.

Levine, James, and Todd L. Pittinsky. 1997. *Working Fathers: New Strategies for Balancing Work and Family.* New York: Harcourt Brace.

Lewis, Jane, ed. 1997. *Lone Mothers in European Welfare Regimes.* London: Jessica Kingsley.

Lewis, Jane, and Gertrude Astrom. 1992. "Equality, Difference, and State Welfare: Labor Market and Family Policies in Sweden." *Feminist Studies* 18(spring): 59–88.

Lewis, Jane, and Ilona Ostner. 1991. "Gender and the Evolution of European Social Policies." Paper presented to Center for European Studies, Workshop on Emergent Supranational Social Policy: The EC's Social Dimension in Comparative Perspective. Washington, D.C. (November 15–17).

Lister, Ruth. 1990. "Women, Economic Dependency, and Citizenship." *Journal of Social Policy* 19(4): 445–67.

———. 1997. *Citizenship: Feminist Perspectives.* New York: New York University Press.

Lundberg, Shelly, and Elaina Rose. 2001. "The Effects of Sons and Daughters on Men's Labor Supply and Wages." *Review of Economics and Statistics* 84(2): 251–68.

Mahony, Rhona. 1995. *Kidding Ourselves: Breadwinning, Babies, and Bargaining Power.* New York: Basic Books.

Malin, Martin. 1994. "Fathers and Parental Leave." *Texas Law Review* 71: 1047–96.

Mallin, Caroline. 2000. "Ontario Workers to get Crisis Leave." Accessed May 23, 2002, at: *www.childcarecanada.org/ccin/2000/ccin11—24—00.*

Marshall, T. H. 1950. *Citizenship and Social Class.* Cambridge: Cambridge University Press.

Marsiglio, William, Paul Amato, Randal D. Day, and Michael E. Lamb. 2000. "Scholarship on Fatherhood in the 1990s and Beyond." *Journal of Marriage and the Family* 62(4): 1173–1191.

Mattingly, Marybeth J., and Suzanne M. Bianchi. Forthcoming. "Gender Differences in the Quantity and Quality of Free Time: The U.S. Experience." *Social Forces* 81(3).

McDonald, Peter. 2000a. "Gender Equity, Social Institutions, and the Future of Fertility." *Journal of Population Research* 17(1): 1–16.

———. 2000b. "Gender Equity in Theories of Fertility Transition." *Population Development Review* 26(3): 427–39.

Meyer, Bruce D., and Dan T. Rosenbaum. 2001. "Welfare, the Earned Income Tax Credit, and the Labor Supply of Single Mothers." *Quarterly Journal of Economics* 116(3): 1063–1114.

Meyer, Christine Siegwarth, Swati Mukerjee, and Ann Sestero. 2001. "Work Family Benefits: Which Ones Maximize Profits?" *Journal of Managerial Issues* 13(1): 28–44.

Meyers, Marcia, Laura R. Peck, Ann Collins, J. Lee Kreader, Annie Georges, Elizabeth E. Davis, Roberta Weber, Deanna Schexnayder, Daniel Schroeder, and Jerry A. Olson. 2002. *The Dynamics of Child Care Subsidy Use: A Collaborative Study of Five States.* New York: National Center for Children in Poverty.

Michalopoulos, Charles, and Philip K. Robins. 2000. "Employment and Child Care Choices in Canada and the United States." *Canadian Journal of Economics* 33(2): 435–70.

Michalopoulos, Charles, Philip K. Robins, and Irwin Garfinkel. 1992. "A Structural Model of Labor Supply and Child Care Demand." *Journal of Human Resources* 27(1): 166–203.

Ministry of Education and Science in Sweden. 1999. "Early Childhood Education and Care Policy in Sweden: Background Report Prepared for the OECD Childhood Education and Care Policy." Accessed April 3, 2002, at: *www.childcarecanada.org/resources/issues/school—age. html.*

Ministry of Health and Social Affairs. 2002. *Swedish Family Policy.* Fact Sheet 5. Stockholm: Printing Works of the Government Offices.

Ministry of Health, Welfare, and Sport and Ministry of Education, Culture, and Science. 2000. "Early Childhood Education and Care in the Netherlands." Background report to the OECD Thematic Review of Early Childhood Education and Care Policy. Accessed April 3, 2002, at: *www1.oecd.org/els/pdfs/EDSECECDOCA011.pdf.*

Mishel, Lawrence, Jared Bernstein, and John Schmitt. 2001. *The State of Working America: 2000–2001.* Ithaca, New York: Cornell University Press, ILR Press.

Mississauga (Canada) Board of Trade. 2002. "Extension of Maternity/Parental Leave Benefits." Accessed July 25, 2002, at: *www.mbot.com/webarticles/policystatements/extmatlben.htm.*

Modigliani, Franco, Jean Paul Fitoussi, Beniamino Moro, Dennis Snower, Robert Solow, Alfred Steinherr and Paolo Sylos Labini. 1998. "An Economists' Manifesto on Unemployment in The European Union." *BNL Quarterly Review* 206(September): 327–361.

Moffitt, Robert. 1990. "The Effect of the U.S. Welfare System on Marital Status." *Journal of Public Economics* 41(1): 101–24.

Moisan, Catherine, and Jacky Simon. 1997. *Les determinants de la reussite scolaire en zone d'education prioritaire.* Paris: Institut National de Recherche Pédagogique.

Moore, Kristin A., and Anne K. Driscoll. 1997. "Low-Wage Maternal Employment and Outcomes for Children: A Study." *Future of Children* 7(1): 122–27.

Morgan, Kimberly, and Kathrina Zippel. 2002. "Paid to Care: The Origins and Effects of Care Leave Policies in Western Europe." Paper prepared for the Thirteenth Conference of Europeanists. Chicago (March 14–16).

Moss, Peter. 1990. *Child Care in the European Communities: 1985–1990.* Brussels: European Commission Childcare Network.

Moss, Peter, and Fred Deven, eds. 1999. *Parental Leave: Progress or Pitfall?* Brussels: NIDI CBGS Publications.

Mott, Frank L. 1991. "Developmental Effects of Infant Care: The Mediating Role of Gender and Health." *Journal of Social Issues* 47(2): 139–58.

Mott Foundation. 1998. "Polls Indicate Widespread Support for Increased Investment in Child Care." Accessed January 18, 2002, at: *cdfweb.vwh.net/childcare/cc—polls.html.*

Mutari, Ellen, and Deborah M. Figart. 2001. "Europe at a Crossroads: Harmonization, Liberalization, and the Gender of Work Time." *Social Politics* 8(1): 36–64.

National Association for the Education of Young Children. 2002. *The Care and Education of Young Children in the United States.* Washington, D.C.: National Association for the Education of Young Children.

National Center for Education Statistics (NCES). 2001. "Featured Topic: Third International Mathematics and Science Study." *Education Statistics Quarterly* 3(1): 7–20.

National Institute of Child Health and Human Development (NICHD) Early Child Care Research Network. 1997a. "Child Care in the First Year of Life." *Merrill Palmer Quarterly* 43(3): 340–60.

———. 1997b. "Poverty and Patterns of Child Care." In *Consequences of Growing Up Poor*, edited by Greg J. Duncan and Jeanne Brooks-Gunn. New York: Russell Sage Foundation.

———. 2002. "Child-Care Structure = Process = Outcome: Direct and Indirect Effects of Child-Care Quality on Young Children's Development." *NICHD Early Child Care Research Network* 13(3): 199–206.

———. Forthcoming a. "Does Amount of Time Spent in Child Care Predict Socioemotional Adjustment during the Transition to Kindergarten?" *Child Development.*

———. Forthcoming b. "Early Child Care and Children's Development Prior to School Entry: Results from NICHD Study of Early Child Care." *American Educational Research Journal* 39(1): 133–64.

National Parenting Association. 1998. "Family Matters: A National Survey of Women and Men conducted for the National Parenting Association." Accessed September 26, 2001, at *www.nationalpartnership.org/survey/survey1.htm.*

National Partnership for Women and Families. 1998. "Family Leave Caring for a Seriously Ill Child, Spouse, or Parent." Accessed November 1, 2000, at: *www.familyleavesurvey.homstead.com/files/GuidetotheFMLA.pdf.*

Newman, Katherine. 2000. "On the High Wire: How the Working Poor Juggle Job and Family Responsibilities." In *Balancing Acts: Easing the Burdens and Improving the Options for Working Families*, edited by Eileen Appelbaum. Washington, D.C.: Economic Policy Institute.

Nickell, Stephen. 1997. "Unemployment and Labor Market Rigidities: Europe versus North America." *Journal of Economic Perspectives* 11(3): 55–74.

O'Connor, Julia S. 1996. "From Women in the Welfare State to Gendering Welfare State Regimes." *Current Sociology* 44(2): 1–108.

O'Hare, William. 2001. *The Child Population: First Data from the 2000 Census.* Washington, D.C.: Anne E. Casey Foundation and the Population Reference Bureau.

Olmsted, Jennifer. 1999. "Workers of the World, Unite!" Accessed June 4, 2002, at: *www.listproc.bucknell.edu/archives/femecon-1/199902/msg00017.html.*

Olsen, Darcy. 1997. "The Advancing Nanny State: Why the Government

Should Stay Out of Child Care." *Cato Policy Analysis* 285(October). Accessed January 10, 2003, at: *www.cato.org/pubs/pas/pa-285.html*.

Organisation for Economic Co-operation and Development. 1997. *Education at a Glance: OECD Indicators*. Paris: OECD.

———. 1998. "Working Hours: Latest Trends and Policy Initiatives." *Employment Outlook* 153–188.

———. 1999a. "OECD Country Note: Early Childhood Education and Care Policy in Norway." Accessed April 3, 2002, at: *www1/oecd.org/els/pdfs/EDSECECDOCA004.pdf*.

———. 1999b. "OECD Country Note: Early Childhood Education and Care Policy in Sweden." Accessed April 3, 2002, at: *www1/oecd.org/els/pdfs/EDSECECDOCA001.pdf*.

———. 2000a. "Early Childhood Education and Care in Finland: Background Report Prepared for the OECD Thematic Review of Early Childhood Education and Care Policy." Accessed February 13, 2003, at: *www1/oecd.org/els/pdfs/EDSECECDOCA010.pdf*.

———. 2000b. "OECD Country Note: Early Childhood Education and Care Policy in the Flemish Community of Belgium." Accessed January 3, 2003, at: *www1/oecd.org/els/pdfs/EDSECECDOCA002.pdf*.

———. 2000c. "OECD Country Note: Early Childhood Education and Care Policy in the United Kingdom." Accessed April 3, 2002, at: *www1.oecd.org/els/pdfs/EDSECECDOCA020.pdf*.

———. 2000d. *OECD Country Note: Early Childhood Education and Care Policy in the United States of America*. Accessed April 3, 2002, at: *www1/oecd.org/els/pdfs/EDSECECDOCA012.pdf*.

———. 2001a. "Balancing Work and Family Life: Helping Parents Into Paid Employment." *Employment Outlook* 129–66.

———. 2001b. *Social Expenditure Database 1980–1998*, 3d ed. Paris: OECD.

———. 2001c. *Society at a Glance: OECD Social Indicators*. Paris: OECD.

———. 2001d. *Starting Strong: Early Childhood Education and Care*. Paris: OECD.

———. 2002a. *Babies and Bosses: Reconciling Work and Family Life*. Volume 1, *Australia, Denmark, and the Netherlands*. Paris: OECD.

———. 2002b. "Education at a Glance." Accessed January 18, 2003, at: *www.cvm.qc.ca/agecvm/dossiers/OCDE/TABLES/B*.

Orloff, Ann Shola. 1993. "Gender and the Social Rights of Citizenship: The Comparative Analysis of Gender Relations and Welfare States." *American Sociological Review* 58(3): 303–28.

Palley, I. Thomas. 2001. *Right-To-Work (For Less): An Empirical Examination of the Impact of Right-To-Work Legislation on State Economic Outcomes*. Washington, D.C.: Public Policy Department, AFL-CIO.

Palme, Joakim S., Ake Bergmark, Olof Backman, Felipe Estrada, Johan Fritzell, Olle Lundberg, Ola Sjoberg, Lena Sommestad, and Marta Szebehely. 2002. *Welfare in Sweden.* Stockholm: Ministry of Health and Social Affairs.

Parcel, Toby L., and Elizabeth G. Menaghan. 1994. "Early Parental Work, Family Social Capital, and Early Childhood Outcomes." *American Journal of Sociology* 99(4): 972–1009.

"Part-Time Workers: European Union or European Disharmony?" 2001. Andersen Legal Newsletter. Accessed May 7, 2002, at *www.andersenlegal.com.*

Pascall, Gillian. 1986. *Social Policy: A Feminist Analysis.* London: Tavistock.

Pateman, Carol. 1988. "The Patriarchal Welfare State." In *Democracy and the Welfare State,* edited by Amy Gutman. Princeton, New Jersey: Princeton University Press.

Patterson, James T. 1986. *America's Struggle Against Poverty: 1900–1985.* Cambridge: Harvard University Press.

Peer, Shanny. 2001. Testimony before the Senate Committee on Health, Education, Labor, and Pensions, *Hearing on Early Education and Care: How Does the U.S. Measure Up?* March 27, 2001.

Peisner-Feinberg, Ellen S., and Margaret Burchinal. 1997. "Concurrent Relations Between Child Care Quality and Child Outcomes: The Study of Cost, Quality, and Outcomes in Child Care Centers." *Merrill Palmer Quarterly* 43: 457–77.

Peters, H. Elizabeth, Robert Plotnick, and Se-Ook Jeong. 2001. "How Will Welfare Reform Affect Childbearing and Family Structure Decisions?" Discussion paper 1239–01. Madison: University of Wisconsin, Institute for Research on Poverty.

Pfau-Effinger, Birgit. 1999. "The Modernization of Family and Motherhood in Western Europe." In *Restructuring Gender Relations and Employment: The Decline of the Male Breadwinner,* edited by Rosemary Crompton. Oxford: Oxford University Press.

Pierson, Paul, ed. 2001. *The New Politics of the Welfare State.* Oxford: Oxford University Press.

Plantenga, Janneke, and Robert A. J. Dur. 1998. "Working Time Reduction in the Netherlands: Past Developments and Future Prospects." *Transfer* 4(4): 679–91.

Plantenga, Janneke, and Johan Hansen. 1999. "Assessing Equal Opportunities in the European Union." *International Labour Review* 138(4): 351–79.

Powell, Lisa M. 2002. "Joint Labor Supply and Childcare Choice Decisions of Married Mothers." *Journal of Human Resources* 37(1): 106–28.

Presser, Harriet B. 1986. "Shift Work among American Women and Child Care." *Journal of Marriage and the Family* 48(3): 551–63.

———. 1989a. "Can We Make Time for Children? The Economy, Work Schedules, and Child Care: Population of America, 1989 Presidential Address." *Demography* 26(4): 523–43.

———. 1989b. "Some Economic Complexities of Child Care Provided by Grandmothers." *Journal of Marriage and the Family* 51(3): 581–91.

———. 1994. "Employment Schedules Among Dual-Earner Spouses and the Division of Household Labor by Gender." *American Sociological Review* 59(3): 348–64.

———. 1995a. "Are the Interests of Women Inherently at Odds with the Interests of Children or the Family? A Viewpoint." In *Gender and Family Change in Industrialized Countries*, edited by Karen Oppenheim Mason and An-Magritt Jensen. Oxford: Oxford University Press.

———. 1995b. "Job, Family, and Gender: Determinants of Nonstandard Work Schedules Among Employed Americans in 1991." *Demography* 32(4): 577–98.

———. 1999. "Toward a 24-Hour Economy." *Science* 284(541): 1778–79.

———. Forthcoming. *Working in a 24/7 Economy: Challenges for American Families*. New York: Russell Sage Foundation.

Putnam, Robert D. 2000. *Bowling Alone: The Collapse and Revival of American Community*. New York: Simon & Schuster.

Quadagno, Jill. 1994. *The Color of Welfare: How Racism Undermined the War on Poverty*. New York: Oxford University Press.

Queralt, Magaly, Ann Dryden Witte, and Harriet Griesinger. 2000. "Changing Policies, Changing Impacts: Employment and Earnings of Child-Care Subsidy Recipients in the Era of Welfare Reform." *Social Service Review* 74(4): 588–619.

Ramey, Craig T., and Sharon L. Ramey. 1998. "Prevention of Intellectual Disabilities: Early Interventions to Improve Cognitive Development." *Preventive Medicine* 27(12): 224–32.

Robinson, John P., and Geoffrey Godbey. 1997. *Time for Life: The Surprising Ways Americans Use Their Time*. University Park: Pennsylvania State University Press.

Rose, Joseph B., and Gary N. Chaison. 1996. "Linking Union Density and Union Effectiveness: The North American Experience." *Industrial Relations* 35(1): 78–105.

Rosenfeld, Rachel A., and Arne L. Kalleberg. 1991. "Gender Inequality in the Labor Market: A Cross-National Perspective." *Acta Sociologica* 34: 207–25.

Ross, Katherin E. 1998. "Labor Pains: The Effects of the Family and Medical Leave Act on Recent Mothers' Return to Work After Childbirth."

Paper presented at the Annual Meeting of the Population Association of America. Chicago (April 2).

Ross Products Division. 2001. "Breastfeeding Trends Through 2000." Accessed August 20, 2002, at: *www.ross.com/aboutRoss/Survey.pdf.*

Rostgaard, Tine, and Torben Fridberg. 1998. "Caring for Children and Older People: A Comparison of European Policies and Practices." In *Social Security in Europe 6.* Copenhagen: Danish National Institute of Social Research.

Rubery, Jill, Mark Smith, and Colette Fagan. 1998. "National Working-Time Regimes and Equal Opportunities." *Feminist Economics* 4(1): 71–101.

———. 1999. *Women's Employment in Europe.* London: Routledge.

Rubery, Jill, Mark Smith, Colette Fagan, and Damian Grimshaw. 1998. *Women and European Employment.* New York: Routledge.

Ruhm, Christopher J. 1998. "The Economic Consequences of Parental Leave Mandates: Lessons from Europe." *Quarterly Journal of Economics* 113(1): 285–317.

———. 2000. "Parental Leave and Child Health." *Journal of Health Economics* 19(6): 931–60.

———. Forthcoming. "Parental Employment and Child Cognitive Development." *Journal of Human Resources.*

Ruhm, Christopher J., and Jackqueline L. Teague. 1997. "Parental Leave Policies in Europe and North America." In *Gender and Family Issues in the Workplace,* edited by Francine D. Blau and Ronald G. Ehrenberg. New York: Russell Sage Foundation.

Sainsbury, Diane. 1994. "Women's and Men's Social Rights: Gendering Dimensions of Welfare States." In *Gendering Welfare States,* edited by Diane Sainsbury. London: Sage Publications.

———. 1999. "Gender, Policy Regimes, and Politics." In *Gender and Welfare State Regimes,* edited by Diane Sainsbury. Oxford: Oxford University Press.

Saluter, Arlene F., and Terry A. Lugaila. 1998. "Marital Status and Living Arrangements: March 1996." Census Bureau Report P20-496. Washington: U.S. Bureau of the Census.

Schor, Juliet B. 1991. *The Overworked American: The Unexpected Decline of Leisure.* New York: Basic Books.

Schumacher, Rachel, Mark Greenberg, and Janellen Duffy. 2001. *The Impact of TANF Funding on State Child Care Programs.* Washington, D.C.: Center for Law and Social Policy.

Schwartz, Deborah. 1994. *An Examination of the Impact of Family-Friendly Policies on the Glass Ceiling.* New York: Families and Work Institute.

Seifert, Hartmut. 1998. "Working Time Policy In Germany: Searching for New Ways." *Transfer* 4(4): 621–40.

Shapiro, Robert Y., and John T. Young. 1989. "Public Opinion and the Welfare State: The U.S. in Comparative Perspective." *Political Science Quarterly* 104(1): 59–89.

Shirk, Martha, Neil G. Bennett, and J. Lawrence Aber. 1999. *Lives On the Line: American Families and the Struggle to Make Ends Meet.* Boulder, Colo.: Westview Press.

Shulman, Karen, Helen Blank, and Daniel Ewen. 1999. *Seeds of Success: State Prekindergarten Initiatives, 1998–1999.* Washington, D.C.: Children's Defense Fund.

Siebert, Horst. 1997. "Labor Market Rigidities: At the Root of Unemployment in Europe." *Journal of Economic Perspectives* 11(3): 37–55.

Singh, Susheela, and Jacqueline Darroch. 2000. "Adolescent Pregnancy and Childbearing: Levels and Trends Across Developed Countries." *Family Planning Perspectives* 32(1): 14–23.

Skuterud, Mikal. 2001. "The Impact of Sunday Shopping Deregulation on Employment and Hours of Work in the Retail Industry: Evidence from Canada." Unpublished paper. McMaster University (Canada).

Smeeding, Timothy. 2002. "No Child Left Behind." Unpublished paper. Syracuse University. Accessed December 15, 2002, at: *www.cpr.maxwell.syr.edu/faculty/smeeding/selectedpapers/nochild.pdf.*

Smith, Kristen, Barbara Downs, and Martin O' Connell. 2001. "Maternity Leave and Employment Patterns: 1961–1995." *Household Economic Studies* Report P70–79. Washington: U.S. Bureau of the Census.

Smith, Mark, Colette Fagan, and Jill Rubery. 1998. "Where and Why Is Part-Time Work Growing in Europe?" In *Part-Time Prospects: An International Comparison of Part-Time Work in Europe, North American, and the Pacific Rim.* London: Routledge.

Stafford, Frank P. 1987. "Women's Work, Sibling Competition, and Children's School Performance." *American Economic Review* 77(5): 972–80.

State of Massachusetts. 2003. "General Laws of Massachusetts, Title XXI: Labor and Industries." Accessed February 17, 2003, at: *www.state.ma.us/legis/laws/mgl/149 52D.htm.*

Stier, Haya, and Noah Lewin-Epstein. 2001. "Welfare Regimes, Family-Supportive Policies, and Women's Employment along the Life-Course." *American Journal of Sociology* 106(6): 1731–60.

Sure Start. 2002. "What is Sure Start?" Accessed April 15, 2002, at: *www.surestart.gov.uk/aboutWhatis.cfm?section.*

Sylvester, Kathleen. 2001. *Listening to Families: The Role of Values in Shaping Effective Social Policy.* Washington, D.C.: Social Policy Action Network.

Sylvester, Tom. 2002. "The Marriage Trap: Why Feminists Won't Talk About Dad." June 14. *National Review Online*. Accessed August 8, 2002, at: *www.nationalreview.com/comment/comment-sylvester061402*.

ten Cate, Adrienne. 2000. "Labour Market Effects of Maternity and Parental Leave Policy in Canada." Paper presented at Canadian Employment Research Meetings. Vancouver (June 1–2).

32 Hours: Action for Full-Employment. 2003. "In Practice: Shorter Work Time Examples, Canada, Europe." Accessed January 20, 2003, at: *www.web.net/32hours*.

Thornthwaite, Louise. 2002. "Work Family Balance: International Research on Employee Preferences." ACIRRT working paper 79. Sydney, Australia: University of Sydney.

Tietze, Wolfgang, and Debby Cryer. 1999. "Current Trends in European Early Child Care and Education." *Annals of the American Academy of Political and Social Science* 563(May): 175–93.

Trattner, Walter I. 1994. *From Poor Law To Welfare State: A History of Social Welfare in America*. New York: The Free Press.

21st Century Community Learning Centers. 2002. "Providing Quality Afterschool Learning Opportunities for America's Families." Accessed July 5, 2002, at: *www.ed.gov/pubs/Providing—Quality—Afterschool—Learning/report.html*.

United Nations International Children's Emergency Fund (UNICEF). 2001. "The State of the World's Children." Accessed August 12, 2002, at: *www.unicef.org/sowc01/pdf/fullsowc.pdf*.

Urban Institute. 2002. "Assessing the New Federalism: Overview of the National Survey of America's Families." Accessed September 2002: *www.urban.org/Content/Research/NewFederalism/NSAF/Overview/NSAFOverview.htm*.

U.S. Bureau of the Census. 1995. "Statistical Abstract of the United States." Accessed January 2, 2003, at: *www.census.gov/stab/www*.

———. 2001. "Statistical Abstract of the United States." Accessed January 2, 2003, at: *www.census.gov/statab/www*.

———. 2002a. "International Database Summary Demographic Data." Accessed January 9, 2003, at: *www.census.gov/ipc/www/adbsum.html*.

———. 2002b. "Who's Minding the Kids? Child Care Arrangements." Current Population Reports, P70-86. Washington: U.S. Bureau of the Census.

U.S. Bureau of Labor Statistics. 1999. *Employed Persons by Detailed Occupation, Sex, Race, and Hispanic Origin*. Washington: U.S. Department of Labor.

U.S. Center for the Child Care Workforce. 2000. *Current Data on Child Care Salaries and Benefits in the United States, March 2000*. Washington: U.S. Center for the Child Care Workforce.

U.S. Department of Health and Human Services (DHHS). 1999. "Temporary Assistance for Needy Families (TANF) Program Second Annual Report to Congress." Washington: U.S. Department of Health and Human Services.

———. 2000. "Access to Childcare for Low-Income Working Families." Accessed October 21, 2002, at: *www.acf.dhhs.gov/news/press/1999/ccreport.html*.

———. 2001a. "Child Care and Development Block Grant/Child Care and Development Fund." Accessed January 24, 2001, at: *www.acf.dhhs.gov/news/cctable.htm*.

———. 2001b. "2001 Head Start Fact Sheet." Accessed January 28, 2002, at: *www.2.acf.dhhs.gov/programs/hsb/about/fact210.htm*.

U.S. Department of Labor (DOL). 1999. *FutureWork: Trends and Challenges for Work in the 21st Century.* Washington: U.S. Government Printing Office.

———. 2000. "Balancing the Needs of Families and Employers: The Family and Medical Leave Surveys, 2000 Update." Accessed July 9, 2000, at: *www.dol.gov/asp/fmla/main2000.htm*.

———. 2002a. "The 'New Economy' and Its Impact on Executive, Administrative, and Professional Exemptions to the Fair Labor Standards Act (FLSA); Executive Summary."Accessed June 3, 2002, at: *www.dol.gov/esa/reg/neweconomy/summary.htm*.

———. 2002b. "State Right-to-Work Laws and Constitutional Amendments in Effect as of January 1, 2002, With Year of Passage." Accessed August 21, 2002, at: *www.dol.gov/esa/programs/whd/state/righttowork.htm*.

———. 2002c. "Work Hours: Part-Time Employment." Accessed January 1, 2003, at: *www.dol.gov/dol/topic/workhours/parttimeemployment.htm*.

U.S. General Accounting Office (GAO). 1994. *Child Care: Child Care Subsidies Increase Likelihood that Low-Income Mothers Will Work.* Washington: U.S. General Accounting Office.

———. 1999. *Report to the Subcommittee on Workforce Protections, Committee on Education and the Workforce.* Washington: U.S. General Accounting Office.

———. 2000. *Contingent Workers: Incomes and Benefits Lag Behind Those of Rest of Workforce.* Washington: U.S. General Accounting Office.

———. 2001. *Private Health Insurance: Small Employers Continue to Face Challenges in Providing Coverage.* Washington: U.S. General Accounting Office.

U.S. Office of Personnel Management. 2001. "Paid Parental Leave." Accessed May 23, 2002, at: *www.opm.gov/oca/leave/HTML/Parental Report.htm.*

Vandell, Deborah Lowe, and Mary A. Corasaniti. 1990. "Child Care and the Family: Complex Contributors to Child Development." In *New Directions for Child Development,* edited by Kathleen McCartney. San Francisco, Calif.: Jossey Bass.

Vandell, Deborah Lowe, and Janaki Ramanan. 1992. "Effects of Early and Recent Maternal Employment on Children from Low-Income Families." *Child Development* 63(4): 938–49.

Vandell, Deborah Lowe, and Barbara Wolfe. 2000. "Child Care Quality: Does It Matter and Does It Need to Be Improved?" Special report (November). Madison: University of Wisconsin, Institute for Research on Poverty.

Waite, Linda J., and Mark Nielsen. 2001. "The Rise of the Dual-Earner Family, 1963–1997." In *Working Families: The Transformation of the American Home,* edited by Rosanna Hertz and Nancy L. Marshall. Berkeley: University of California Press.

Waldfogel, Jane. 1997. "The Effect of Children on Women's Wages." *American Sociological Review* 62(2): 209–17.

———. 1998. "Understanding the 'Family Gap' in Pay for Women with Children." *Journal of Economic Perspectives* 12(1): 137–56.

———. 1999. "The Impact of the Family and Medical Leave Act." *Journal of Policy Analysis and Management* 18(2): 281–302.

———. 2002. "Child Care, Women's Employment, and Child Outcomes." *Journal of Population Economics* 15(3): 527–48.

Waldfogel, Jane, Wen-Jui Han, and Jeanne Brooks-Gunn. 2002. "The Effects of Early Maternal Employment on Child Cognitive Development." *Demography* 39(2): 369–92.

Wall Street Journal–NBC. 1998. "Polls Indicate Widespread Support for Increased Investment in Child Care." Accessed January 18, 2002, at: *cdfweb.vwh.net/childcare/cc—polls.html.*

Weber, Tina. 1997. "Social Partners Reach Framework Agreement on Part-Time Work." Accessed March 12, 2002, at: *www.eiro.eurofounf. ie/1997/06/feature/eu9706131f.html.*

Wenger, Jeffrey. 2001. "The Continuing Problems with Part-Time Jobs." Issue brief 155. Economic Policy Institute. Accessed August 21, 2002, at: *www.epinet.org/Issuebriefs/ib155.html.*

Wheeler, Hoyt. 1989. "Management-Labour Relations in the USA." In *International and Comparative Industrial Relations,* edited by Greg J. Bamber and Russell D. Lansbury. London: Allen and Unwin.

White, Julia. 2002. "A New Look at Shorter Hours of Work in the Communications, Energy, and Paperworkers Union." *Just Labor* 1: 41–49.

Whitebook, Marcy. 1999. "Child Care Workers: High Demand, Low Wages." *Annals of the American Academy of Political and Social Science* 563(May): 146–61.

Whitebook, Marcy, Carollee Howes, and Deborah Phillips. 1989. "Who Cares? Child Care Teachers and the Quality of Care in America." Oakland, Calif.: National Child Care Employee Project.

Williams, Joan. 2000. *Unbending Gender: Why Work-Family Conflict and What to Do About It.* New York: Oxford University Press.

Wilson, Pete. 1995. "Text of Letter Requesting Daily Overtime Review." Accessed July 8, 2002, at: *http://www.dir.ca.gov/bulletin/Oct—Nov—95/IWC—Letter.html.*

Winegarden, C. R., and Paula Bracy. 1995. "Demographic Consequences of Maternal Leave Programs in Industrial Countries from Fixed Effects Models." *Southern Economic Journal* 61(4): 1020–35.

Winning, Ethan A. 2002. "Rest, Meal Breaks, Days Off from Work, and Maximum Hours." Accessed July 8, 2002, at: *www.ewin.com/articles/restper.htm.*

Wisensale, Steven K. 2001. *Family Leave Policy: The Political Economy of Work and Family in America.* London: M. E. Sharpe.

Woodill, Gary A., Judith Bernard, and Lawrence Prochner. 1992. *International Handbook of Early Childhood Education.* New York: Garland.

Woodward, Evan. 2002. "Are Americans 'Vacation Starved'?" Accessed December 2, 2002, at: *www.accuracy.org/ipam081601.htm.*

Work Life Research Center. 2002. "Childcare and Family Statistics Database." Work Life Research Center. Accessed April 2, 2002, at: *www.workliferesearch.org.*

Zero to Three. 2000. *Survey Results: What Grown-Ups Understand About Child Development.* Washington, D.C.: Zero to Three, National Center for Infants, Toddlers, and Families.

—— Index ——

Numbers in **boldface** refer to figures and tables